Palgrave Politics of Identity and Citizenship Series

The politics of identity and citizenship has assumed increasing importance as our polities have become significantly more culturally, ethnically and religiously diverse. Different types of scholars, including philosophers, sociologists, political scientists and historians make contributions to this field and this series showcases a variety of innovative contributions to it. Focusing on a range of different countries, and utilizing the insights of different disciplines, the series helps to illuminate an increasingly controversial area of research and titles in it will be of interest to a number of audiences including scholars, students and other interested individuals.

More information about this series at
http://www.springer.com/series/14670

Elke Murdock

Multiculturalism, Identity and Difference

Experiences of Culture Contact

Elke Murdock
University of Luxembourg
Esch-sur-Alzette, Luxembourg

Palgrave Politics of Identity and Citizenship Series
ISBN 978-1-137-59678-9   ISBN 978-1-137-59679-6   (eBook)
DOI 10.1057/978-1-137-59679-6

Library of Congress Control Number: 2016953778

Cover illustration: © Antoni Bastien / Alamy Stock Photo

Printed on acid-free paper

This Palgrave Macmillan imprint is published by Springer Nature
The registered company is Macmillan Publishers Ltd. London.

Acknowledgements

I want to express my gratitude to all who have made this book project possible. The research presented in this book was supported by a grant from the Fonds National de la Recherche, Luxembourg. I would like to express a special thank you to my academic supervisor, Prof. D. Ferring. He was open to my research proposal from the start and guided me through the various stages of the project with great insights, critical questioning and continuous support. I would also like to express my heartfelt gratitude to the late Prof. P. Weinreich whose work on identity construal processes greatly influenced the early stages of my research. In the later stages I critically benefited from Prof. J. Valsiner's and Prof. M. Barrett's vast knowledge, expertise and energy. I am lucky enough to work in the intellectually stimulating, constructive and supportive Research Unit INSIDE at the University of Luxembourg. This book would not be possible without the continuous support of my colleagues at INSIDE.

In terms of the support I received when conducting my field research, I would like to thank the Directors of the European Schools of Luxembourg for their openness towards my proposal and giving permission to conduct research projects within this multilingual and multicultural European school context. Special thanks also go to Mme A. Agustsson and Mme M. Jacobs at the Communications Department of the Ville de Luxembourg for their exceptional support. Thank you also to Mme A. Reitz of the Family of Man Exhibition and Mme E. Bossi of the Luxembourg Government Press and Information Office for their instant help concerning copyrights for images. Thank you also to the Dalai Lama's office for their prompt and positive reply.

I also offer special thanks to Harriet Barker and Amelia Derkatsch, the editors at Palgrave Macmillan, for their support, professionalism and efficiency throughout the stages of the publication process. I would also like to thank the anonymous reviewer for the helpful comments on the manuscript.

Finally, I would like to express my heartfelt thanks to my family for their interest in my work and their continuous support. My children, Philip and Anna, have also helped in a very practical way as they have quite often pre-tested questionnaires aimed at their age group. Thankfully, they don't hold back with critical comments. A special thank you goes to them for their considered insights.

Contents

List of Figures

List of Tables

1

Introduction

International Scope

The United Nation's (2009) migration report affirms "that international migration is a growing phenomenon, both in scope and in complexity, affecting virtually all countries in the world" (p. 37). The report notes further that the rise in global mobility, the growing complexity of migratory patterns and its impact on countries, migrants, families and communities have all contributed to international migration becoming a priority for the international community. Castles and Miller (2009) have in fact described the twenty-first century as "the age of migration." According to the United Nation's (2013) report, the number of international migrants was estimated at 232 million in 2013, representing about 3 % of the world population. As Skeldon (2013) pointed out, the global migration system has changed over recent decades with regard to the origins and destinations, as well as the volume and types of migrants. As he explained, countries that were once origins of migration became destinations of migrants and vice versa. In the twentieth century Europe was a major area of emigration and in the course of the twenty-first century has become

© The Author(s) 2016
E. Murdock, *Multiculturalism, Identity and Difference*,
DOI 10.1057/978-1-137-59679-6_1

the target for immigration (and within Europe Luxembourg is a case in point). A consequence is that most European countries, even those as far north as Iceland now have significant minority immigrant populations (http://www.migrationpolicy.org/programs/data-hub/international-migration-statistics). Moran (2011) argued that multiculturalism has been used as a nation-building tool in "classical" immigration countries such as Australia, building an inclusive national identity whilst embracing diversity. Skeldon (2013) concluded that in these settler societies where immigration from many different origins has been a central policy and integral part of nation-building, cultural diversity has become part of the social fabric. Yet concerns about multiculturalism are now emerging in Asian countries such as China, Japan and the Republic of Korea where the proportion of foreigners is still very small. On the one hand there is European unification, globalization and immigration and at the same time we observe a return and revitalization of strong national and regional identities (Schmidt-Denter, 2008). Within Europe several countries have seen a rise in the popularity of right-wing parties, which tend to use strong anti-immigration rhetoric (Fischer, 2016). Therefore it is important to understand the dynamics of culture contact—especially from the perspective of a *receiving* society. As noted in a recent Council of Europe Report (2016) increased migration, growing diversity and globalization have a profound effect on people's identities. The central theme of this book is an exploration of what it means for the individual to live in a multicultural society. In this, Luxembourg is used as a case study as Luxembourg can be described as "super-diverse" as defined by Vertovec (2007). The "diversification of diversity" can be illustrated by the "natural laboratory" Luxembourg provides: Luxembourg's population does not only represent a wide range of nationalities, but more importantly, Luxembourg has experienced and still experiences different immigration waves. As a result, recent arrivals, first, second and third generation immigrants live side by side. These immigrants have divergent labour market experiences and also discrete gender and age profiles. Specific patterns of spatial distribution can also be observed including local area responses. As Vertovec (2007) noted, the interplay of these factors result in "the notion of 'super-diversity'" (p. 1025). In terms of surface area (2586 km^2) and total population (563,000 inhabitants) Luxembourg may seem small. Nestled in the heart of Europe between Belgium, France and Germany, Luxembourg is a founding member of the European Union, the Organization for Economic Co-operation and Development (OECD), the United Nations and NATO. Luxembourg also hosts several key EU institutions including the Court of Justice, the Court of Auditors, the European Investment Bank, the secretariat of the European Parliament and several European Commission services. Thus Luxembourg plays an important role on the European and international political stage. Notably, 46 % of the total population comes from 170 countries and 71 % of the active population are foreign nationals (http://www.surprisinglux.com). The lessons learnt within this country with a large, diverse immigrant population can be applied to other contexts and countries.

Outline

Some markers about Luxembourg were given above, but given Luxembourg's centrality to this book I will start out with providing some more contextual information. Also on theoretical grounds it is important to include contextual information: In his *Bioecological Model* Urie Bronfenbrenner's (1986) has highlighted the influence of the external environment on the human development (see Fig. 1.1).

The flow of my analysis will follow first the direction from the outside to the core: The context or *macro environment* will be given in Chap. 2, followed by an explanation of relevant research concepts in Chap. 3 and continuing with motivation and identity processes located at the *core* at the individual level (Chap. 4). After laying this groundwork, the flow is then from the core to the outside: The focus of Chap. 5 is the negotiation of two or more (national) identities within one individual whilst Chap. 6 concerns the individual living in a multicultural context.

In Chap. 2 I will start out by giving an overview of Luxembourg's more recent history, consistent with chronosystem models (Bronfenbrenner, 1986; Bronfenbrenner & Ceci, 1994). Within its current borders Luxembourg has only existed since 1839 and the Luxembourg "national identity" is but a twentieth-century invention. These historical developments are reflected in the *macrosystem*, the attitudes and ideologies of the

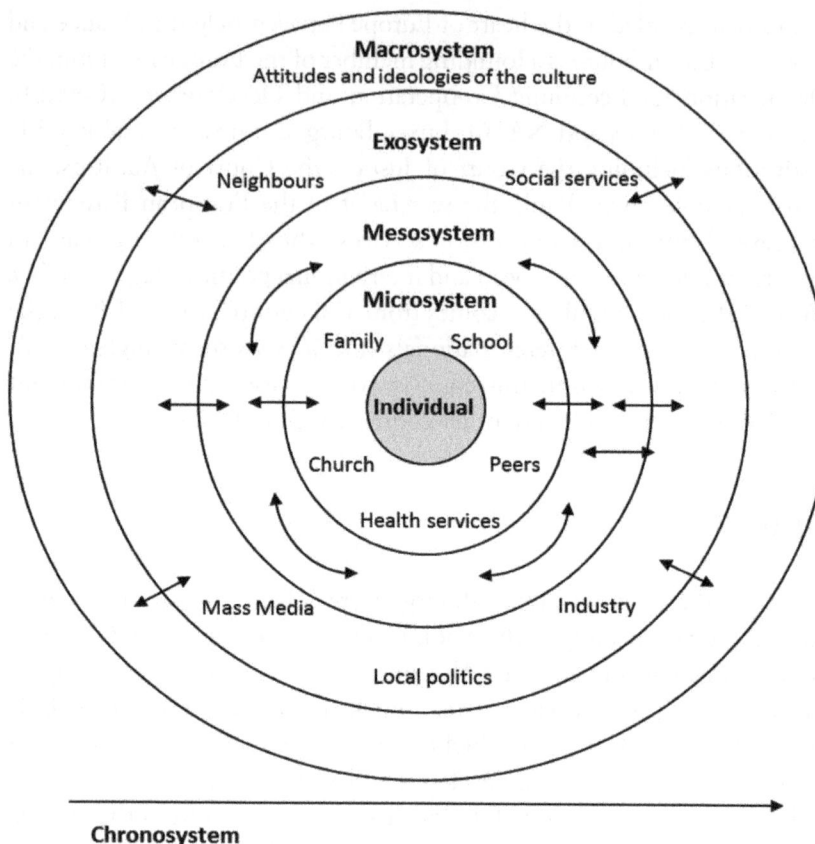

Fig. 1.1 Bioecological Model (*Source*: Bronfenbrenner, 1986)

country. Luxembourg has experienced several immigration waves which can be distinguished by permanency, country of origin and target industry. In terms of demographics, the Luxembourg of today is a diverse society—even super-diverse as alluded to above. This increasingly multicultural composition has an impact at societal level, shaping economic, political and cultural activities and resources—the *exosystem*. At government level, for example, there has been a reaction to the increasing number of foreigners in the form of the revision of the Luxembourg Law on Nationality which came into force in 2009. One key change introduced by the new law is that it allows for dual nationality, if certain conditions are met. Today, there is a debate whether the hurdles in form of residence requirement and level of language competence are too high, but in principle, the legislation allows for dual nationality. This is an example for a policy at societal level to multiculturalism. Another example for a policy initiative is the external branding by the capital, Ville de Luxembourg (VdL), which has coined the slogan *multiplicity*. To the outside world, the Ville de Luxembourg uses the plural composition of the town to show its openness towards diversity, embracing different cultures ("Une identité forte: multiplicity." http://www.vdl.lu). Thus in its external communication, the multicultural composition is presented as desirable, a synonym for moving forward, modernity and openness. Yet what are the individual-level responses to the multicultural society? What is the native population's attitude towards the culturally heterogeneous composed society? These questions are addressed in empirical research. It should also be noted that even within a globalizing world, Luxembourg takes an exceptional position with a foreign population percentage of 46 % (Statec, 2015). Within the European Union, relative to the size of the resident population, Luxembourg has the highest percentage of immigrants per capita (Eurostat, 2011). Within a comparatively short period of time, in less than 200 years, Luxembourg has transformed from being a relatively poor, agrarian country of emigration to becoming a wealthy, sovereign state and target country for immigration. Luxembourg is also a country with three officially recognized national languages. The three languages, Lëtzebuergesch, French and German, are spoken throughout the country, with Lëtzebuergesch being the national language. Language competence plays an important role within this context, so much so that the ability to speak Luxembourgish was cited as the most important criterion for being Luxembourgish in a survey amongst Luxembourg nationals (TNS Ilres, 2007). "Speaking Luxembourgish" was mentioned as a criterion for being Luxembourgish ahead of "being born in Luxembourg" and "being born to parents of Luxembourgish origin." Thus the simple question of who is a Luxembourger is actually quite difficult to answer. Official statistics will refer to the passport country—but even that will become more complex with the rise in dual citizenship. Subjective nationality is much harder to ascertain—it is in the mind of the beholder. I distinguish between Luxembourgers and Non-Luxembourgers in the full knowledge that this is an imperfect solution. The self-definition in terms of nationality was the explicit subject at one of the empirical studies carried out in Luxembourg and the simple question produced quite complex answers—which in turn is a reflection of living in a multicultural society. In summary, Luxembourg can be described as a "natural laboratory" to study several phenomena related to multiculturalism at societal and individual level.

Following on from the description of Luxembourg's macro environment, I will firstly provide a review of the theoretical body of research concerning multiculturalism, its origins and related concepts such as globalization and acculturation (Chap. 3). The origins of the concept multiculturalism will be explained, as well as current understandings and a "misleading" understanding of the concept. Immigration, multiculturalism and citizenship are understood to form a triad (Kymlicka, 2012) and therefore new models of citizenship will be briefly outlined. The effects of globalization can be felt even without moving to another country. There are different motivations for moving to another country and different types of migrants. Motivation and migrant type influence the acculturation challenges migrants face. The consequences of culture contact in all its facets are the focus of acculturation research. Historical roots of the concept of acculturation will be explained and a taxonomy of acculturation variables will be presented. The acculturation orientation integration will be examined in more detail, as this orientation is frequently cited as the most desirable acculturation outcome (Celenk & van de Vijver, 2014).

In Chap. 4 the challenges multicultural societies present to the individual are explained within a psychological framework: Insights from evolutionary psychology are provided as well as psychological theories concerning human motivation and identity construal processes. Mobility is one key characteristic of the globalized world and a key achievement within the European Union is the free movement of capital, goods, services and people. As Chen (2013) pointed out, opening up is one reaction to globalization and ethnic protectionism being another. Weinreich, Bacova and Rougier (2003) observed "some writers have been perplexed by the persistence of ethnicity in the absence of obvious gain, and the affect that is associated with it" (p. 115). Going far back in time, considering human phylogeny, may provide some answers, which is why evolutionary aspects of human motivation will be discussed. Core human motives will be examined further with a special emphasis on the need to belong and the need for self-enhancement. Human beings need to negotiate stability and change—core elements of identity development. In the last section of this chapter, identity theories will be reviewed, including the structure of the self and the link between the self and the cultural context.

These theoretical insights are then transposed into different empirical studies, each addressing a different aspect of the culture contact situation in a plural society and each one providing novel insights. The first study, for example, shows that living within a nationally mixed environment actually increases the awareness of one's own nationality. In a comparative study amongst adolescents we empirically demonstrated that growing up in a nationally mixed context heightens the awareness of nationality in the spontaneous self-concept. This study also showed that it is possible to combine increased awareness of nationalities with tolerance and respect. This study also demonstrated the difficulties related to the identification with supra-national entities such as "European."

Another consequence of an increasingly global world is the rise in complex biographies. Mixed national families are becoming more common and children may grow up in a country different to their country of birth. The scientific study of biculturalism is a relatively new field of research and the concept of biculturalism will be explained in Chap. 5. Different models will be presented explaining how second-culture exposure is experienced at individual level. One particular question is also, whether lessons from the individual experience of multiple cultures[1] can be learnt for multiculturalism at societal level. Taking advantage of the multilingual context Luxembourg provides, the relationship between language competence and biculturalism is empirically explored. Bilingualism, defined

---

[1] Various conceptions and definitions of culture can be found in Berry et al. (2011) or Matsumoto and Juang (2008). However, most definitions of culture include the idea that it is the "person-made" part of the environment, is usually passed from one generation to the next, is often thought to reside inside the person in a highly subjective manner (as opposed to the objective world), and embraces a wide range of human experiences and thought such as language, beliefs, a wide range of cognitions, values, family and parenting styles, interpersonal interaction and so on. These experiences are often thought to be shared by the collective group that form a nation. In that sense, the terms culture and nation are used interchangeably. The different understanding of nations as socially constructed vs. built on kinship ties will be discussed in Chap. 4.

as competence in two languages, was identified as necessary but not sufficient condition for biculturalism. As will be shown, for biculturalism to occur an *internalization* of the cultures has to take place. An important finding of this study was within-group differences regarding the perception whether language influences personality. An association was found between the belief that language influences personality and in turn the self-identification as bicultural. This result can be explained within the cultural frame switching theory (Hong, Morris, Chiu, & Benet-Martínez, 2000). For those participants who perceive language influencing their personality, language serves as a cultural prime—these participants have internalized the culture associated with the language.

The question how different nationalities or cultures are experienced and reconciled within one individual is the subject of a further empirical study. In particular, I studied factors contributing to a bicultural identification and researched whether biculturalism is experienced as enrichment or a source of conflict. Findings include firstly, that it is possible to identify with and feel attached to more than one nationality and secondly, to experience this dual nationality as a doubling of resources and not a source of conflict. Having more than one nationality can thus be a source of pride, serving the sense of being unique. This study also demonstrates that culture contact alone is not sufficient to become bicultural.

The final series of studies focused specifically on the attitudes towards a plurally composed society and identified factors that are conducive towards openness to multiculturalism. In Chap. 6, the body of research concerning the attitudes towards multiculturalism is presented first, followed by an outline of two empirical studies. These studies especially highlighted that the idea of multiculturalism is actually widely accepted, but specific policies of societal participation less so. A person may thus be in favour of a multicultural society but oppose participation of migrants in public services. Opponents and proponents focus on different aspects of multiculturalism. The importance of an inclusive understanding of nationality is also stressed within this body of research as well as the role of human values. These studies thus have direct consequences for policy implications within Luxembourg, but also importantly, insights can be transferred to other countries and contexts.

In the final chapter, conclusions across the empirical studies are drawn and implications considered. Around the globe, people are voluntarily and involuntarily on the move—at the time of writing, there is the dislocation of large parts of the population in Syria as well as other conflict zones. This can only be described as a humanitarian catastrophe which has ramifications across many countries in the Middle East, Europe, and beyond (International Monetary Fund, 2016). Increasingly diverse societies are a reality of the twenty-first century. Taking Luxembourg as a case study, this book looks at the consequences of culture contact. It comes to no surprise that the reactions to culture contact are also diverse. Individuals may choose very different acculturation strategies depending on personal characteristics and context, but this plurality could actually be the "glue" that holds a multicultural society together. A plural society offers a wider range of choices and opportunities for self-expression, whilst embedded in human rights and civic values.

References

Berry, J. W., Poortinga, Y. H., Breugelmans, S., Chastiosis, A., & Sam, D. (2011). *Cross-cultural psychology: Research and applications* (3rd ed.). New York: Cambridge University Press.

Bronfenbrenner, U. (1986). Ecology of the family as a context for human development: Research perspectives. *Developmental Psychology, 22*(6), 723–742. doi:10.1037/0012-1649.22.6.723.

Bronfenbrenner, U., & Ceci, S. J. (1994). Nature-nuture reconceptualized in developmental perspective: A bioecological model. *Psychological review, 101*(4), 568–586. doi:10.1037/0033-295X.101.4.568.

Castles, S., & Miller, M. J. (2009). *The age of migration: International population movements in the modern world* (4th ed.). Basingstoke: Palgrave-Macmillan and Guilford.

Celenk, Ö., & van de Vijver, F. J. R. (2014). Assessment of psychological acculturation and multiculturalism: An overview of measures in the public domain. In V. Benet-Martínez & Y.-Y. Hong (Eds.), *Oxford handbook of multicultural identity: Basic and applied psychological perspectives*. Oxford, UK: Oxford University Press.

Chen, S. X. (2013). *Psychological responses to globalization: Bicultural identities and beyond.* Presentation held at Conference "Identity in a globalized world," 31st May – 3rd June 2013, Isle of Vilm, Germany.

Council of Europe (2016). *Competences for democratic culture. Living together as equals in culturally diverse democratic societies.* Strasbourg, France: Council of Europe Publishing.

Eurostat (2011). *Migrants in Europe. A statistical portrait of the first and second generation. Eurostat statistical books* (2011 ed.). Luxembourg: Publications Office of the European Union. doi:10.2785/5318.

Fischer, J. (2016, January 2/3). Die Alterskrankheiten des Westens. Project Syndicate/Institute für die Wissenschaften vom Menschen, 2015. www.project-sncicate.org. Quoted in: Luxemburger Wort, Analyse & Meinung, p. 15.

Hong, Y., Morris, M. W., Chiu, C., & Benet-Martínez, V. (2000). Multicultural minds: A dynamic constructivist approach to culture and cognition. *American Psychologist, 55*(7), 709–720. doi:10.1037//0003-066X.55.7.709.

International Monetary Fund. (2016). *The refugee surge in Europe: Economic challenges.* Staff Discussion Note, SDN/16/02.

Kymlicka, W. (2012). *Multiculturalism: Success, failure, and the future.* Transatlantic Council on Migration, Washington, DC: Migration Policy Institute.

Matsumoto, D., & Juang, L. (2008). *Culture and psychology* (4th ed.). Belmont, CA: Wadsworth/Cengage.

Moran, A. (2011). Multiculturalism as nation-building in Australia: Inclusive national identity and the embrace of diversity. *Ethnic and Racial Studies, 34*(12), 2153–2172. doi:10.1080/01419870.2011.573081.

Schmidt-Denter, U. (2008). *Patterns of national identity in cross-cultural comparison.* Symposium: Cultural Influences on Identity Development. 29th International Congress of Psychology (ICP). 20–25 July 2008, Berlin, Germany.

Skeldon, R. (2013). Global migration: Demographic aspects and its relevance for development. United Nations Department of Economic and Social Affairs (DESA), Population Division, Technical Paper No. 2013/6. New York: United Nations. Retrieved from: http://www.un.org/esa/population/migration/documents/EGM.Skeldon_17.12.2013.pdf

Statec. (2015). Luxembourg in figures. Luxembourg: Institut national de la statistique et des études économiques (statec).

Surprising Luxembourg. (n.d.). http://www.surprisinglux.com website accessed 06.05.2016.

TNS Ilres. (2007). *L'IdentitéLuxembourgeoise.* Enquête Internet auprès de 524 personnes en juin 2007 pour Le Jeudi.

United Nations Department of Economic and Social Affairs (DESA). (2009). *International Migration Report 2009* : *A Global Assessment.* Retrieved from: http://www.un.org/esa/population/publications/migration/WorldMigration Report2009.pdf

United Nations Department of Economic and Social Affairs (DESA). (2013). *International Migration Report 2013.* Retrieved from: http://www.un.org/en/ development/desa/population/publications/pdf/migration/migrationre- port2013/Full_Document_final.pdf

Ville de Luxembourg. (n.d.). *Une identité forte: Multiplicity.* Retrieved from: http://www.vdl.lu

Vertovec, S. (2007). Super-diversity and its implications. *Ethnic and Racial Studies, 30*(6), 1024–1054. doi:10/1080/01419870701599465.

Weinreich, P., Bacova, V., & Rougier, N. (2003). Basic primordialism in ethnic and national identity. In P. Weinreich & W. Saunderson (Eds.), *Analysing iden- tity: Cross-cultural, societal and clinical contexts* (pp. 115–171). Hove: Routledge.

2

Luxembourg—In a Multicultural Context

Introduction

Luxembourg can be described as a "natural laboratory" to describe processes pertaining to national identity development and experiences of culture contact at several levels. Luxembourg's outer borders have been drawn and redrawn by those in power at the time. Historically, borders were drawn over people (*Grenzen über Menschen ziehen*) without consultation of the resident population. Today, people cross borders (*Menschen ziehen über Grenzen*) more or less at will. Foreigners make up nearly half of Luxembourg's total population today. Even though the historical developments which have led to the sovereign state of Luxembourg are unique to Luxembourg, the questions concerning what constitutes the "national identity" and how to accommodate the rising foreign population concern other countries as well. Rather than discussing these phenomena at an abstract level, they are anchored in the specific case study that is Luxembourg.

© The Author(s) 2016
E. Murdock, *Multiculturalism, Identity and Difference*,
DOI 10.1057/978-1-137-59679-6_2

13

Due to its central position right at the fault lines of the great powers, Luxembourg was frequently the centre of attention during European negotiations and as a result carved up to preserve the balance of power. I will start with giving a brief overview of Luxembourg's history. As Luxembourg historian Trausch (2008) explained[1]: "Schließlich geht es auch darum, zu erklären, wie das kleine, von drei mächtigen Nachbarn umgebene Land überleben und eine eigene Identität ausbilden konnte[2]" (p. 13). An understanding of the historical frame of reference is important to place the current discourse on Luxembourg's national identity in context. Following the historical overview, I will explain the different immigration waves to Luxembourg and discuss the current multicultural demographic profile. I will finish with outlining current efforts regarding the (re-) search for the Luxembourg identity.

Luxembourg—A Brief History

In less than 200 years Luxembourg transformed from a relatively poor agricultural land of emigration into a highly developed attractive target country for immigration. The population has nearly trebled and the population mix has changed. Today, the number of cross-border workers entering Luxembourg on a single working day is just slightly lower than the entire population of the country in 1839.

The Grand Duchy of Luxembourg, within its current borders, is the result of nineteenth-century diplomacy. The development of a national sentiment is even more recent. Before obtaining its independence during the nineteenth century, Luxembourg lived under successive Burgundian, Spanish, French, Austrian and Dutch sovereignty. A detailed description of the history of Luxembourg goes beyond the remit of this book. For comprehensive overviews see, for example, Trausch (2007) or Péporté (2011a, 2011b). I will limit myself to highlighting

---

[1] All translations are provided by the author, unless otherwise specified.
[2] Finally, an explanation is warranted of how this small country surrounded by three powerful neighbours could survive and develop its own identity.

some key historical facets which are important to understand the current debate on Luxembourg nationality.

The Early Origins and the Period of Expansion

963—"Neun sechs drei—Luxembourg schlüpft aus dem Ei."[3] Children are taught this mnemonic at school. Indeed, the name "Lucilinburhuc," meaning "small castle," was mentioned for the first time in an exchange charter around 963. Count Siegfried acquired the small fort Lucilinburhuc located on what is now known as the Bockfelsen through an exchange act with the abbey of St Maximin in Trier. At the time, this territory was part of the western fringe of the Holy Roman Empire. Territorial expansion followed through Siegfried's descendants by means of marriages, land purchases, vassalage ties and war. By the end of the thirteenth century, the County of Luxembourg occupied a vast area between the rivers Meuse and Moselle. The territory straddled the linguistic border, with one part being German-speaking and the other French-speaking. In the fourteenth to fifteenth century, Luxembourg even found itself at the head of the Holy Roman Empire. Henry VII, count of Luxembourg, was elected king of Germany and crowned emperor in Rome in 1312. His son, John the Blind, became king of Bohemia through his marriage to Elisabeth, heiress to the Kingdom of Bohemia. John the Blind died at the Battle of Crecy in 1346 in service of the King of France. In 1354, Emperor Charles IV elevated the County of Luxembourg to the rank of duchy and ceded it to his half-brother Wenceslaus I. In the following years the lands were ceded to lords on mortgage terms and in 1443, Philip the Good, duke of Burgundy, conquered the city of Luxembourg and the duchy became a province of the Netherlands and remained so for the next centuries, tied closely to the fate of the Dutch sovereigns. Thus, when the Netherlands passed to the Habsburgs, the Duchy of Luxembourg also belonged to the Spanish Habsburgs during the sixteenth and seventeenth centuries.

---

[3] Nine six three—Luxembourg emerges from the egg.

Period of Division

Luxembourg occupied an important strategic position on the European political chessboard and found itself drawn into various wars from the sixteenth century onwards. The City of Luxembourg was progressively transformed and fortified which is why it became known as "*Gibraltar of the North*." The Duchy of Luxembourg experienced three major divisions: The first division was in 1659, when the southern parts fell to France as stipulated by the Treaty of the Pyrenees, which put a provisional end to the Franco-Spanish conflict. In 1684, the fortress of Luxembourg was besieged and captured by Vauban and the troops of Louis XIV. From 1684 to 1697, the Duchy of Luxembourg remained under French rule. Following the War of the Spanish Succession, Luxembourg fell under the Austrian branch of the Habsburgs in 1715. A period of calm followed until, in 1795, the French revolutionary troops conquered the fortress and Luxembourg was annexed to France as the *Département des Forêts* (Forest Department). The introduction of conscription triggered a peasant uprising in 1798, which is known as the "*Klëppelkrich*" (cudgel war).

The second division was decided at the Congress of Vienna in 1815 followed by the third and final territorial division stipulated at the Congress of London in 1839. The areas concerned are shown in Fig. 2.1. The decisions behind the divisions will be elaborated next.

Congress of Vienna in 1815

Following the collapse of the Napoleonic Empire, the European map was redrawn at the Congress of Vienna in 1815: The Kingdom of the Netherlands was created, but the Duchy of Luxembourg was not to be part of it. The great powers wanted to erect a barrier against France and therefore Luxembourg became a separate political entity, but assigned as a patrimonial asset to the king of the Netherlands, William I of Orange-Nassau. The duchy was also elevated in rank becoming a *Grand* Duchy and as a result the King of the Netherlands also bore the title of Grand Duke of Luxembourg. The elevation in rank did not protect the Grand Duchy from a loss of territory, Luxembourg's second division.

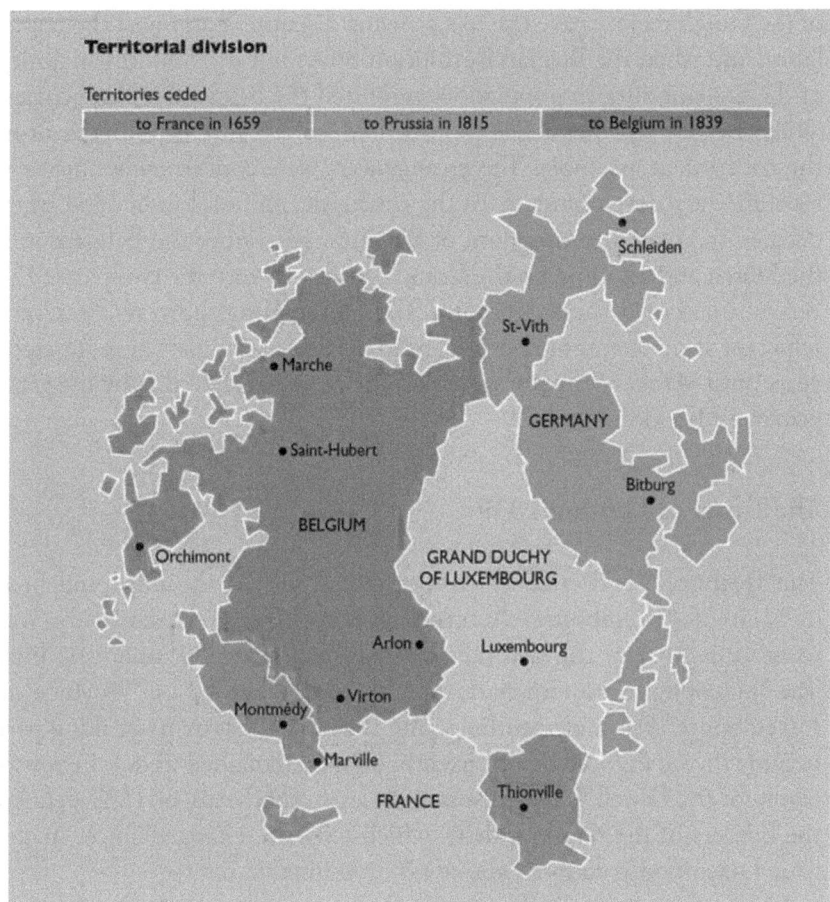

Fig. 2.1 Territorial division

To the east, large parts along the Moselle, Sûre and Our rivers fell to Prussia. The Grand Duchy of Luxembourg was also integrated in the German Confederation (Deutscher Bund) and the town of Luxembourg became a federal fortress. A Prussian garrison was stationed there as a precautionary measure against a possible French attack.

William I governed the Grand Duchy as though it was the 18th province of his kingdom. The Dutch fundamental law was applied to Luxembourg and Dutch was taught at school. Economic and fiscal policies of the Dutch regime gave rise to a growing discontent amongst the population and when the Belgian Revolution broke out in 1830, the majority of the Luxembourgish population supported the Belgian revolutionaries. When Belgian independence was declared, several Luxembourgers sat in the constituent assembly. The great powers were concerned about these revolutionary developments. At the conference in London in 1831, they decided to create the Kingdom of Belgium, separating the Belgians and the Dutch and dividing up the Grand Duchy between the two parts. The Belgians accepted these decisions. The Dutch King, however, was very reluctant and Luxembourg experienced a double administration for eight years until William I finally agreed on the proposal arrived at by the great powers in London.

The Treaty of London 1839

The Treaty of London of 19 April 1839 stipulated the third and final division of Luxembourg. According to the Treaty, Luxembourg was to be split in two, the two halves largely following the linguistic line: The francophone western part, which is today known as "Province de Luxembourg" was added to Belgium. The largely German-speaking part became the Grand Duchy of Luxembourg and remained under the sovereignty of the Dutch Orange-Nassau dynasty. The Treaty of 1839 defined the borders of the Grand Duchy, which have not changed since. At the time Luxembourg counted about 170,000 inhabitants.

For the first time in its history, Luxembourg did not belong to a wider political entity but formed a separate state. The decisions taken by the great powers during the Congress of Vienna and in London were taken over the heads of the population. Even the separation of the "Province de Luxembourg" from the Netherlands which was added to Belgium did not face opposition. This process of "Grenzen über Menschen ziehen" (drawing borders over people) was accepted by the population. As historian Pauly (2013) explained: "Die Bevölkerung ließ diese Händel widerstandslos über sich ergehen. Sie hatte bis dahin noch immer kein nationales Bewusstsein entwickelt."[4] Trausch (2008) explicated that an independent

---

[4] The population allowed this to happen without showing any resistance. At that point a national sentiment had not yet developed.

state simply went beyond the population's imagination: "Ein unabhängiger und selbständiger Staat Luxembourg war eine Perspektive, die zunächst ihre Vorstellungskraft überstieg"[5] (p. 18).

The Road to Independence

At the time of the Treaty of London, Luxembourg was still closely linked to its powerful neighbours in various ways: Luxembourg was part of the German Federation and attached to the Netherlands through its dynastic link. During the French occupation the Napoleonic Code had been introduced, which was still in place. William II (1840–1849) was keener than his predecessor to grant Luxembourg a separate administration. He actually visited the Grand Duchy and in 1841 he declared that he wanted Luxembourg to be governed by the Luxembourg people. He granted a constitutional charter. Whilst the Napoleonic Code was maintained, a series of fundamental laws were introduced which laid down community organization, justice and education. For example, the Law on Primary Education dates back to this period, stipulating that German and French should be taught at school.

Second Treaty of London 1867

During the Austro–Prussian war, Luxembourg was again caught in the cross-fire of the great powers. Napoleon III actually offered the Grand Duchy in exchange for five million gold francs to William III (1849–1890) who accepted the proposal, but the German Chancellor Bismarck refused. Again the powers met in London and a compromise was found in 1867. Luxembourg's fate as a sovereign, neutral, disarmed state was sealed: France renounced its territorial claims and Prussia withdrew its garrison and dismantled the fortress. Luxembourg was declared perpetually neutral under the guarantee of the signatory powers. Luxembourg's international status was confirmed. The first task the young state faced was setting up an institutional framework. The first

---

[5] An independent and sovereign state of Luxembourg was a perspective going beyond their imagination.

constitution dates back to 1848 and was subsequently revised several times. The young state adopted the regime of a representative democracy in the form of a constitutional monarchy. Political parties were formed after the turn of the century and universal suffrage for men and women was introduced in 1919.

The Nassau-Weilburg Dynasty—Luxembourg's Own Dynasty

After William III's death in 1890, Luxembourg fell to a different branch of the Nassau dynasty, the Nassau-Weilburgs. From then on, Luxembourg had its own branch of the Nassau dynasty who have provided the country with six sovereigns: Adolf (1890–1905), William IV (1905–1912), Marie-Adélaïde (1912–1919), Charlotte (1919–1964), Jean (1964–2000) and Henri (since 2000). William IV was a Protestant, the religion of the House of Nassau, but Catholicism was the dominant religion in Luxembourg. William IV married Princess Marie Anne Bragance of Portugal—a Roman Catholic. The couple agreed that sons would be raised Protestants and any daughters would be raised following the Catholic faith. The couple had six daughters. In Marie-Adélaïde Luxembourg had its first female and its first Catholic monarch and the population and their monarch shared the same faith. However, Marie-Adélaïde's reign was quite controversial and in 1919 she abdicated to be succeeded by her sister Charlotte. During the German occupation of the country during World War II, Grand-Duchesse Charlotte went into exile in 1940 and thus clearly distanced herself from the occupying forces. She became a symbol for national independence and was held in high esteem by the Luxembourg population.

Development of a National Identification

On paper, the Grand Duchy had become an independent state in 1839. Yet at that time, the thought of a truly independent country overstrained the imagination of the majority of the population. The existing local administration had been trained either in France, the Netherlands or in

Belgium. A professional administrative system had to be set up which would do a new, sovereign state justice. As will be shown in the next section, little by little the people grew accustomed to the idea of having their own country. In the nineteenth century, when Luxembourg was created, a feeling of national identity was to be imparted on Luxembourgers through its (medieval) history. The rediscovery or reinterpretation of history was part of the process.

"Discovery" of History

An example for this reinterpretation may be the *Klëppelkrich* in 1798, which was now seen as fight for independence against France. In the early twentieth century, Luxembourg historians discovered "their" emperors, concentrating mainly on the medieval period and reinterpreted history for the purpose of nation-building. This emergence of a national reading of history was the central theme of Peporté's (2011a) oeuvre "*Constructing the Middle Ages. Historiography, Collective Memory and Nation-Building in Luxembourg.*" Péporté specifically looked at the Middle Ages and showed how "national heroes" were created retrospectively, serving a sense of nation-building. The Luxembourg emperors were rediscovered and especially John the Blind adopted as the last "true knight." This idea of the "master narrative" whereby historical events are retrospectively construed through the lens of the investigator is also the theme of another book by Péporté and colleagues which carries the provocative title "Inventing Luxembourg" (2010). The historians analysed the historical construal process of Luxembourg during the nineteenth to the twenty-first century.

The Myth of Foreign Domination (*Fremdherrschaft*)

The brief overview of the history of Luxembourg demonstrated that the territory that now forms the Grand Duchy of Luxembourg has frequently changed in terms of boundaries and rulers. However, the use of the term *Fremdherrschaft* to describe the period of the Ancien Régime (fifteenth–eighteenth century) is inappropriate:

Luxembourg historiography has for a long time described the regimes that succeeded one another from the 15th to the 18th century as periods of "foreign domination". This suggests a simple interval from the autonomy of the Middle Ages, when Luxembourg had its own dynasty, to when it regained its independence during the 19th century. In this interpretation, the periods of Burgundian, Spanish and Austrian rule become periods of occupation with Luxembourg falling into the hands of foreigners. The men and women of the Ancien Régime, however, did not share this sentiment. They recognised the sovereign, whether Spanish or Austrian, as their natural prince, the legitimacy of whom had been acknowledged by the assembly of the estates of the Duchy at the time of accession. (…) While a local and provincial sense of identity was very much present under the Ancien Régime, a national sentiment is but a 19th-century invention. (Government Brochure, 2008, p. 5)[6]

"Discovery" of a National Sentiment

As noted above, the little fortress *Lucilinburhuc* was first mentioned in 963 and the current territorial dimensions and sovereignty date back to the Treaty of London in 1839. When William I violated the status granted to the Grand Duchy in 1815, there were no protests by the Luxembourg population. However, when the Belgians started to show discontent in the 1830s, many Luxembourgers joined them and many regretted the separation from Belgium in 1839:

A true national sentiment started to form after the creation of the Luxembourg state. In 1839, the population of the Grand Duchy, which in its majority had supported the Belgians in their revolution, was still regretting its separation from Belgium. But before long, the Luxembourg people became attached to their state and started to appreciate the advantages conferred by autonomy. Twenty years following the split, the Feierwôn, a patriotic song composed to celebrate the inauguration of the railway, declared: "Mir wëlle bleiwe wat mir sin" ("We want to remain

---

[6] The quote is taken from the Government Brochure with the full title: "About … History of the Grand Duchy of Luxembourg, edited by Information and Press Service of the Luxembourg Government/ www.gouvernement.lu" and I shortened this source document to "Government Brochure (2008)."

what we are"). It became a true national song. (Government Brochure, 2008, p. 9)

Thus the identification with the sovereign state had a somewhat slow start, but the process of nation-building had been set in motion. Trausch (2008) argued that even in 1866/67 there was still a rather passive reaction to the potential loss of independence. The Luxembourg ruling classes did not have a lot of influence and the negotiations in London happened largely behind closed doors. The Luxembourg dignitaries informed the Dutch King/Grand Duke of their preferences: The first option was to remain a sovereign state, failing that the preferred option was annexation by France rather than Germany. Only a few years later, towards the end of the German–French war in 1871, there was a German movement for a "return" of Luxembourg to the German union. This motion was perceived as a threat and openly opposed by the Luxembourg population: Patriotic demonstrations were staged against Bismarck's proposal and 40,000 signatures of men older than 25 years were collected, representing nearly the total male population of the time.

By that time, the first railway network was in place and the first steel mills had been erected and "foreign" workers had entered the country. As Pauly (2013) noted: "Dieser verstärkte Austausch mit dem Ausland weckte allerdings die Luxemburger aus ihrer Gleichgültigkeit."[7] The increased exposure to other cultures therefore led to a process of reflection of their own nationality. This effect of second culture exposure as a central catalyst for self-reflection is a finding that will be elaborated further as a central theme of this book.

Pauly (2013) also noted that this "*nation-building*" was not planned. Rather, it is the end-point of a process when the Luxembourgers learnt to fend for themselves. Moyse (2010) also commented on the fact that the State was created before a national sentiment was developed. Trausch (as cited in Moyse, 2010) explained: "Avant d'être une nation le Luxembourg fut d'abord un Etat."[8] The first national flag was introduced in 1845. The

---

[7] This increased exposure with foreign countries awakened the Luxembourgers from their apathy.
[8] Before becoming a nation, Luxembourg had to become a State.

first, albeit quite constricted, constitution was drafted in 1848 and the patriotic song *Feierwôn* (locomotive engine) was composed in 1859. In 1871 the first open protests and petitions were staged against Bismarck. This progression shows that the nation-building process had gathered momentum.

During World War I the young state was still involved in establishing itself and strictly observed the neutrality granted under the second Treaty of London, which the German troops clearly violated in 1914 and then again in 1940. During World War II the national sentiment was strengthened even further. At the 1941 census by the German occupying forces, the majority responded with "Luxembourgish" to the three crucial questions of national, ethnic and linguistic affiliation. When the occupying forces announced compulsory conscription in 1942, a large-scale, peaceful strike was staged which was brutally ended by the Wehrmacht. The use of Luxembourgish became a symbol for the resistance movement. Kollwelter (2007) goes as far as stating "As a result of the Nazi occupation, Luxembourgers developed a distinct national identity" (p. 1). The authors of "Inventing Luxembourg" (Péporté et al., 2010, p. 344) provide a more qualified statement. They argued that history is increasingly being "de-nationalized," at least as far as the academic side and official history are concerned. However, language is still in the process of "nationalization." The role of language in the process of nation-building will be elaborated in the next section.

The Role of Language(S) in the Process of Nation-Building

As was shown above, a (re)interpretation of history first served the purpose of nation-building. As will be shown next, multilingualism and especially the own language *Lëtzebuergesch* have increasingly taken on that role.

Multilingualism

The third division of Luxembourg in 1839 reduced the territory of the Grand Duchy to its German-speaking part. The country could have renounced its bilingualism. Instead, a conscious decision was made to keep both languages. The Law on Education of 1843 set down that learning French was compulsory alongside German. Thus, by learning German and French at school, Luxembourg would stay connected with both neighbouring countries. The social elite remained in favour of the use of French, but did not want a linguistic separation from the working classes. However, in everyday life, the Moselle-Franconian dialect was spoken, which right up until the end of the nineteenth century was referred to as *Lëtzebuerger Däitsch* (Luxembourgish German) or "*our German.*"

Keeping French was also an assertion against the German neighbour. French enabled craftsmen to seek employment in France and young women worked in Paris as maids or governesses. French became and is to date the language of administration and justice. French became also the language of the cultural and intellectual circles, whereas German was more the language of the Press and Church. In parliament both German and French were used until 1944 when the use of German was forbidden and the use of Lëtzebuergesch introduced. Today, Lëtzebuergesch is the dominant language in politics (Trausch, 2008).

Cultivating bi- or rather trilingualism was thus one way of distancing oneself from both powerful neighbours. Today, it is expected of all Luxembourg people to be able to speak and write all three languages. As Trausch (2008) wrote: "Das ist eine außergewöhnliche kulturelle Bereicherung, in der die Luxemburger eine wichtige Komponente ihrer Identität sehen"[9] (p. 27). It should also be noted that in the Luxembourg of today, a fourth language, namely Portuguese, is the second most frequently spoken language, after Luxembourgish (Dickens & Berzosa, 2010). *Lëtzebuergesch* is increasingly at the heart of the national identity debate.

Lëtzebuergesch

At the end of the nineteenth century, Lëtzebuergesch gradually asserted itself as the mother tongue rather than German. As alluded to above,

---

[9] This is an exceptional cultural enrichment which is viewed by Luxembourgers as a central part of their identity.

the use of Lëtzebuergesch was to become the symbol of resistance and national cohesion during World War II. As was also noted, the increased exchange with "foreigners" who came to Luxembourg to work in the steel and mining industry contributed to the awakening of Luxembourg people from their national indifference. They remembered their roots and more and more their own local language. Lëtzebuergesch became a language that was not only spoken, but written. German and French were increasingly viewed as foreign languages and Lëtzebuergesch as *Mammensprooch* (mother tongue). This trend culminated in the 1984 Law, which finally awarded Lëtzebuergesch the status of national language. Article 1 of the Law reads: "Luxembourg's national language is Luxembourgisch." However, the simultaneous use of French and German was never called into question. A recent study (IPSE, IDENT, 2010) identified Luxembourgish as the preferred mother tongue by Luxembourgish participants. A detailed overview of the current linguistic landscape can be found, for example, in the first and second Baleine reports (Fehlen, Piroth, Schmitt, & Legran, 1998; Fehlen, 2009). Linguistic aspects of the language are covered in a recent publication by Gilles and Wagner (2011).

Today, the ability to speak Luxembourgish is perceived by many Luxembourg people as the central, qualifying criterion for being Luxembourgish. An article in a Luxembourg weekly magazine headlined "Auf der Suche nach der Identität. Typisch luxemburgisch?" (In search for identity. Typically Luxembourgish?) came to the conclusion: "Luxemburger ist, wer Luxemburgisch spricht"[10] (Scheffen, 2013). The Luxembourgish language has taken on a very strong identification function. In the above mentioned IPSE (2010) report Fehlen wrote: "Man wird also kaum fehlgehen, dem Luxemburgischen eine stark identitätsstiftende Funktion beizumessen"[11] (p. 79).

Some groups have been founded with the explicit goal of defending the use of the Luxembourg language. The *Actioun Lëtzebuergesch* (AL), an organization dedicated to the defence of *eis Sprooch* (our language),

---

[10] Those who speak Luxembourgish can be called Luxembourgish.

[11] One cannot go wrong, by ascribing a strong identity-generating function to the Luxembourgish language.

was founded in 1971. Fehlen (2008, p. 57) explained that these proponents of the Luxembourg language want to protect the Luxembourgish
language against "*Germanisierung*" and the use of other "*foreign*" (friem)
languages, in particular French, in their own country. The new law on
Luxembourg Nationality will be explained in Chap. 3. Here I just want
to mention that high competence levels in Luxembourgish are a requirement of the naturalization procedure. Currently, applicants must achieve
level B1 in Luxembourgish listening comprehension and A2 in speaking.[12]
Government suggestions for lowering the levels have so far been met by
resistance from the population. In October 2015, the coalition government has drafted another revision of the Nationality Law which includes
the suggestion to scale down all language competence levels to A2.

According to Fehlen (2008) traditionally teachers and lower civil servants
have been the main champions in defending the use of Lëtzebuergesch.
For example, in 2011, the Association des professeurs de L'enseignement
secondaire et supérieur (APESS, Higher Education Teacher's Union)
published an essay entitled "Eis Identitéit" by Nico Thewes in its magazine *Ausbléck*. In reference to the national motto *Mir welle bleiwe wat mir
sinn* (We want to remain what we are), the author stressed that the population should keep its values such as the (Luxembourgish) language *eis
Sprooch*. Thewes refers to the language-based open-mindedness (*sprooch-
lech bedéngte Weltoffenheet*) of Luxembourgish people and argues that foreigners who don't speak the three languages, benefit from Luxembourg's
openness, but threaten to destabilize Luxembourg's trilingualism. The
author deplores the rise of the use of the French language, first as a result
of Portuguese immigration[13] and subsequently as a consequence of the
influx of Francophone frontaliers: "Mir hunn elo do en Identitéitsproblem:
mir ginn an eisem eegene Land emmer méi vu francophonen Auslänner
gezwongen am all deegleche Liewe franséisch zu schwätzen"[14] (p. 205).

---

[12] The Common European Framework of Reference for Languages (CEFR) is a guideline used to
describe achievements of learners of foreign languages. Six Common Reference Levels (A1, A2, B1,
B2, C1, C2) refer to degrees of competence with, A1 standing for Beginner and C2 Mastery.

[13] As will be explained in the following section, the Portuguese immigrant wave started in the late
1960s and today Portuguese immigrants form the largest minority within Luxembourg. Given the
linguistic roots, Portuguese often speak French as a second language.

[14] We now have a problem of identity: we are forced by the francophone foreigners to use French
more and more in our daily life in our own country.

Thewes claims that more should be done to protect the local population and its identity bestowed through language (sproolech Identitéit). He perceives the destruction of the language as a destruction of the identity and solidarity ("Zersetzung vun der Sprooch als Zerstéierung vun Identitéit a Solidaritéit," p. 209). To summarize—the author postulates a strong relationship between language and national identity. Language use and the relationship with the attitude to the plural composition of society will be explored in the empirical studies presented later, as well as the association between language competence and biculturalism.

National Symbols

As noted above, Lëtzebuergesch was only included as officially recognized language in national law in 1984. Moyse (2010) showed that other national symbols were also only relatively recently anchored in the Luxembourg national legislation.

Flags are important political symbols (Billig, 1995). The current Luxembourg national flag was specified in the *Loi sur les emblèmes nationaux* (Law of national emblems) of June 1972 which was amended in July 1993 specifying the exact colour hues. The tricolour with three bold stripes in red, white and blue dates back to 1815. William I simply included the Duchy under the Dutch flag. Following the Treaty of London in 1839, the Grand Duchy wanted its own flag. To differentiate itself from the Dutch flag, a lighter shade of blue was adopted. The "*Fändel*" (flag) will emerge as topic of discussion again in 2006. Moyse (2010) commented: "Le débat sur la nécessité ou non de changer le drapeau tricolore (…) montre que même au niveau des symboles collectives, la définition d'une identité collective demeure problematique"[15] (pp. 4–5).

The Coat of Arms of Duke Henry V of Luxembourg (1216–1281) also had the tricolour and a red lion. This "*Roude Léiw*" became a symbol of the resistance during World War II. In 1990, an official flag inspired by the Coat of Arms was designed for ships sailing under the Luxembourg

---

[15] The debate about the necessity to change or not to change the tricolour shows that even at the level of national symbols the definition of collective identity is problematic.

flag. This flag sporting the Roude Léiw became very popular and in 2006 a Christian Social People's Party (CSV) parliamentarian started a motion to replace the current national flag with the one showing the Roude Léiw. This initiative was widely, and in parts passionately, debated and accompanied by bumper sticker campaign saying *"Ech sinn dofir"* (I am for it). Trausch (2008) explained: "Das soziale und politische Leben der Luxemburger ist durch ihren ausgesprochenen Pragmatismus gekennzeichnet"[16] (p. 29). The solution to the *Fändel* debate can be seen as an example for this proverbial pragmatism. In 2007, a government compromise was found: The tricolour remains the official flag, but the Roude Léif can be shown *as well*.

The evolution of the national song also illustrates the growing self-assertion of the fledgling new state. Luxembourg joined the German *Zollunion* (customs union) in 1842 and Germany was instrumental in helping to develop Luxembourg's infrastructure, constructing railway lines, connecting Luxembourg and Thionville in France. This rail connection between Luxembourg and the outside world took on a symbolic function as it also connected the population to their land. The patriotic song Feierwôn (locomotive engine) was composed for the inauguration of this railway line in 1859. A strong national sentiment is expressed in this song composed by the national poet Michel Lentz. The song's refrain directly invites the three big neighbours to come to the country and local people will only be too happy to show them *their* beautiful homeland. They would be told by everyone they meet that they are only too happy to remain who they are ("Kommt her aus Frankräich, Belgie, Preisen, Mir wellen iech ons Hémecht weisen, Frot dir no alle Säiten hin, Mir welle bleiwe wat mir sin"). A bold statement of national emancipation. The statement *Mir welle bleiwe wat mir sin* becomes the national motto. A different song *"Ons Hémecht"* ("Our homeland"), also composed by Michel Lentz, was adopted as the official national anthem and performed for the first time in public in 1864, but was only included in national legislation in 1993.

Finally, I want to mention Luxembourg's national day. The precursor to today's Fête Nationale was introduced by Luxembourg's

---

[16] The social and political life of Luxembourgers is characterized by a pronounced pragmatism.

first own dynastic ruler. Grand Duke Adolphe wanted to be more recognized by the population than his predecessor and took on a stronger ceremonial role. In 1891, Adolphe thus introduced the *"Bal Populaire"* which is the precursor to today's festival before the national day. A year later the "day off" for school children was introduced and in 1947 Grand-Duchesse Charlotte declared the day a national holiday (Péporté, 2011b). Initially, the national day was celebrated on her birthday, 23 January. Today's date for the *fête nationale* can be interpreted as another example for the above mentioned pragmatism. The Grand-Duchesse moved the celebrations to June for climatic reason—and it stayed 23 June ever since. Moyse (2010) explained: "Cette grande fête populaire, que constitue l'une des grandes manifestations de l'unité nationale, n'est donc pas liée à un moment de grande rupture dans l'histoire nationale, mais elle est le résultat d'un simple processus évolutif"[17] (pp. 4–5). The national day celebrations have traditionally preceded the solemn religious service *Te Deum* at the Cathedral. This part of the celebration has now been questioned and changed by the current government and shows that the *processus évolutif* continues.

Interim Conclusion

This brief overview of historical key events served to illustrate that Luxembourg, as sovereign State, is less than 200 years old and Luxembourg as a *nation* is still being formed. Even today, national symbols are discussed and amended. The overview also shows why language and multilingualism play such a central role in the self-conception of Luxembourg. Within the Luxembourg context, language goes beyond language competence in terms of speaking, reading and writing—from Luxembourg's inception as a country within its current borders, language has taken on a symbolic function. The third division of Luxembourg took place along linguistic lines: Luxembourg was reduced to the German-speaking part and for reasons spelled out above, a conscious decision was taken to keep French, to stay

---

[17] This great popular celebration, which is one of the great demonstrations of national unity, does not mark a rupture in national history, but is the result of a natural evolution.

bi-lingual. During World War II Lëtzebuergesch gained status as a symbol of resistance. Following World War II Luxembourg also emerged as a leading force within Europe, gaining strength from this newfound status. It is therefore no surprise that the rise in status of the country and the rise in status of the Luxembourgish language, culminating in the language law of 1984, are intertwined. Official *tri*-lingualism is a mere 20 years old. The linguistic landscape is still changing. As noted above, Portuguese is already the second most frequently spoken language and the importance of English is on the rise. As will be discussed in the next section, Luxembourg's success in Europe and beyond is closely tied to the influx of foreigners. Thus, the process of establishing a Luxembourg national identity, of looking *inward*, runs in parallel with opening up or looking *outward*.

Migration Waves in Luxembourg

Emigration in the Nineteenth Century

Prior to becoming a sovereign state, the Luxembourg economic fate was largely tied to the rulers of the time. As was shown above, rulers and borders changed frequently and the economic development of the country was left behind. Before the development of the steel industry, Luxembourg was a poor agricultural country, struggling to feed its growing population. This triggered several waves of emigration. From 1825 onwards, Luxembourgers emigrated first towards Brazil and Argentina, then primarily to the USA, where some significant Luxembourg colonies developed in Wisconsin and Illinois. In honour of the many Luxembourgers who settled in Wisconsin, the *"Luxembourg American Cultural Center"* was opened in the Town of Belgium, Wisconsin, in 2010 (Luxemburger Wort (2010, August 7)).

Between 1841 and 1891, approximately 72,000 Luxembourgers left their country, amounting to approximately a third of the total population at the time. In 1908, 16,000 Luxembourgers lived in Chicago (Government Brochure, 2008). However, not all travelled as far as the Americas. As Willems and Milmeister (2008) reported, significant numbers also emigrated to Hungary and the ability to speak French allowed Luxembourgers to find work in France. At the beginning of the nineteenth century, only some minor "cottage" industries existed in Luxembourg such as tanneries, wine production or paper mills. To stem the outflow of people, economic development had to be initiated. Given size and resources, development was only possible in partnership. In 1842 Luxembourg joined the German customs union (Zollverein) on Grand Duke William II's insistence, against the will of the population (Trausch, 2008). For the first time Luxembourg orientated itself economically to Germany and this union proved to be beneficial for both sides. Germany supplied Luxembourg with capital, labour and an export market for its products whilst Germany was to benefit from the Luxembourg iron and steel production which ranked amongst the world's six largest producers on the eve of World War I (Government Brochure, 2008). This union lasted until 1918 when Luxembourg withdrew from the *Zollverein* under pressure from the allied forces. In 1921 Luxembourg joined the economic and monetary union with Belgium (*Union économique Belgoluxembourgoise*), which was later superseded by European Union.

With great foresight, the Luxembourg government of the time stipulated that the processing of iron ore discovered in Luxembourg had to take place locally. This meant that foreign iron and steel companies had to set up in Luxembourg as raw materials could not be exported. From 1870 onwards, large-scale steel works were erected in the Minette region in the southern part of the country and marked the beginning of Luxembourg's industrial revolution. This set in motion what Schalast (1995) described as a "radical transformation from an agrarian state at the beginning of the 19th century into part of the SaarLorLux (Saar-Lorraine-Luxembourg) coal and steel region and finally into a leading European financial center" (quoted in Lorig & Hirsch, 2008a, p. 8). The consequences are changes in the demographic and social structures of the country which are still felt today.

Immigration Waves

I will describe five immigration waves to Luxembourg, which can be differentiated by country of origin of immigrants, permanency and sector of the economy. During the first wave, mainly seasonal workers came to work in the steel industry, returning to their home countries upon completion of their jobs. The second wave is characterized by more permanence as workers are bringing their families. The third wave is mainly composed of European "expatriates" who come to Luxembourg for the duration of their contract. Waves 2 and 3 overlap in parts and continue to this day. The fourth and more recent wave is characterized by growth of non-EU citizens. The fifth wave is slightly different as it refers to the daily wave of *transfrontaliers* or commuters who travel to work in Luxembourg from the three neighbouring countries. In the following section these immigration waves will be discussed in more detail.

Early Immigration (Wave 1)

The Luxembourg *emigration* in the nineteenth century described above meant a shortage of workers in the fast expanding iron and steel industry. Farmers from the northern part of the country moved south but were not sufficient in numbers to satisfy the demand in labour. Thus, from 1892 onwards, the trend towards immigration to Luxembourg started, disrupted only by two shorter periods of emigration during the world wars (Willems & Milmeister, 2008).

The earliest phase of pre-war immigration attracted mainly German workers—convenient because of their geographic proximity and linguistic skills. Furthermore, economic links had already been established through Luxembourg's membership in the *Zollverein*. Italian workers followed and by 1910 "immigrants already represented 15.3 % of the total population" (Government Brochure, 2008, p. 12). The early Italian migrants were mainly seasonal workers who would return to their home country on completion of their work. Many also returned to Italy during the interwar years. As Kollwelter (2007) explained: "At the end of the 19th century, workers from German and Italy were recruited to work in the iron industry on a temporary basis."

Immigration in the Second Half of the Twentieth Century (Wave 2)

Following World War II, German immigration rapidly declined. Italian workers returned after the war and from the late 1950s onwards, they started to bring their families. The second wave of immigration is characterized by more permanency. The first foreign workers mainly settled in the Minette region of Luxembourg, working in the iron and steel industry. Today, the largest absolute numbers of Italians can still be found in that region (Heinz, Peltier, & Thill, 2013a). The peak in Italian immigration in the 1970s coincided with the beginning of the immigration from Portugal. The guest worker agreement with Portugal allowed immigrants to bring their immediate family members (Kollwelter, 2007). The steep post-war rise in immigration from Portugal has been accompanied by a steady decline in Italian immigration since the 1970s. The most recent census actually showed a decline by 4.9 % of the Italian population (Heinz et al., 2013a). With over 37 %, Portuguese make up the largest part of Luxembourg's foreign population and comprise 16.1 % of the total population (Heinz et al., 2013b). A quarter of the Portuguese living in Luxembourg were actually born in Luxembourg, 70 % in Portugal and 1.6 % in Cap Verde. Before gaining independence in 1975, Cap Verdeans could enter Luxembourg under a Portuguese passport. According to the 2011 census, 2472 people of Cap Verdean origin resided in Luxembourg (Heinz, Peltier, & Thill, 2012).

Changes in the economic circumstances may explain at least in part the different immigration patterns. The structural crisis of the steel industry also hit Luxembourg and steel production declined over 50 % between 1974 and 1992 (Government Brochure, 2008). Yet the Luxembourg authorities had implemented a policy of diversification from the late 1950s onwards. The tertiary sector was to take over from the steel industry as locomotive for the Luxembourg economy. Furthermore, Luxembourg had succeeded in attracting several European institutions to Luxembourg (see Wave 3). For the large infrastructure development needed, the Luxembourg government turned to Portugal. Willems and Milmeister (2008) explained that many Italians started out working in the steel industry, but the second and third generation is now working in the service sector, thanks to better education. On the whole, the Portuguese population has not experienced the same upward mobility. In comparison, the Portuguese immigrant population is more numerous and heterogeneous. Very recent immigrants live alongside those who have lived in Luxembourg very large parts or even their entire lives. In percentage terms there is a concentration of Portuguese citizens in some parts of the country. In Larochette, for example, just under half of the population (45.5 %) are Portuguese (Heinz et al., 2013b). Portuguese immigrants have their own shops, bars and clubs—there is also an annual "*Luxembourg Miss Portugal*" election. Young Portuguese living in Luxembourg tend to marry younger than the national average and also tend to marry amongst themselves (Leduc & Villeret, 2009).

In conclusion, Wave 2 immigration can be characterized by permanence, dominant countries of origin (Italy and Portugal) and sector of industry (steel and building trade). Integration patterns vary between the Italian and Portuguese immigrants. The meaning of integration will be discussed in more detail in Chap. 3.

Immigration in the Second Half of the Twentieth Century (Wave 3)

During the twentieth century Luxembourg acted as a catalyst in the unification of Europe. Siding with the allies in World War II gave Luxembourg a good standing with the allied forces and confidently, Luxembourg participated in the reconstruction of Europe. Luxembourg is a founding member of the United Nations (UN, 1945), NATO (1949) and the European Coal and Steel Union[18] in 1951 with its seat in Luxembourg. Hosting the Headquarters of the *Montanunion* was the start of the "Europeanization" of Luxembourg. As Trausch (2008, p. 26) reported, Jean Monnet would have liked to create a "*European district*" in Luxembourg, but the government of the time feared that this might pose a threat to the political identity of the country. Thus, in 1957 Brussels was elected seat for the European Economic Union (EEU). Nevertheless, the weight of Luxembourg in the European Union is disproportionate to its size. Luxembourg today is host to a great number of European Institutions including the European Court of Justice, the European Court of Auditors, the European Investment

---

[18] Europäische Gemeinschaft für Kohle und Stahl (EGKS), Communauté européenne du charbon et de l'acier (CECA).

Bank, Eurostat, the European Publications Office and the Secretariat of the European Parliament employing in total about 10,100 European civil servants in 2014 (Statec, 2015). These international civil servants are classed by the national statistics office (Institute national de la statistique et des études économiques, Statec) as "*ansässige Grenzpendler*" (resident borderers). This classification reflects the circular nature of migration for this group of European migrants. Most will have the intention to return to their home countries on completion of their working contracts.

In an attempt to diversify, the Luxembourg government created a regulatory environment and an infrastructure which allowed Luxembourg to become an important player in the financial sector. Today, Luxembourg is the second largest investment fund centre in the world after the USA (Luxembourg for Finance, 2014). With a market share of nearly 27 %, Luxembourg is by far the largest fund domicile in Europe in terms of total assets under management. Today, the financial sector is the largest contributor to the Luxembourg economy. As of the end of July 2016, 141 banks from 28 different countries were counted in Luxembourg (CSSF, 2016, monthly statistics).

In the Global Financial Ranking Index ranking 80 financial services centres around the world, Luxembourg achieved rank 13 in 2013. In 2014, "*Luxembourg for Finance*" summarized the success of Luxembourg as a financial centre as follows: "The success of the financial centre is founded on the social and political stability of the Grand Duchy and on a modern legal and regulatory framework that is continuously updated, inspired by regular consultation between the government, the legislator and the private sector." This successful position in the financial sector has earned Luxembourg a standing in the world of finance as centre of excellence but has also attracted some negative attention as an alleged "tax haven."

At the end of 2015, 44,993 people were employed in the financial services sector (CSSF, 2016, annual statistics). The financial services sector attracts an international work force—again many of whom will return to their countries of origin after their contract finishes. *Transfrontaliers* (Wave 5) are also employed in this highly specialized sector.

Wave 3 migration is thus characterized by semi-permanence, as the majority of work force will stay for the length of a contract. This semi-permanence means that many lead an "expatriate" way of life, with children often not attending the Luxembourg school system, but going to one of European Schools, the International School (ISL), British St. Georges School or French schools such as the Lycée Vauban. Fehlen (2014) referred to Wave 3 as "immigration dorée ou expatriés" (golden immigration), as quite often there is financial security associated with this type of migration. The countries of origin for Wave 3 immigrants are wide-ranging, but the majority are European.

Most Recent Immigration Wave (Wave 4)

The composition of the immigrant population has changed in the 30 year period from 1981 to 2011. As Fig. 2.2 illustrates, immigration from non-European countries did not exist in 1981, but made up 13 % of the foreign population in 2011 and has risen to 14 % in 2015 (Statec, 2015).

It is too early to assess the impact of this most recent development. The main countries of origin for the non-EU foreign population are given in Fig. 2.3. As shown in Fig. 2.3, the non-European group of immigrants spans highly developed countries such as the USA or Switzerland, but also countries which have recently experienced war, unstable governments and weaker economies.

It goes beyond the scope of this research project to discuss the plight of refugees and asylum seekers in detail. In the past, asylum seekers mainly originated from European countries, but given the recent refugee crisis, the majority now originate from Asia, with just under half of the asylum seekers coming from Syria and Iraq. The most recent government figures show that 2018 asylum seekers were registered under the Geneva conventions in Luxembourg in 2015 (as of 30 November, Ministry of Foreign Affairs, 2015). Of these 26 % came from Syria, 20.9 % from Iraq, followed by 11.6 % from Kosovo.

Despite this rise in non-European immigrants and non-European asylum seekers, the overall composition of the immigrants remains quite homogeneous in Luxembourg.

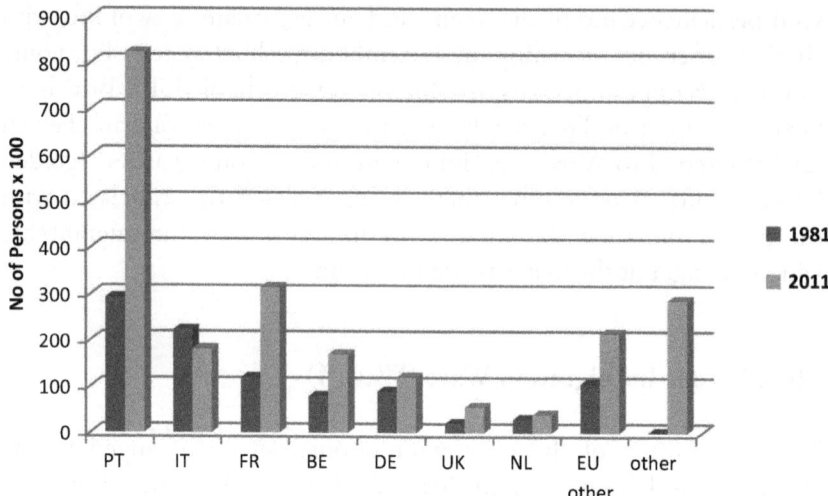

Fig. 2.2 Foreign population by country of origin (*Source*: Statec, 2013, Luxembourg in figures)

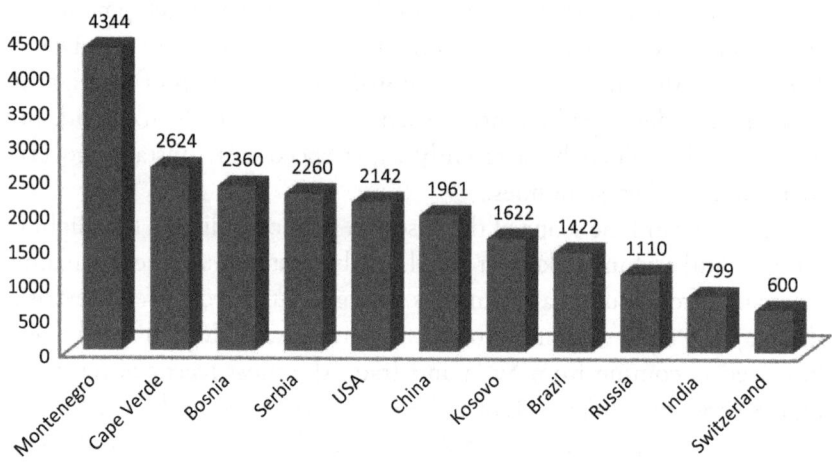

Fig. 2.3 Non-EU foreign population—main countries of origin (*Source*: Cefis [2013])

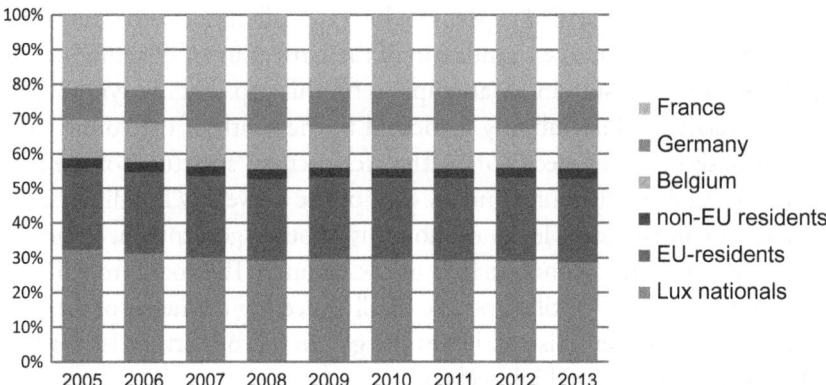

Fig. 2.4 Composition of workforce by nationality and residence, 2005–2013 (*Source*: Statec [2014], Luxembourg in figures)

Frontaliers (Wave 5)

Another Luxembourg-specific phenomenon is the number of commuters. Over 40 % of Luxembourg's total work force travels to Luxembourg on a daily basis from France (77,800), Belgium (39,500) and Germany (39,900) (Statec, 2013). This group of migrants is the most "transient" as they only spend their working day in Luxembourg. The importance of the *Frontaliers* for the Luxembourg employment market is shown in Fig. 2.4:

This daily influx poses a special challenge to the road and rail infrastructure of the country. The differential employment rates (Statistique en bref, Grossregion, 2013) in the neighbouring countries are one explanation for the daily influx of workers. As Wille (2011) pointed out, the *frontaliers* play the "*rôle de régulateur*" in Luxembourg. They are often the most recent to join an enterprise, on short-term contracts and the first to be released. One of the particularities of the Luxembourg employment market is that there are open positions, which are difficult to fill, alongside people who are looking for work. The open positions habitually demand very specific, highly skilled expertise which can often not be recruited on the domestic market. The foundation of the University of Luxembourg in 2003 was one measure in an attempt to fill this gap. Highly symbolical, the University of Luxembourg is located in the south of the country on the grounds of closed steel works. The architectural structures of the former industrial age surround and are part of the university buildings. This investment in the knowledge economy is another government effort to further diversify the economic base of the country. The goal is to educate and to develop highly skilled people locally, meeting the needs of the private sector. However, this still leaves the gap in job opportunities for less educated, less specialized job seekers.

Summary Immigration Waves

The aim of this section was to show the heterogeneity of immigration to Luxembourg and the fact that the demographic profile is still evolving. The key characteristics of the immigration waves are summarized in Table 2.1:

Other countries have, of course, also experienced immigration waves or patterns, but Luxembourg is quite unique in terms of scale and types of immigration groups. Each set of immigrant group brings with it its own integration issues, aspirations and challenges. The nature of these challenges will be different, depending on the permanence—whether I come to Luxembourg for a working day, the length of a contract or to settle permanently, country of origin and other push-and-pull factors

Table 2.1 Summary of immigration waves

	Wave	Country of origin	Permanency	Sector
1	Late 19th century	Mainly DE Some IT	Seasonal	Steel
2	Post WWII From 1970s	IT PT	Permanent—with family	Steel Steel/Building sector
3	2nd half of 20th century	EU EU; high HDI	Length of a contract	EU civil servants Banking/Finance
4	Early 21st century	Non-EU	?	?
5		FR, BE, DE	Working day	Tertiary sector

driving the immigration decision. These issues as well as the concept and aspects of integration will be elaborated in Chap. 3. Next I will discuss the demographic profile in more detail.

Luxembourg's Demographic Profile

In 1839, the year Luxembourg became a sovereign state, the Luxembourg population amounted to 175,223 people. A hundred years later, the population broke the 300,000 barrier and by 2010 the half million marker was surpassed. Thus, in the space of less than 150 years the population more than doubled, as Fig. 2.5 illustrates:

Figure 2.5 also shows that Luxembourg's native population has stayed nearly constant in that period. The population growth is largely attributable to immigration. In terms of capacity expressed as population density, Luxembourg with 207 inhabitants/km^2 (Statec, 2013) takes a position above the European (27 countries) average of 116 inhabitants/ km^2 (Eurostat, 2013). For example in comparison with the neighbouring German *Bundesland* Saarland, there is still scope for growth. The Saarland, at 2568 km^2, is of similar size to Luxembourg (2586 km^2), but has a population density of 393 inhabitants/km^2 (Saarland, Statistische Amt, 2012).

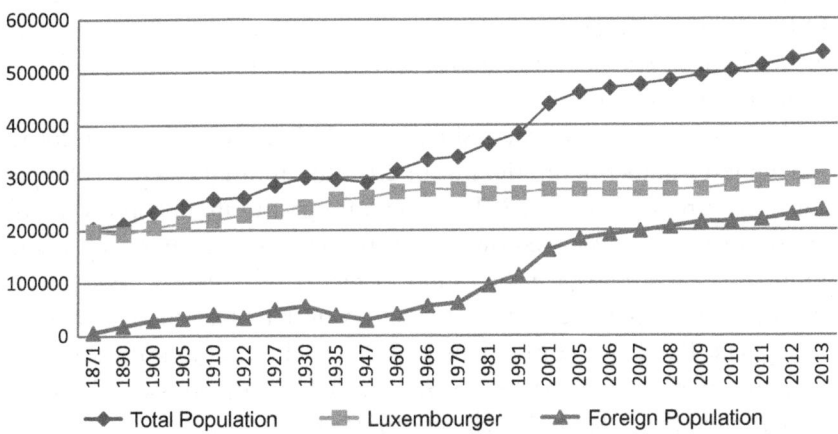

Fig. 2.5 Luxembourg population evolution from 1871 to 2013 (*Source:* http://www.statistiques.public.lu/Etat de la population)

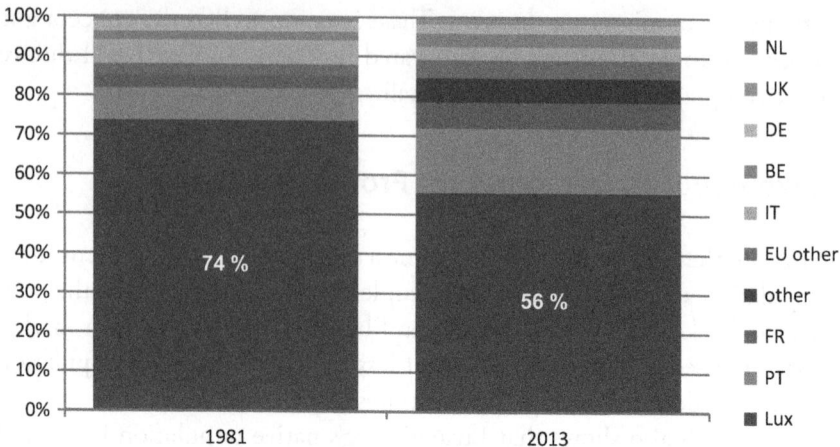

Fig. 2.6 Demographic composition—total population 1981 and 2013 (*Source*: Statec [2013]. Luxembourg in figures)

However, not only the absolute number of inhabitants has changed, also their composition. The Luxembourg population mix in 1981 compared to 2013 is shown in Fig. 2.6.

This chart not only highlights the increase in the foreign population proportion, but also the change in the foreign population mix: The share of the Portuguese immigrants has doubled and the share of the Italian immigrants has halved. There is also a marked rise of French residents. Other major changes include the rise of *other-EU* immigrants and especially the *non-EU* immigrants. Immigrants are thus coming from a wider range of countries.

Relative to the size of the resident population, Luxembourg recorded the highest number of immigrants in 2011 (39 immigrants per 1000 persons) in Europe (Eurostat, 2013). The immigrants are not spread evenly across the country. A breakdown of the percentage of foreigners per commune in Luxembourg can be found in Heinz, Thill and Peltier (2012). As the authors pointed out, in five cities over half of the residents are foreigners. Based on census figures of 2011, the capital leads the tables with (64.9 %), followed by Larochette (61.5 %), Strassen (55.1 %), Differdange (51.9 %) and Esch-sur-Alzette (51.9 %).

A fifth of the Grand Duchy's population lives in the capital and recent Government figures (2014) show that the foreign percentage has risen to 69 %, spread across 160 different nationalities. Thus, at 31 %, native Luxembourgers represent less than a third of the population in the capital. In some *quartiers*, the percentages drop to as low as 25.2 % (Neudorf/Weimershof), 24.6 % (Kirchberg) and even 16.3 % (Gare).

One consequence of the influx of foreigners to Luxembourg is that in some schools, Luxembourg native children are in the minority. In fact Eurostat (2011) figures show that Luxembourg is the country with the highest proportion (40 %) of 15-year-olds at school with immigration background in Europe. In most countries, less than 10 % of the 15-year-olds have migration background. At European average, 3.9 % of the 15-year-olds are first generation students (both students and their parents were born outside the country of assessment) and 5.4 % of the 15-year-olds are second generation students (students were born in the country of assessment, but their parents were not). In Luxembourg, proportions are 16.1 % for first generation and 24.0 % for second generation pupils. For comparison: The figures for Germany are 5.9 % for first generation and 11.7 % for second generation students and in France 3.2 % for first and 10.0 % for the second generation students (OECD, PISA 2009 database, quoted in Eurostat, 2013).

The influx of foreigners also leads to a differential cohort experience as Willems and Milmeister (2008) pointed out: "Einer weitegehend homogenen luxemburgischen älteren Generation steht eine multiethnische jüngere Generation gegenüber"[19] (p. 71).

As the capital hosts a high concentration of the foreign population (69 %) a more detailed population breakdown will be provided for the City of Luxembourg. Less than 10 % of the foreign population has a non-European background, with 3.8 % being of Asian descent, 2.9 % American, 2.5 % African and the rest Oceania or other. A breakdown of the European population is provided in Fig. 2.7.

---

[19] A largely homogeneous Luxembourgish older generation sits side by side a multiethnic younger generation.

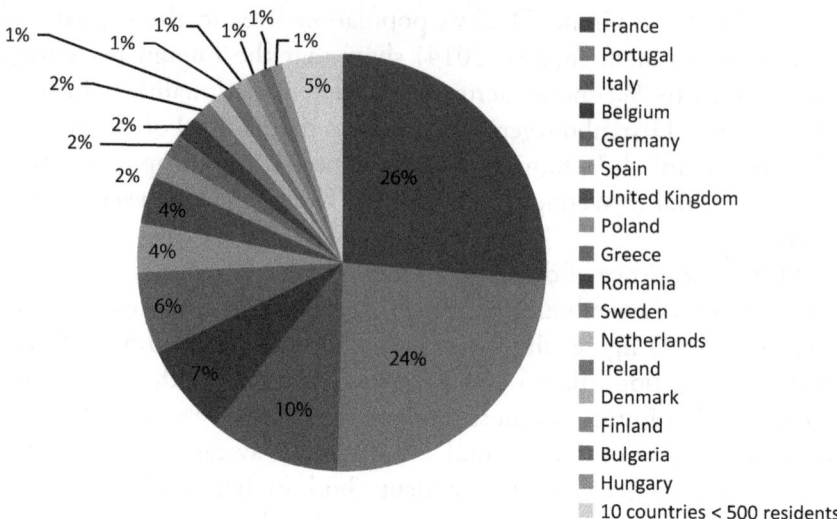

France
Portugal
Italy
Belgium
Germany
Spain
United Kingdom
Poland
Greece
Romania
Sweden
Netherlands
Ireland
Denmark
Finland
Bulgaria
Hungary
10 countries < 500 residents

Fig. 2.7 Breakdown—Ville de Luxembourg's European population mix (*Source*: Statistiques sur la Ville de Luxembourg, 2014)

This breakdown shows that the population composition is in fact quite homogeneous. Together, French and Portuguese migrants make up half of the European foreign residents. If Italian, Belgian and German residents are added, these five countries together make up nearly 75 % of the foreign European population living in the capital. Conversely this means that a wide range of other European countries make up a quarter of the "other" European group. Non-European residents clearly are in the minority which also explains the relative lack of *visible* minorities in Luxembourg. The relative homogeneity of the population is also reflected in a high concentration of high-ranking Human Development Index (HDI)[20] countries amongst the main immigration countries (United Nations Development Programme, n.d.) and in the position of the countries on the Inglehart-Welzel map of the world (Inglehart & Welzel, 2005, 2010). On this map, countries are positioned according to its people's values rather than their geographical location. The map measures

---

[20] Index developed by the United Nations Development Programme combining indicators of life expectancy, educational attainment and income.

cultural rather than geographical proximity. Luxembourg is positioned in the *Catholic European* cluster. Close neighbours to Luxembourg on this value map are France and Belgium, but also Italy. As noted above, immigrants from Catholic Europe dominate. Moyse (2010) remarked that Luxembourg has been steeped in Catholicism for centuries and "les autres confessions n'y étaient guère tolérées"[21] (pp. 4–5). This close cluster of countries is thus no surprise. Portugal, although also mainly Catholic in terms of denomination, is positioned more closely to the Latin American countries, in terms of value structure. In contrast to the other dominant immigrant countries in Luxembourg, Portugal, at 43, has also a relatively lower HDI ranking than the other countries.

Conclusion—Migration and Demographic Change

The demographic composition of the Luxembourg population can be described as multicultural. At country level, the percentage of the foreign population is 44 %, rising to 69 % in the capital. However, in terms of countries of origin and value structure, the composition of the foreign population is relatively homogeneous with the vast majority (91 %) being of European origin. Yet the non-European share of migrants has risen steadily. This rise in the non-European share also brings with it a more pluralistic religious scene. There is thus not only the challenge of dealing with a wider range of nationalities, but religious beliefs as well.

As shown above, the speed of change from country of emigration to target country for immigration is remarkable. In 1871, a foreign population was virtually non-existent and 100 years later, nearly a quarter of the population was foreign-born. Today, two-thirds of the capital's population is comprised of foreigners. Immigration patterns are not static and the composition of the foreign population is still changing. Another aspect, which will be discussed in in the next chapter, is the recently introduced new Law on Luxembourg nationality, which allows for dual nationality. Since its introduction in 2009, around 3000 persons were

---

[21] Other denominations were hardly tolerated.

naturalized per year. The number of persons with *dual* nationality is thus rising also.

The foreign population is heterogeneous in terms of permanence and in that sense differs regarding the enduring commitment to Luxembourg. The most transient group is that of the *frontaliers*, followed by the *circular* migrants. Amongst the traditional immigrants, that is those who arrive with an intention to stay, Portuguese are by far the largest immigrant group, comprising 16 % of the total population, today.

Within the country, there are different settlement patterns and the concentration of foreigners varies across regions, Cantons and at town level. Within the capital, the number of foreigners differs between the various *quartiers*. The influx of foreigners means challenges for Luxembourg's infrastructure/transport, (affordable) housing and especially the school system.

Within the Luxembourg society changes include the fact that a largely homogeneous older generation lives alongside a multicultural younger generation and the rise of foreign-born and second generation children in the school system. The School law of 1843 stipulates that German and French are taught at school. Luxembourgish, as *Integratiounssprooch*, is used at preschool level. English, as foreign language, is gaining in importance. As mentioned above, at 40 %, Luxembourg has the highest percentage of 15-year-old students with migration background in Europe. For many immigrant children, the trilingual school system is particularly challenging as they have to learn two, if not three languages in addition to their mother tongue(s). In the 2012 Programme for International Student Assessment (PISA) study, which compares mathematics, reading and natural science competencies of 15-year-olds, Luxembourg students fared better than in the previous report in mathematics (at OECD average), but still below OECD average in the other two domains. More detailed analysis shows that students with migration background are disproportionately high amongst the students performing less well (PISA (2012), national report Luxembourg). Thus, there is pressure for reform of a school system, which has served Luxembourg's needs well for so many years, but seems to require adjustment given the contemporary composition of society.

Economic cycles change and the patterns of immigration change as well. Luxembourg, for example, has seen a marked decrease in immigrants from Italy, but a rise in a greater range of European and non-European immigration. The employment sector was briefly touched on above. At the end of 2012, 379,000 employees were recorded in Luxembourg. Of these, 42 % are non-resident *frontaliers*. Willems and Milmeister (2008, p. 74) stated that Luxembourgers make up 36 % of the work force. These authors also mentioned that the open labour market is not free of tensions within the local population and they quote Fernand Fehlen who stated that the local population has developed certain strategies to protect itself from potential competition from the *frontaliers*. These strategies include language requirements, which usually cannot be met by outsiders. However, at a recent conference, Fehlen (2014) addressed the myth that many Luxembourgers work for public companies and stressed that "Tous les 'Luxos' ne travaillent pas dans le secteur public,"[22] but the list of top ten employers in terms of numbers of employees is headed by the State as the largest employer by far (Statec, 2013). Included in the list are also several public or semi-public companies such as the Groupe Entreprise des P&T (Telecommunications) or the Group CFL (Railway). Traditionally, these organizations may stipulate language competencies or nationality which favours native employment, but this is indeed changing.

Fetzer (2011) described Luxembourg, as implied by the title of his book, an "immigration success story." He concluded that Luxembourg's success depends on (1) a strong economy, (2) low economic inequality, (3) culturally similar immigrant migrants and (4) a pro-immigration elite consensus. Fetzer was struck by the absence of right-wing rhetoric or xenophobic attitudes and behaviour despite the high percentage of foreigners. Luxembourg's economy is still strong, but unemployment figures have been rising steadily, especially for the non- or low-skilled employees. There may be signs that the first two factors contributing to Luxembourg's success story, as mentioned by Fetzer are weakening. For years, Luxembourg was successful at propagating mainly European and Catholic immigration. Only recently, the Muslim community became the second largest Faith group in Luxembourg. Therefore, also the third cornerstone mentioned by Fetzer is changing. However, the elites remain firmly committed to a pro-immigration stance. For example, the then Minister responsible for communication and media, François Biltgen,

---

[22] Not all "Luxos" work for the public sector.

asserted in an interview in 2012, that he does not want a "Kachkéis a Bouneschlupp"[23] mentality. He wants to put Luxembourg on the international map and benchmark Luxembourg against competition from outside (LW-online, 10.02.2012.).

Yet there are recent initiatives addressing an underlying current of anti-immigrant sentiments. One campaign, "*Making Luxembourg*" was launched by the immigrant support group Association de Soutien aux Travailleurs Immigrés (ASTI) in 2012 to counteract xenophobia and any latent racism (http://www.makingluxembourg.lu). "*Making Luxembourg*" is an initiative which encourages people to state their individual components of identity in percent and to have these printed on T-shirts. Every person can indicate their unique component mix, but the total would always add up to "100 % Luxembourger and 0 % racist" (e.g. "50 % Minettsdapp, 25 % open-minded, 25 % Savoir-vivre, 0 %—Rassist = 100 % Lëtzebuerg"). The idea behind this campaign was to show that "Man ist Luxemburger, auch, aber eben nicht nur" (You are Luxembourgish, also, but not only). The little word "*auch*" (also) is the key. Identity construal from a psychological perspective will be discussed in Chap. 4. Kmec has (2013) noted critically that the percentages change constantly, depending on the situation and as she would argue, may surpass 100 %. She also made a general reference regarding the difficulties in quantification in social sciences "l'identité personelle que collective—comme tout objet d'étude des sciences humaines—se laisse difficilement quantifier. Quel serait le poids du passé exprimé en kilogrammes ou en tonnes?"[24] (Kmec, 2013, p. 60). In January 2014, the *Making Luxembourg* was complemented by the *Mixing Luxembourg* campaign—Your sound against racism using the slogan "Mix your sound and win" ("Mixing Luxembourg": Dein Sound gegen Rassismus. LW-online, 21.01.2014).

Another recent campaign is the social media initiative "Eng Mandarine geint riechts," which obtained over 11,000 "likes" within three days. (http://www.wort.lu/de/view/eng-mandarine-gegen-rechts-ein-facebook-phaenomen). This initiative was launched as a counter

---

[23] Reference to traditional Luxembourg dishes—a melted, soft cheese and hearty bean stew.
[24] Personal and collective identity, like all subjects in the social sciences, are difficult to quantify. How do you express the weight of the past in either kilogrammes or tons?

movement to another Facebook community "gegen die Diskriminierung von Luxemburgern" (against discrimination of Luxembourgers) which is estimated to have around 4000 members.

Could these anti-racism campaigns be interpreted as a reaction to a change in climate? In February 2014, the popular initiative against "Mass immigration" won by a slender majority in Switzerland. Switzerland's foreign percentage has reached 23.2 % and mainly the counties with lower foreign population voted for the anti-immigration motion. Blunchi (2014) wrote that "Viele Schweizerinnen und Schweizer fühlen sich in ihrer Identität herausgefordert."[25] Could the same happen in Luxembourg? The empirical studies conducted as part of this research project have the aim to identify factors which influence to openness towards the plural composition of society. As mentioned above, Luxembourg is a fairly young state and the search for a national identity commenced only in the nineteenth century. From its inception and to this day, Luxembourg has depended on a foreign workforce. Sovereignty and the influx of foreigners are of course important triggers for self-reflection. To this day, a lively debate concerning the "Luxembourg identity" exists.

Current (Re) Search for the Luxembourg Identity

"Auf der Suche nach der Identität. Typisch luxemburgisch?" (In search of Identity. Typically Luxembourgish?) was the headline of an article in Luxembourg's weekly magazine *Telecran* (29.12.2012, p. 27). The author, Jean-Louis Scheffen, observed, that "the" Luxembourger probably does not exist. Yet this headline reflects the fact that the content of and search for the Luxembourgish identity are still the subject of intense debate and study today, both in the academic setting and in the wider public domain. In this section different academic research projects will be presented, followed by coverage of this topic in the areas of arts and culture including popular culture. The aim is to show how topical "Luxembourg identity"

---

[25] Many Swiss people feel challenged in their identity.

still is today and how intense and from how many different angles the Luxembourg identity is studied. A more detailed account of the concept of identity and identity construal from a psychological perspective will be provided in Chap. 4.

Luxembourg Identity—Subject of Academic Study

The Luxembourg identity is subject of study within several academic disciplines. No exhaustive list of all academic research projects can be provided and only some examples of projects which have the study of Luxembourg or Luxembourgish (national) identity at their core will be provided to illustrate the range of coverage within the academic setting.

Luxembourg is the explicit content of *Luxembourg studies*, a Master's Degree course focusing on the Luxembourger language and culture within the country's multilingual and multicultural context. Students learn to identify and to distinguish specific Luxembourgish characteristics and to analyse the influence of other cultures in Luxembourg. These are then evaluated and compared from the perspective of the Larger Region, Europe and the World (http://wwwde.uni.lu/formations/flshase/master_en_langues_cultures_et_medias_letzebuerger_studien_academique). Course graduates are qualified to teach Luxembourgish in secondary schools or work in political or cultural institutions and the media.

Not only the University of Luxembourg offers courses on Luxembourgish culture, but the University of Sheffield in the UK also provides a specific course entitled Luxembourg Studies (https://www.shef.ac.uk/luxembourg-studies). As explained on this website: "Upon the initiative of Professor Gerald Newton, the Centre for Luxembourg Studies was founded at the University of Sheffield in 1995 and was endorsed by Jacques Santer, former Prime Minister and European Commissioner. The Centre established an archive of material in Luxembourg Studies for visiting scholars from all relevant disciplines." The course advertises the fact that Sheffield is the only place outside of Luxembourg offering this degree and is the only place where one can learn the Luxembourgish language "from scratch."

Within the research unit *Identités. Politiques, Sociétés, Espaces* (IPSE), the Faculty of History has launched several projects regarding the study of Luxembourg's national identity. These initiatives include, for example, lecture series such as "*Identity—deconstruction of a concept*" organized by Kmec and Thommes (23.02.–25.05.2011) or "En neie Bléck op d'Lëtzebuerger Geschicht"[26] (Pauly, 09.10–04.12.2012). Book projects concerning the construal aspect of Luxembourg history (Inventing Luxembourg and Constructing the Middle Ages) were already mentioned earlier in this chapter.

The Luxembourg identity was at the core of an interdisciplinary, 3-year (2007–2010) research project "IDENT—Sozio-kulturelle Identitäten und Identitätspolitiken in Luxembourg." The results of the project were published in a book titled "Doing Identity in Luxembourg. Subjektive Aneignungnen—institutionelle Zuschreibungen—soziokulturelle Milieus (2010)."[27] The aim of the project was to explore the acquired and ascribed identities within a globalized context. One of the co-authors, Kmec (2012), explained that three different levels can be distinguished in terms of the Luxembourg identity: (1) Self-definition (I am Luxembourger. *Selbstaneignung*), (2) (external) ascription (You are Luxembourger. *Fremdzuschreibung*) and (3) corporate identity (Luxembourg is …). The results of the research project were also the basis for an exhibition at the Musée dräi Eechelen which will be explained in the next section. Given Luxembourg's trilingualism, the study of multilingualism in schools, higher education and professional settings is another research focus. (http://wwwfr. uni.lu/recherche/flshase/education_culture_cognition_and_society_eccs/ institutes/research_on_multilingualism).

Within the *Integrative Research Unit on Social and Individual Development* (INSIDE), one research project concentrates on intergenerational relations in the light of migration and aging (IRMA). In a triangular approach, intergenerational value transmission is compared between Portuguese migrants living in Luxembourg, Portuguese living in Portugal and native Luxembourgers. Another research project focuses on older migrants and their network structures in Luxembourg.

This is not an exhaustive list of research projects within the academic setting focusing on the Luxembourg identity and specific aspects of the macro environment the Luxembourg context provides. The examples

---

[26] Luxembourg's History from a new perspective.

[27] Doing Identity in Luxembourg. Subjective appropriations—institutional ascription—sociocultural milieus.

serve to illustrate that there is a very active research community, feeding off the opulent context the "natural laboratory" Luxembourg provides.

Luxembourg Identity in the Arts and Culture

The Luxembourg identity has not only been the focus of attention within academia, but also in the sphere of the arts and culture. Several exhibitions centred on the theme of the Luxembourg identity.

Museum Exhibitions

The Luxembourg identity or the ascription, what it means to be Luxembourgish, has been the subject of two recent museum exhibitions. The Musée d'Histoire de la Ville die Luxembourg hosted the Exhibition *ABC—Luxemburg für Anfänger und Fortgeschrittene* (Luxembourg for Beginners and the more Advanced) from 8 June 2012 to 31 March 2013. This exhibition was concerned with stereotypes, symbols or clichés associated with Luxembourg. For every letter of the alphabet, the exhibition covered particularities about Luxembourg ranging from A "anescht" (different) to Z "zefridden" (content).

Luxembourg identity was also the topic of the inaugural exhibition of the newly created Musée dräi Eechelen (13.07.2012–29.07.2013). As alluded to above, the exhibition *iLux. Identités au Luxembourg. Fortress, History, Identities* was curated by academic researchers at IPSE, incorporating some of the results of the research project IDENT. Kmec explained that idea behind the project was to show the "Making of Luxembourg" as opposed to "made in Luxembourg," emphasizing a process: "L'Homme n'est pas un produit du terroir, mais un acteur social qui construit lui-même son identité au quotitien"[28] (Kmec, 2013, p. 60).

The theme of the diversity of Luxembourg was also subject of a photo exhibition *Ech si Lëtzebuerg* at the Galerie Urbengsschlass in Hersperange

---

[28] A person is not the product of his land, but a social agent who constructs himself, his identity on a daily basis.

in 2011. Well-known Luxembourg personalities were photographed in a pose of their choice. http://larochemarc.com/ech-si-letzebuerg.

Media

The Luxembourg identity was also the subject matter of a satirical film "Ons Identitéit. Mir hunn se fonnt" (Luxembourg identity—we have found it). The film was first shown on 13 November 2010 in Echternach. Once placed online, it reached over 3000 viewers within 2 weeks, which was considered a great success. The film addresses some latent negative sentiments against foreigners in a satirical fashion. A critical tone is also found in the song by the Luxembourg song writer Serge Tonnar in his song *Ech si Lëtzebuerg* (http://www.youtube.com/watch?v=Mxp8JXwljVk).

Popular Initiatives

A recent popular initiative was launched by the newspaper "*Luxemburger Wort*," the weekly magazine "*Télécran*" and the supermarket chain Cactus: "*Mäi Lëtzebuerg—Wat ass fir dech Lëtzebuerg?*" What does Luxembourg mean to you? A sticker album for Luxemburg was created and customers could collect stickers, representing the diversity of Luxembourg and complete their own album. The instigator explained: "Jeder von uns verbindet ganz bestimmte Dinge mit 'seinem Luxemburg'. Das Sammelalbum 'Mäi Lëtzebuerg' mit 160 Klebebildern erlaubt es, die Vielfältigkeit unseres Landes zu entdecken."[29] (http://www.wort.lu/de/view/wat-ass-fir-dech-letzebuerg published on 20.01.14).

Luxembourg Identity—The Corporate Brand

Luxembourg's "corporate brand" is the focus of a dedicated committee at the Luxembourg Foreign Ministry. The aim is to promote the image of the

---

[29] Everybody has their own association with "his/ her Luxembourg". The collectors album "my Luxembourg" with 160 stickers allows us to discover the diversity of our country.

brand "Luxembourg" abroad (Ministry of Foreign Affaires, 2013, p. 5). Within this remit a study was commissioned to assess "Le Luxembourg vu de l'étranger" and the results were presented at a round table discussion on 29 February 2012 (government.lu, Press report, 01.03.2012.) In terms of external perspective of Luxembourg, the survey came to the following conclusion:

> La qualité de vie élevée, le caractère international et multilingue du pays, le patrimoine naturel et historique attrayant, la paix sociale et la stabilité politique sont les associations positives le plus souvent citées avec le Luxembourg. Le centre financier international et la compétitivité économique sont nettement moins souvent cités parmi les associations positives. De l'autre côté, les associations négatives le plus souvent citées avec le Luxembourg sont le paradis fiscal et le secret bancaire, la taille réduite du pays, son caractère conservateur, provincial et bourgeois ainsi que le coût de vie élevé.[30] (Government.lu 01.03.2012, Le Luxembourg vu de l'étranger)

The 8th edition of "*The Economy Days*" were held on 4–5 February 2014 under the title "Réinviter Luxembourg." The purpose of this conference was to bring political decision-makers, public officials, entrepreneurs and economists together and to analyse the economic programme of the new government and discuss new development opportunities to build the future of Luxembourg. One of the participants, Journalist Pierre Leyers, wrote an editorial headlined "Was wir sind" (What we are)—in reference to the Luxembourg motto. He made reference to the Foreign Ministry working group and alleged that the search continues and urges that themes identified have to be grounded in reality (LW-online, 12.02.2014). Leyers thus picked up on a finding of the 2012 survey, commissioned by the government working group, which had stressed that "Countries are judged by what they <u>do</u> and what they <u>make</u>, not

---

[30] High living standards, the international character and multilingual nature of the country, nature and cultural heritage, social peace and political stability—these are the positive associations with Luxembourg. The international financial centre and economic competitiveness are less frequently cited under the positive associations. On the other hand, regarding negative associations, fiscal paradise and banking secrecy, the relative small size, the conservative, provincial bourgeois character as well as the high cost of living are cited.

by what they <u>say</u> about themselves." The report had also concluded that Luxembourg is not well known outside Europe: "Whatever Luxembourg has been doing in the past has <u>not</u> been sufficient to make it world famous" (underlined text as in the original source document, Le Luxembourg vu de l'étranger). Yet positive perception and public awareness ("notoriété") are linked. The most recent government initiative (NationBranding.lu) carried out in 2015, identified three core strength or values representing the *brand* Luxembourg namely reliability, dynamism and openness. Luxembourg is perceived as a reliable ally, but an ally who has been able to reinvent himself several times in the course of history.

Emerging Themes

In reviewing these various projects into the search for the Luxembourg identity, some central themes emerge, namely (1) size and (2) the difficulties in finding a positive answer to the motto Wat sin mir (What are we?) and (3) language.

Size

Size is a recurrent theme. Of course, in terms of dimensions, Luxembourg is small—2586 km², spanning North–South 82 km, and East–West 57 km. Given this closeness, personal contacts and family are important and harmonious relations are sought. It is difficult "to get away" or to remain anonymous in such a small country. Therefore, it is not surprising that "*Maach ewéi d'Leit.*" (do as other people do) was identified as the central theme the Luxembourg typology by Jul Christophory (2012). In that sense size can explain the ascribed conservatism and political stability. Reliability was also identified as the primary core value associated with the *brand* Luxembourg. Conflict must be avoided; social harmony is important—the tripartite system and pragmatism can be named as concrete examples. This system ensures that strikes are a rare occasion. In business relations the direct paths (kurze Wege) to politicians and key decision-makers are often stressed.

However, the small size is also a limiting factor. Career or development opportunities may have to be found outside of the country.

After all, prior to 2013 Luxembourg students wishing to pursue an academic career did not have the choice but to study abroad. This leads to the phenomenon that Luxembourg can celebrate two types of heroes—those who achieved fame within its borders and those who became famous abroad ("die es im Ausland 'gepackt' haben"). The importance of this latter category is reflected in the fact that "*Lëtzebuerger an der Welt*" were represented with one chapter (the letter L) in the A to Z exhibition mentioned above. Famous Luxembourgers abroad were actually "collected" and presented in a book entitled 100 Lëtzebuerger rondrëm d'Welt (2003) (Luxembourg für Anfänger, Pressedossier, 2012). Pride is thus expressed in those, coming from small Luxembourg, who hold their own in competition with the much larger neighbours. The most recent accolade in this respect is the Oscar, won for the Short Film *Monsieur Hublot*. Luxembourg beat competition from America and claims the Oscar for itself as Luxembourg played the dominant role in the Luxembourg-French co-production (LW-online, 03.03.2014).

Thus there is the pride in the achievements of such a small country, but also the vulnerability felt, being sandwiched between three much larger neighbours. Confrontation is to be avoided and instead the image of a skilled negotiator and bridge builder has been cultivated, helped by the language capabilities. As noted above, the latest nation-branding exercise identified "ally" as the Luxembourg archetype (Nation Branding.lu, 2015, p. 7). This may also explain Luxembourg's disproportionate influence on the European stage, with, for example, three Presidents of the EU, Gaston Thorn (1981–1985), Jacques Santer (1995–1999) and Jean-Claude Juncker since July 2014. Prior to this appointment, Jean-Claude Juncker was President of the Eurogroup (2005–2013). The Luxembourg people were awarded the Charlemagne Prize for their pro-European attitudes in Aix-la-Chapelle in 1986.

Size is also mentioned in the context of business relations. For example, a headline for an article on Sino-Luxembourg relations reads "Luxembourg is a bridge to Europe." In the article it is stressed that one of the smallest countries in the EU has good trade relations with the country housing 20 % of the world population. It is proudly reported that Luxembourg was the first country in the world to deliver blast furnaces to China in 1894 and good trade relations have been built on this ever since (Luxemburger Wort, 30.05.2013, p. 47). "Size does not matter" was also the title of the official brochure on Luxembourg for the EXPO 2010 in Shanghai.

As repeatedly noted, Luxembourg has undergone a tremendous transformation from being a poor agricultural country to becoming the second richest country in the world (after Qatar) with a per capita GDP on a purchasing-power parity (PPP) basis of $77,958 in 2012 (International Monetary Fund, IMF). Looking at these achievements, "size does not matter." However, Luxembourg is too small to support this level of growth of the economy without foreigners. The sectors of industry established in Luxembourg rely on a foreign workforce. Part of the demand in labour is supplied by the neighbouring countries (*frontaliers*) and part of it through immigrants to Luxembourg. On the one hand, there is the recognition that the different sectors of the economy rely on a foreign workforce and the international flair is seen as an advantage of Luxembourg. On the other hand, the influx also puts pressure on the existing infrastructure in the form of transport systems, affordable housing and education. As discussed in detail above, native Luxembourgers are already in the minority in the capital and the influx of foreigners is perceived by some as threatening their identity. However, the question remains—what constitutes this identity?

Wat sin mir?

As recurrently mentioned, Luxembourg's motto is "mir wëlle bleiwe wat mir sin." A central theme addressed in the more critical contributions regarding the Luxembourg identity such as the film *Eis Identitéit* is the search of an answer to the question "wat sin mir?" Wat sin mir—apart from *not* "Heckefransous, Peggiën oder Preisen?"[31] What is a positive answer to this question? What differentiates the Luxembourgers from other nationals? The film *Eis Identitéit* ends with a long list of countries we are *not*. In terms of customs, even the national dish, Kachkéis, which plays a prominent role in the national comic strip series "*Superjhemp*," is consumed, under slightly different names, in other countries. The same is true for the other national dish Bouneschlupp.

---

[31] Pejorative terms for French, Belgian or German.

The survey regarding the external perception of Luxembourg (2012) had identified the high living standard as one component of the Luxembourg brand. Indeed, national wealth is important and as Trausch (2008) commented "Offensichtlich hat der Wohlstand die Identifizierung der Luxemburger mit ihrem Staat begünstigt"[32] (p. 22). In the same vein, then prime minister Juncker argued: "Anstatt bleiwe wat mir sinn, wolle mir hale wat mir hun: dat ass eise Problem"[33] (Juncker, 2006, p. 1, quoted in Lorig & Hirsch, 2008a, p. 109).

As was explained above, the state was created before the nation and a first attempt to create a feeling of national identity was the reinterpretation of history. However, this interpretation of history serving national identity formation has been put in perspective by current historians such as Péporté, Margue or Pauly. Moyse (2010) also warned against building an identity on "mir wëlle bleiwe wat mir woren" (what we were) and at the same time on building one on "mir wëlle bleiwen wat mir gäre wieren" (what we would like to be). The task force at the Foreign Ministry is still fine-tuning the corporate brand for Luxembourg—how we would like to be perceived. The goal here is obviously to attract foreign businesses and tourists to Luxembourg and "unique selling points," differentiating Luxembourg from other potential locations, have to be found. One unique aspect is language, both Lëtzebuergesch and Luxembourg's multilingualism, and both of these are at the core of the national identity debate.

Language: Lëtzebuergesch (eis Sprooch) and Multilingualism

The trilingualism practiced in Luxembourg is unique as there is no territorial division of language use as in other multilingual countries such as Belgium, Switzerland or Canada. In addition to the three officially recognized languages, Portuguese is widely spoken and heard and English plays an increasingly important role. Visitors coming to the country are often amazed with what ease people switch between the languages from one situation to the next. Given Luxembourg's current demographic profile, this multitude of languages does put pressure on the education infrastructure.

---

[32] Evidently, the wealth has helped with identification of Luxembourgers with their state.

[33] Instead of remaining what we are, we want to hold on to what we have, that is our problem.

The role of Lëtzebuergesch as a symbol for national identification was discussed in detail above. In the public sphere, French is the dominant language and many Luxembourgish people object to the fact that they often cannot speak their native language outside their home in their own country. As Morbach (2014) commented in an editorial "Wer im Internet einen urluxemburgischen 'Shitstorm' auslösen möchte, muss nur einige Sätze zum Thema Französisch in Krankenhäusern, Geschäften oder Banken posten—schon kocht der Volkszorn über."[34] A letter to the editor in the Luxemburger Wort (06.11.2013) entitled "*Lëtzebuerg, mäi friemt Land!*" by a mother recounting her experience of not being able to converse in Luxembourgish in the Kannerklinik (children's hospital) had indeed caused outrage. Great annoyance at not being able to speak Luxembourgish in shops was also found the empirical study, to be reported later. The ability to speak the Luxembourgish language thus signifies much more than linguistic competence.

The Government Brochure (2008) summarizes the process of national identity formation as follows: "In actual fact, by emulating its three neighbours, Luxembourg succeeded in carving itself an original identity, which was neither German, French nor Belgian, but a mixture of all three cultures" (p. 11).

References

Amann, W., Gretscher, M., & Unité de Recherche Politique, Société, Espace IPSE - Identités Université du Luxembourg - IDENT (2010). Doing identity in Luxemburg: subjektive Aneignungen-institutionelle Zuschreibungen-sozio-kulturelle Milieus. Bielefeld: transcript-Verlag.

Billig, M. (1995). *Banal nationalism*. Loughborough University: Sage.

Blunchi, P. (2014, February 9). *Der Sieg der heilen Geranien-Schweiz. Debatte um Zuwanderungsvotum*. Spiegel online, Retrieved from http://www.spiegel.de/forum/politik/debatte-um-zuwanderungsvotum-der-sieg-der-heilen-geranien-schweiz-thread-113069-1.html

Cefis (Centre d'études et formation interculturelles et sociales). (2013). Démographie. Evolution historique 1875–2013. http://www.cefis.lu/page9/page22/page22.html, accessed April 2014.

---

[34]To provoke a typically Luxembourgish "shitstorm" on the Internet, one only needs to post a few sentences referring to the use of French in hospitals, shops or banks, and immediately the good people of Luxembourg are sent into a rage.

Christophory, J. (2012). «Maach ewéi d'Leit… » Typologie des Luxemburgers. *Telecran, 26,* 17.

Commission de Surveillance du Secteur Financier (CSSF). (2016). https://www.cssf.lu/en/supervision/banks/statistics/monthly-statistics/number-of-banks-per-country-of-origin/ accessed August 2016. https://www.cssf.lu/en/supervision/pfs/support-pfs/statistics/annual-statistics/total-employment/

Dickens, P. & Berzosa, G. (2010). Pays multiculturel, pays multilingue? Un modèle pragmatique pour l'analyse des relations langières au Luxembourg. (No 2010-2016) Luxembourg: CEPS Instead.

Eurostat (2011). *Migrants in Europe. A statistical portrait of the first and second generation. Eurostat statistical books* (2011 ed.). Luxembourg: Publications Office of the European Union. doi:10.2785/5318.

Eurostat (2013). Migration and migrant population statistics—Statistics explained (2013/9/1) http://epp.eurostat.ec.europa.eu/statistics_explained/index.php/Migration_and_migrant_population_statistics

Fetzer, J. S. (2011). *Luxembourg as an immigration success story. The Grand Duchy in Pan-European perspective.* Lanham: Lexington Books.

Fehlen, F., Piroth, I., Schmitt, C., & Legran, M. (1998). *Le Sondage Baleine, une étude sociologique sur les trajectoires migratoires, les langues et la vie associative au Luxembourg.* Recherche Etude Documentation éditeur: SESOPI Centre Intercommunautaire. Luxembourg. Luxembourg: Imprimerie St Paul.

Fehlen, F. (2009). *Baleine Bis, une enquête sur un marché linguistique multilingue en profonde mutation.* Luxemburgs Sprachenmarkt im Wandel: SESOPI Centre Intercommunautaire Luxembourg (=RED n°12). Luxembourg: Imprimerie St Paul.

Fehlen, F. (2008). Multilingualismus und Sprachenpolitik. In W. H. Lorig & M. Hirsch (Eds.), *Das politische System Luxemburgs. Eine Einführung* (pp. 45–61). VS Verlag für Sozialwissenschaften: Wiesbaden.

Fehlen, F. (2014). *Le Luxembourg, une petite société dans un monde globalisé.* Conference presentation at Vers due multi—ou de l'interculturel? organized by la Ville de Luxembourg et la Commission consultative communale d'intégration. Luxembourg, 06.03.2014.

Gilles, P., & Wagner, M. (Eds.) (2011). *Linguistische und sozio-linguistische Bausteine der Luxemburgistik.* Mikroglottika 4: Peter Lang publischer.

Heinz, A., Peltier, F., & Thill, G. (2012). La population par nationalité (1), RP 2011—Premiers résultats N°04. In S. Allegreza, D. Ferring, H. Willems, & P. Zahlen (Eds.), *La Recensement de la Population 2011.* Statec.

Heinz, A. Peltier, F., & Thill, G. (2013a). Les Italiens au Luxembourg—Italiener in Luxemburg, RP 2011—Premiers résultats N°16. In S. Allegreza, D. Ferring, H. Willems, & P. Zahlen (Eds.) *La Recensement de la Population 2011.* Statec.

Heinz, A. Peltier, F., & Thill, G. (2013b). Les Portugais au Luxembourg—Portugiesen in Luxemburg, RP 2011—Premiers résultats N°18. In S. Allegreza, D. Ferring, H. Willems, & P. Zahlen (Eds.), *La Recensement de la Population 2011*. Statec.

Information and Press Service of the Luxembourg Government, Publishing Department (Ed.) (2008). *About...History of the Grand Duchy of Luxembourg*. http://www.gouvernement.lu

Inglehart, R., & Welzel, C. (2005). *Modernization, cultural change and democracy. The human development sequence*. New York: Cambridge University Press.

Inglehart, R., & Welzel, C. (2010). Changing mass priorities: The link between modernization and democracy. *Perspectives on Politics, 8*(2), 551–567. doi:10.1017/S1537592710001258.

IPSE – Identités Politiques Sociétés Espaces (Ed.), (2010). *Doing identity in Luxemburg: subjektive Aneignungen-institutionelle Zuschreibungen-soziokulturelle Milieus*. Bielefeld: transcript-Verlag.

Kmec, S. (2012, June 6). Mein, dein, unser Luxemburg. *Revue—de Magazin fir Lëtzeburg*, 14–15.

Kmec, S. (2013). «100% Lëtzebuerg» ou: comment calculer l'incommensurable? *Forum, 328*, 60–61.

Kollwelter, S. (2007). *Immigration in Luxembourg: New challenges for an old country*. Migration Information Source (mpi). http://www.migrationinformationsource.org/Profiles

Leduc, K., & Villeret, M. (2009). *Regard croisé sur la vie familiale selon l'origine*. Collection—Vivre au Luxembourg n°57, CEPS/Instead.

Lorig, W. H., & Hirsch, M. (Eds.) (2008a). *Das politische System Luxemburgs: Eine Einführung*. Wiesbaden: VS Verlag für Sozialwissenschaften.

Lorig, W. H., & Hirsch, M. (2008b). Einleitung: Luxemburg—"Small, beautiful, and successful"? In W. H. Lorig & M. Hirsch (Eds.), *Das politische System Luxemburgs Eine Einführung* (pp. 7–12). Wiesbaden: VS Verlag für Sozialwissenschaften.

Luxembourg for Finance. (2014). Agency for the development of the financial centre. Retrieved from: https://www.luxembourgforfinance.lu/why-luxembourg

Luxemburger Wort. (2010, August 7). Neue Heimat in der neuen Welt. *Wort.lu Online*.

Ministry of Foreign Affaires – Ministère des Affaires étrangères et européennes (2013), *Rapport d'activité 2013*, retrieved from http://www.gouvernement.lu/3535255/2013-rapport-affaires-etrangeres-europeenes

Ministry of Foreign Affaires—Ministère des Affaires étrangères et européenne (2015, November). Direction de la Immigration, Statistiques concernant la protection internationale au Grand-Duché de Luxembourg. Mois de novembre 2015. Date de publication 8 décembre 2015.

Moyse, L. (2010). *Le drapeau, la vache et le coffer-fort. Reflexions sur l'identité nationale à travers l'exemple luxembourgeois.* Die Warte, Luxemburger Wort, 23.09.2010, No 25/2303 pp. 4–5.

Morbach, F. (2014). Wir Wutbürger. Luxemburger Wort, 13.02.2014.

Nation Branding.lu. (2015). Luxembourg country profile. *Nation Branding Interministerial Coordination Committee* version 14 August 2015. http://www.nationbranding.lu/lu/

Pauly, M. (2013). Der Weg ist das Ziel. Historische Vortragsreihe an der Uni Luxemburg: "En neie Bléck op d'Lëtzebuerger Geschicht" reported in: Tageblatt Luxembourg (16.01.2013).

Péporté, P. (2011a). *Constructing the middle ages: Historiography, collective memory and nation-building in Luxembourg* (Vol. 3). Leiden: Brill.

Péporté, P. (2011b). Das Land feiert sich und seinen Grossherzog. Entstehungsgeschichte und Bedeutung des Nationalfeiertages aus sich des Historikers Pit Péporté. *Luxemburger Wort*, 22.06.2011.

Péporté, P., Kmec, S., Majerus, B., & Margue, M. (2010). *Inventing Luxembourg. Representations of the past, space and language from the nineteenth to the twenty-first century.* Leiden: Brill.

PISA. (2012). Nationaler Bericht Luxemburg. Ministère de l'Education nationale et de la Formation professionnelle et Université de Luxembourg.

Saarland, Statistisches Amt, Statistische Berichte A/ 1. vj 3/2012. (2012). Bevölkerungsentwicklung im 3.Vierteljahr 2012, Bevölkerungsdichte, Stand 30.09.2012. Report of Saarland Statistisches Amt on the population development in Saarland, Germany. Retrieved from http://www.saarland.de/dokumente/thema_statistik/STALA_BER_AI1-VJ3-12.pdf

Schalast, C. (1995). The Luxembourg model. *German Comments, 39*, 77–83.

Scheffen, J.- L. (2013). Auf der Suche nach der Identität. Typisch luxemburgisch? *Telecran*, 29.12.2013, p. 27.

Statec. (2014). Luxembourg in figures. Luxembourg: Institut national de la statistique et des études économiques (statec).

Statec. (2015). Luxembourg in figures. Luxembourg: Institut national de la statistique et des études économiques (statec).

Statistique en bref, Statistische Kurzinformation (2013). SaarLorLuxRheinland-PfalzWallonie. Eds. Statistische Ämter der Grossregion.

Thewes, N. (2011). Eis Identitéit. In *Ausbléck 26*, Récré, L'Annuaire culturel des Professeurs Luxembourgeois. Éditions de L'APESS, 187–220.

Trausch, G. (2007). *Le Luxembourg, Emergence d'un Etat et d'une nation.* Esch/Alzette: Edition Schortgen.

Trausch, G. (2008). Die historische Entwicklung des Grossherzogtums—ein Essay. In W. H. Lorig & M. Hirsch (Eds.), *Das politische System Luxemburgs: Eine Einführung* (pp. 13–30). Wiesbaden: VS Verlag für Sozialwissenschaften.

United Nations Development Programme (n.d.) *Human Development Index* (HDI), retrieved from http://hdr.undp.org/en/content/human-development-index-hdi

Wille, C. (2011). Luxembourg macht nicht immer eine gute Figur. *Forum, 309*, 7–9.

Willems, H., & Milmeister, P. (2008). Migration und Integration. In W. H. Lorig & M. Hirsch (Eds.), *Das politische System Luxemburgs: Eine Einführung* (pp. 62–92). Wiesbaden: VS Verlag für Sozialwissenschaften.

Further Reading

Luxemburger Wort (2014, March, 3), „Cocorico" für einen Luxemburger Oscar Wort.lu Online

Luxemburger Wort (2014, March, 3), Oscar für Luxemburg. Xavier Bettel gratuliert Wort.lu Online

Luxemburger Wort (2014, February, 13), Fernand Morbach: Wir Wutbürger. Wort.lu Online

Luxemburger Wort (2014, February, 12), Pierre Leyers: Was wir sind. Wort.lu Online

Luxemburger Wort (2014, January, 30), Eng Mandarine geintriechts, ein facebook Phänomenon. Wort.lu Online

Luxemburger Wort (2014, January, 21), "Mixing Luxembourg": Dein Sound gegen Rassismus. Asti und Serge Tonnar stellen neue Kampagne gegen Fremdenhass vor. Wort.lu Online

Luxemburger Wort (2014, January, 10), Wat ass firdechLëtzebuerg? Wort.lu Online

Luxemburger Wort (2013, November, 6), Lëtzebuerg, mäifriemt Land! Wort.lu Online

Luxemburger Wort (2012, February,10), Biltgen: „Keine Kachkéis – a Bouneschlupp-Mentalität." Wort.lu Online

Luxemburger Wort (2010, August, 7) Neue Heimat in der neuen Welt. Wort.lu Online

Further Reading

3

Multiculturalism in Context

Introduction

We live in a global era of increasing international mobility and intercultural contact. The scale and intensity by which people from different parts of the world have become connected has accelerated dramatically, even if there are differences in the degree of exposure to globalization in different parts of the world. People are increasingly interconnected through information technology, trade and transportation. International travel has increased 700 % since 1960 (Held, 1998, quoted in Arnett, 2002). Global consumer brands such as Coca Cola, Nike or McDonald's are ubiquitous and international corporations such as HSBC or Nissan are expanding world-wide. Exposure to global consumer brands and goods are examples for increasing intercultural exposure, even for people who stay in situ. Therefore, even if people remain in their culture of origin they face what Chen, Benet-Martínez and Bond (2008) have termed "globalization-based acculturation." Thus even people who do not move themselves experience intercultural contact *indirectly* through global products, new media, films or TV series and so on or *directly* by coming in contact with people taking advantage of increased mobility.

© The Author(s) 2016
E. Murdock, *Multiculturalism, Identity and Difference*,
DOI 10.1057/978-1-137-59679-6_3

The chapter is divided into three sections. In the first part the concept of globalization will be reviewed with particular emphasis on lay perceptions of the social impact of globalization. Globalization is also associated with geographic mobility, people physically relocating from one country to another. The scale of migration flows will be discussed and types of migrants described. People moving to another country for an extended period of time will face *immigration-based acculturation* challenges (Chen et al., 2008). The concept of acculturation and its many facets will be elaborated in the second part of this chapter. Different acculturation strategies will be explained and implications discussed. Whilst these acculturation strategies are located at the individual level, multiculturalism can be located both at the societal and individual level. The origins of multiculturalism will be explained, followed by an overview of the concept of multiculturalism. Kymlicka (2003) has described immigration, multiculturalism and citizenship as a "three legged stool" (p. 202), each leg supporting the other two. Therefore, this section will end with an outline of citizenship policies and the chapter will close with observations, tying the different parts of this chapter together.

Globalization

In his article entitled "The psychology of globalization" Arnett (2002) defined globalization as the process "by which cultures influence one another and become more alike through trade, immigration, and the exchange of information and ideas" (p. 774). This definition implies an end point of eventual alignment between different cultures. Later definitions focus on the *process* of globalization. Yang et al. (2011), for example, commented that the common denominator amongst social scientist discussing globalization is that "globalization is a complex, multifaceted concept" (p. 678). In addition to the global flows of goods, services, ideas, technologies, cultural forms and people, the social dimension and ramifications have to be taken into consideration. Globalization is thus much more than the product of technology and economics. It is a highly complex and even ambiguous concept. As Chiu, Gries, Torelli and Cheng (2011) pointed out, globalization has created, on the one hand, optimism in a global acceptance of the finest universal values of humanity, but at the same time the force of globalization creates the fear of erosion of local cultural traditions.

To date there has not been a lot of research into the social psychology of the effects of globalization and as a first step Yang et al. (2011) examined lay perceptions and theories of globalization and their assessment of the consequences. Two opposing views were detected: According to one position, globalization is viewed as having a positive impact because globalization facilitates the movement of people and ideas. As a consequence, provincialism is weakened and creativity heightened. The opposing viewpoint emphasizes the downside of globalization: Globalization is perceived to highlight cultural divides, to fuel parochial exclusionism and to cause or accelerate the spread of global calamities (e.g. AIDS, global warming, SARS). It should also be noted that globalization flows have been asymmetrical, with the USA being, for example, an "exporter" of popular culture and China being a beneficiary in terms of manufacturing and trade.

Lay Perceptions of Globalization

Globalization has become an unstoppable and potent force that impacts everyday life in most parts of the world, even though to varying degrees (Chiu et al., 2011). Globalization is a force that can hardly be evaded. How do people make sense of and respond to globalization and its socio-cultural ramifications? As a first step Yang et al. (2011) determined whether participants from different parts of the world (USA, Mainland China, Hong Kong and Taiwan) with different degrees of globalization experience would and could distinguish between globalization and the three related topics modernization, Westernization and Americanization. Previous research in Hong Kong (Fu & Chiu, 2007) found that people actually differentiate between modernity and Westernization. Modernity is associated with objectivity, competence and scientific knowledge whereas Westernization is associated with cosmological values such as human rights, democracy and individuality. Yang et al. (2011) replicated this finding in their study. The participants from the four different regions listed above also perceived globalization as related, but not synonymous with modernization,

Westernization and *Americanization*. People in all four regions did not differentiate between Westernization and Americanization. Thus issues related to Westernization were also associated with Americanization and vice versa.

Yang et al. (2011) found that issues commonly perceived to be strongly associated with globalization fall into one of five categories: (1) global consumer brands (e.g. McDonald's, Starbucks), (2) information technology that promotes global connectivity (such as Facebook, YouTube, Internet), (3) geographic mobility (passport, air travel, immigration), (4) global calamities (global warming, HIV/AIDS) and (5) international trade and regulatory bodies (e.g. Wall Street, the World Bank). Lay people understand globalization to be a multifaceted concept that is anchored in international trade and technology. Besides, globalization is associated with positive consequences such as increased geographic mobility, but also negative consequences such as global calamities. A key finding was that participants from all four regions perceived most globalization-related objects to have more positive impact on people's competence rather than warmth, the two dimensions at the core of the Stereotype Content Model (SCM, Fiske, Cuddy, Glick, & Xu, 2002). This finding parallels research on the assessment of the impact of economic development. This body of research also found an association between economic development and efficiency at the social cost of breakup of communities, creating colder, more dehumanized societies (Cheng et al., 2010; Kashima et al., 2009, 2011). Yang et al. (2011) summarized this finding as follows: "People across cultures view economic development as a process that empowers the individual and weakens human communities" (p. 680).

Despite the overall similarities, regional differences could also be found: Notably, "immigration" was negatively evaluated on the dimension "warmth" in America, but not in the greater China regions. This may reflect that the USA is the receiving country of immigrants whilst people in the greater China region have been motivated to leave the region, seeking opportunities in the West. Other differences included the more negative perception of consumer brands in the USA or the negative perception of the United Nations only in Taiwan, reflecting Taiwan's frustration of being denied membership. These examples illustrate that regional variations in perceptions reflect the respective region's unique experiences with particular issues.

The inverse relationship between competence and warmth as a result of globalization was also found by Kashima et al. (2011) in their research on folk theory of social change (FTSC) in diverse regions such as Australia, China and Japan. These researchers found that people typically believe that a society undergoes a natural course of evolution from a traditional community with relatively low levels of competence and high levels of morality to a modern society with relatively high levels of competence and low levels of morality: "More scientifically developed, technologically advanced societies are seen to be wealthier, and more sophisticated, intelligent, and generally more competent, but less considerate, trustworthy, and generally less communal" (Kashima et al., 2011, p. 699). Kashima et al. (2011) pointed out "globalization plays an important role in the construction of future societal perceptions by providing a significant backdrop for people's particular experiences about the past history and the present trend" (p. 698). People will use their own FTSC in constructing their imagined future society, applying their naïve knowledge structure about social change.

This is an important finding as people's imagination about their society in the future is likely to play a significant role in public opinion and policy preferences in the present. As was shown in the preceding chapter, the large inward migration is considered economically necessary, but also viewed by parts of the resident population as threating social cohesion. At European level a shift in opinion has also been noted. In the most recent opinion poll, immigration has overtaken economic themes as most important issues the EU faces (Standard Eurobarometer 83, European Commission, 2015). Whilst immigration of people from other EU Member States evokes a positive feeling for just over half of the respondents (51 %), immigration for people from outside the EU invokes a positive feeling for only about a third (34 %).[1]

Summing up, people experience an increase in the frequency and intensity of intercultural exposure even without necessarily physically relocating. There is a compression of time and space—especially in cities, where symbols of different geographical regions and traditional and modern

---

[1] The fieldwork for this research was carried out in May 2015 and the data were published in July 2015.

times can be seen at the same time. Opposing views exist whether this increased cultural exposure is an enriching process or not. Proponents argue that by opening up the mind to new experiences and by removing cultural barriers the diffusion of human rights and democracy are accelerated. Opponents contend that cultural exposure incites parochial and exclusionary resistance against foreign cultures or the reaffirmation of local cultures. Research in various parts of the world has shown that globalization is generally perceived to have a positive impact on competence to the detriment of warmth. One aspect of globalization, namely immigration, was viewed differently in the USA, a prime target for immigration, and in the Greater China regions. In the next section migration flows globally and more specifically at European level will be described and a typology of migrants will be provided.

Quantification of Migration Flows

According to the United Nations Department of Economic and Social Affairs (2009) report on Migration, the number of international migrants was estimated at 214 million, representing 3.1 % of the world population. As was noted in the introduction, the twenty-first century has actually been referred to as "*the age of migration*" (Castles & Miller, 2009). More developed regions hosted 60 % of the migrant stock. In fact, ten countries accounted for 52 % of the total numbers of international migrants. The ten countries with the highest number of international migrants in 2010 are listed in Table 3.1.

Even though the USA lead this table at country level, the largest number of international migrants actually lived in Europe (70 million), followed by Asia (61 million) and then North America (50 million). Abel and Sander (2014) quantified global international migration flows using sequential stock tables published by the United Nations (UN). They plotted the actual size of migration flows within and between 15 world regions in 2005 to 2010. In line with previous observations the authors show the continued attractiveness of North America as immigrant destination, the diverse pattern of movements within and between the European regions, the large movements from South Asia to the Gulf States of Western Asia and finally the general tendency for more developed regions to register more net gains.

Table 3.1 Top ten countries with highest number of international migrants in 2010

		International migrants as a percentage of			
Rank	Country	Migrant stock (in millions)	Country's population	World's migrants	Cumulative
1	USA	42.8	13.5	20	20
2	Russian Federation	12.3	8.7	5.7	25.7
3	Germany	10.8	13.1	5	30.8
4	Saudi Arabia	7.3	27.8	3.4	34.2
5	Canada	7.2	21.3	3.4	37.5
6	France	6.7	10.7	3.1	40.7
7	United Kingdom	6.5	10.4	3	43.7
8	Spain	6.4	14.1	3	46.7
9	India	5.4	0.4	2.5	49.2
10	Ukraine	0.5	11.6	2.5	51.7

Source: United Nations DESA (2009)

The analysis by Abel and Sander (2014) also uncovers other features of the global migration system: First of all, migrants for Sub-Saharan Africa move primarily within the region. Secondly, migration flows from Asia and Latin America tend to be more spatially focused than those originating from Europe. Thirdly, although the largest flows occur within or to neighbouring regions, there are some long-distance flows, which are dominated by movements from lower- to higher-level income countries.

These are some high-level considerations regarding migration flows. As will be shown in the next section, reasons for migration may influence the reception migrants experience in their destination country.

Migration Types

As Schwartz, Unger, Zamboanga and Szapocznik (2010) pointed out, migration does not occur at random. Migration occurs because of the confluence of push-and-pull factors: The desire to leave the country (push) is stronger than the desire to stay (pull). The primary distinction of migration types is the voluntariness of the move. Within voluntary migrants the duration of the stay is a further criterion as well as the motivation for the move. There is an association between migrant type and type of reception in the host country: Migrants who are perceived to contribute to the local economy are usually welcomed, whereas migrants with low economic status or refugees and asylum seekers may be perceived as drain on resources and may be faced with discrimination. Host countries compete for highly skilled migrants but other migrants may have difficulty finding a country that will accept them. A brief description of migration types follows.

Distinction between Migrants and National Minorities

The term "migrant" is used to refer to those people who have immigrated themselves and their children who form the second generation. In contrast, the term "national minorities" refers to historically and legally established groups in multiethnic states. The inclusion in the state is not the result of recent migration, but the result of the way in which borders have been drawn or redrawn between states. Because of their special situation, national minorities often express the desire for cultural and political autonomy which is frequently met by resistance from the majority population and may ultimately lead to tensions and intergroup conflict.

Voluntary Migrants

Labour migrants move to another country in search of employment or economic opportunity. Labour migration may be intended to be permanent or a temporary measure. For temporary workers the term "sojourners" is often applied. Sojourners relocate to a different country on a time-limited basis for a specific purpose and intend to return to their countries of origin afterwards. Examples for sojourners include international students, seasonal workers or corporate executives (expatriates). Labour migration may actually be permitted or even encouraged by destination countries to fill gaps in the national labour market. Countries may actually compete for some specialist skill labour migrants. Transitions between semi-permanence and may be fluid. Schemes that are intended to be temporary such as the original *Gastarbeiter* Program in Germany may move to become permanent. Similarly, student migration, which is also temporary in nature, may become permanent. Students may decide to remain in their host country on completion of their studies as labour migrants or following family formation. Here the other major reasons for voluntary migration are mentioned, namely family reunion or family formation.

Involuntary Migrants

Refugees and asylum seekers fall within this category. The number of refugees was estimated at 16.3 million, representing 8 % of the total migrant stock in the world (United Nations Department of Economic and Social Affairs [DESA], 2009). Refugees have been involuntarily displaced by war, persecution or natural disasters. They are usually resettled by virtue of agreements between international aid agencies and governments. If asylum seekers seek out sanctuary in a new country, it is because of fear of persecution or violence in their home country.

Asylum seekers or refugees may face different barriers to integration than labour migrants. For this group of involuntary migrants the push factors to leave their countries are rather complex and of a different nature than to the voluntary migrants. A detailed discussion of this subjugated group or the current Middle East refugee crisis goes beyond the scope of this book. For an analysis see for example the dedicated website by the Migration Policy Centre (MPC).

Migration Flows in Europe

Within Europe it is important to make the distinction between intra-EU migration and migration from outside the EU. Subjects of the EU have the right to live and work in the other EU Member States.[2] Third-country nationals, persons who are not citizens of EU Member States, may face restrictions regarding duration of residence and access to the labour market.

In 2008, 3.8 million people migrated to and between the EU-27 Member Statues (Eurostat, 2011). Nearly two million migrants were of other EU

---

[2] Subject to some transitory restrictions on citizens of New Member States.

nationalities, with Rumanians being the most dominant group, followed by Poles and Bulgarians. The remaining 1.8 million immigrants to EU-27 Member States were non-EU citizens and amongst these the Moroccans were the largest group with 157,000 persons, followed by citizens of China, India, Albania and the Ukraine. The majority of the EU-27 Member States reported more immigration than emigration in 2008. As shown in Table 3.1, in absolute terms, Spain, Germany and the UK were the EU countries with the highest immigration, but at the same time they also experienced high emigration. Historical and linguistic links influence the migration flows. Because of the colonial past, the UK, for example, experiences influx from the Indian subcontinent and the West Indies. Refugees from Zimbabwe have almost exclusively sought protection in the UK, again reflecting historical and linguistic links. France on the other hand has been the target country for immigration by Algerians and Moroccans.

Labour migration had been encouraged by certain countries in the 1950s and 1960s to fill in gaps in the local labour markets. This is the time when Germany, for example, attracted *Gastarbeiter* mainly from Turkey. The guest workers were invited literally as *guests* on a temporary basis which turned into a permanent arrangement. As outlined in Chap. 2, in Luxembourg guest workers were recruited first from Italy and then Portugal. The Netherlands also had their own scheme of attracting foreign guest workers relying on colonial links. Whilst countries like Germany, France and the UK experienced significant labour immigration in the 1950s and 1960s, other countries such as Ireland, Spain and Italy experienced significant labour outflows. More recently, Ireland and Spain have moved from being predominantly emigration countries, to countries attracting a large-scale immigration both from outside the EU and from other EU Member States (Eurostat, 2011). It should also be noted that in some countries second-generation migrants are the most alienated, accepted neither in the country of origin of their parents, nor in the country where they grew up and of which they are citizens (Simon & Ruhs, 2008). This failed social integration in Europe has also been brought to attention by terrorist attacks in Paris in November 2015 (Fargue, 2015). The free movement of goods, services, capital and people (*Freizügigkeit*) is one of the major EU achievements which is under threat following the terrorist attacks and the scale of the current refugee crisis.

Interim Summary

In the first part of this chapter, the ubiquitous nature of globalization, the global flow of goods, ideas and people was highlighted. Cross-cultural research of lay perspectives on the impact of globalization showed that globalization is universally perceived to increase competence accompanied by a decrease in warmth. Views on the movement of people differ depending on the country in question being one of immigration or emigration. Migration flows were quantified globally and presented in more detail for Europe. Within Europe, a distinction must be made between within and outside-EU immigration. In this context it is also noteworthy that within the latest European Elections (25.05.2014) political forces opposing Europe gained strength across Europe (Europa: Der Rechtsruck. Spiegel online, 26.05.2014). Anti-immigration rhetoric featured strongly in the election campaigns by the right-leaning parties and is fuelled by the terrorist attacks on Paris and large-scale Syrian refugee crisis. Yet *Freizügigkeit* (movement of people) is one of the cornerstones of the EU. As also noted above, immigration patterns are still changing with traditional emigration countries becoming target countries for immigration.

In the next part, one of the consequences of people on the move will be discussed, namely the process of changes that occurs when people of different ethno-cultural backgrounds come into prolonged contact with each other. This process is commonly referred to acculturation.

Acculturation

Historical Roots of the Concept of Acculturation

The term "acculturation" was introduced by American anthropologists as early as the 1880s to describe the culture change that occurs when different cultural groups come into contact with each other (Arends-Tóth & van de Vijver, 2006). These early anthropological studies focused on the acculturation of developing nations to industrial, Western societies. Recognizing the importance of the study of acculturation, and the varying points of view from which this concept has been approached, the Social Science Research

Council appointed a committee for the study of acculturation in 1935. The committee members provided the following definition of acculturation: "Acculturation comprehends those phenomena which result when groups of individuals having different cultures come into continuous first-hand contact, with subsequent changes in the original cultural patterns of either or both groups" (Redfield, Linton, & Herskovits, 1936, p. 149). This definition of acculturation refers to the essential condition of *culture contact* which is necessary for differences to become *salient*. This definition also acknowledges that the culture contact situation has consequences for both, the migrant but also the receiving society.

Even though the Social Science Council recognized the importance of acculturation as early as 1935, acculturation is by no means a new phenomenon. As Rudmin (2003) noted "inscriptions dating from 2370 B.C. show that Sumerian rulers of Mesopotamia established written codes of law in order to protect traditional cultural practice from acculturative change and to establish fixed rules for commerce with foreigners" (p. 9). Rudmin (2003) pointed out further that Plato was in fact the first to discuss the psychology of intercultural adaption. Plato wrote that the mixing of people.

(...) has the tendency to produce all manner of admixture of characters, as the itch for innovation is caught by host from visitor or visitor from host. Now this may result in the most detrimental consequences to a society where public life is sound and controlled by right laws (...) inhabitants should welcome the foreign visitor and blend with him, or take a jaunt into another state themselves... to refuse all admission to the foreigner and permit the native no opportunity of foreign travel is, (...) not always possible and (...) may earn the state a reputation for barbarism and inhumanity. (Plato, quoted in Rudmin, 2003, p. 10)

Thus Plato recognized that acculturation could cause social disorder and was the first to suggest acculturation policies. As more recent acculturation examples Rudmin (2003) cited the history of Western civilization and in particular the creation of present-day English, a language which is the result of an amalgamation of Celtic and Latin with the Germanic dialects of the Anglo-Saxons and French from Viking Normandy. He also mentioned the Renaissance which arose from

Europeans' encounters with their own classic past. This parallels the Luxembourg experience outlined earlier when, in the process of nation-building, first the own history was consulted, (re)discovered and reconstructed. Thus culture contact can be experienced in different ways.

These examples also demonstrate that acculturation is certainly not a new phenomenon. However, the topic has come into prominence because of the scale of migration flows and the interconnectedness of the world in terms of technology and transport. The definition of acculturation by Redfield, Linton and Herskovits (1936) cited treats acculturation mainly as a group-level phenomenon. As Arends-Tóth and van de Vijver (2006) pointed out, in recent times the interest has grown in the study of individual-level phenomena which is referred to as psychological acculturation (Graves, 1967). In that sense, acculturation refers to changes that an individual experiences as a result of the culture contact situation. Arends-Tóth and van de Vijver (2006) explain that theoretical frameworks on acculturation have been borrowed from various areas of mainstream psychology. Examples include the social learning approach which focuses on the aspect of the acquisition of culturally appropriate new skills in the culture contact situation or the stress and coping approach which puts the emphasis on coping mechanisms, cognitive appraisal of change, personality characteristics or social support. Even though agreement exists amongst social scientists about a definition of acculturation, confusion exists about the conceptualization. To establish some order in this confusion, Arends-Tóth and van de Vijver (2006) suggested a taxonomy of acculturation variables.

Taxonomy of Acculturation Variables

As noted by the Social Science Research Council in 1935, there are very different angles from which to study acculturation and together with the "borrowed" theoretical frameworks from various disciplines in psychology the result is confusion about the conceptualization of acculturation. In an attempt to disentangle the confusion, the taxonomy of acculturation variables understands acculturation as the interplay of three components, namely acculturation conditions, orientations and outcomes. The taxonomy is presented in Fig. 3.1.

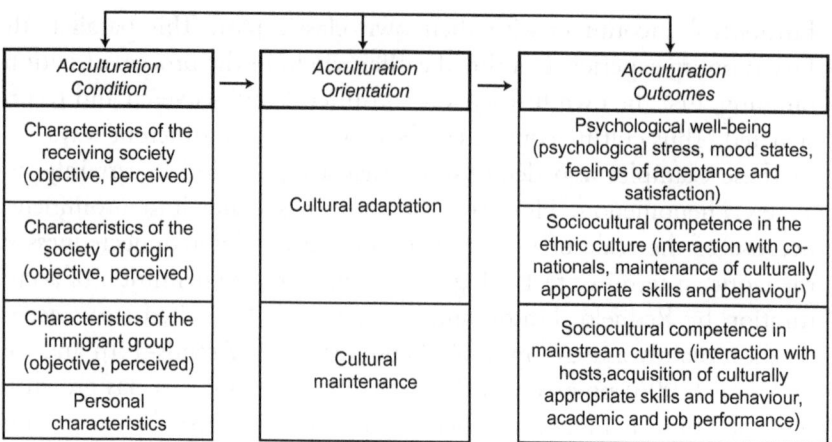

Fig. 3.1 Taxonomy of acculturation variables. *Source*: Arends-Toth & van de Vijver (2006)

A recent review and content analysis of acculturation measures by Celenk and van de Vijver (2014) confirmed that measures of acculturation tend to focus on the three components conditions, orientations and outcomes and I will discuss each of these components in turn, starting with acculturation conditions, followed by acculturation outcomes. Acculturation orientations will be presented last and in more depth as these are the main focus of acculturation research.

Acculturation Conditions

Even though important, it is yet uncommon to assess the cultural context in which acculturation takes place. Acculturation conditions refer to the contextual limits and demands of the acculturation process. Context factors are grouped into four different categories, the characteristics of the receiving society and the society of origin, the immigrant group itself and personal characteristics. These characteristics can be objectively different or perceived to be different. At society level these include demographic composition, cultural openness, social distance, value structure and social inequality. The perceived difference between the heritage culture and the culture of the host society is a crucial factor in the acculturation process. Larger differences between cultures tend to be accompanied by larger difficulties and intergroup problems (Arends-Tóth & van de Vijver, 2004). Within the immigrant group factors such as ethnic vitality and permissiveness to adjust are important. These factors may be influenced in turn by the characteristics of the country of origin. Finally, at level of the individual personality traits or coping style and demographic, factors including age, gender, generational position and length of stay may play a role in the acculturation process. Furthermore, situational or social context may also be influential.

The Interactive Acculturation Model (IAM) by Bourhis, Moise, Perreault and Senécal (1997) is usually credited as the acculturation model taking contextual conditions explicitly into consideration. This model is conceptualized as interactive with immigration and integration policies influencing the acculturation orientation of both the immigrants and the host society. Ethnic vitality of the immigrant group can be used to illustrate the interaction. An immigrant group characterized by high ethnic vitality is likely to want to retain their distinctiveness. Therefore acculturation orientations may be adopted that serve the continuity of the group rather than those of the larger society. If the acculturation orientation of the immigrant group and the host country are aligned, consensual acculturation outcomes follow. In case of discordance, problematic relational or even conflictual outcomes are the result. The difference between these outcomes is that in case of problematic outcomes at least partial agreement regarding acculturation orientations between host society and immigrant group exists.

For the case study that is Luxembourg, the characteristics of the receiving society were outlined in Chap. 2. The main immigrant groups were described, but no detailed account of each society of origin was provided. However, the majority of the immigrants share a European background, and reference to cultural distance (Inglehart & Welzel, 2010), a key component for intergroup relations, was made. Personal characteristics were not touched upon yet, but one of the aims of this empirical research, which will be presented later, is to determine individual difference variables influencing the attitude towards a plurally composed society.

Acculturation Outcomes

In line with cross-cultural research on psychological and socio-cultural acculturation (Ward, Bochner, & Furnham, 2001; Ward, Leong, & Low, 2004; Ward & Kennedy, 1999), acculturation outcomes have been divided into two domains: psychological (emotional/affective) and socio-cultural (behavioural) within the taxonomy presented in Fig. 3.1. The first domain refers to internal adjustment "being well," whereas the socio-cultural domain or external adjustment refers to the ability to "fit in" or "doing well." Psychological well-being can be understood in terms of the stress of coping framework and may be measured in a variety of ways (e.g. life satisfaction, general well-being). In contrast, socio-cultural adaptation is best explained within a social skills and culture learning paradigm. Socio-cultural adaptation refers to the specific life skills required to function in a specific cultural context. Internal and external adjustments are related, but are predicted by different variables and show different fluctuations over time. Socio-cultural problems tend to decrease steadily over time whereas psychological distress is more variable over time.

Importantly, within the acculturation taxonomy, socio-cultural competence within *both*, the host and heritage culture, are included in the outcome measures. Arends-Tóth and van de Vijver (2006) stressed that both the proficiency in the mainstream culture and the maintenance or loss of the ethnic culture should be assessed as both are relevant outcomes of the acculturation process. This point is also made by Celenk and van de Vijver (2014) who emphasized that "doing well" has two components for the immigrant namely survival skills in the host country such as speaking the host country language and in the heritage culture in the form of retention of the ethnic language. Acculturation orientations take heritage and host country explicitly into consideration, but this tradition has not yet been established when assessing the outcomes of acculturation. Yet as the recent review of publicly available acculturation measures highlighted, there is an emphasis on assessing the level of adjustment to the host society leaving out the maintenance-related aspect of the acculturation process (Celenk & van de Vijver, 2014). In terms of outcome measures, Rudmin (2009) criticized the intertwining of acculturation with mental health issues. He recommended a reframing: Acculturation should be understood as second culture acquisition. Acculturative motivations, learning and changes should be measured and studied independently of mental health issues.

Acculturation Orientations

Many studies on acculturation processes of migrants focus on acculturation *orientations* also referred to as acculturation strategies or styles. Acculturation orientations concern the way immigrants deal with their heritage and host culture. Theoretical models on acculturation orientations can be grouped along two lines namely (1) dimensionality and (2) domain-specificity. The different models and their assumptions are summarized in Table 3.2. This classification helps to place the different acculturation approaches and their respective critiques in context.

Dimensionality

Unidimensional Model

Dimensionality refers to the gravitation between host and home culture orientation. According to the unidimensional model, acculturation is thought to involve a single underlying dimension (Gordon, 1964) with host and heritage cultures being positioned at either ends (↔). Cultural maintenance and cultural adaptation are conceptualized as opposites, the dimension being bipolar. This model implies that immigrants will move from full immersion in their ethnic culture to complete immersion in the host culture after a period of adjustment. Regarding language acquisition, for example, the inference is that as the proficiency in the host society language increases, the ability to speak the heritage language decreases.

Unidimensional models of change have become under critical scrutiny (van de Vijver & Phalet, 2004). These authors cited two aspects responsible for this change: The sheer volume of migrants and the *Zeitgeist* amongst mainstreamers, where assimilationist tendencies have given way to more acceptance of cultural maintenance. In line with these societal developments, bidimensional models have replaced unidimensional models.

Table 3.2 Classification of acculturation orientation models

Domain specificity		Dimensionality		
Trait models		Unidimensional models	Bidimensional models	Fusion models
Level 1	Assume cross-situational consistency	Migrants adapt to main culture	Migrant has two attitudes: maintenance of original culture and adaptation to the host culture	A new culture emerges
Domain specific models				
Level 2	Cluster of domains: Public vs. Private	Speed of adaptation varies across domains/ situations	Speed of adaptation varies across life domains/ situations	A new culture emerges in a domain/ situation
Level 3	Specific life domains: Childrearing, news etc.			
Level 4	Specific situations: Food at home vs. food outside the home etc.			

Source: Arends-Tóth & van de Vijver (2006)

However, implicit ideas about the course of the acculturation process over generations actually support the unidimensional model of acculturation. Turkish-Dutch immigrants perceived the subsequent generations moving more towards the Dutch culture (Arends-Tóth & van de Vijver, 2004).

Bidimensional Model

Nevertheless, this assumption of having the adoption of the host culture at the end point of the acculturation process and as such as the *only* option has been criticized (e.g. see Benet-Martínez, 2012). An alternative framework has been offered in the form of the bidimensional model. As the name suggests, maintenance and adaptation are treated

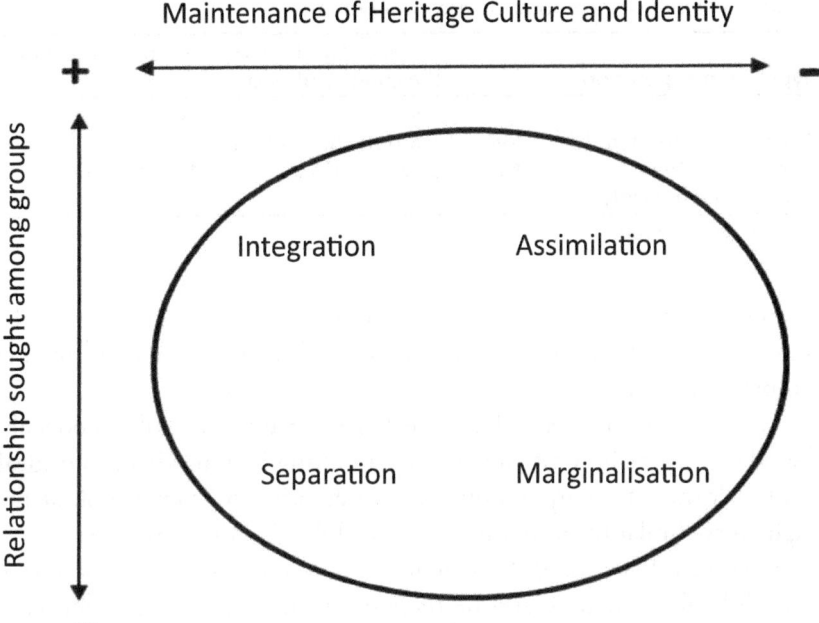

Fig. 3.2   Acculturation attitudes of immigrant groups. *Source*: Berry (2005, p. 705)

as *two* separate dimensions. Within this model the question becomes to what extend the migrant wishes to stay in touch with the home culture and to what extend the migrant wishes to engage in the host culture or attempt to do both (or neither). The most popular bidimensional model, also known as the fourfold theory of acculturation, is attributed to John Berry (1984, 1997) and consists of four acculturation orientations namely integration, assimilation, separation and marginalization. These orientations are based on the question whether the immigrant wants to adopt the host culture and whether he or she wants to maintain the heritage culture. This Model is summarized in Fig. 3.2.

Integration refers to the simultaneous attempt of retaining attachment to the heritage culture, whilst adopting elements of the host culture. The assimilation orientation closely mirrors the unidimensional outcome, whereby the individual adopts the host culture and rejects the heritage culture. The opposite is the case for the separation orientation and under

Table 3.3 Types of incorporation according to Esser

Types of incorporation		Social integration in the ethnic context or the country of origin	
		Yes	No
Social integration in the	Yes	Multiple integration	Assimilation
context of the	No	Segmentation	Marginalisation
mainstream society			

Source: Esser (2000)

marginalization, both cultures are rejected. According to the model, integration is the most desirable outcome which has been confirmed by empirical research.

The German sociologist Hartmut Esser suggested a similar model also based on two dichotomy dimensions, resulting in a matrix of four ideal-typical forms of incorporations. The orientation outcomes look at first sight very similar to Berry's strategies, as Table 3.3 demonstrates:

However, Esser (2000) maintained that multiple integration is in fact difficult to achieve and he therefore focuses his research efforts on assimilation, instead. According to Esser's interpretation, assimilation refers to the diminishing of socially relevant differences between groups. Understood in this way, assimilation is not conceptualized as a unidirectional or a suppressive concept.

At this stage only an outline of the fourfold model is provided. Despite its popularity, the model has also been criticized extensively and the major points of criticism will be given later. As Esser's conceptualization illustrates, part of the problem stems from the fact that the terminology used may be interpreted in different ways. This holds especially true for the term "integration." Other criticisms result from the fact that the model concentrates only on one aspect of the acculturation process.

Fusion Model

In accordance with the *Fusion* model, acculturation is seen as a mixture of cultural characteristics. Examples for fused cultures have been mentioned in the literature, for example *Neoricans* (New Yorkers of Puerto Rican descent, Brannen & Thomas, 2010). But Arends-Tóth and van de Vijver (2006) observed that no studies are available in which the validity of this model has been investigated empirically. One difficulty may be the domain- and situation specificity of acculturation strategies. As Barrett, Garbin, Cinnirella and Eade (2007) observed, the mixed-heritage Bangladeshi participants included in their study simultaneously affirmed both of their heritage backgrounds (integration), switched to either background depending on domain (alternation) or were involved in the Bhangra and Bollywood Remix scenes which are hybridized South Asian/Western pop music sub-cultures—an example for fusion, but in a specific context.

Domain-Specificity

Trait Models

Trait models assume cross-situational consistency of behaviour and often leave out the context in which acculturation occurs. However, the context may be an important factor, influencing an individual's preference for acculturation orientation. As noted above, Barrett et al. (2007) found that the acculturation attitudes of the Bangladeshi and mixed-heritage adolescents varied across contexts. What was considered "correct" behaviour varied between the home, when at school or with the peer group.

Domain-Specific Models

Arends-Tóth and van de Vijver (2006) observed that current models of acculturation tend to focus on dimensionality, yet as their own empirical research shows, acculturation is often more domain and situation specific than current models suggest. Their research on Turkish-Dutch immigrants showed, very similar to Barrett et al.'s findings, that the domain, public versus private, had a strong influence on immigrants' preference for acculturation strategy (Arends-Tóth & van de Vijver, 2003). For example, assimilation was sought in the work sphere (economic assimilation), but social and family life may revolve around one's own heritage group (separation in private relationships). On the other hand, linguistic competence may be sought in the host country language, whilst at the same time maintaining competence in the heritage language (linguistic integration). As was the case for the Bangladeshi participants mentioned above, the Dutch-Turkish immigrants also used at least three different acculturation orientations depending on context. The importance of a distinction between private and public domain regarding acculturation attitudes and behaviour was also underscored by Arends-Tóth, van de Vijver and Poortinga (2006). Interestingly, this is where the Dutch majority differed from the Turkish-Dutch immigrants: The Dutch majority population expected adaptation in both public and private sphere whereas the immigrants prefer adaptation only in the public sphere (Arends-Tóth & van de Vijver, 2003).

A further question is whether acculturation processes or what aspects of the process are universal or group-specific (Berry, Poortinga, Segall, & Dasen, 2002). Some researchers argue that all people regardless of ethnicity undergo similar processes following prolonged culture contact exposure. Immigrants have common experiences as immigrants and face similar demands and expectations. Others suggest that each cultural group is unique and undergoes specific cultural changes. Arends-Tóth and van de Vijver (2006) quoted a study by De Bot (1999) on language loss. He observed that Dutch immigrants in Canada and Australia show considerable language loss, whereas Chinese immigrants retain their heritage language across several generations.

In style of Epstein's (1973, 1979) self-concept theory (see Chap. 4), Arends-Tóth and van de Vijver (2006) suggested that acculturation can be seen as a hierarchical concept with unidimensionality at the top. At the apex, there is thus a general global preference for either adaptation or cultural maintenance. The second level is constituted of the public versus private domain. The public domain can be described as functional and utilitarian and involves participation-based activities such as education and work. The private domain revolves around personal, emotional and value-related matters such as child-rearing or marriage. Several studies amongst Turkish-Dutch immigrants in the Netherlands showed that minorities prefer adaptation to the Dutch public sphere, but wish to retain cultural maintenance in their private sphere (Arends-Tóth & van de Vijver, 2004, 2007). The adaptive value of different acculturation strategies depending on domains was also pointed out by van de Vijver and Phalet (2004).

The acculturation taxonomy model, as shown in Fig. 3.1, highlights that acculturation involves various processes and components. From the review of the components of the model, it becomes clear that no single measure or method can adequately capture the complexity of acculturation. The model helps to clarify which aspect of the acculturation process is investigated. Arends-Tóth and van de Vijver (2006) emphasized that a balance should be struck between heritage and receiving culture in terms of outcome variables. Using language as an example they observed that plenty of studies address the question of the acquisition of the host country language, but few will also address the maintenance of the ethnic language. Furthermore, different foci are often applied in assessing mainstream and heritage culture. Whereas the mainstream culture is assessed in terms of behaviours, attitudes are assessed in relation to the heritage culture. If assessments are not paired, then differences may relate to aspects of measurements rather than aspects of cultures.

Criticism of the Fourfold Model

As mentioned above, the acculturation orientation is the most frequently researched component in acculturation research and the fourfold model has attracted some major criticisms. Some criticisms levelled at the four-fold model are outlined below.

The Assumption of Two Cultures

The fourfold model assumes that there are only two cultures at play—one host and one heritage culture. Berry, Phinney, Kwak and Sam (2006) actually made this quite explicit in their immigrant youth study when they formulated as one of their goals to find answers to the following question: "How do immigrant youth live within and between two cultures?" (p. 2). The authors refer to this as the *intercultural question*. Berry's (2005) article on acculturation is titled "*Acculturation: Living successfully in two cultures*" (Berry, 2005). However, the reality today is that the actual demographic composition of countries is more complex than this. As was shown in Chap. 2, in the capital of Luxembourg for example, the native population is in the minority and the foreign population is composed of 160 different nationalities. Furthermore, the composition of the population in Luxembourg in fact changes on a working day due to the *frontaliers*. Therefore, people may come in contact with a wide range of nationalities on a daily basis and may need to negotiate their position within different migrant groups or sub-cultures. Barrett et al. (2007) reported a wide range of nationalities represented in London in his study on British Bangladeshi and mixed-heritage adolescents. Acculturation in such a context is not a question of negotiating two cultures.

The assumption of two cultures has also been criticized from another angle. Brannen and Thomas (2010) commented on the assumption of the universe of cultures being limited to a minority and majority culture and that the intersection of cultures is treated as an empty set. They criticize that the possibility of synergistic effects is thereby not acknowledged.

Insufficient Context Considerations

Even though some society context variables are taken into consideration, some authors consider this as insufficient. Weinreich (2009), for example, noted that variables such as distance between cultures or the attitude of the receiving culture play an important role. Accepting the norms of the dominant culture may contravene the cultural norms of the heritage culture. Another criticism levied by Weinreich (2009) is that the model assumes that both the dominant and heritage cultures are "benign and congenial, without racism, intolerance of difference in form of oppression" (p. 125). Yet, as he elaborated further, xenophobia remains a theme in many communities. He concluded that in this case immigrants would be ill advised to adopt the cultural norms of the host cultures. In such a climate, integration or assimilation may not be viable options for the immigrant.

The lack of context consideration includes the lack of consideration of domain-specificity. The fourfold model focuses on dimensionality as evidenced by Phinney, Berry, Vedder and Liebkind, (2006) who maintained that the two fundamental aspects of acculturation, namely intercultural contact and cultural maintenance, define an intercultural contact space within which individuals occupy a preferred attitudinal position. Yet as Arends-Tóth and van de Vijver (2003) and Barrett et al. (2007) pointed out, there is extensive evidence that minority individuals adopt different attitudinal positions in different life domains and across different contexts. Related to this issue is the fact that attitudes, associations and practices may be dissociated. There may not always be coherence between cultural identifications and cultural practices (Silver, 2013).

Linked to the lack of acknowledgement of domain-specificity of the acculturation process is also an oversimplification of the integration strategy. Even though Phinney, Berry, Vedder and Liebkind (2006) conceded that the choice of acculturation strategy depends to a large degree on the conditions of the larger society and integration may only be an option if the national society is open and inclusive, the model does not differentiate between different forms of integration. The key assumption is that both cultures are simultaneously maintained, but the "how" is not developed. As research on biculturalism has shown, individuals may employ alternation or code switching (Benet-Martínez, Leu, Lee, & Morris, 2002; Brannen & Thomas, 2010; Hong, Morris, Chiu, & Benet-Martínez, 2000; Nguyen & Benet-Martínez, 2007). The emergence of a third, hybrid culture may also be an outcome. These aspects will be discussed in more detail in Chap. 5.

The Assumption of Cross-Situational Consistency

A further criticism is the assumption of cross-situational consistency in cultural attitudes and behaviour. As noted above, different acculturation strategies may be employed depending on the situational context (Barrett et al., 2007). Furthermore, the question of time comes into play. As Weinreich (2009) noted, acculturation is in fact a gradual process which would be better captured by the term "*enculturation*," a process whereby people "enculturate aspects of a variety of cultural values and beliefs represented in the different communities of the individual's social world" (p. 125). Thus Weinreich emphasizes the gradual character of the acculturation process, in fact a continual incorporation of cultural elements of any available ethnicity that are significant to the individual. Enculturation may happen at a different speed in different domains.

A Question of Choice?

Weinreich (2009) further remarked on the assumption of choice. He questioned whether people can really choose between the four acculturation strategies. On the one hand this assumes that people have conscious awareness of their identity choices and on the other hand wholesale acceptance or rejection appears as an oversimplification of the process. He stresses that cultural experience is an issue of continual development and reformulation of identity in the contexts of alternative cultural norms.

Methodological Concerns

As Phinney et al. (2006) explained: "Based on the fit with the dominant theoretical framework guiding the study and on the interpretability of the resulting clusters, we decided to use four clusters or four distinct profiles of acculturation" (p. 102). Thus the four-cluster analysis was imposed, *a priori*, on theoretical grounds. This might explain the rather low internal reliabilities of the scales ranging from Cronbach's $\alpha = 0.48$ for the Integration scale, Marginalization $\alpha = 0.55$, Assimilation $\alpha = 0.58$ to Separation $\alpha = 0.64$ (Vedder & van de Vijver, 2006, p. 57). Each scale is composed of five items so lower internal reliabilities can be expected, but these α values can at best be considered adequate and thus indicating that the scales do not measure a single underlying construct. For a detailed critique of acculturation measures see (Rudmin, 2009).

A further methodological problem is that for people scoring on the mid-point, the measurement cannot distinguish between integration and marginalization. Furthermore, in Arends-Tóth and Van de Vijver's (2007) comparative study, participants had problems with complex statements and double negatives in the four-statement method (p. 1282).

Terminology

Rudmin (2003) reviewed 68 different acculturation theories dated between 1918 and 1984 pointing out on the one hand that psychological theories regarding acculturation existed prior to Berry's model and at the same time criticizes these for their varied and inconsistent use of terminology, poor citation of earlier research, conflicting and poorly tested predictions of acculturative stress and general lack of logic. The criticism of imprecise use of terminology can also be applied to the acculturation orientation *integration*.

The Meaning of Integration

According to the fourfold theory of acculturation orientations, integration refers to a simultaneous attachment to the heritage culture and the adoption of the host culture. It is also the preferred and practiced strategy by immigrants (Berry & Sam, 1997; Rudmin, 2003). Yet there is a large variation regarding the interpretation of integration. A key issue with the concept of integration is in fact its high face validity. Everybody seems *to know* what integration means. Implicit meaning systems are transposed onto the term, yet the specific understanding needs to be spelled out. As Arends-Tóth and van de Vijver (2006) wrote, integration is an umbrella concept that covers a variety of meanings. They list as the first problem the fact that integration can have a connotation of assimilation especially for majority group members. In Western European countries, the terms assimilation and integration are often used interchangeably in public discourse. Secondly, the term can refer to any combination of adaptation and cultural maintenance. But what is the proportion of each? Is the balance 20 % adaptation and 80 % maintenance? Even if both are assumed to contribute equally, does this mean 50:50 or 100 % each? The latter would then literally refer to the doubling of resources. The third question relates to the fact how the cultures are organized. Do people perceive themselves as a blend of two cultures or are they "*dual mono-culturals*" who switch or alternate depending on domain or specific situation? Alternatively, does a new fused culture emerge from the two original cultures? In their research on implicit acculturation theories of Turkish-Dutch immigrants, Arends-Tóth and van de Vijver (2004) asked participants in semi-structured interviews how they combine their two cultures. The results show that integration is not always "the sum of two independent dimensions, cultural maintenance and adaption, as the bidimensional models maintain" (p. 33). Only a small group of participants (14.3 %) answered that they keep the cultures separate. For the largest group (44.8 %), the situation or domain (private versus public) influenced if and to what extent the two cultures are combined. Another group (40.9 %) indicated that the two cultures resulted in a mixture, but they found it difficult to indicate the unique contribution of each culture in various parts of their daily lives. However, for most parts of their private lives, the Turkish culture was considered. A further 8.2 % indicated that the two cultures actually resulted in a new culture, which the authors referred to as "*intercreation.*" These examples give some indication about the complexity involved in "*integrating*" two cultures and will be elaborated in depth in Chap. 5 on *Biculturalism.*

Concluding Remarks

As noted in the introductory comments, acculturation refers to the changes that occur when people of different ethno-cultural backgrounds come into prolonged contact with each other. The concept of acculturation is certainly not new, but given the effects of globalization described in the preceding section, the scientific preoccupation with acculturation is on the rise. The Taxonomy of Acculturation Variables, introduced by Arends-Tóth and van de Vijver (2006), was used to organize the research efforts according to their different points of emphasis. Berry's fourfold model of acculturation is nearly always cited in acculturation research as it is very useful in conceptualizing the basic options regarding acculturation orientations. However, as is illustrated by the taxonomy of acculturation, many variables influence the acculturation process, domain-specificity being an important variable, for example. Much of the acculturation research has focused on the immigrant's perspective, how the immigrant deals with the heritage culture and the mainstream culture in the country of settlement.

Acculturation preference can also be studied from the perspective of the mainstream culture in terms of which acculturation orientations are expected from the immigrants. The four acculturation orientations as identified by the fourfold model can also be used to describe government policies in plural societies. As van de Vijver, Breugelmans and Schalk-Soekar (2008) explained, integration at the individual level has close correspondence to multiculturalism at the policy level. Assimilation refers to the melting pot philosophy, where immigrants are expected to "melt into" or adopt the mainstream culture. Separation is likened to segregation and marginalization can refer to either exclusion or individualization. In the next part, these acculturation orientations at the society level will be explored further, starting with a review of multiculturalism.

Multiculturalism

Introduction

In his presidential address to the Canadian Political Science Association in Montreal in June 2010, Keith Banting stated that maintaining and strengthening the bonds of community in ethnically diverse societies is one of the compelling challenges Western democracies face today. He asked: "How can we reconcile growing levels of multicultural diversity and the sense of a common identity which sustains the norms of mutual support, the capacity to pursue collective projects and social solidarity?" (Banting, 2010, p. 797). "The rise and fall of multiculturalism" has become the master-narrative of scholars, policymakers and journalists in discussing diversity (e.g. see Kymlicka, 2012; Modood, 2005; Meer & Modood, 2011). Given this polemic use of the term, the origins of multiculturalism will be explained first, followed by an overview of the concept of multiculturalism and of multiculturalism policies (MCPs). The narrow understanding of multiculturalism as celebration of cultural differences will then be discussed, including critical comments of the concept in general. The concerns raised by these critics have led towards a move of emphasizing shared citizenship and this concept will be explained.

The term "multiculturalism" does not only refer to policy issues. The term also denotes demographic features and, importantly, psychological aspects (Van de Vijver, Breugelmans, & Schalk-Soekar, 2008). The demographic aspect refers to the plural, in particular the poly-ethnic composition of society. In terms of the demographic composition, the question is *who* is counted and *how* in the statistics. In the Netherlands, for example, "people with migration background" include foreign-born individuals, immigrants with Dutch or dual citizenship as well as second-generation migrants. In Sweden, people with migration background are defined as people born abroad and people with both parents born abroad (which leads to the curious fact that Swedish citizens born abroad are also counted as foreigners). A key question is also if and how the ethnic minorities resident in the country are included in the statistics. Istanbul, for example, has attracted a large number of internal migrants, mainly of Kurdish origin. In Estonia, the Russian "ethnic minority" is included in the population statistic with migration background and minority status. In Finland, foreigners are "people born outside Finland." Thus even a seemingly simple definition of multiculturalism as demographic feature becomes more complex than appears at first sight.

The psychological aspects of multiculturalism involve individuals' acceptance and support for a plural composition of society as well as an appreciation of diversity. Multiculturalism refers to a positive attitude towards a culturally plural society in which members accept and support diversity (van de Vijver et al., 2008). Multiculturalism is taken to include behaviours and practices with regard to diversity. The attitude towards multiculturalism will be discussed in more detail in Chap. 6 as part of the empirical research.

For completeness, it should also be noted that the term "multiculturalism" may also refer to approaches of dealing with cultural pluralism in educational settings and counselling (Celenk & van de Vijver, 2014). Used in that sense, multiculturalism focuses specifically on measures of how services are to be provided to ethnically diverse groups. More recently, the term has also been used to describe individuals of different cultural backgrounds, quasi as an extension of *bi*culturalism to *multi*culturalism (Benet-Martínez, 2012).

The Origins of Multiculturalism

In one sense, multiculturalism (MC) is as old as humanity. As noted above, the Greek philosopher Plato was the first to suggest acculturation policies. Yet the Romans were the first to implement multicultural policies. As pointed out by Rudmin (2003), the extensiveness and endurance of the multicultural Roman Empire can at least be partly attributed to its codified law and liberal treatment of local cultures. The Roman system of ruling was not based on ethnic identity, but on rights of citizenship. Once peoples were conquered, they were made citizens. The Ottoman Empire is another example for a ruling system where different cultures found ways of coexisting and respect for diversity was a dominant feature. In the more recent history, multiculturalism came to prominence in Western democracies in the late 1960s, in the wake of the experience of World War II. The founders of the United Nations (UN) responded to the horrors of the World War II by emphasizing human rights in the Organization's Charter. Multiculturalism is inspired and constrained by human rights. Human rights provide the operating framework for multiculturalism and the cornerstones of this framework will be outlined next.

The Charter of the United Nations, adopting the emphasis on human rights, was signed at the San Francisco Conference on 26 June 1945. Some 40 non-governmental organizations successfully lobbied delegates for relatively strong language on human rights. In 1946, the UN established the Commission on Human Rights the principal policy-making body for human rights within the UN system and finally, the General Assembly adopted the *Universal Declaration of Human Rights* in Paris on 10 December 1948. To date, this Declaration provides the foundation for human rights law, and the Articles relevant in the context of movement of people and nationality are given below. As can be seen, freedom of movement and nationality were declared *universal human rights*. The equality of all human beings is emphasized in Article 1.

Article 1
All human beings are born free and equal in dignity and rights. They are endowed with reason and conscience and should act towards one another in a spirit of brotherhood.

Article 13
(1) Everyone has the right to freedom of movement and residence within the borders of each state.
(2) Everyone has the right to leave any country, including his own, and to return to his country.

Article 14
(1) Everyone has the right to seek and to enjoy in other countries asylum from persecution.
(2) This right may not be invoked in the case of prosecutions genuinely arising from non-political crimes or from acts contrary to the purposes and principles of the United Nations.

Article 15
   a. Everyone has the right to a nationality.
   b. No one shall be arbitrarily deprived of his nationality nor denied the right to change his nationality.
(http://www.un.org/en/documents/udhr/)

The equality of all members of the human race was emphasized clearly in a statement issued by the "Expert Group on Problems of Race" of the United Nations Educational, Scientific and Cultural Organization (UNESCO) in 1951: "Mankind is one: all men belong to the same species, *Homo sapiens*" (Italics in the original document, Metraux, 1951, p. 142). These experts stress that any differences are due to evolutionary factors and suggest dispensing with the use of the term "race" altogether: "National, religious, geographic, linguistic and cultural groups do not necessarily coincide with racial groups. Cultural traits of such groups have no demonstrated genetic connection with racial traits. Because serious errors are committed when the term race is used in popular parlance—it would be better to drop the term altogether and speak of *ethnic groups*" (Metraux, 1951, p. 142).

This statement on equality was also formulated after World War II. As Kymlicka (2012) explained: "Prior to WWII ethnocultural and religious diversity in the West was characterized by a range of illiberal and undemocratic relationship of hierarchy, justified by racialist ideologies that explicitly propounded the superiority of some peoples and cultures and their rights over others. These ideologies were widely accepted throughout the western world and underpinned by both domestic laws (e.g. racially biased immigration and citizenship policies) and foreign policies (e.g. in relation to overseas colonies)" (p. 5). The Human Rights Declaration was a first step in the direction of change. Kymlicka (2012) distinguished three waves within the human rights movement. In the first period from 1948 to 1965, the struggle for decolonization dominated. This wave was followed by the struggle against racial segregation and discrimination, initiated and exemplified by the African-American civil rights movement from 1955 to 1965, and finally in the late 1960s the struggle for multiculturalism and minority rights emerged.

"Misleading Model" of Multiculturalism

Barrett (2013) acknowledged that the term "multiculturalism" has acquired multiple meanings in everyday speech and explained that "in its proper use, the term 'multiculturalism' denotes a particular kind of policy approach that may be used for the management of culturally diverse societies. Under this approach the cultures of the non-dominant minority groups are accorded the same recognition and accommodation that are accorded to the dominant group" (p. 16). Kymlicka (2012) also stressed that "multiculturalism is first and foremost about developing new models of democratic citizenship, grounded in human-rights ideals, to replace earlier uncivil and undemocratic relations of hierarchy and exclusion" (p. 8). This understanding differs substantially from "feel-good celebration of ethnocultural diversity" which Kymlicka (2012, p. 4) described as "misleading model" of multiculturalism. This feel-good celebration of ethno-cultural diversity, encouraging citizens to acknowledge and embrace the panoply of customs, traditions, music and cuisine that exist in a multiethnic society has been described as the "3 s" model of multiculturalism (saris, samosas and steel-drums), referring to clothing, cuisine and music (Alibhai-Brown, 2001). According to this understanding of multiculturalism, familiar cultural markers of ethnic groups are taken and treated as authentic practices to be preserved by their members and safely consumed by others. This "celebratory model of multiculturalism" has been criticized for several reasons, which are outlined next:

Fundamental Inequalities Are Ignored

The "3 s" model of multiculturalism ignores issues of economic and political inequality such as unemployment, poor educational outcomes, residential segregation, poor language skills and political marginalization. Yet these economic and political issues cannot be solved simply by celebrating cultural differences.

Celebration of "Authentic" Practices of the Past

The focus on celebrating "authentic" cultural practices which are "unique" to each group is potentially dangerous. Firstly, not all customs that may traditionally be practiced within a particular group are worthy of being celebrated (e.g. forced marriage). To avoid stirring up controversy, there is usually a focus on inoffensive practices such as cuisine or music, which can be enjoyably consumed in a liberal democracy. Secondly, focussing on these "soft" practices runs the risk of trivialization or *Disneyfication* of cultural differences and thus ignores the real challenges that differences in cultural and religious values can raise. Bissoondath (1993) quite critically described multicultural fairs that are often showcases for different cultural customs as:

> Simplification of culture—a folksy Disneyland with multicultural versions of Mickey, Minnie and Goofy. Your exposure has been not to culture but to theatre, not to history, but to fantasy: enjoyable, no doubt, but of questionable significance. You come away knowing nothing of the language and literature of these places, little of their past and their present (...) You have acquired no sense of everyday lives. (...) Such displays are uniquely suited to seeking out the lowest common denominator. Comfortable only with superficialities, they reduce cultures hundreds, sometimes thousands of years old to easily digested stereotypes. (...) Greeks we learn are all jolly Zorbas, and Spaniards dance flamenco between bouts of "Viva España"; Germans gulp bear, sauerkraut and sausages while belting out Bavarian drinking songs; Italians make good ice-cream, great coffee, and all have connections to shady godfather. (pp. 373–374)

Multiculturalism understood in this way actually encourages the devaluation of what it claims to protect and promote: Culture becomes an object for display. A further danger in emphasizing cultural practices in this way is the risk of excessive fantasy. As Bissoondath (1993) explained it is human to edit the past, to gloss even harsh reality into coveted memory: "We were starving, but we were happy." It is easy to forget in the comforting grip of edited memory that everything has changed. Benet-Martínez (2012) referred to this phenomenon as the *"encapsulation effect."* She observed that some immigrants and their descendants may adhere to the ethnic cultural values even more strongly than members of their home country. They become *"encapsulated"* with the norms and values of an earlier era in their homeland and they ignore the fact that even their (former) home country will undergo changes. The nostalgia effect or cultural self-priming will be discussed further in Chap. 5. Foroutan (2012) stated that this idealization of the past may lead to *"invented traditions"* that may not even exist in the homeland any more. It is understandable that immigrants may cling on to memories of the past, but the danger is that memories will be idealized and eventually fantasy may not be separated from reality. Bissoondath (1993) warned that theatrical display may turn fantasy into something concrete and then the golden fantasy is taken for reality. Alibhai-Brown (2001) argued that uncertainties produced by globalization are creating new insecurities across the planet. In many cases the reaction to this bewildering opening up of our lives has been a greater (and more idealized) identification with old histories and smaller, neater identities.

"Static" Perception of Culture

As noted above, change may be ignored and the past "edited" for comfort. Yet in celebrating "authentic" practices, the "3 s" model of multiculturalism actually encourages a conception of groups as hermetically sealed and static, each reproducing its own distinct practices (Alibhai-Brown, 2001). Processes of cultural adaptation or mixing are ignored as well as emerging cultural commonalities. Thereby, perceptions of minorities as eternally "*other*" are reinforced. This in turn can lead to the strengthening of prejudice and stereotyping and generally the polarization of ethnic relations.

Preservation of the Status Quo

The "3 s" model can reinforce power inequalities and cultural restrictions within minority groups. In deciding which traditions are authentic and how to interpret and display them is generally done by the traditional elites within the groups (traditionally older males) who may be challenged by internal reformers. The danger is that people may be imprisoned in "*cultural scripts*" that they are not allowed to question or dispute.

These observations highlight that the uncritical celebration of diversity may actually increase the cleavage between "them" and "us" by emphasizing the past, rather than building up a shared vision of the future and by being static, ignoring the possibility of change at the individual and societal level.

Critical Observations Regarding the Concept of Multiculturalism

The criticism levied above largely concerned the reduction of multiculturalism to the "soft" factors of cultural practices. The underlying assumption of the Canadian Multiculturalism Act that immigrants may wish to "preserve, enhance and share their cultural heritage" has also been criticized for the implicit assumption that integration is the best acculturation strategy—the idea that immigrants would want to and should preserve their heritage culture as well as becoming Canadian. Belonging to two cultures is often expressed in the form of "*stroke-identities.*"

Stroke Identity

As Bissoondath (1993) observed, "to be simply Canadian untinged by the exoticism of elsewhere seems insufficient" (p. 377). In a Canadian context the answer to "Who are we?" is often simply "not American," but in terms of search for distinctiveness, this answer is not sufficient. Heritage can be a source of self-enhancement and pride and can provide an important sense of self. However, the game cuts both ways: The stroke identity can prevent from being ordinary, but it can also prevent from being accepted. Bissoondath quoted the Jamaican-born Canadian sprinter Ben Johnson as an example. He experienced the public demotion from the being a celebrated "one of us" to "one of them." Ben Johnson was a Canadian when convenient and an immigrant when not, "Thus the weight of the multicultural hyphen, the pressure of the link to exoticism can become onerous" (Bissoondath, 1993, p. 378).

Identity Denial

"Where are you *really* from?" (Italics in original) is the title of a publication on Asian Americans and identity denial by Cheryan and Monin (2005). As these authors explain, the term "identity denial" describes acceptance threat wherein an individual who does not match the prototype of an in-group sees that identity called into question or unrecognized by fellow group members (p. 717). According to self-categorization theory (Turner, Hogg, Oakes, Reicher, & Wetherell, 1987), *prototypicality* is defined as the degree to which an individual matches a set of characteristics or attributes strongly associated with that group. The more a person deviates from these attributes, the less prototypical he or she is considered by the others. The plight of identity denial is not only restricted to the domain of nationality. Identity denial may be experienced by anyone who differs from the prototype of a group.

As explained by Cheryan and Monin (2005), many Americans of Asian descent experience the "perpetual foreigner syndrome" even though they were born in America and feel, think and act American, as this is the only culture they have known. This experience is mirrored by other non-prototypical groups, as for example Muslims in Germany. Foroutan (2012) reported on the experience of Muslims in Germany. When asked: "Where do you come from?" and the answer is given as "Koblenz,"[3] the

---

[3] Medium-sized town in Germany.

questioner will, more often than not, proceed with the follow-up question "Jaja, aber so richtig?" (yes, yes, but really?). Bissoondath (1993) reported the same experience. When he replies to the question "What nationality are you?" simply by "Canadian," he can expect the follow-up question "What nationality are you *really?*"

As Cheryan and Monin (2005) explained, identity denial is the fear of not being part of the in-group at all, as opposed to stereotype threat, which refers to the fear of being seen in a negative light because of one's group membership. The athlete Ben Johnson was mentioned in relation to hyphenated identity and Cheryan and Monin (2005) also give an example from the sporting world to illustrate identity denial. In the 1998 Winter Olympics a headline read "American beats out Kwan," referring to the victory of figure skater Tara Lipinski over Michelle Kwan, also an American figure skater born and raised in California. The headline does not portray Kwan as a member of an out-group; she is simply denied membership of the in-group.

Inadvertently, differences between members of society may be over-emphasized and group membership within the confines of nationalistic categories perpetuated. Bissoondath (1993) warned that depending on stereotypes held, ensuring that ethnic groups will preserve their distinctiveness may lead an already divided country down the path to further social divisiveness. He himself wanted "to go beyond the confines of his cultural inheritance" (p. 371). In line with the argument put forth by the "*individualist marginal*" a concept which will be introduced in Chap. 6, Bissoondath reasoned that people want to be recognized for who they are and not what they represent.

Import of Cultural Conflict

A focus on ethnic heritage also bears the risk of importing ethnic and political conflicts. The authors of the CLIP (2011) report warned that, especially within minority groups, there is danger of ethnic conflict import, for example Turkish-Kurdish. Therefore, the new discourse emphasizes civic integration, social cohesion, common values and shared citizenship. Bissoondath (1993) used the same argument stressing that imported *Old World feuds* along ethnic, religious or political lines must not be allowed to override loyalties to citizenship laws in Canada. This also implies addressing the question of limit—not everything deemed cultural is sacred.

A Question of Limit

As repeatedly noted, multiculturalism is firmly grounded in human rights law, the Charter of Human Rights providing the operating framework. However, in a climate of openness and promotion of diversity, "freedom of cultural expression" may become subject of political or legal protection. As reported in Bissoondath (1993, p. 380) a group in Toronto demanded, in the name of respect for its culture, the right to opt out the Canadian judicial system in favour of Islamic law, which is considered fundamental to its practicing members. According to the spokesman, this right should be granted in a multicultural society. Two observations can be made—on the one hand, the Islamic group turned to the judicial system asking for permission—conform to the Canadian civic system. On the other hand, it is remarkable that this group felt that this request can be made in the first instance. Closer to home, the Muslim veil—in various forms such as the body-covering burka and the niqab, which covers the face apart from the eyes, has been discussed in various European countries. France was the first European country to ban the full-face Islamic veil in public places. The European Court of Human Rights upheld the ban on 2 July 2014 after a case was brought by a 24-year-old French woman who argued that the ban violated her freedom of religion and expression. The court argued that the veil proves a barrier to society and considers it a violation of individual liberties (Gerichtshof für Menschenrechte, Spiegel online, 01.07.2014). It is interesting to note that the decision regarding weighing up of competing interests (*Güterabwegung*) was referred to the *Human Rights* Court.

Not only the question of limit is touched upon here but also the question of reciprocity: Multiculturalism can be described as a transformative project as it requires both the dominant or majority group as well as the subordinated group or minority group to engage in new practices, to enter new relationships and to embrace new concepts or discourses—all of which transform people's identities. For example, subordinate groups can appeal to multicultural policies to challenge their illiberal exclusion, but those very policies also impose the duty on the subordinate group to be inclusive. All need to abide by the overarching principle of human rights, civil rights liberalism and democratic constitutionalism.

Acceptance versus Tolerance

The question of limit can be considered an issue of breadth, and this final point concerns the question of depth. Acceptance goes much deeper than tolerance. Acceptance requires true understanding, the recognition over time that surface differences such as skin colour or accent may give only a glimpse of the person beneath. Understanding in this sense requires effort. Questioning one's own set of beliefs and values as a result of culture contact may be experienced as stressful. Getting underneath this surface does require effort. Tolerance may stay at the surface level and does not necessarily require the acquisition of new knowledge. Building multiculturalism merely on tolerance may be fragile.

Variability of Multiculturalism

Across Time

As shown above, multiculturalism grew out of the human rights movement. However, ethnic and racial hierarchies persist in many societies today, whether measured in terms of economic inequalities, political underrepresentation, social stigmatization, or cultural invisibility. Various forms of multiculturalism have been developed to help overcome these lingering inequalities. As Barrett (2013) explained, multiculturalism has evolved through successive decades in terms of primary focus, identified problems and proposed solutions[4]:

---

[4] Based on Kunz and Sykes (2007) quoted in Barrett (2013, pp. 19–20).

1. In the 1970s *ethnic* multiculturalism dominated with a focus on culture and the celebration of ethnic differences; prejudice was viewed as the primary problem, which could be tackled through individual adjustment to diversity through cultural sensitivity.

2. In the 1980s, the emphasis shifted to *equity* multiculturalism, which focused instead on race relations; systematic discrimination was seen to be the primary problem; removing barriers to economic participation was a primary concern and with employment equity and cultural accommodation as targets.

3. During the 1990s, *civic* multiculturalism emerged focussing on fostering constructive engagement, shared citizenship and a sense of belonging. Social cohesion, based on common values, was emphasized. Social exclusion was viewed as the problem, which needed to be tackled through participation and inclusiveness.

4. In the 2000s, in response to ethnic- and religious-based conflicts and debates concerning multiculturalism in both Europe and Canada, *integrative* multiculturalism has emerged, where the focus has shifted to concerns about accommodating religious sensitivities and an emphasis on multiculturalism as a strategy for managing cultural diversity.

Kymlicka (2012) also observed a clear trend towards increased recognition and accommodation of diversity through a range of MCPs in Western democracies from the 1970s to the 1990s, but witnessed, since then, a retreat from these ideas in favour of a reassertion of ideas of nation-building. In its extreme form, this is referred to as "*nativism*" and describes the outbreak of right-wing, anti-immigrant political radicalism that often occurs in majority populations in times of economic crisis (CLIP,[5] 2011). The immigrant population is then *perceived to* be on the increase, getting out of control and threatening the majority population's way of life. In times of economic downturn, certain people feel receptive to nativist ideologies and as Farley (2005, p. 441) explained: "Competition and

---

[5] CLIP refers to Network Cities for Local Integration Policies (2011). Intercultural policies in European cities. European Foundation for the Improvement of Living and Working Conditions. Dublin, Ireland.

perceived threat, feelings of personal insecurity, and a need to scapegoat have all been identified as factors that contribute to prejudice," (cited in CLIP, p. 140). If right-wing political leadership encourages prejudice and hate, this leads to the rise of a nativist anti-immigrant movement. This rhetoric has been observed in the campaign used by the US Republican presidential candidate Trump (*Donald Trump hetzt wie ein Faschist*, Zeit online, 27.11.2015). Also within Europe, right-wing political parties have used the current refugee crises and the terrorist attack in Paris in November 2015 for their political goals (*Regionalwahlen in Frankreich: Front National profitiert von der Terrorangst*, Zeit online, 06.12.2015).

Radical, openly anti-immigrant parties have been established in several EU countries. Although working within a democratic context, the danger of these anti-immigrant parties is that they make intercultural and interreligious dialogue more difficult and reinforce segregation and radicalization within the minority groups. Just recently, Slovakia and Hungary have actually put their case against taking in refugees to the European Court of Justice (*Protest gegen Quote: Slowakei reicht Klage gegen EU-Flüchtlingsverteilung ein*, Spiegel online, 02.12.2015). The current refugee crisis is putting the European Union to a test. At the time of writing, it is not clear how the outer borders will be protected in the future, whether free movement of people, as stipulated in Schengen agreement, can be maintained and if and how the thousands of refugees can be fairly distributed amongst member states.

Banting (2010) observed that the disenchantment with multiculturalism is driven by fears of economic costs, perceived threats to liberal values including anxieties about Islam, a perceived threat to historic cultures and fears about security. Incidentally, these are the arguments used by the nationalist parties throughout Europe. Based on these considerations, Kymlicka (2012) identified five factors that will facilitate or impede the implementation of multiculturalism (MC).

1. *Economic contribution.* As already noted highly skilled immigrants who are perceived to contribute economically are welcome. If immigrants are perceived as net burdens to the welfare state, support for MC dwindles.

2. *Diversity of migrant groups.* MC works best when it is genuinely multicultural, that is, when immigrants come from many source countries rather than coming overwhelmingly just from one source country. If there is a numerically dominant group, this may lead to more polarized relations with the majority population.
3. *Human rights.* MC is firmly grounded in human rights. Support for MC weakens if immigrant groups are perceived as unwilling to embrace liberal-democratic norms.
4. *Desecuritization* of ethnic relations. MC works best if relations between the state and minorities are seen as an issue of social policy and not as an issue of state security. If the state perceives immigrants as a security threat, support for MC will drop and the space for minorities to even voice MC claims will diminish.
5. *Border control.* MC is more controversial when citizens fear they lack control over their borders.

The current refugee crisis is exacerbated by the fact that none of these more favourable conditions are perceived to apply. It is important to note that these factors refer to *perception* of immigrants in terms of numbers and behaviour and this perception may not be borne out in terms of actual facts. However, this perception is construed as reality.

Across Countries

Indices Assessing Multicultural Policies

Global migration flows as well as a more detailed analysis of the historic immigration patterns within the European context were described earlier. These patterns also impact on immigration policies and approaches in dealing with diversity at country level. Banting and Kymlicka (2006) have developed the Multiculturalism Policy Index (MPI) which allows a comparison of multiculturalism policies across countries. The MPI was a first attempt to measure the evolution of MCPs in a standardized format and thus allowing comparative research. The authors identified eight concrete policy areas concerned with the development of more multicultural forms of citizenship in relation to immigrant groups. These policies are:

1. Constitutional, legislative, or parliamentary affirmation of multiculturalism, at the central and/or regional and municipal levels.
2. The adoption of multiculturalism in school curricula.
3. The inclusion of ethnic representation/sensitivity in the mandate of public media or media licensing.
4. Exemptions from dress codes, either by statute or by court cases.
5. Allowing of dual citizenship.
6. The funding of ethnic group organizations to support cultural activities.
7. The funding of bilingual education or mother-tongue instruction.
8. Affirmative action for disadvantaged immigrant groups. (*Source*: Multiculturalism Policy Index (MPI), www.queensu.ca/mcp)

Countries are assessed in relation to what extent they have espoused some or all of these policies over time. The maximum score per country to be reached is eight. The MPI scores for selected countries from 1980 to 2010 are provided in Appendix 1. Countries differ widely in terms of the absolute score—the range being 7, with an average score of 3.1 for European countries. The scores reported refer to immigrant-based multicultural citizenship. As Kymlicka (2012) pointed out, different dynamics apply to native minorities or indigenous people who may claim land rights, territorial autonomy or official language status.

Countries also differ in terms of trajectories towards multiculturalism policies. The MPI lists data only up to 2010: Canada, at 7.5, achieved the second highest MPI score after Australia. The Netherlands have experienced the largest drop from 5.5 in 2000 to 2 in 2010 and have experienced an extreme trajectory from being a very open country towards diversity to becoming restrictive.

The Migrant Integration Policy Index (MIPEX, Huddleston, Bilgili, Joki, & Vankova, 2015) is another tool which measures policies to integrate migrants in all EU Member States, Australia, Canada, Iceland, Japan, South Korea, New Zealand, Norway, Switzerland, Turkey and the USA. This tool permits the evaluation and comparison of countries on the basis of 167 policy indicators, spread over eight policy areas, regarding integration efforts of migrants by countries. Luxembourg is listed here as one of only a handful of countries that has passed major reforms between 2007 and 2011. In fact, with +11 points, Luxembourg was the highest climber on the MIPEX 100 points scale under this period under review (http://www.mipex.eu/key-findings.) Luxembourg has made progress in all policy areas. In the following, three case studies will be presented—the Canadian example as a high scorer, the Dutch case for its downward trajectory and Luxembourg as an example for an upward trajectory.[6]

Canada

To date, Canada is the only country in the world that has anchored multiculturalism in its constitution. As Banting, Courchene and Seidle (2007) noted, diversity and the broad acceptance of multiculturalism are the defining characteristics of Canada. However, they also concede that this does not mean that everyone agrees how Canadian's respect for diversity should translate into practice. The roots of the federal government's multiculturalism policy are linked to linguistic duality. As reported in Book IV of the Royal Commission on Bilingualism and Biculturalism: "Immigration does not imply the loss of an individual's identity and original characteristics or of his original language and culture. Man is a thinking and sensitive being: severing him from his roots could destroy an aspect of his personality and deprive society of some of the values he can bring to it" (p. 5, quoted in Berry et al. (1977), p. 1). The underlying assumption is that immigrants wish to retain links with their heritage, and sharing this heritage with Canadians is considered beneficial for all. Cultural diversity is considered important for the development of

---

[6] For a more detailed analysis at country level for other countries, for example Norway, see Erikson (2013), Spain, see Arango (2013) or France see Simon (2012).

Canada. The specific multiculturalism policies introduced in 1971 had the following goals:

1. To assist all Canadian cultural groups that have demonstrated a desire and effort to continue to develop a capacity to grow and contribute to Canada;
2. To assist members of all cultural groups to overcome cultural barriers to full participation in Canadian society;
3. To promote creative encounters and interchange among all Canadian cultural groups in the interest of national unity;
4. To assist immigrants to acquire at least one of Canada's official languages in order to become full participants in Canadian society. (Banting, Courchene, & Seidle, 2007, p. 5)

These objectives were incorporated in the Canadian Constitutional Reform of 1982. The Canadian Multiculturalism Act (CMA) was adopted in 1988 and renewed in 1997. In the CMA the Canadian Government declares its policy to recognize and promote the understanding that multiculturalism reflects the cultural and racial diversity of Canadian society and acknowledges the freedom of all members of the Canadian society to preserve, enhance and share their cultural heritage. This highlighted that the CMA is firmly rooted in the ideals of human rights, emphasizing the equality of all people and the civil rights liberalism. The CMA shows the Canadian Government's commitment to civil liberties and in particular the freedom of the individual "to make the life that the individual is able and wishes to have" (Kymlicka, 2007, p. 60).

These statutory policies are also reflected in the citizenship procedures which are widely accepted and not perceived as "assimilationist." For this consensus, Kymlicka (2003) cited the following reasons: Firstly, the requirements for naturalizing are not perceived to be onerous. A modest residency test (3 years), the knowledge test regarding Canadian history and institutions is considered "simple" and the language test achievable. Secondly, becoming Canadian through naturalization is not perceived as a first step towards assimilation. This is underlined on the one hand by the official acceptance of dual citizenship and on the other hand the official policy of multiculturalism. "Both policies acknowledge that 'being Canadian' is not an exclusive identity, and accept that immigrants are likely to have dual identities and loyalties" (Kymlicka, 2003, p. 197). Thirdly, public funds are spent to encourage and facilitate naturalization (i.e. language training). Fourthly, the legal status of non-citizens is quite tolerable. Apart from the lack of voting rights, non-citizens have equal access to civil rights, social benefits and the labour market. Finally, the citizenship policy trajectory in Canada is perceived to be "open" or progressive—and what is important in the Canadian context—more open than the US citizenship policies.

Public attitudes towards immigration in Canada are quite positive in comparison to several European countries. As Table 3.4 indicates, the USA takes a position half-way between European and Canadian responses:

Canadian responses mirror those of their European counterparts only with regard to adaptation. Kymlicka (2003) attributed the widespread endorsement of immigrants to three factors. Firstly, Canada is competing with other immigrant countries for highly skilled workers and the Canadian openness is perceived as unique selling point for Canada. Secondly, naturalization is perceived as a reciprocal act: Greater protection is given to the immigrants, but naturalization is also perceived as facilitating growing roots in Canadian society and thereby engaging with and giving back to Canadian society. Furthermore, naturalization is not viewed as an end point rather than a mid-point in the integration process, encouraging and enabling further integration. These latter points

Table 3.4 Attitudes to immigration and immigrants in selected countries

	Reduce immigration levels	Immigrants increase crime	Immigrants are good for the economy	Immigrants should adapt
Canada	32.2	27.2	62.9	71.1
Germany	70.3	62.6	28.6	64.2
Netherlands	69.9	47.8	26.7	87.8
Norway	71.3	79	30.5	79.8
Spain	51.5	57.6	49.2	68.1
UK	77.8	39.8	21.6	75.3
USA	56.3	26.8	45.5	52.6

Source: Banting (2010) Figures are based on the 2003 International Survey Program

may explain why (majority) Canadians expected immigrants to adapt. For a more detailed analysis of the current debate regarding immigration, multiculturalism and the welfare state see Banting et al. (2007), attitude towards multiculturalism Berry, Kalin, and Taylor 1977; Berry and Kalin, 1995 and an explanation of Canadian approaches to recognizing and accommodating diversity Kymlicka (2007).

The CMA has not been without its critics. Bissoondath (1993), who is an immigrant to Canada and simply describes himself as *Canadian*, has critically commented on some of the CMA's underlying assumptions. He criticized the assumption that people will *want* to hold on to their past heritage (cultural maintenance) and the implication that holding on to the *former* homeland is more important than the *here and now*. Connected to this aspect is the assumption that personalities and ways of doing things can be frozen in time. Bissoondath asserted that the act of moving alone will have an impact on the person. Of course, the reasons for emigration are multifaceted, but the decision to emigrate implies that the émigré wants to look for a new life and will leave something behind. He also noted the Canadian feeling of inferiority that Canadian cultural influences pale before the exoticism of the foreign. The final criticism he voiced is that the question of limits is not addressed: How far does one go as a country in encouraging and promoting cultural difference? How far is far enough? How far is too far? Some of these points will be commented on in more detail in the next section. These critical comments should not detract from the fact that overall multiculturalism and associated multiculturalism policies are widely accepted by the Canadian population as a whole.

The Netherlands

The Netherlands is a country where the trajectory for immigration policies has been one of great openness towards quite a restrictive policy. Not unconnected, the Netherlands is also a country which has attracted a substantive body of research on attitudes towards multiculturalism. Therefore, the Dutch case study provides a backdrop for these studies. The case study presented next is based on Entzinger (2006), unless otherwise indicated.

The Dutch immigration population consists of former "repatriates" from Indonesia and Moroccan and Turkish guest workers in the 60s and 70s who were thought to be temporary residents of the Netherlands. As a consequence no efforts were made at the time to promote integration. Instead, these presumed temporary immigrants were encouraged to retain their own cultural identity which included the introduction of mother-tongue teaching for migrant children. This approach was in line with the Dutch system of *verzuiling* ("pillarization") under which various religious and ideological communities had their own institutional arrangements. Under this system, each community or "pillar" (Catholics, Protestants, Jews, but also socialists, liberalists, humanists) could set up their own institution, largely paid for by the state, whilst the state remained neutral. "Living apart together" was the result of this policy whereby unification was achieved through the elites at the top. The elites of all pillars met regularly to discuss issues of common concern. This system of *verzuiling* has lost ground since the late 1960s for several reasons: secularization, increased questioning of the elite, paternalistic leadership and the realization that the "temporary" guest workers will be staying in the Netherlands. This realization led to the belief that integration should be encouraged. A catalogue of measures was devised to promote integration all the while aiming to preserve the communities' cultural identity. To this purpose the label "ethnic minorities" was introduced and the policy on their behalf became known a as the *Minorities' Policy*. Ethnicity was now introduced as a basis for differential policy-making in a country that had been, up to that point, quite homogeneous. Some critical voices predicted that stressing ethnic differences would risk perpetuating these. Even though the term "multiculturalism" was not used by the Dutch government, the Dutch *Minorities Policy* can be characterized this way. Even though parallel institutions were generously supported with public funds, the *Minorities Policy* could not prevent an alarming rise in immigrant unemployment. Immigration became a growing burden for welfare and social policy regimes. Underneath the surface, dissatisfaction was forming and a public debate on the presumed incompatibility of Islam and "Western values" was triggered by parliamentary opposition leader Frits Bolkenstein (1991).

This led to a shift in policy and the *Minorities Policy* was renamed *Integration Policy*. As the new name implies, the focus shifted to immigrants' social participation rather than respecting cultural diversity. Culture was now considered a private affair and employability became the key objective and important for achieving this objective is language competence. Thus, mother-tongue teaching was abolished and mandatory (Dutch) language classes were introduced as well as *inburgering* (civic integration) classes. In 2000, the Dutch politician Paul Scheffer published an article in a leading newspaper stating that "Dutch multiculturalism has failed." Respect for cultural difference had prevailed over defending principles of liberal democracy, undermining social cohesion. In Scheffer's view the only solution was a "civilisation offensive," coercing immigrants to adopt principles of liberal democracy and furthering identification with Dutch mainstream culture. Although Scheffer's view commanded widespread support, his stance was also criticized for several reasons: Firstly, national policies had already moved away from multiculturalism. Secondly he appealed to stereotypes of immigrants and ignored the diversity amongst immigrants. Finally, he assumed that cultures are static. Surveys amongst young Muslim immigrants at the time (Van Oudenhoven et al., 1998) had shown that they actually had developed a Westernized interpretation of Islam. There were virtually no differences in terms of liberal ideas between Dutch and Muslim youngsters of the same educational background (Phalet, van Lotringen & Entzinger [2000], quoted in Entzinger, 2006).

Since 2004, the ideal of a multicultural society has been officially rejected by the Dutch government. Former Interior Minister Jan Pieter Donner said: "(…) it shows that many Dutch people do not experience ethnic and cultural diversity as an enrichment, but as a threat. The Dutch society, in all her diversity, is the society in which those who settle have to learn to live, to which they have to adjust and fit into" (quoted in Kremer, 2013, p. 9). Since 2007 a civic integration exam and language test have been introduced—immigrants now have to become Dutch and dual citizenship is prohibited. This also affects Dutch emigrants abroad who cannot apply for citizenship in their new host countries, without losing their Dutch nationality. This also explains why so few Dutch nationals have applied for Luxembourg citizenship (see next section).

In summary, the debate on "what it means to be Dutch" has become politicized in recent years and immigrant policies have become increasingly restrictive. For the acceptance of multiculturalism, the trajectory is important. As noted above, in Canada there has been a persistent movement towards openness whereas the Netherlands has seen a dramatic shift from an institutionalized acceptance of diversity towards an assimilationist policy. However, as will be shown in Chap. 6, even despite terror attacks around the world and politically motivated assassinations in the Netherlands, the attitude towards multiculturalism has remained remarkably stable.

Luxembourg

Luxembourg has experienced a trajectory of increased openness, culminating in the new law on Luxembourg nationality which entered into force on 1 January 2009. This law crucially allows for dual citizenship. The revision has been a long process, reflecting circumstances of the time and different conceptualizations of nationality. The evolution of the Luxembourg law on nationality will be briefly outlined as this process highlights the change in the interpretation of nationality which is directly linked to the integration approach of immigrants.

Nationality can be granted through lineage (*ius sanguinis*) or through place of birth (*ius soli*). As Willems and Milmeister (2008, p. 63) explained, traditional immigration countries such as USA, Canada or Australia have applied ius soli as it is expected in those countries that immigrants take on the nationality of the host country. However, in countries that only recently have been become target countries for immigration such as Germany or Sweden, nationality has traditionally been passed on through blood lineage—ius sanguinis. The authors mention a third category, namely countries with colonial past such as France or the UK, who may adopt a mixture of the two. Luxembourg has oscillated between the two positions as the progression of the nationality law illustrates. Scuto (2013) divided the development of the Luxembourg citizenship law into five phases:

1. The period of the French civil code (1803–1878).

As noted in Chap. 2, Luxembourg became the Département de la Forêt under the Napoleonic rule and the (French) Civil Code was introduced. Following the Treaty of London in 1839, ius sanguinis was introduced to replace the ius soli, as ius soli was associated with the Ancien Régime, where a person was attached to the soil of his lord of the manor. Citizenship now became the right of a person, transmitted by lineal descent from father to his children. Women assumed the nationality of their husband. Yet place of birth was also taken into consideration as "any person born from a foreigner in [the country of] Luxembourg may, during the year of attaining his or her majority, claim the quality of a Luxembourger" (quoted in Scuto, 2013, p. 3). Naturalization became a legislative act and a naturalized foreigner would enjoy all civil and political rights. As Scuto (2013) explained: "The will of the authors of the Constitution of 1848 was—as a sign of openness and trust in the capacity of the young state to integrate newcomers—to transform naturalized persons to fully-fledged Luxembourgers" (p. 3).

2. The liberal period (1878–1940).

This was the time when iron ore was discovered in the south of the country, attracting workers from the bordering countries and further afield to Luxembourg. The sovereign state had been created and alongside the emergence of a feeling of nationhood, the concept of "foreigners" emerged. Decisions on which foreigners are welcome were to be made largely on pragmatic grounds, namely industry needs and the financial situation of the foreigners. Those who were considered financially secure were welcome. A new codifying and modernizing citizenship law was adopted in 1934. Possibilities for acquisition of Luxembourgish citizenship were increased, whilst dual citizenship was restricted. Under the new law the right was granted to Luxembourgish women to keep their citizenship in case of marriage. The driving force behind this new law was the consideration that the formation of national minorities should be avoided: "In immigration countries like ours or in those countries with small numbers of births, which is also our case, the state should increase as much as possible the number of its citizens by assimilating all whose who are born on national soil and thus we avoid the formation of colonies of foreigners in our country" (quoted in Scuto, 2013, p. 4).

3. The phase of national restrictiveness (1940–1968).

In response to the German occupation during World War II, Luxembourg actually adopted a principle introduced by Germany in its defence against the oppression: *Luxemburgertum* (Luxembourgishness) was increasingly emphasized counterbalancing the German *Deutschtum*. As a result, Luxembourgish citizenship law was amended again on 9 March 1940 and double ius soli was abrogated in favour of ius sanguinis. Furthermore, the need for assimilation was laid down in the law: "Naturalization will be refused to a foreigner who does not show *sufficient assimilation*" (Italics added, quoted in Scuto, 2013, p. 5). Even then, in May 1939, Minister of Justice Blum critically remarked on the concept of "sufficient assimilation." He had asked in parliament "How can you prove that a foreigner is assimilated? Give me the symptoms of this adaptation" (quoted in Scuto, 2013, p. 6). A residence requirement of 15 years was introduced for the acquisition of Luxembourgish citizenship. Furthermore, a woman's right to retain or regain her citizenship following marriage was abolished. The experience of war is reflected in these legislative amendments and repercussions can be seen in the subsequent only cautious amendments to the citizenship law.

4. The phase of hesitation between openness and distrust vis-à-vis foreigners (1968–2001).

The law of 22 February 1968 reinstated the possibilities of option, whilst reinforcing the conditions of residence. An underlying sentiment of distrust was still felt towards foreigners. However, in the following years, discriminatory provisions were gradually lifted. On 26 June 1975 the women's right to retain or regain their citizenship was reintroduced. The law of 11 December 1986 brought equality between fathers and mothers regarding the transmission of citizenship. Furthermore, transmission of citizenship to children is possible if one of the parents holds Luxembourgish citizenship. The acquisition of Luxembourgish citizenship by option is allowed for a foreign spouse.

The initiative by then Minister of Justice Krieps to reduce the residence requirement from 10 to 5 years was refuted by the Council of State. It was assumed that only an adequately long (specified as 10 years) period of residence can ensure "sufficient assimilation" to the Luxembourgish society. Demographic realities such as low birth rates and high immigration rates were well recognized, but the approaches in dealing with these issues were now influenced by ideological convictions. The left-leaning side pledged in favour of increased naturalizations and options, whilst the right-leaning side showed reluctance, arguing that citizenship must be granted with caution given the size of the country and declining birth rates. In terms of "symptoms of assimilation" visible criteria were identified in 1986 in the form of competence in the languages of the country, especially Luxembourgish—which had been declared the official, national language in 1984. Thus language, emerging as central theme from the deliberations regarding the search for Luxembourg national identity, finds its way into the debate on the Law on Luxembourg nationality.

5. The 2001 Law on Luxembourg Nationality and the path towards the 2008 law.

The 2001 Law on Luxembourg Nationality (LNL) can be seen as an attempt to move forwards in terms of making it easier to acquire citizenship, but at the same time, building in enough safeguards to restrict access to Luxembourg citizenship. Steps towards opening up include the reduction of the residency requirement from 10 to 5 years and the removal of costs in the application procedure. Conditions include the *honorabilité* requirement (absence of serious penal convictions or loss of civil rights) and sufficient integration—mainly to be shown by active knowledge of Luxembourgish. "Assimilation" has been replaced by "integration." In contrast to Canada, naturalization is understood as the end point or reward for sufficient integration. Precise criteria for language levels had not been specified at that time making the process non-transparent. Art. 4 of the LNL introduced two categories of citizens: "Luxembourgers by origin" and others. Luxembourgers by origin include those born in the Grand Duchy of Luxembourg before 1 January 1920 and their descendants.

The European Convention on Nationality had been signed by the Council of Europe in 1997, inviting member states to find solutions to multiple citizenships. The LNL was the starting point for a new discussion on Luxembourg citizenship including the allowance of dual citizenship.

In October 2006 the "law project 5620 on Luxembourgish citizenship" was registered in parliament and the New Law on Luxembourg Nationality (NLNL) came into force on 1 January 2009. As was the case in Canada, a sentiment of avoiding a rupture in a person's biography was a key consideration. This is expressed in the preface to the explanatory brochure of the NLNL:

> Nationality is generally defined as the legal link between a state and an individual, which is based on a social fact of attachment, a connection of existence, interests and feelings, entailing reciprocal rights and duties. The legislative reform adapts the law about nationality to the changes that have occurred in Luxembourg society. By way of the conditions governing the acquisition of nationality, the law consolidates the integration of foreigners residing in Luxembourg. Many foreigners, through the acquisition of the Luxembourg nationality, wish to show their attachment to our country and their will to integrate, whilst also, through their nationality of origin, wanting to maintain a link with the homeland and culture of their ancestors. It is in this light that the principle of dual nationality has been introduced into Luxembourg law. In addition, the procedures applying to the acquisition and re-acquisition of Luxembourg nationality have been simplified and harmonised. (*Source*: The Luxembourg nationality law of 23 October 2008, Ministry of Justice, Information and Press Service of the Luxembourg Government, January 2009_EN)

In this short introduction, several important points are addressed: First of all, the definition of nationality highlights that nationality is understood as a multifaceted concept: Nationality is specified by not only a legal link between an individual and the state, but also an emotional bond. Furthermore the concept of reciprocity is introduced, implying rights and duties. Specific reference is made to the changes within the Luxembourg society and the objective of the new law is "to contribute to a more consolidated integration of foreigners residing in Luxembourg" (Government, January 2009, p. 10). Furthermore, it is conceded that people can have a loyalty towards two countries—the country of birth and the host country. Between 2009 and 2013, just over 3000 persons on

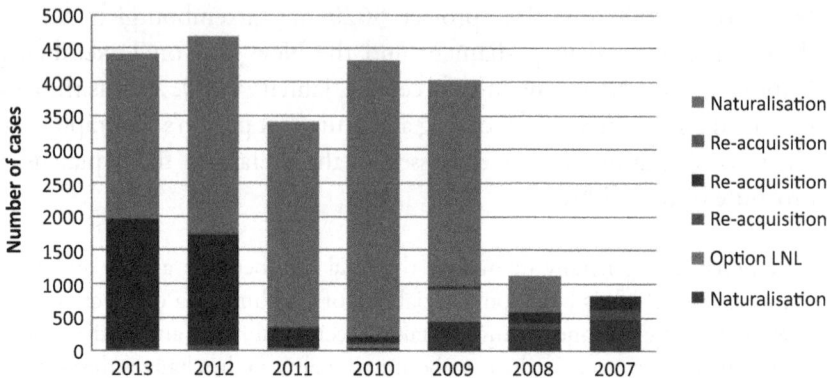

Fig. 3.3 Acquisition of Luxembourg nationality 2007 to 2013. *Source*: Ministry of Justice

average per year have taken up the Government's offer of "integration." According to a survey by TNS Ilres (2007), 75 % of foreigners gave as reason for applying for Luxembourg citizenship "Pour s' intégrer au pays" (Scuto, 2012). The number of acquisitions of Luxembourg nationality since 2007 is shown in Fig. 3.3.

Figure 3.3 shows that there has been a fourfold increase in naturalization requests since the introduction of the NLNL. 2012 and 2013 have seen a marked rise in re-acquisition requests under Art. 29 (Descendants of Luxembourg grandparents). The vast majority (96 %) of re-acquisition requests originate from Belgium and France—with Belgium taking the lion share with 83 % in 1012 and 75 % in 2013. Regarding naturalizations, the traditional immigrant countries to Luxembourg lead the table: Forty percent of the applicants were of Portuguese descent followed by applicants from Italy (14 %). The three neighbouring countries follow and together these 5 countries make up nearly 75 % of those seeking voluntary acquisition of Luxembourg nationality in 2012. This distribution closely mirrors the current foreign demographic profile of Luxembourg (see Fig. 2.6).

Allowing for the principle of dual citizenship can be considered a step change from previous legislation. This is an important principle which also plays a role regarding openness towards a plural society, as will be shown in the empirical research in Chap. 6. Even though the NLNL can be considered a milestone, the law has also been criticized for the length of the residency requirement (which was elevated from 5 to 7 years) and the high level of language competence required for Luxembourgish, in a country that is officially trilingual. As was already noted in Chap. 2, the current coalition government has drafted another revision of the Nationality Law in October 2015, which addresses the language competence levels and residence requirement.

As Scuto (2013) explained, the current political debate about citizenship in Luxembourg is influenced by two opposing trends—the "elite-driven" and "electorate-driven" policy. Whereas the socio-political elite can be described as "modernizing" and fully aware of the foreign work force's contribution to the economy and the country, there are political groups who are defending the "national preferences." Those Luxembourgers who feel threatened in the private labour market or who suffer because of the increased cost of living, "may give value to their Luxembourg citizenship and their national language and raise them as protectionist ramparts" (Fehlen, 2009, p. 233). The political elite consider citizenship as a means to facilitate integration (mid-point) whereas the public debate often focuses on the "symptoms" of integration. Foreigners have to prove integration first and may be rewarded by citizenship (end point). The "symptom" of integration is mainly reduced to the question of (Luxembourgish) languages competence in the public debate. As Fehlen (2009) indicated, a rift is emerging between the political elites and the more nationalistic fraction within the population. One of the objectives of this book is to explore the psychological factors which contribute to a more accepting or rejecting attitude towards the plural composition of society and a wide range of factors play a role as will be elaborated further in Chap. 6.

Finally, it should also be noted that not all countries allow for dual or multiple citizenship. The onus is on the applicant to find out if he or she can keep his or her foreign nationality in case of acquisition of the Luxembourg nationality through naturalization. In Germany, double nationality is still hotly debated. For example, children of Turkish descent born in Germany need to decide by the time they turn 23 whether they want to be a German or Turkish citizen (Peters, 2013).

The Concept of Shared Citizenship

Nationality versus Citizenship—The European Legal Framework

As was already noted above nationality is formally defined as the legal bond between a person and a state (NATAC report, 2006). Each state determines under its own law who are its nationals. The term "citizenship" refers to the sum of legal rights and duties of the individuals attached to nationality under domestic law. "Nationality not only links an individual to a state, it also links individuals to international law; in the EU it also provides individuals with a specific set of rights within this supranational Union" (NATAC, 2006, p. 1). As was pointed out above, the right to nationality is considered a human right.

The European Convention on Nationality (ECN) was adopted in 1997 and came into force in 2000. The ECN has developed the right to a given nationality and influenced the terms of relaxing the requirements for the acquisition of nationality and tolerance of multiple nationalities. As noted previously, two different perspectives on naturalization can be discerned: Naturalization as "mid-point" instrument supporting the integration of immigrants, or as "crowning of a completed integration process." A shift towards the latter understanding has been observed within EU Member States. As was described also for Luxembourg, implications of this shift include the introduction of formal examinations of language skills and courses on knowledge of society as well as lengthening residence and marriage duration requirements. However, contrary to the restrictive tendencies in these areas, multiple nationalities have been accepted in most countries, including Luxembourg. Overall, the authors of the NATAC report have noted a trend towards more restrictive nationality laws in the EU Member States. Yet the authors commented that more restrictive policies may actually exacerbate problems such as social marginalization or cultural alienation rather than solve them. Furthermore, the message to immigrants may be read to be that they are not welcome as future citizens.

A passport carries rights, for example, voting rights or freedom of travel, and also duties, that is, the duty to vote or military service in some countries. When establishing the criteria for nationality, not only the perspective of the immigrant has to be taken into consideration, but also the intention of the state: The state may want to increase its electorate, strengthen recruits for military operations and so on. An important issue however is that a passport does not determine the feelings towards a country. The emotional bond, "based on a social fact of attachment, a connection of existence, interests and feelings" is much more difficult to determine and thus subject of debate. Furthermore, as was mentioned above, there is also the question of perspective—whether nationality is self-assigned, (externally) ascribed or hoped for.

Shared Citizenship

Given the critical observations concerning multiculturalism mentioned above, the discourse on diversity has shifted towards an emphasis on "civic integration," "social cohesion," "common values" and "shared citizenship." In this discourse, the need to develop a more inclusive national identity is stressed as well as the need to fight racism and discrimination. This new approach aims to overcome naïve or misguided forms of multiculturalism whilst avoiding the oppressive reassertion of homogenizing nationalist ideologies. After World War II the world recoiled against Hitler's fanatical and murderous use of such ideologies, but today a rise of nativist discourse and right-wing populist parties has been observed in several European countries. Also persons on the centre-left political spectrum have come to realize that multiculturalism may have failed to help minorities, unintentionally possibly even contributing to social their social isolation. As

Kymlicka (2012, p. 5) summarized, the new models of citizenships therefore emphasize:

1. Political participation and economic opportunities over the symbolic politics of cultural recognition.
2. Human rights and individual freedom over respect for cultural traditions.
3. Building of inclusive national identities over the recognition of ancestral cultural identities.
4. Cultural change and cultural mixing over the reification of static cultural differences.

The focus on inclusiveness (point 3) and the need to create binding values based on human rights and social responsibilities which apply to everyone, even if these lead to some multicultural losses (point 2) was also highlighted by Alibhai-Brown (2001):

> Two thirds of the British still live within five miles of where they were born. Millions of Britons still love books by authors such as Bill Bryson, about how delightful eccentric and unchanged the British are, and listen to the comfortable Radio 4 programme The Archers which, in spite of being set in the Midlands, has no black local characters darkening our doorsteps. ... 80 per cent of Pakistanis have incomes which are below half the national average. Grant money goes to "ethnic minorities." They can get money if they can show that group A is more "excluded" than group B. Different people lay claims to areas, buildings etc. Some translate claims into violence. How can people with such different attitudes absorb the meaning of citizenship? Do they feel a bond and obligations only with other members of their own tribe? (pp. 48–49)

She stressed further that more relevant and inclusive curricula need to be provided at schools, ensuring also that past injustices are not redressed by inflicting guilt on or diminishing those who are three generations removed from those who were responsible. Nordgren and Johansson

(2015), for example, developed a conceptual framework for advancing intercultural learning in history education.

The term "the progressive's dilemma" has been coined to describe the tension between diversity and solidarity (Banting, 2010, p. 797). Banting noted disenchantment with multiculturalism driven by various fears. As a result, newcomers are often seen as "strangers" and not part of "us." He quoted several theories, rooted in different traditions, providing different explanatory frameworks for the erosion of support for redistribution of welfare resources over time. Evolutionary biology suggests that humans have a natural instinct to be less altruistic towards others with whom they share fewer genes. In-group–out-group studies in social psychology have shown that people are comfortable with, supporting and trusting in-group members, but are more suspicious of out-groups. Theories in rational choice emphasize the reciprocal nature of altruism. People are willing to assist and cooperate with people who have assisted and cooperated with them in the past. Scientists representing all these traditions accept that features of the wider social context can trigger or mute these mechanisms. "The search is on for the secret to forestalling such tensions. Most observers place their faith in some form of *cultural glue*, some form of overarching identity or sense of community which transcends ethnic and racial differences" (italics in original, Banting, 2010, p. 801). The civic conception of national identity has been suggested as a form that can bind people together who would otherwise be divided by economic or ethnic differences. In that civic sense, national citizenship is still relevant in the age of migration. Kymlicka (2003) argued that immigration, citizenship and multiculturalism form a triad or "three legged stool"—each supporting one other. He illustrated this using Canada as an example: There is general consensus that Canada is and should remain a country of immigration. The commitment to multiculturalism is enshrined in the legislation (1988 Multiculturalism Act) and in the Constitution (1982). Finally, the citizenship policy is couched within these two strong pillars which alleviate fears that citizenship policies are used as a tool of exclusion or assimilation. The consensus or positive attitude towards multiculturalism will be elaborated in Chap. 6.

Concluding Remarks

This chapter is titled "multiculturalism in context" referring to the multifaceted nature of this concept. The chapter started out by high-lighting the increased flow of goods, ideas and people (globalization). Modern technology allows people to be connected in real time around the world. Not only information travels swiftly and easily around the world, also goods and people. This global reach means that people around the world come in culture contact directly (immigrant-based) or indirectly (globalization-based). Thus world-wide a greater inter-mixing of nationalities and cultures can be observed. The processes brought on by the culture contact situation are described under the heading of acculturation. Prior to the age of globalization, accultura-tion processes could simply be described from the perspective of an immigrant (single minority) moving to a host country (homogeneous majority), but this scenario does not reflect the reality of today. Both migrant populations and societies are increasingly diverse. Especially in urban areas, "minorities" and "majorities" are becoming more dif-ficult to determine. Individual biographies are becoming more com-plex with dual/multiple nationalities and work/living experiences in several countries on the rise, representing challenges to prototypical categorization.

As noted in the introduction to the section on multiculturalism, the term can have different meanings—referring to the demographic composition of society, a policy promoting diversity and equality and finally an attitude towards the plurally composed society. In the pub-lic discourse there is generally no differentiation between the differ-ent layers. "Multiculturalism is dead"—may actually refer to specific policies which may not have been effective, rather than the ideology itself. The broadness of the concept touching on group perceptions, intergroup relations, policies, acculturation strategies by majorities and minorities also means that in their daily lives, people will relate the concept to different aspects of their lives. For one person the necessity to switch languages within the country may be cumbersome and therefore lead to lower levels of endorsement, for another person this switching of languages may be a welcome opportunity to practice languages. Growing numbers of foreigners may be perceived as threat, taking jobs and weakening the own identity, or as a source of stimulation and fresh ideas. Everyone is being touched by a different aspect of multiculturalism and the concept will evoke different connotations. The high face validity was mentioned as a problem for the concept "integration." Everybody seems to know "what it means." The concept "multiculturalism" shares a similar problem but in addition, the implicit assumption of what the concept "means" is superimposed by ideological convictions. As described, multiculturalism is rooted in the human rights movement following World War II. The ideology behind the concept thus entails that cultural differences should be accepted and valued by all groups of society. The normative character is explicit in this statement—indicated on the one hand by the modal verb should and by stipulating going beyond tolerance to actually value the differences. Because of the normative character of multiculturalism ideologies, indicating what should be done and ought to happen, the reactions will be stronger. Yet persons using the term "multiculturalism" may not necessarily be conscious of their own ideological frame of reference.

A different question is whether multiculturalism policies are able to deliver the desired outcome or whether the government ideology is shared by its citizens. In post-apartheid South Africa, for example, the concept of the "rainbow-nation" is promoted by the government. To what extend is this concept a valid self-reflection of its citizens? Or transferred to the Luxembourg context, to what extend do Luxembourg nationals embrace the concept of "multiplicity" as part of their self-definition? The ensuing question is then also how the attitude manifests itself in behaviour. In day-to-day interactions with the mainstream society, immigrants may be more influenced by the attitudes held by the majority population than by more remote immigration policies. The focus of the next section therefore is the individual perspective—the individual living within a multicultural society.

Appendix 1: Immigrant multiculturalism policy scores, 1980–2010

	1980	2000	2010
Australia	4	8	8
Canada	5	7.5	7.5
Sweden	3	5	7
Finland	0	1.5	6
Belgium	1	3	5.5
United Kingdom	2.5	5.5	5.5
Norway	0	0	3.5
Portugal	1	2	3.5
Spain	0	1	3.5
USA	3	3	3
Ireland	1	1.5	3
Germany	0	2	2.5
Greece	0.5	0.5	2.5
France	1	2	2
Netherlands	2.5	5.5	2
Austria	0	1	1.5
Italy	0	1.5	1
Switzerland	0	1	1
Denmark	0	0.5	0
European Average	0.7	2.1	3.1

Source: Kymlicka (2012)

References

Abel, G. J., & Sander, N. (2014). Quantifying global international migration flows. *Science, 343*, 1520–1522. doi:10.1126/science.1248676.

Alibhai-Brown, Y. (2001). After multiculturalism. *The Political Quarterly Publishing Co., 72*(1), 47–56. doi:10.1111/1467-923X.72.s1.7.

Arango, J. (2013). *Exceptional in Europe? Spain's experience with immigration and integration.* Transatlantic Council on Migration, Washington, DC: Migration Policy Institute.

Arends-Tóth, J., & van de Vijver, F. J. R. (2003). Multiculturalism and acculturation: Views of Dutch and Turkish-Dutch. *European Journal of Social Psychology, 33*(2), 249–266. doi:10.1002/ejsp.143.

Arends-Tóth, J., & van de Vijver, F. J. R. (2004). Domains and dimensions in acculturation: Implicit theories of Turkish–Dutch. *International Journal of Intercultural Relations, 28*(1), 19–35. doi:10.1016/j.ijintrel.2003.09.001.

Arends-Toth, J., & van de Vijver, F. J. R. (2006). Conceptual and measurement issues in family acculturation research. In M. H. Bornstein & L. R. Cote (Eds.), *Acculturation and parent-child relationships: Measurement and development* (pp. 33–62). Mahwah, NJ: Lawrence Erlbaum.

Arends-Tóth, J., & van de Vijver, F. J. R. (2007). Acculturation attitudes: A comparison of measurement methods. *Journal of Applied Social Psychology, 37*(7), 1462–1488. doi:10.1111/j.1559-1816.2007.00222x.

Arends-Tóth, J., van de Vijver, F. J., & Poortinga, Y. H. (2006). The influence of method factors on the relation between attitudes and self-reported behaviors in the assessment of acculturation. *European Journal of Psychological Assessment, 22*(1), 4–12. doi:10.1027/1015-5759.22.1.4.

Arnett, J. J. (2002). The psychology of globalization. *American Psychologist, 57*(10), 774–783. doi:10.1037//0003-066X.57.10.774.

Banting, K. G. (2010). Is there a progressive's dilemma in Canada? Immigration, multiculturalism and the welfare state. *Canadian Journal of Political Science, 43*(04), 797–820. doi:10.1017/S0008423910000983.

Banting, K. G., & Kymilicka, W. (Eds.) (2006). *Multiculturalism and the welfare state: Recognition and redistribution of contemporary democracies.* Oxford: Oxford University Press.

Banting, K. G., Courchene, T. J., & Seidle, F. L. (2007). *Belonging? Diversity, recognition and shared citizenship in Canada.* Institute for Research on Public Policy = Institut de recherche en politiques publiques.

Barrett, M. (Ed.) (2013). *Interculturalism and multiculturalism: Similarities and differences.* Strasbourg: Council of Europe Publishing.

Barrett, M., Garbin, D., Cinnirella, M., & Eade, J. (2007). *Identifications and cultural practices amongst British Bangladeshi and mixed-heritage adolescents.* 13th European Conference on Developmental Psychology, 21–25 August 2007. Jena, Germany.

Benet-Martínez, V. (2012). Multiculturalism: Cultural, social, and personality processes. In K. Deaux & M. Snyder (Eds.), *Handbook of personality and social psychology* (pp. 623–648). Oxford, UK: Oxford University Press.

Benet-Martínez, V., Leu, J., Lee, F., & Morris, M. W. (2002). Negotiating biculturalism: Cultural frame swsitching in biculturals with oppositional versus compatible cultural identities. *Journal of Cross-Cultural Psychology, 33*(5), 492–516. doi:10.1177/0022022102033005005.

Berry, J. W. (1984). Multicultural policy in Canada: A social psychological analysis. *Canadian Journal of Behavioural Science/Revue canadienne des sciences du comportement, 16*(4), 353–370. doi:10.1037/h0080859.

Berry, J. W. (1997). Immigration, acculturation, and adaptation. *Applied Psychology, 46*(1), 5–34. doi:10.1111/j.1464-0597.1997.tb01087.x.

Berry, J. W. (2005). Acculturation: Living successfully in two cultures. *International Journal of Intercultural Relations, 29*(6), 697–712. doi:10.1016/j. ijintrel.2005.07.013.

Berry, J., & Kalin, R. (1995). Multicultural and ethnic attitudes in Canada: An overview of the 1991 National Survey. *Canadian Journal of Behavioural Science, 27*(3), 301–320. doi:10.1037/0008-400X.27.3.301.

Berry, J. W., & Sam, D. L. (1997). Acculturation and adaptation. *Handbook of Cross-Cultural Psychology, 3*, 291–326.

Berry, J. W., Kalin, R., & Taylor, D. M. (1977). *Multiculturalism and ethnic attitudes in Canada.* Ottawa: Ottawa Supply and Services.

Berry, J., Phinney, J., Kwak, K., & Sam, D. (2006). Introduction: Goals and research framework for studying immigrant youth. In J. Berry, J. S. Phinney, D. L. Sam, & P. Vedder (Eds.), *Immigrant youth in cultural transition* (pp. 1–14). Mahwah, NJ: Lawrence Erlbaum.

Berry, J. W., Poortinga, Y. H., Segall, M. H., & Dasen, P. R. (2002). *Cross-cultural psychology: Research and applications* (2nd ed.). Cambridge: Cambridge University Press.

Bissoondath, N. (1993). A question of belonging: Multiculturalism and citizenship. In W. I. Kaplan (Ed.), *Belonging: Essays on the meaning and future of Canadian citizenship* (pp. 368–387). Kingston: McGill-Queen's University Press..

Bourhis, R., Moise, L., Perreault, S., & Senécal, S. (1997). Towards an interactive acculturation model: A social psychological approach. *International Journal of Psychology, 32*(6), 369–386. doi:10.1080/002075997400629.

Brannen, M. Y., & Thomas, D. C. (2010). Bicultural individuals in organizations: Implications and opportunity. *International Journal of Cross Cultural Management, 10*(1), 5–16. doi:10.1177/1470595809359580.

Castles, S., & Miller, M. J. (2009). *The age of migration: International population movements in the modern world* (4th ed.). Basingstoke: Palgrave-Macmillan and Guilford.

Celenk, Ö., & van de Vijver, F. J. R. (2014). Assessment of psychological acculturation and multiculturalism: An overview of measures in the public domain. In V. Benet-Martínez & Y.-Y. Hong (Eds.), *Oxford handbook of multicultural identity: Basic and applied psychological perspectives.* Oxford, UK: Oxford University Press.

Chen, S. X., Benet-Martínez, V., & Harris Bond, M. (2008). Bicultural identity, bilingualism, and psychological adjustment in multicultural societies: Immigration-based and globalization-based acculturation. *Journal of Personality, 76*(4), 803–838. doi:10.1111/j.1467-6494.2008.00505.

Cheng, S. Y. Y., Chao, M. M., Kwong, J., Peng, S., Chen, X., Kashima, Y., et al. (2010). The good old days and a better tomorrow: Historical representations and future imaginations of China during the 2008 Olympic Games. *Asian Journal of Social Psychology, 13*(2), 118–127. doi:10.1111/j.1467-839X.2010.01307.

Cheryan, S., & Monin, B. (2005). "Where are you really from?": Asian Americans and identity denial. *Journal of Personality and Social Psychology, 89*(5), 717–730. doi:10.1037/0022-3514.89.5.717.

Chiu, C., Gries, P., Torelli, C. J., & Cheng, S. Y. Y. (2011). Toward a social psychology of globalization. *Journal of Social Issues, 67*(4), 663–676. doi:10.1111/j.1540-4560.2011.01721.x.

CLIP. (2011). Cities for local integration policies (European Commission funded project—Ended in 2010). Interkulturelle Politik in europäischen Städten Intergruppenbeziehungen und die Rolle von Migrantenorganisationen in der Integrationsarbeit, Doris Lüken-Klaßen, Friedrich Heckmann, Bamberg. www.eurofound.europa.eu/areas/populationandsociety/clip.htm

De Bot, K. (1999). The psycholinguistics of language loss. In G. Extra & L. Verhoeven (Eds.), *Bilingualism and migration* (pp. 345–362). Berlin: Mouton de Gruyter.

Entzinger, H. (2006). Changing the rules while the game is on; From multiculturalism to assimilation in the Netherlands. In Y. M. Bodemann & G. Yurdakul (Eds.), *Migration, citizenship, ethnos: Incorporation regimes in Germany, Western Europe and North America* (pp. 121–144). New York: Palgrave Macmillan.

Epstein, S. (1973). The self-concept revisited. Or a theory of a theory. *American Psychologist, 5*, 404–416.

Epstein, S. (1979). Entwurf einer Integrativen Persönlichkeitstheorie. In S. H. Filipp (Ed.), *Selbstkonzept-Forschung: Probleme, Befunde, Perspektiven* (pp. 15–45). Stuttgart: Klett-Cotta.

Erikson, T. H. (2013). *Immigration and national identity in Norway.* Transatlantic Council on Migration, Washington, DC: Migration Policy Institute.

Esser, H. (2000). *Soziologie. Spezielle Grundlagen. Band 2: Die Konstruktion der Gesellschaft.* Franfurt: Campus.

Eurostat (2011). *Migrants in Europe. A statistical portrait of the first and second generation. Eurostat statistical books* (2011 ed.). Luxembourg: Publications Office of the European Union. doi:10.2785/5318.

Fargue, P. (2015). *Jihadist attacks: Is closing borders really the answer?* Migration Policy Centre, European University Institute 19.11.2015.

Farley, J. E. (2005). *Majority-minority relations* (5th ed.). New Jersey: Pearson Prentice Hall.

Fehlen, F. (2009). *Baleine Bis, une enquête sur un marché linguistique multilingue en profonde mutation.* Luxemburgs Sprachenmarkt im Wandel: SESOPI Centre Intercommunautaire Luxembourg (=RED n°12). Luxembourg: Imprimerie St Paul.

Fiske, S. T., Cuddy, A. J. C., Glick, P., & Xu, J. (2002). A model of (often mixed) stereotype content: Competence and warmth respectively follow from perceived status and competition. *Journal of Personality and Social Psychology, 82*(6), 878–902. doi:10.1037//0022-3514.82.6.878.

Foroutan, N. (2012, October). *Die neuen deutschen Heimatsucher.* Zeit online 19.10.2012. Retrieved form: http://www.zeit.de/politik/deutschland/2012-10/integration-muslime

Fu, J. H.-Y., & Chiu, C.-Y. (2007). Local culture's responses to globalization: Exemplary persons and their attendant values. *Journal of Cross-Cultural Psychology, 38*(5), 636–653. doi:10.1177/0022022107305244.

Gordon, M. M. (1964). *Assimilation in American life: The role of race, religion, and national origins.* New York: Oxford University Press.

Graves, T. (1967). Psychological acculturation in a tri-ethnic community. *Southwestern Journal of Anthropology, 23*, 337–350.

Hong, Y., Morris, M. W., Chiu, C., & Benet-Martínez, V. (2000). Multicultural minds: A dynamic constructivist approach to culture and cognition. *American Psychologist, 55*(7), 709–720. doi:10.1037//0003-066X.55.7.709.

Huddleston, T., Bilgili, O., Joki, A.-L., & Vankova, Z. (2015). Migrant integration policy index 2015. Retrieved from: http://www.mipex.eu

Inglehart, R., & Welzel, C. (2010). Changing mass priorities: The link between modernization and democracy. *Perspectives on Politics, 8*(2), 551–567. doi:10.1017/S1537592710001258.

Kashima, Y., Bain, P., Haslam, N., Peters, K., Laham, S., Whelan, J., et al. (2009). Folk theory of social change. *Asian Journal of Social Psychology, 12*(4), 227–246. doi:10.1111/j.1467-839X.2009.01288.

Kashima, Y., Shi, J., Tsuchiya, K., Kashima, E. S., Cheng, S., Chao, M. M., et al. (2011). Globalization and folk theory of social change: How globalization relates to societal perceptions. *Journal of Social Issues, 67*(4), 696–716. doi:10.1111/j.1540-4560.2011.01723.x.

Kremer, M. (2013). *The Netherlands: From national identity to plural identifications.* Transatlantic Council on Migration, Washington, DC: Migration Policy Institute.

Kunz, J. L., & Sykes, S. (2007). *Form mosaic to harmony: Multicultural Canada in the 21st century.* Policy Research Initiative, Ottawa.

Kymlicka, W. (2003). Immigration, citizenship, multiculturalism: Exploring the links. *The Political Quarterly, 74*(1), 195–208. doi:10.1111/j.1467-923X.2003.00590.

Kymlicka, W. (2007). Canadian approaches to recognizing and accommodating diversity. In K. Banting, T. J. Courchene & F. L. Seidle (Eds.), *Belonging? Diversity, Recognition and Shared Citizenship in Canada* (pp. 37–86). Institute for Research on Public Policy = Institut de recherche en politiques publiques.

Kymlicka, W. (2012). *Multiculturalism: Success, failure, and the future.* Transatlantic Council on Migration, Washington, DC: Migration Policy Institute.

Meer, N., & Modood, T. (2011). How does interculturalism contrast with multiculturalism? *Journal of Intercultural Studies, 33*(2), 175–196. doi:10.1080/07256868.2011.618266.

Metraux, A. (1951). United Nations economic and security council statement by experts on problems of race. *American Psychologist, 3*(1), 142–145. doi:10.1525/aa.1951.53.1.02a00370.

Modood, T. (2005). Remaking multiculturalism after 7/7. *Open Democracy*, 29.09.2005. https://www.opendemocracy.net/conflict-terrorism/multiculturalism_2879.jsp

NATAC. (2006). The Acquisition of Nationality in EU Members States: Rules, Practices and Quantitative Development (European Commission funded, project ended in 2006) http://ec.europa.eu/research/fp6/ssp/natac_en.htm

Nguyen, A.-M. D., & Benet-Martínez, V. (2007). Biculturalism unpacked: Components, measurement, individual differences, and outcomes. *Social and Personality Psychology Compass, 1*(1), 101–114. doi:10.1111/j.1751-9004.2007.00029.x.

Nordgren, K., & Johansson, M. (2015). Intercultural historical learning: A conceptual framework. *Journal of Curriculum Studies 47*(1), 1–25. doi: 10.1080/00220272.2014.956795

Peters, F. (2013). *Doppelstaatler sind Deutsche mit Verfallsdatum.* Welt.de downloaded on 25.02.2013. Retrieved from: http://www.welt.de/

Phinney, J., Berry, J., Vedder, P., & Liebkind, K. (2006). The acculturation experience: Attitudes, identities, and behaviors of immigrant youth. In J. Berry, J. Phinney, D. Sam, & P. Vedder (Eds.), *Immigrant youth in cultural transition* (pp. 71–116). Mahwah, NJ: Lawrence Erlbaum.

Redfield, R., Linton, R., & Herskovits, M. J. (1936). Memorandum for the study of acculturation. *American Psychologist, 38*(1), 149–152. doi:10.1525/aa.1936.38.1.02a00330.

Rudmin, F. (2009). Constructs, measurements and models of acculturation and acculturative stress. *International Journal of Intercultural Relations, 33*(2), 106–123. doi:10.1016/j.ijintrel.2008.12.001.

Rudmin, F. W. (2003). Critical history of the acculturation psychology of assimilation, separation, integration, and marginalization. *Review of General Psychology, 7*(1), 3–37. doi:10.1037/1089-2680.7.1.3.

Schwartz, S. J., Unger, J. B., Zamboanga, B. L., & Szapocznik, J. (2010). Rethinking the concept of acculturation: Implications for theory and research. *The American Psychologist, 65*(4), 237–251. doi:10.1037/a0019330.

Scuto, D. (2012). Drei Fragen an D. Scuto. Interview in: Luxemburger Wort (12.11.2012), p. 3.

Scuto, D. (2013). Country Report Luxembourg. EUDO Citizenship Obeservatory, European University Institute, Florence, Italy.

Silver, R. (2013). Upstream it's all English: Moving through language-in-education policies in English. Presentation at International Symposium "Multilingualism, Identity, Education. Asian and European Perspectives." University of Luxembourg, 4–5 November 2013.

Simon, P. (2012) French national identity and integration: Who belongs to the national community? Transatlantic Council on Migration, Washington, DC: Migration Policy Institute.

Simon, B., & Ruhs, D. (2008). Identity and politicization among Turkish migrants in Germany: The role of dual identification. *Journal of Personality and Social Psychology, 95*(6), 1354–1366. doi:10.1037/a0012630.

Spiegel. (2014, July 1). Gerichtshof für Menschenrechte: Frankreichs Burka-Verbot für rechtens erklärt. *Spiegel.de Online*.

Spiegel. (2014, May 26). Europa: Der Rechtsruck. *Spiegel.de Online*.

Standard Eurobarometer 83, European Commission. (2015). *Public opinion in the European Union*. First Results.Retrieved from: http://ec.europe.eu/public opinion/index

TNS Ilres. (2007). *L'IdentitéLuxembourgeoise*. Enquête Internet auprès de 524 personnes en juin 2007 pour Le Jeudi.

Turner, J. C., Hogg, M., Oakes, P., Reicher, S., & Wetherell, M. (1987). *Rediscovering the social group: A self-categorization theory*. Oxford: Basil Blackwell.

United Nations Department of Economic and Social Affairs (DESA). (2009). *International Migration Report 2009 : A Global Assessment*. Retrieved from: http://www.un.org/esa/population/publications/migration/WorldMigrationReport2009.pdf

Van de Vijver, F. J. R., Breugelmans, S. M., & Schalk-Soekar, S. R. G. (2008). Multiculturalism: Construct validity and stability. *International Journal of Intercultural Relations, 32*(2), 93–104. doi:10.1016/j.ijintrel.2007.11.001.

Van de Vijver, F. J. R., & Phalet, K. (2004). Assessment in multicultural groups: The role of acculturation. *Applied Psychology, 53*(2), 215–236. doi:10.1111/j.1464-0597.2004.00169.x.

Van Oudenhoven, J. P., Prins, K. S., & Buunk, B. P. (1998). Attitudes of minority and majority members towards adaptation of immigrants. *European Journal of Social Psychology, 28*(6), 995–1013. doi:10.1002/(SICI)1099-0992(1998110)28.

Vedder, P., & van de Vijver, F. J. R. (2006). Methodological aspects: Studying adolescents in 13 countries. In J. Berry, J. Phinney, D. Sam, & P. Vedder (Eds.), *Immigrant youth in cultural transition* (pp. 47–70). Mahwah, NJ: Lawrence Erlbaum.

Ward, C., Bochner, S., & Furnham, A. (2001). *The psychology of culture shock.* Hove, East Sussex: Routledge.

Ward, C., & Kennedy, A. (1999). The measurement of sociocultural adaptation. *International Journal of Intercultural Relations, 23*(4), 659–677. doi:10.1016/S0147-1767(99)00014-0.

Ward, C., Leong, C. H., & Low, M. (2004). Personality and Sojourner adjustment. An exploration of the big five and the cultural fit proposition. *Journal of Cross-Cultural Psychology, 35*(2), 137–151. doi:10.1177/0022 022103260719.

Weinreich, P. (2009). "Enculturation", not "acculturation": Conceptualizing and assessing identity processes in migrant communities. *International Journal of Intercultural Relations, 33*(2), 124–139. doi:10.1016/j.ijintrel.2008.12.006.

Willems, H., & Milmeister, P. (2008). Migration und Integration. In W. H. Lorig & M. Hirsch (Eds.), *Das politische System Luxemburgs: Eine Einführung* (pp. 62–92). Wiesbaden: VS Verlag für Sozialwissenschaften.

Yang, D. Y.-J., Chiu, C.-Y., Chen, X., Cheng, S. Y. Y., Kwan, L. Y.-Y., Tam, K.-P., et al. (2011). Lay psychology of globalization and its social impact. *Journal of Social Issues, 67*(4), 677–695. doi:10.1111/j.1540-4560.2011.01722.

United Nations. (n.d.) The universal declaration of Human Rights. Available at: http://www.un.org/en/documents/udhr/) (accessed 29 April 2013).

United Nations. (n.d.) Human Development Index (HDI) https://data.undp.org/dataset/Table-1-Human-Development-Index-and-its-components/wxub-qc5k

Zeit. (2015, December 6). Regionalwahlen in Frankreich: Front National profitiert von der Terrorangst. *Zeit.de Online.*

Zeit. (2015, November 27). Donald Trump hetzt wie ein Faschist. *Zeit.de Online.*

4

The Individual in a Multicultural Context

Introduction

The focus of this chapter is on the individual *within* a multicultural context. As Chen (2013) noted, opening up is one reaction to globalization, ethnic protectionism being another. Within this chapter, some aspects pertinent to individuals living within an increasingly multicultural context will be highlighted. Firstly, the persistence of primordial sentiments will be explored, turning to evolutionary psychology in search for some explanations. Core human motives will then be examined further with a special emphasis on the need to belong and the need for self-enhancement. Human beings need to negotiate stability and change—core elements of identity development. Selected identity theories will be reviewed, including the structure of the self and the link between the self and the cultural context. In the final part of this chapter an empirical study will be presented which explores the salience of national identity as a function of the multicultural context.

© The Author(s) 2016
E. Murdock, *Multiculturalism, Identity and Difference*,
DOI 10.1057/978-1-137-59679-6_4

Phylogenetic Insights—Persistence of Ethnicity

Weinreich, Bacova and Rougier (2003, p. 116) commented on the persistence and strength of emotion associated with ethnicity even in a global world:

> Primordialist sentiments are frequently expressed in people's everyday discourses about nationality and ethnicity. What needs to be explained is why such sentiments are manifested and, when they are, why with such intensity and affect as is so often evident. In other words, the refocused problematic is the human propensity to think about ethnicity or nationality in primordialist terms, when historical evidence provides man counter examples of fluidity and change, as when national state boundaries emerge anew, alter or disappear altogether.

Why do people in the age of globalization and European unification hold on to their national identifications with such fervour? Why is national identification still important and in particular why do people hold on to primordial sentiments, if historical facts speak so clearly against it? The strength of the sentiment led me turn to evolutionary psychology in the first instance. As the term *primordial* itself suggests, the roots for the intensity of feeling may be traced to the roots of human evolution. Therefore, insights from phylogenies will be presented next.

The Long Path to Anthropogenesis

The transition from *Pongides* to *Hominides* dates back to 10 ± 4 million years ago (Bischof-Köhler, 1985). The Australopithecus *afarensis* lived around three million years ago in East Africa and showed evidence for an upright walk. The *Homo habilis* lived around three to two million years ago, and prehistoric finds suggest that he used simple tools and resting places. The *Homo erectus* (1.7 m to 400,000 years ago) used fire, as evidence found at a cave near Peking suggests. Evidence also shows that *Homo sapiens neanderthalensis*, who lived around 100,000 years ago, buried their dead. The high period of hunters and gatherers with cave paintings dates back to around 80,000 years ago.

During this period, bands of 20 to 30 people lived and hunted together, roaming the country according to the seasons. The early humanoids built tent-like huts and hunted larger, dangerous animals. Hunting required co-operation and role division. Band members must have found a ways of communicating with each other. With the onset of language development, knowledge could be communicated and passed on. Minimal stock keeping was possible and personal belongings were reduced to what people could carry. This changed with the *Neolithic Revolution* which is thought to have taken place around 10,000 BC. This transition to settlement and farming led to an increase in the size of group members living together and allowed planning for food and storage keeping. Settlement implied not only an increase in population size and greater degree of specialization and interdependence, but also a qualitative change in motivations in the form of an accumulation of wealth and an escalation of needs. Initially, the group membership was defined by blood ties, which was then extended to the clan. The first urban high cultures are dated to 3500 BC. A common language, symbols, clothing, traditions and values strengthen the feeling of belonging within these larger settlements. Bischof (1980) noted that family can be extended to the clan, but *familiarity* must be supplemented by meticulously maintained *uniformity* (language, customs, etc.) and especially a common moral code. Since readiness for altruistic behaviour increases with familiarity, empathetic moral norms of altruism towards clan members exist. Altruistic behaviours (e.g. care for the young, social grooming, group defence, etc.) which are to the advantage of the recipient to the cost of the donor are evolutionary stable, as long as these behaviours are directed at kinship members. The most important cue for kinship is familiarity. Offspring seek out familiar persons (attachment motivation) and avoid the unfamiliar (fear of the stranger). Despite the support mechanisms seeking to build familiarity noted above, members within larger settlements won't have the same level of familiarity with each other that the band members of the hunter and gatherers enjoyed. People create sub-groups *within* groups based on interests, competencies, origin, and so on to generate familiarity and to reduce levels of stress and aggression. Solidarity measures create familiarity within groups, but behaviour towards out-groups still needs to be regulated. Bischof-Köhler (1985) noted that "semi-familiarity" actually increases levels of aggression and increasingly, own interests are placed above group interests "Das Zusammenleben mit vielen unvertrauten Menschen stellt also einen Stressfaktor dar, der trotz der vielen symbolischen Kontaktvermeidungsstrategien, die der Mensch entwickelt hat, nicht zu unterschätzen ist"[1] (p. 37). Thus living with many unfamiliar persons is a source of stress and with a rise in group size, own interests are increasingly placed above group interests.

Revolutions in the Evolution

Only three revolutions are counted in the evolution of human kind. The first was the Neolithic revolution which led to the changes just outlined. The next revolution happened around 12,000 years later: The *Industrial Revolution* took place at the end of the eighteenth century. A key characteristic of the Industrial Revolution was the formation of large urban settlements around the places of industrial production. This phase is characterized by even greater population density, an even higher degree of specialization, as well as greater accumulation of wealth and needs than during the preceding phase. The *Digital Revolution* soon followed in the twentieth century and brought with it a globally connected world—both digitally and physically (see Chap. 3). Whilst millions of years passed between the transition of humankind to the stone age and then around 70,000 years between the days of glory of the stone age period and the period of settlement, "only" about 10,000 years have passed between the Neolithic period and the Industrial revolution and a mere 200 years separate the Industrial and Digital revolution. The pace of change has increased dramatically, possibly allowing insufficient time, in evolutionary terms, to adapt. Human evolution is on the one hand an example for the great plasticity and capacity for adaptation of humanoids, but if genetics and environment don't match, ecological damage can take place. Not all environments humans are able to create suit the genetic depositions. The new escalation of needs is not necessarily of adaptive benefit—on the contrary. Maladaptation may take the form of abuse of

---

[1] Living together with so many unfamiliar people represents a stress factor which should not be underestimated despite all the contact-avoidance measures people have developed.

resources, physical damage (i.e. obesity) and psychological problems. For the longest stretch of human development, people lived mainly with their kith and kin in small bands of people. Adaptation to living in larger settlements with the benefits of storage of resources making life more predictable had just happened, when the industrial revolution took place. One key characteristic of the industrial life-style is very densely populated, yet anonymous urban areas, which have brought with them problems such as increasing crime rates and social isolation. Bischof-Köhler (1985) wrote: "Die moderne industrielle Massengesellschaft stellt eine Überforderung an das menschliche Motivationsinventar dar"[2] (p. 42). In evolutionary time-scale, with the blink of an eyelid, the industrial revolution is followed by the digital age. The new global era, with its speed of travel of both information and people, adds new challenges for the human community. The greater inter-mixing is thus a very recent development—from an evolutionary perspective the adherence to a primordial perspective of nationality is therefore understandable.

The difficulties of living in a modern, complex world, where external points of reference are disappearing were, for example, described by sociologists Ehrenberg (*La Fatigue d'être soi*, 1998) and Sennett (*The corrosion of character*, 1998). From a psychological perspective, Baumeister (1987) pointed out that the identity components of the self-definition process have become more complex. In the modern world there is a shift from unproblematic definitions which are characterized by clear criteria for obtaining identity to those where the achievement of this identity requires continual redefinition. Examples for the former include *assigned* identity such as gender or a *single transformation*, for example, motherhood. Problematic self-definitions are those where a hierarchy of criteria has to be applied, for example, wealth, or choices have to be made. If choice is optional, such as political affiliations or dual citizenship, the ease of decision will depend on the alternative options and clarity of the guidelines regarding how to obtain each option. If an individual is faced with required choice, for example, career or forced choice citizenship and is presented with incompatible alternatives, meta-criteria have to be identified to make a choice between them. A shift towards the more

---

[2] Modern, industrial mass society overstrains the human motivation inventory.

problematic components where the individual is continually faced with choices between incompatible alternatives and has to weigh up criteria, whose worth will also be changeable, has contributed to the fact that "identity has become a problem" (Baumeister, 1987, p. 163).

Acquisition of Key Competencies on the Path to Anthropogenesis

Bischof-Köhler (1991) pointed out several competencies that mark the transition to anthropogenesis. Key achievements include the development of social cognitions and an awareness of the concept of time. Cognition includes all processes which allow an organism to recognize what is important for survival. Some animals also use tools to solve problems or show co-operation when hunting. However, when chimpanzees solve a problem, for example using a box to reach a banana, the frame of reference is the specific situation. They do not anticipate future needs.

Social Cognition

The development of social cognition represents a qualitative leap in the evolution. A key role is played by the cognitive ability to make oneself the object of reflection, recognizing the distinction between "I" versus "me" (*Selbstobjektivierung*), making the self a subject of reflection. Further steps on the path to anthropogenesis are the ability for simultaneous identification (self and mirror image), reification (objects can carry attributes) and crucially, decentralization, the ability to take different perspectives (Bischof-Köhler, 1985). At cognitive level this is then referred to as role- or perspective taking. The motives or intention of another can be anticipated and understood. If an emotional component is added, social decentralization implies *empathy*. An observer has the subjective experience of feeling the emotions of another. In several experiments Bischof-Köhler (1994) could show that self-objectivation (the ability to recognize oneself in the mirror) is the only precondition for empathy during the second year of life. Ontogenetically, empathy is the earliest socio-cognitive function and the link between empathy and self-concept development could be demonstrated empirically. In this context it is also interesting to note that primates have the ability to recognize themselves in the mirror. However, primates raised in isolation do not develop this ability. Once reunited with conspecifics, the mirror deficit is levelled: "Es sieht so aus, als würde der Umgang mit Artgenossen das `Material´ liefern, aus dem sich die Vorstellung vom eigenen 'Ich' aufbaut"[3] (Bischof-Köhler, 1991, p. 172). It comes as no surprise that mothers "mirror" the behaviour of their children and thus provide valuable feedback to the child regarding how the child's behaviour is perceived by the outside world.

The ability to show empathy in turn is a precondition for co-operation and developing a feeling of self-worth. Increasing one's own self-worth becomes a motivational goal: "Die Steigerung und Intensivierung des Selbstgefühls wird damit ein motivationales Ziel"[4] (Bischof-Köhler, 1985, p. 20). Empathy does not only lead to altruistic behaviour, but it can also serve anti-social purposes. Whether empathy leads to pro-social or harming behaviour depends on the attitude towards the other. Bischof-Köhler (1991) pointed to the link between empathy and aggression: The recognition of inflicting harm on others is based on empathy. If one can imagine how pain is felt, then this pain can also consciously be inflicted on others. As this intentional aspect is usually missing in animal aggression, it is considered "innocent." Bischof-Köhler reckoned that some chimpanzees have transgressed and "lost their innocence" in the way they treat some of their enemies (p. 177). As a counterpoint to this anti-social behaviour, empathy also plays a role in the genesis of guilt.

Concept of Time

Another important element on the path to human evolution is the development of a temporal perspective. This includes the anticipation of needs—the hunt takes place in anticipation of hunger; wood needs to be gathered before a fire can be lit. The temporal perspective also extends beyond the immediate needs. Burial rituals indicate that an idea of an

---

[3] It appears that living with conspecifics produces the "material" on which the idea of the own "self" is built.

[4] Increasing and intensifying the feeling of self-worth becomes a motivational goal.

after-life existed even amongst early hominids. The fear of the future, "existential anxiety" is specifically human. It is the first price we pay for time representation (Bischof, 1980). Ritualized practices are introduced to reduce the fear of the unknown, a form of appeasement in expectation of reciprocity. The time-perspective also stretches backwards—actions can be remembered. A "bad" deed can be rectified by doing something "good." Gifts or sacrifices are made in order to receive benevolent treatment. Inherent in this is the understanding of delayed gratification. A time delay is also implied in the idea of reciprocity—help is offered now—and a reciprocal offer is expected at some unspecified time in the future. In this way, mutual obligations are created. Violation of such commitments will meet retaliation. Mutuality, giving and taking, is a key strategy for survival. Amongst primitive people, living in harmony with nature as a principle has been observed. If something is taken from nature, something, even if symbolically, is given back.

Developmentally, the theory of the mind, the ability to take perspectives develops around the age of four as well as mental time travel, the use of a temporal buffer to anticipate motivational states (Bischof-Köhler, 2007). The theory of recapitulation, often summarized in Ernst Haeckel's phrase as "ontogeny recapitulates phylogeny," appears to hold true for the human development, as key developmental tasks are mastered, in the order paralleling phylogeny. The stages in the child's cognitive development follow much the same progression of evolutionary stages.

Only a brief outline of the evolutionary development was provided above. The key objective was to highlight some major achievements which differentiate the human species from other species. The first is the social cognition of empathy, the ability to take the position of others. The ability of perspective-taking has pro-social consequences. On the one hand, it may lead to co-operation, but anti-social behaviour is also possible. The second differentiator is an understanding of time, which then implies anticipation as well as the suppression of needs. A further step is the development of language, facilitating the communication and coordination within group members and offering the possibility to pass on knowledge. Finally there is the principle of reciprocity. Reciprocal altruism regulates pro-social, but also the negative behavioural tendencies. Familiarity determines the boundaries for altruism. With the Neolithic revolution a phase of population growth, greater specialization and an escalation of needs have been rung in. Henceforth mechanisms had to be developed, regulating living in larger groups and with different groups.

From Instinct to Society

An extension of the temporal perspective is the capacity for internalization—a child learns to internalize their key carers and learns to cope with (temporal) separation. This capacity for internalization also extends to the internalization of norms and rules, which are important, as human beings are not governed by instinct. As Lothar Krappman noted: "Die Gesellschaft geht dem Interagierenden genetisch voran."[5] Von Schlippe and Schweitzer (1996) explained that man can not *not* belong: "Die Zugehörigkeit zum System ist für jeden Menschen unabdingbar"[6] (p. 44). The authors assert that systems form spontaneously and self-organize (*autopoiesis*). Furthermore, systems don't exist per se, but are created through our perception. Social systems create their borders according to the question of what makes sense. The earliest systems consisted of bands or tribes. These were extended to clans, but following the Neolithic revolution and a population explosion and the development of complex societies, governing systems had to be developed. With regard to plurally composed societies, von Schlippe and Schweitzer (1996) noted: "Staaten müssen sich die Frage stellen, ob sie den Sinn ihrer Mitgliedschaft in ethnischer Blutsverwandschaft (Nationalstaat) oder auf faktischen Zusammenleben begründen wollen (multikulturelle Gesellschaft)"[7] (p. 59).

The term "nation" can be traced back to the Latin term "natio" which referred to birth, origin or people. In Roman times, the term described "others" or "heathens" (Rumpel, 1991). The anthropologist Clifford Geertz (1973) described a nation as a group based on primordial affiliations, reflecting an understanding based on ancestry. As discussed in the

---

[5] Society precedes the individual genetically.

[6] It is essential of human beings to belong to a system.

[7] Countries must answer the question whether they define their sense of membership (in-group) in terms of ethnic blood ties (Nationalstaat) or on the basis of actual living together (multicultural society).

context of Luxembourg (see Chap. 2) most historians would agree that nations themselves can be considered a construct (Péporté, 2011). Billig (1995) explained that unifying objective criteria such as language, religion or geography cannot be used to predict where state boundaries are: psychological considerations are decisive. Nations are in fact "imagined communities" (Anderson, 2006).

In the Middle Ages reference is made to a territorial understanding of the term "nation" for the first time. The context was university registration—students had to state where they were from (Helmchen, 2005). This author also explained that the term initially had an ethnic connotation, followed by use in a geographic sense and finally the term acquired political connotations. Helmchen emphasized that nations are historic creations and are based on heritage. She further emphasized that the history of nations serves a specific purpose and is in that sense *normative*. During the French revolution the terms "nation" and "state" were for the first time used in the same sense. The common ideals of *Liberalité*, *Egalité* and *Fraternité* forged members together to form a nation. This point illustrates the purposefulness (*Zweckgerichtetheit*) of the process of nation-building as well as the notion that there has to be a will to form a nation. A characteristic of a nation is simply that the members have "a lot in common" and over time, a sense of commonality is formed that can become stereotypical. These stages in the process of nation-building can be witnessed in the case of Luxembourg (Chap. 2). The sovereign state of Luxembourg was created by the Treaties of London. Over time, a feeling of togetherness and perceived distinctiveness from others developed. The communal bond was strengthened by a (re-) interpretation of history, common symbols (Feierwôn, Flag) and common experiences (suffering experienced during World War II, development into a wealthy state). Gradually, the importance of Lëtzebuergesch as a common language emerges. The will to form a nation exists and the national day is now staged to celebrate the state and its people.

Human Motivation

Anthropogenesis is characterized by few revolutions, but the pace of change has accelerated. In the course of human evolution, humanoids have lived for the longest stretch of time in small bands of people, where familiarity regulated altruistic behaviour. The Neolithic and Industrial revolutions were each accompanied by growth in population density, a higher degree of specialization and role division as well as an escalation of needs. Human evolution thus also represents an evolution and escalation of needs and human motivations.

Evolution and Human Motivation

Bischof-Köhler (1985) noted that the problem of competition for resources within a group has to be solved without endangering the coherence within the group. One solution to this problem is the introduction of hierarchies, but within hierarchies, the rank order has to be determined. This gives rise to the need for dominance, as well as the need for recognition. To be the centre of attention is an indication of rank. Attention can be demanded through aggression, if physically strong, or through the calming effect of experience, which is the basis for the higher rank order of older (yet physically weaker) primates. Those who are admired can expect beneficial treatment, which in itself provides an incentive to seek that status. The need for attention forms the counterpoint to the need for dominance, giving rise to leadership roles. A high rank order is then based on group recognition, rather than dominance. Bischof-Köhler (1985) suggested that need for recognition and praise by others may have been a strong motivator to share food and to gather and store food exceeding own needs.

Social emotions and motivations are centred on the self. Social decentralization is reciprocal—I can also evaluate myself taking the perspective from another person. According to Bischof-Köhler (1985) the experience of competence, the satisfaction experienced on successfully completing a task and the beneficial experience on self-worth make the satisfaction of *self-worth* the most fundamental human need. According to the Zurich model of social motivation (Bischof, 1975; Bischof-Köhler, 2007) three fundamental motivational systems can be distinguished, namely the need for security, the need for arousal and the need for autonomy. All three systems interact and mutually influence each other. Throughout human development a shift in emphasis between the systems occurs. The need for security guides behaviour in relation to familiar persons and facilitates the development of trust. Children learn to turn to familiar persons for care and attention and affiliation is sought with those persons—initially family and kinship members, who provide care. At the emotional level the experience of affiliation and care leads to a sense of being safe and secure (*Geborgenheit*). On the other hand, "strangers" evoke fear and anxiety. Novel input is regulated by the arousal system. Too much security can lead to boredom and "*Unternehmungslust*"[8] sets in. In the course of human development, a shift from security to arousal occurs, but individuals differ regarding the amount of stimulation they can tolerate. The third system, the autonomy system, relates to the experience of exercising control, being able to influence events. Success in completion of tasks increases self-esteem and confidence in own abilities. Bischof-Köhler (1985) noted: "Mit der Rückwirkung, die der Abschluss jeder motivierenden Handlung durch das zusätzliche Erlebnis der Kompetenz auf die Selbstachtung hat, wird die Befriedigung des Eigenwertes zur umfassenden menschlichen Motivation überhaupt und ein zusätzlicher Faktor der Verhaltenssteuerung"[9] (p. 27).

Human Core Motives

In developing the core motives of human development, Fiske (2010) also turns to evolution as an explanatory framework. She noted that belonging to a group helps people survive psychologically and physically. Thus evolutionary adaptation favoured the group-oriented person and "people respond to other people and seek social acceptance through social motives that have evolved to help them survive and thrive in groups—and more generally" (p. 11). Multiple evolutionary reasons can be suggested for the readiness to form groups easily. Groups can share labour, resources and information, diffuse risk and co-operate to overcome stress or threat. Reciprocity or the concern with equity was also noted above. Fiske described five core human motives, which are summarized in Table 4.1 below.

---

[8] Need for stimulation, however literally the terms can be translated as "Lust for adventure."
[9] With the feedback loop that each completion of a motivational task provides, including the additional feeling of competence conducive for self-esteem, the satisfaction of the self-worth becomes the guiding principle for human motivation and an additional factor in guiding behaviour.

Table 4.1 Core human motives

Belonging Need for strong, stable relationships			
Relatively cognitive motives		Relatively affective motives	
Understanding	*Controlling*	*Self-enhancement*	*Trusting*
Need for shared meaning and prediction	Need for perceived contingency between behavior and outcomes	Need for viewing self as basically worthy or improvable	Need for viewing others as basically benign

Source: Fiske (2010)

Relationships and groups are fundamental for survival, and therefore Fiske described the *need to belong* as the first and fundamental motive. Two more cognitive motives follow on from the need to belong, namely understanding, the need for prediction and control, which ensures the contingency between behaviour and outcomes. The affective motives include the need for enhancing the self, establishing self-worth and the development of trust.

The Need to Belong

Baumeister and Leary (1995) noted in their seminal article on the need to belong that "much of what people do is done in the service of belongingness" (p. 498). The authors noted further that human beings have a pervasive drive to form and maintain at least a minimum quantity of lasting, positive and significant interpersonal relationships. They provide a detailed evaluation of the hypothesis that the "need to belong" is a fundamental human motivation, arriving at an affirmative conclusion. In the following I will highlight some key aspects, which are based on Baumeister and Leary's review article.

Belongingness can be almost as compelling a need as food. Human culture is significantly conditioned by the pressure to provide belongingness. The need to belong is universal and can be satisfied also by non-interpersonal relationships such as membership in a political or interest group. Societies may differ in terms of the number and permanence of groups, but people across the world quite naturally form groups.

Respect for people's ties to one another permeates collectivist cultures more than individualist cultures. It takes little to form social groups, as has been shown experimentally (e.g. the classic Robbers Cave study, Sherif et al., 1988). Simply assigning people to artificial groups (A and B or red and blue, minimal intergroup situation) produces group attachment and favourable in-group treatment. Closeness and frequent contact promote in-group attachment. People are as reluctant to break social bonds as they are keen to form them.

Belongingness shapes cognition. Basic patterns of thought reflect a fundamental concern with social relationships. Relationships are natural categories—people spontaneously classify incoming relationships in terms of social relationships (Sedikides, Olsen, & Reis, 1993). Out-group information is stored on the basis of attribute categories (traits, preferences, duties), whereas in-group information is processed on the basis of person categories. Social bonds create a pattern in cognitive processing that gives priority to organizing information on the basis of the person with whom one has a connection. Close relationship partners have cognitive effects similar to those of the self. Information about relationship partners is singled out for special processing. Thus more complex information processing is used when processing information about in-group members than for out-group members. Individuals process information more analytically when they have to justify their views to others, when the "self is at stake." The need to belong leads to a cognitive merging of self with particular other people: Selective memory operates for in-group members. People expect more favourable and fewer objectionable actions by their in-group than by their out-group and people tend to forget the bad things (relative to good things) for in-group members. People make group-serving or "socio-centric" attributions for the performance of the groups to which they belong. People tend to process information about out-group members in extreme, black-white, simplistic, polarized ways, whereas information about their own group is processed in a more complex fashion. Thus, the mere existence of a social bond leads to more complex (and sometimes more biased) information processing (Linville & Jones, 1980). Furthermore, people seem most likely to be prejudiced against members of groups to which they have little or no opportunity to belong. Thus, the most common and widespread bases for prejudice are race, gender and national origin. People bolster their own in-group at the expense of out-groups from which they are excluded.

Absence of close social bonds is linked to unhappiness. Social isolation is practically incompatible with high levels of happiness. Lonely people spend less time with friends and family—those who are the most likely to fulfil their needs to belong. People seek a limited number of relationships, consistent with the view that the need to belong is subject to satiation and diminishing returns. The first few close social bonds seem to be the most important, beyond which additional ones furnish ever lesser benefits. Belongingness is linked to well-being. Many of the emotional problems for which people seek professional help result from people's failure to meet their belongingness needs (Fiske, 2010).

Cognitive Motive—Understanding and Control

The nature of the self includes a strong desire for control and choice (Baumeister, 1999). On the other hand, a lack of control is experienced as a source of stress. As Campbell (1981) found, people who believe that they have a high degree of control over their lives are happier. The motivational experience of exercising control and being able to influence events was already mentioned in relation to the autonomy system above. As noted in Table 4.1, understanding refers to the need for shared meaning and prediction and control is defined as need for perceived contingency between behaviour and outcomes. A shared understanding is usually developed from membership in stable groups. These shared meaning systems guide behaviour automatically. As Triandis (1989) noted: "When a person is socialized in a given culture, the person can use custom as a substitute for thought, and save time" (p. 512). If a problem occurs, socially acceptable ways of asking for and getting help will be established within this group, assisting in the process of regaining a sense of control. Within a culture contact situation it is precisely this contingency which may be missing, inducing feelings of discomfort or stress. Knowing how to ask for help and getting it constitutes social control and effectiveness.

Fiske (2010) pointed out that people and cultures vary in how much they are motivated to understand others. Individuals vary in their need for unambiguous answers and cognitive closure. For persons high in need for unambiguous answers and cognitive closure, the culture contact situation, challenging existing meanings, is more likely to be experienced as a loss of control, challenge to understanding and as a result stressful. As the late German novelist Christa Wolf wrote: "Freude aus Verunsicherung ziehen … Wer hat uns das je beigebracht?[10]" (quoted in Keupp & Höfer (1997), p. 21).

Affective Motives—Self-Enhancement and Trust

Trusting people deserve trust. A trusting orientation facilitates people's interactions with others (Fiske, 2010). People who always expect the worst from people (paranoid) are socially ineffective. Trust and cooperation reinforce each other. As noted above, Bischof-Köhler (1985) referred to the satisfaction of self-worth as a fundamental human motivation. Self-enhancement refers to the need to feel unique and comprises self-esteem, self-improvement and self-sympathy (Fiske, 2010). The term *self* is introduced and only some key aspects will be explicated in this section. Identity and the structure of self will be addressed in the subsequent section in more detail.

Three major human experiences form the basis of self-hood: (1) Reflexive consciousness—people are self-aware and the conscious human mind can turn its inquiring attention back towards its own source and seek the self (self-verification). (2) Interpersonal being—the question is how the self is a member of groups and relationships and (3) Executive function (agentic self), which enables the self to make choices, initiate actions and to exert control (Baumeister, 1999). As Baumeister asserted further, self-awareness and self-knowledge remain incomplete and depend on inference. He stated three reasons for the quest for self-knowledge. Firstly, the appraisal motive which refers to the fact that accurate information is diagnostic for the self's traits. Secondly, the quest for consistency—people seek information to confirm what they believe (self-verification) and finally the self-enhancement. Self-enhancement is the main social motivation for the individual self (Brewer & Gardner, 1996).

---

[10] Experiencing insecurity as joy, who has ever taught this to us?

The interpretation of the self-enhancement motive depends on the cultural content. Triandis (2001) introduced the distinction between individualistic and collectivistic cultures and Markus and Kitayama (1991) distinguished between independent and interdependent cultures. The key difference here is that within individualistic cultures, which are usually associated with the Western life-style, individuals want to distinguish themselves. Within Eastern cultures, blending in with the group is more important. The relationship between culture and the self will be discussed later in this chapter.

Aspects of Identity

Theories of identity and the self are key concepts of psychology and some aspects of identity construal have already been mentioned in the course of the chapter. For an overview of key approaches and concepts of self and identity I would like to refer to Epstein (1973), Greve (2000) and Filipp and Mayer (2005), as a detailed review goes beyond the scope of this book. At this stage I would like to note that the development of self-related knowledge systems (identity) is a *life-long process*. The sources for and content of self-related knowledge change in the course of development. Self-related information is incorporated in a way that maximizes *coherence, consistency* across situations and *continuity* over time, the goal being an increase in self-worth at the affective level and the experience of consistency at the cognitive level. As noted in the previous section, self-enhancement is a core human motivation and has also behavioural consequences. People differ regarding the level and stability of the self-assessments (self-esteem), as well as the level of complexity and organization of the self. People also differ regarding domains included in the self-concept as well as the valence accorded to aspects within the self.

In the following section I will highlight some frameworks which address specific aspects of identity formation which are pertinent in a multicultural context. First the question of national identity formation will be addressed, including the persistence of a primordial understanding. This persistence will be explained using the cognitive-experiential framework. The relationship between culture and the self, including the interplay between the individual, interpersonal and group self will be the focus of the final section.

As Valsiner (2007) noted "The self is a trouble-maker" (p. 1). Epstein (1973) asked if there is a need for a self-concept in psychology, as "one can neither see a self-concept nor touch it, an no one has succeeded as yet in adequately describing it as a hypothetical construct" (p. 404). Baumeister (1999) also observed that even though most people use *I* and *self* many times each day, articulating that understanding is not easy and he observed: "This conceptual elusiveness is one reason that the study of self has proven fiendishly difficult" (p. 1). Using immunology as an analogy, Valsiner (2007) defined the self as a general term to describe the myriad of personal-cultural processes that are created through semiotic mediation. As such, the concept of self becomes a frame for viewing unity in the processes of creating personal experiences. The self is not open to direct measurement, as self is a process not an entity—Valsiner speaks of *selfing*. Direct queries about "your self" are culturalized phenomena. As he explained, "the 'detection' of identity is in the mind of the beholder— it is a co-constructive interpretative act" (Valsiner, 1997, p. 2).

Identity Structure Analysis (ISA)

The *construal* aspect of identity formation is also emphasized in Identity Structure Analysis (ISA), developed by Weinreich and Saunderson (2003). At the core of ISA lies the person's appraisal of the social world. Weinreich stressed the inter-generational transmission aspect through kith and kin and the affective component in the process. The ISA framework has been applied specifically to study ethnic and national identity (Weinreich, Bacova & Rougier, 2003). According to Weinreich (2003) the terms "ethnic" or "national" can be used interchangeably, if the terms refer to the fact that people are born into and experience their childhood within a well-defined peoplehood with a shared socio-cultural history, and the identity is then derived of that peoplehood. He thus derived the following definition for ethnic/national identity: "One's ethnic/national identity is defined as that part of the totality of one's self-construal made up of those dimensions that express the continuity between one's construal of past ancestry and one's future aspirations in relation to ethnicity" (Weinreich, 2003, p. 28). Within the study of ethnic/national identity two stances have been delineated: *primordialism* and the *socially constructed* stance.

Primordialism emphasizes ethnic persistence: Shared characteristics have an ancient root, and nations are national phenomena over different historical eras. As is the case with Luxembourg, most nations experienced border changes and migration over the last centuries and intermarried with other national groups. Thus, shared ancestry is more often a national myth rather than a genetic reality. This fluidity is taken into account under the socially constructed or situational approach: On reflection and questioning of what was considered to be the natural order of things, some people will develop a situationalist perspective. This may result from personal biographical experience, changing historical contexts or educational curricula which analyse social change or promote openness to alternative perspectives.

Despite all the historical evidence, there is still a human tendency, as alluded to in the introduction to this chapter, to explain nationality in primordial terms. Primordial sentiments are often expressed with great intensity and affect. Weinreich offers a socio-developmental explanation: The child's early identifications with kith and kin which may be emotionally strong and unquestioned. Primordialism is the basic and initial lay perspective on nationality. It is an emotive "gut feeling" sense of affinity. In evolutionary terms, it reinforces the orientations towards those from whom care can be expected. In times of turmoil, people may retreat to a primordialist perspective in an attempt to retain a sense of core stability to their identity. Those who hold a socially constructed view on nationality may not be entirely free of primordialist sentiments and gravitate towards this end of the spectrum in times of crisis. Primordialists may also, for reasons of political correctness, first-hand biographical experience or social desirability incorporate certain socially constructive notions, for example express tolerance for "dual nationality" or certain immigrants. However, this will not represent a core dimension of identity for them. Most people will best be described as being of mixed primordialist versus socially constructed orientation. Both convictions form endpoints on a spectrum.

Cognitive-Experiential Theory

The affective component, the fervour with which some people hold on to their national identity, may be explained by a theory that combines personality and the self, namely Epstein's (1979, 1994, 2003) Cognitive-Experiential Self-Theory of Personality (CEST). Epstein assumes that people process information by two independent, interactive conceptual systems, a pre-conscious "experiential" system and a conscious "rational" system. The experiential system is an adaptive, associative learning system and is emotionally driven. The rational system is a logical, inferential system that operates with the aid of language. CEST assumes that everybody automatically constructs an implicit theory of reality which consists of a hierarchical organization of schemas. Towards the apex of the conceptual structure are highly general, abstract schemas which are normally highly stable and not easily invalidated (higher order postulates). At the opposite end of the hierarchy are narrow, situation-specific schemas which are readily susceptible to change. Their changes have little effect on the stability of the personality structure at the core. The hierarchic structure of the implicit theory allows it to be stable at the centre and flexible at the periphery. Schemas derived from childhood experiences are emphasized in CEST because later experiences are assimilated by earlier schemas. With increasing maturity from childhood to adulthood, the balance of influence between the two processing systems shifts in the direction of increased rational dominance.

One explanation for the persistence of primordialism could thus be the developmental primacy—it is the first perspective of in-group belonging passed on to the child and likely to be processed by the experiential system. As noted, only later in the course of development the conceptualization of the in-group may be widened. However, processing is then through the rational system. Information is then cognitively or *rationally* processed—historical complexities are acknowledged. However, the primordial attachment was emotionally experienced. This differential processing of information may also explain why there are so few instances of emotional attachment to such supra-national institutions such as "Europe" (Grundy & Jamieson, 2003; Wallace, Condor, & Boehnke, 2005). The insistence on the primordial understanding of nationality could also be explained by the hierarchical structure. If primordial understanding was a core dimension of personality, information would also be filtered in a way that confirms this understanding.

The influence of cognitive structures on the selection and organization of self-relevant information is also noted by Markus (1977). She stated that people do not process information at random but develop what she has termed *self-schemata*. These self-schemata are derived from experience and "Once established, these schemata function as selective mechanisms which determine whether information is attended to, how it is structured and how much importance is attached to it" (Markus, 1977, p. 64). She explained that self-schemata are derived from *specific* experiences as well as *general* representations derived from repeated categorizations and the subsequent evaluation by the individual and others reacting to the individual. Information about the self, organized in self-schemata, is more easily accessed by the individual and is more salient to the individual. Markus also noted that the influence of cognitive schemata is most noticeable when processing information about ourselves.

Aspects of Self and Cultural Variation

The influence of the cultural context on the sampling of experiences that constitutes the self are explained by Triandis (1989).[11] He provided a succinct definition of the self: "The self consists of all statements made by a person, overtly or covertly, that contain the words 'I', 'me', 'mine' and 'myself'"(p. 506). As he explicated further, aspects of social motivation in relation to the self can be derived from this definition: Attitudes (*I* like X), beliefs (*I* think that X results in Y), intentions (*I* plan to do X), norms (in *my* group people should act this way), roles (in *my* family, fathers act this way) and values (*I* think equality is important). Like Baumeister (1999), Triandis also stressed that the self is an active agent, promoting differential sampling, processing and evaluation of information from the environment. Empirical evidence suggests that self-definition will also lead to behaviour that is consistent with that understanding of the self. If people consider themselves as "charitable" they will actually give more to charity under experimental conditions and so on. Furthermore, the more an aspect of the self is accessible to memory, the more likely it is to determine behaviour.

Baumeister (1986) introduced the distinction between three aspects of the self, namely private self (cognitions that involve traits, states and behaviour, e.g. *I* am introverted, *I* will buy X), the public self (cognitions concerning the generalized other's view of self, e.g. *People* think I am

---

[11] The following is largely based on Triandis (1989) and page numbers refer to his article.

introverted, *people* think I might buy X) and the collective self (view that is found in some collective such as family, co-workers, tribe etc., e.g. *My family* thinks I am introverted, *my coworkers* believe I travel too much). These different selves are sampled with different probabilities in different social environments and cultures. Triandis classifies cultural variations according to three dimensions namely individualism–collectivism, tightness–looseness and cultural complexity.

Cultural Complexity

This concept can be illustrated by comparing the bands of hunters and gatherers introduced above with life in a major metropolitan city. As archaeological evidence suggests, the bands of hunters usually comprised about 30 individuals. The number of relationships to be maintained with such a small group of people is therefore small. In contrast, the number of potential relationships in urban areas is almost infinite. Triandis therefore suggested the *number of potential relationships* as one measure of cultural complexity. Additional measures of complexity can be obtained by examining various domains of culture, including language, technology, economic systems (e.g. number of occupations), political systems, educational systems, religious and aesthetic patterns (e.g. number of different functions) and social structures. Each of these domains also contains even more distinct elements. As Triandis (p. 509) observed, one of the consequences of the increased complexity is that individuals have more and more in-groups towards whom they may or may not feel loyal. As the number of in-groups increases, the loyalty towards any one group decreases. Priority can be given to own goals, rather than the goals of the in-group. Furthermore, in increasingly affluent societies, financial wealth can also be turned into social and emotional independence, with the individual giving priority to personal rather than in-group goals. In summary, as societies become more complex, they can also become more individualistic.

Individualism-Collectivism

Individualists give priority to personal goals over the goals of collectives. In contrast, collectivists make either no distinction between personal and collective goals or subjugate personal to collective goals. Triandis specified that the terms "individualistic" and "collectivistic" should be used to characterize cultures and societies and the terms *idiocentric* and *allocentric* should be used to characterize individuals (p. 509). Collectivists tend to emphasize the in-group and feel involved with lives of the in-group members. Even within collectivist societies, the definition of the in-group keeps shifting with the situation: Important determinants of in-group–out-group boundaries include common fate, common outside threat and proximity. Within collectivist societies, social behaviour is a function of in-group norms more so than in individualist societies. Triandis introduced the concept of communal versus exchange relations, which are outlined in Table 4.2 below, as collectivist cultures are characterized by more communal relations, whereas more exchange relationships are found in individualist societies.

In the course of evolution, a shift has been observed to more exchange relations and towards individualism in general. As Triandis noted affluence and complexity are the major antecedents of individualism (p. 510). The more complex the culture, the greater the choice of in-groups an individual may join. Affluence means that the individual can be independent of in-groups. Mobility, referring both to social and physical mobility, is also an important factor, as individuals have the choice to join in-groups which they deem more compatible with their own goals. The size of the in-groups also tends to be different in the two different types of societies. In individualist societies, an in-group can be quite large and comprise, for example, all individuals who share the same attitude on a particular issue. In collectivist societies in-groups tend to be smaller, mainly involving family. Child-rearing practices will also vary,

Table 4.2 Communal versus exchange relations

Communal relations	Exchange relations
Lack of clarity about what is exchanged where and when	Clarity about what is exchanged where and when
Concern for other person's needs	Concern for equity
Maintaining equality of affect	Emotional detachment
Inequality of benefits exchanged	Equity as basis of benefits exchanged
Benefits not comparable	Benefits comparable

Source: Triandis (1989, p. 509)

with collectivist societies emphasizing conformity-related values and behaviour (obedience, reliability) and individualistic societies stressing autonomy, self-reliance and independence.

In terms of distribution of collectivism-individualism, Latin America, Asian and African cultures are mostly classified as collectivistic and North America and Northern and Western European cultures as individualistic. However, as Triandis (p. 510) noted, other variables are also relevant. For example, urban samples tend to be more individualistic and traditional-rural samples tend to be more collectivistic even within the same culture. Exposure to other cultures (through travel, cultural heterogeneity) also increases individualism, inasmuch as the individuals become aware of different norms and may choose their standards of behaviour.

Tight versus Loose Cultures

Within homogeneous societies, norms and values of in-groups are similar. Within heterogeneous societies, groups with dissimilar norms exist. If an in-group member deviates from in-group norms, the in-group members are faced with the decision to exclude this member or not. The decision may be emotionally draining for both sides and cultures may develop tolerance for deviation of group norms. As Triandis (p. 511) explained, homogeneous cultures are often rigid in requiring in-group members to strictly adhere to in-group norms. These societies are then considered *tight*. Tight cultures have clear norms that are reliably imposed. Little deviation from normative behaviour is tolerated. *Loose* cultures, in contrast, have either unclear norms about most social situations or tolerate deviance from the norms. Tightness and collectivism are related, but the concepts can be kept separate. It is possible for a collectivist society to tolerate deviations from the norm before applying sanctions. Cultural complexity and tightness are not related. As illustrated in Table 4.3, types of cultures can be identified for all four quadrants:

Collectivism and tightness have different antecedents. Collectivism is defined by a common fate and limited resources that must be divided to

Table 4.3 Tight versus loose cultures

	Complex	Simple
Tight	Totalitarian Industrial State	Agricultural simple
Loose	Industrial Democracy	Hunter Gatherers

Source: Boldt (1978)

survive. Tight cultures in contrast are characterized by cultural homogeneity derived through isolation from external cultural influences.

Culture and Self

Triandis noted: "Culture is to society, what memory is to a person" (p. 511). What has proven to be effective in the past is reinforced. He noted that the three dimensions of culture outlined above have emerged because of different ecologies, in terms of what has proven useful for survival. Within agricultural societies, for example, co-operation is necessary and collectivist forms of living emerge. If societies become more complex over time and once complexity reaches high levels, moves towards simplification emerge as counter-reaction. Excessive individualism may create a reaction towards collectivism and vice versa. Triandis asserted that the three dimensions of culture variation are systematically linked to different kinds of self (p. 512). In individualistic cultures, for example, child-rearing practices emphasize self-reliance, and independence. Therefore it is likely that more elements of the private self will be sampled. Conversely, in collective societies, child-rearing emphasizes the importance of the collective and the collective self will be sampled more often. Factors that increase ethnocentrism such as external threat, competition with out-groups or a common fate increase the probability that the collective self will be sampled. The size of the in-group also has a bearing on the sampling of the collective self: The larger the size of the in-group, the lower the probability that it will be sampled in the collective self. The more areas of one's life are affected by an in-group, the more likely the individual will sample the collective self. The looser the culture, the more the individual can choose what self to sample. Triandis also reported on cultural variations regarding the relationship between the selves. In the USA, for example, it is important to keep the public and private self consistent as it is considered important not be seen as a hypocrite. In contrast, in Japan "proper" action matters. Consensus seeking is important, not personal opinions. In tight cultures, people avoid disclosing much of the self. "The more complex the society, the more confused is likely to be the individual's identity" (p. 514). The basis and content of identity definitions differ in individualistic and collectivistic cultures and a summary is provided in Table 4.4. Who is placed in an in-group is culture-specific. As individualistic cultures tend to be more complex, individuals can potentially be members of more in-groups.

In summary, aspects of the self (private, public, collective) are differentially sampled in different cultures, depending on cultural complexity, level of individualism and looseness of cultures. The more complex, individualistic and loose a culture, the more likely that the private self is sampled. When the collective self is sampled, people are more likely to be influenced by norms, role definitions and values of a collective. When the culture is collectivist and tight, the public self is most likely to be sampled. The cultural context thus plays an important role in determining the probabilities with which the private, public and collective self are sampled.

Table 4.4 Definition of identity in individualistic and collectivistic cultures

Individualistic culture	Collectivistic culture
Definition of Identity on the basis of:	
· Possession (what I own)	· Relationships (mother of...)
· Experiences I have had	· Member of family
· My accomplishments	· Resident of...
Qualities that are important in forming an identity:	
· Being logical	· Personal style
· Rational	· Ways of moving
· Balanced	· Unique spontaneous self
· Fair	· Sincere self-expression
	· Unpredictability
	· Emotional expression

Source: Triandis (1989)

Relationship between Personal, Dyadic and Collective Self

Rather than focusing on the content of the self-definition, Brewer and Gardner (1996) focus on the *process* and wondered to what extend individuals define themselves in relationships with others and to social groups. They argued that individual, relational and collective levels of self-definition represent distinct forms of self-representation with different origins, sources of self-worth and social motivations. Sedikides and Brewer (2001) asserted that persons seek to achieve self-definition and self-interpretation in terms of unique traits, dyadic relationships and group membership. The individual self is achieved by *differentiating* from others, which is derived on the basis of interpersonal comparison processes. It contains those aspects of the self-concept that differentiate the person from other persons as unique constellation of traits and characteristics that distinguish the individual within his/her social context. The underlying core motive is to protect or enhance the person psychologically. In contrast, the relational self is achieved by *assimilating* with significant others. It contains those aspects of the self-concept that are shared with relationship partners and define the person's role or position within significant relationships. The relational self is based on personalized bonds of attachment (parent-child, friends and romance— role-specific relationships such as teacher-student) and relies on the process of reflected appraisal. The underlying core motive is the protection or enhancement of the significant other and the maintenance of the relationship itself. Finally, the collective self is achieved by inclusion in large social groups and contrasting the group to which one belongs (in-group) with relevant out-group. It contains those aspects of the self-concept that differentiate in-group members from members of the relevant out-group. It is based on impersonal bonds to others derived from common (and often *symbolic*) identification with a group. These bonds do not require close personal relationships amongst group members. The collective self relies on intergroup comparison processes and the core motive is the protection or enhancement of the in-group. These relationships are summarized in Table 4.5.

Table 4.5 Individual, relational and collective self

Level of analysis	Self-concept	Basis of self-evaluation	Frame of reference	Social motive: protect/enhance:
Individual	Personal	Traits	Interpersonal comparison, differentiation	The person *Uniqueness*
Interpersonal	Relational, dyadic	Roles, assimilation with significant others	Reflection	Significant others *Sameness*
Group	Collective	Group prototype	Intergroup comparison	The *in-group*

Source: Brewer & Gardner (1996)

Sedikides and Brewer (2001) asked whether these three self-representations of self are "partners, opponents or strangers" (p. 1). Agreement exists amongst authors concerning the social nature of the selves and that the three self-representations *coexist* within the same individual. Disagreements exist regarding the primacy of the self-representations, with some arguing that the individual self is primary on emotional and motivational grounds, whereas others purport the primacy of the interpersonal self—based on the fundamental need to belong. Others again argue that relational and collective self become primary and subsume the individual self. However, as Sedikides and Brewer (2001) conclude, the verdict is still out on this question and this framework allows explaining why and how individuals simultaneously attempt uniqueness and sameness.

Salience of National Identity as a Function of Context

This empirical study[12] addressed the question of sampling a collective identity as a function of context. Specifically, we examined whether the salience of national identity is heightened in a multicultural context. As early as

---

[12] A full account of this study was published in: Murdock, E., Hirt, F. S. and Ferring, D. (2014). Salience of nationality in students' spontaneous self-concept: A comparative study of a nationally homogeneous and a heterogeneous school context. *Journal of Research in International Education*, 13 (2), 1–6. 1475240914539797.

1978, McGuire, W.J., McGuire, C. V., Child and Fujioka conducted a research project amongst 560 fourth-grade students in America, assessing the salience of ethnic identity in children's spontaneous self-concept as a function of the ethnic mix at the school. Based on the distinctiveness postulate, these researchers hypothesized that inter-mixing would heighten rather than erase consciousness of ethnicity. Their findings supported this hypothesis and the authors noted the social policy implications of the distinctiveness postulate, "some going in counterintuitive directions" (McGuire et al., 1978, p. 512). Policy-makers may formulate well-intentioned policies assuming that integration will be achieved simply by bringing people together. Yet bringing children of different ethnic backgrounds together heightens rather than lessens the awareness of the differences, especially for minority groups. Given the fact that cultural diversity and multicultural societies have become an established fact of life in many countries across the world (Barrett, Flood, & Eade, 2011) and the Luxembourg context in particular, we reasoned that the implications of the distinctiveness paradigm are noteworthy and we set out to replicate McGuire et al.'s (1978) study in a European context with some modifications, which I will briefly explain.

We compared adolescent school children at two secondary schools which differed regarding their national mix of its pupils, one being nationally homogeneous and the other being heterogeneous. The key question was whether this difference in school context would influence the salience of nationality in students' spontaneous self-concept. In replication of the McGuire study, the students were asked the non-directive questions aimed at eliciting the students' spontaneous affirmative and negated self-concept. We hypothesized that students at the nationally diverse school would mention nationality more frequently than students in the fairly mononational school. In other words, we predicted that nationality would be more salient in the heterogeneous school students' spontaneous self-concept.

Before presenting the study, the distinctiveness postulate will be explained given its central importance to the research question followed by the modifications to McGuire et al.'s (1978) original study. Next, the school contexts will be described, as the different composition of the student body in terms of nationalities is conceptualized as the main independent variable within the study. This will be followed by a description of the study and a comprehensive overview of the results. Finally, conclusions will be drawn and implications discussed.

The Distinctiveness Postulate

As McGuire et al. (1978) explain, the distinctiveness postulate was formulated to deal with the more general question of how people manage
the problem that their senses can take in more information than they can
meaningfully deal with in perception and memory. As was first suggested
by Broadbent (1958), people essentially act like information-processing
machines, applying selective filters. The distinctiveness postulate proposes
that people selectively attend to and encode aspects that are most distinctive, which is an efficient information-processing strategy. For example,
a red triangle is noticed in a field of red circles (triangularity being the
distinctive feature) and a green triangle would be noticed in a field of red
triangles. These are very simple examples to illustrate the basic principle.
Yet the distinctiveness postulate can also be applied to self-perception:
We notice in ourselves those aspects that are peculiar in our customary
social environment. Distinctiveness affects the self-concept directly, as
one notices one's distinctive features and indirectly by others responding
to our peculiarities. Transferred to the school setting, the distinctiveness
postulate implies, firstly, that nationality is more salient in people's self-
concepts in a nationally mixed environment than in a monocultural one.
Secondly, nationality is more salient in the in the self-concept of minority
group members than in the majority group.

The distinctiveness postulate therefore has important social policy
implications. It implies that as schools integrate children of different
backgrounds, children become more conscious of their nationality/eth-
nicity and more likely to define themselves in terms of it. This occurs
as a basic perceptual phenomenon, regardless of the emotional climate
as McGuire et al. (1978, p. 512) point out. The distinctiveness postulate implies that we notice in our self-concept what makes us different
from others in our social environment. The self-concept acts as a filter
and organizing principle for self-relevant experiences (Markus, 1977).
Domains important to our self-concept are expected to be more salient
and thus easily accessible in spontaneous retrieval. We thus derived the
following predictions for our study: Firstly, nationality should be mentioned more frequently in the nationally mixed school context than in the
more homogeneous school context (Hypothesis 1). Secondly, nationality

should be mentioned more frequently by students belonging to minority groups (Hypothesis 2).

Modifications of the Original Study

National Identity

Given the European setting, the focus was on national rather than ethnic identity construal. Arts and Halman (2006) explained that national identity refers to "perceived distinctiveness, a possibility to distinguish oneself or a group from others" (p. 73). Condor (2011) defined national identity as the ways in which members of a national group reflexively understand themselves. It is evident that nation and nationality have very different meanings from one country to another. In France, for example, nation has always had a very strong political connotation. In Central and Eastern Europe, as explained by Arts and Halman (2006), "the idea of nation came to have a particularly strong ethnic connotation" (p. 73). As noted above, Weinreich (2003) suggested that the terms "national" and "ethnic" can be used interchangeably, if the context of growing up is taking into consideration. The difficulties of adequately capturing an individual's national or ethnic identity in quantitative surveys were specified by Billiet (2002). As he pointed out, it is a question of degree of identification and (simultaneous) multiple group membership. This is precisely why we opted for a non-directive qualitative measure and did not present our student samples with pre-defined categories (see explanation of the measure, below).

Focus on Adolescents

McGuire et al. conducted their study at elementary and high schools in Chicago, USA. We opted to focus only on adolescents for theoretical and practical reasons. Adolescence is seen as a particularly important period in the life-long process of the development of the self. As Pinquart and Silbereisen (2000) indicated, the period of adolescence is special as the young people change and adapt their self-definition through cognitive abilities acquired for self-reflection, which is why we focused on adolescents.

Looking at this age group also meant that the students in our sample were able to complete questionnaires and could indicate their country of birth and state their nationality or nationalities themselves. In the original study, the ethnic background of the pupils was assessed by the researchers.

Measurement of the Spontaneous Self-Concept

In the style of the non-directive Twenty Statement Test (TST; Kuhn & McPartland, 1954), we asked the students "Who am I?" and "Who am I not?" We piloted the statements with target students and learnt that the instruction to write answers to the simple question "Who am I?" was too abstract. We therefore supplemented these questions by a further instruction: "Just imagine, that you have to describe yourself to someone. Could you please list 5 things which come to your mind? (Please, don't write your name!)." This instruction was followed by a list of five bullet points with empty lines. The same was repeated for the negated self-concept on a different sheet, but the instruction not to provide the name was replaced by the reminder to please be serious.

As the test title implies, the original version of the TST uses 20 statements but only focusing on affirmative self (I am). We wanted to retain the split into affirmative and negated spontaneous self-concept, as we believe, in line with identity-construal theories (Weinreich, 2003), that the negated self-concept is highly informative, given the potential positivity bias of the affirmative self-concept. We decided to ask the students for five instances of the positive and five of the negated self-concept resulting in ten statements per student. Several reasons led us to use this shortened list: Firstly, we anticipated attention problems in school children. Secondly, we wanted to reduce the stressors of writing and spelling. Thirdly, we expected a more consistent pattern of actually obtaining five answers per self-concept per student, rather than a high variability when 20 answers have to be elicited. Most crucially, we assumed that the most salient aspects would be more easily accessible and be mentioned in either of the top five statements.

Changes in the number of statements have been made before (Halkoaho, 2012 or Niebergall, 2010) and this shortening has proven to be useful, depending on the aim of the study. Halkoaho reduced the number of statements to three. Cousins (1989) used all 20 statements in his comparative study of self-perception in Japan and the USA and asked the students to circle their top five statements. The analysis of the TST statements showed that the top five responses were similar to the full form responses. Even though we did develop a coding system for our study and analysed all answers, we were primarily interested in the question whether nationality markers would be mentioned or not. Contrary to other studies using TST (e.g. Bond & Cheung, 1983), there was no explicit time-limit given to the students.

Description of the Schools

We identified two secondary schools which differed regarding their national mix of students. The homogeneous national school context was provided by a German, private, state-approved secondary school near Munich, Germany. Around 700 mainly Catholic students attend this secondary school. Students can choose between a humanistic orientation and an emphasis on modern languages. All students start with Latin as first foreign language, followed by English. Later, ancient Greek or French and optionally Italian or Chinese can be chosen. It is the school's philosophy to motivate students to actively engage in sports, music and other cultural activities.

The heterogeneous national school context was provided by the European School of Luxembourg. European schools are divided into different language sections, representing the member states of the European Union. Basic instruction is given in the official languages of the EU. The study of a first foreign language (English, French or German), known as L2, is compulsory from the first primary class onwards. The aim of the European School system is stated as follows:

> Educated side by side, untroubled from infancy by divisive prejudices, acquainted with all that is great and good in the different cultures, it will be borne in upon them as they mature that they belong together. Without ceasing to look to their own lands with love and pride, they will become in

mind Europeans, schooled and ready to complete and consolidate the work of their fathers before them, to bring into being a united and thriving Europe. (Schola Europaea, n.d.)

European schools are known for high standards in languages. Language classes are composed of mixed nationalities and are taught by native speakers. By definition, students from different, albeit mainly European, countries attend the school and inter-mixing is reinforced by bringing together different nationalities in different subjects. At the time of the study, 2265 students attended the secondary school.

Method

Measure

The dependent variable, salience of nationality in youths' spontaneous self-concept, was measured using the "Who am I?"/"Who am I not?" questions as outlined above. This qualitative measure was complemented by a quantitative part in the form of a short demographic questionnaire.

Procedure

We presented our project outline to the respective headmasters of each school and obtained permission to conduct our study. As the participants were minors, parent consent forms were distributed at each school well ahead of the study. No parent refused participation of their child. The test material (in German) was the same for both schools. For the European School, all materials were also available in French and English. For some language sections (Finnish and Danish), material was therefore provided only in their second language (L2) and students had the choice between the three languages. As we addressed secondary students in years 3 and 4, an excellent command of the second language could be expected. The students completed the survey at school in their classrooms, observed by their teacher. Completing the questionnaire in the classroom, surrounded by the classmates, was also assumed to reinforce the school context.

Samples

The German school sample consisted of n = 117 students and the European school sample of n = 106 students, but two students had to be excluded, as the questionnaires had not been completed properly. This makes for a total sample of N = 221 students. The students were between 12 and 16 years. The average age was 13.64 years (SD = 1.72). Gender was equally distributed in both groups (in total: 49 % female; 51 % male). Participants at the German school attended years 7 and 8 (7. and 8. Klasse), corresponding to secondary years 3 and 4 (S3 and S4) at the European school, where the following language sections (LS) participated: English (EN; n = 45), German (DE; n = 25), French (FR; n = 14), Finnish and Danish (FI; DK; n = 10 each). As anticipated, the nationality makeup of the student samples at the two schools was quite different:

Uniformly, all students at the German school defined their first nationality as German. Only four students (3 %) mentioned a second nationality (two times Italian, one Austrian and one *Bavarian*). Only one student was born in another country than Germany, namely England. Regarding mother tongue, all defined their first mother tongue as German. As second mother tongue, three named Italian, and one named English. It is also noteworthy that three specified the regional dialect Bavarian and one even the more specific *Lower* Bavarian as second language. A third nationality or mother tongue was not mentioned. Nearly all mothers (97.4 %) were born in Germany. The three exceptions were born in Ireland, Spain and Austria. The fathers were also mostly born in Germany (95.7 %) with five exceptions: two were born in Italy, one in Austria, one in Cameroon and one in Congo.

At the European school, 20 different first nationalities were mentioned, not counting the regional variations within the UK (British, including separate mentions of English, Welsh, Scottish and N-Irish). The first named nationalities are represented in Table 4.6.

In addition, 43 % of the 104 subjects also named a second and 11 % a third nationality. Corresponding to these countries, different first mother tongues were mentioned, whilst just over a third of the students named a second mother tongue and five students even a third. Regarding students'

Table 4.6 First named nationalities at the European school

First named nationality	% of mentions	First named nationality	% of mentions
British	17	Austrian	3
German	12	Hungarian	2
Irish	10	Maltese	2
Danish	10	Slovakian	2
Finnish	9	American	1
French	8	Bulgarian	1
Luxembourgish	7	Canadian	1
Belgian	6	Croatian	1
Lithuanian	5	Latvian	1
Italian	4	Polish	1

country of birth Luxembourg (n = 41) was most dominant. Parents' countries of birth were also much more diverse than in the German sample, as can be implied by the first named nationalities of the children.

Concluding, these comparative breakdowns of nationalities, country of birth of students and parents as well as languages spoken serve to illustrate that we managed to identify two schools which differed in the national composition of its student body.

Results

Distribution of Self-Concept-Related Statements

The student sample of N = 221 produced a total of 2311 responses to the questions of "Who am I/Who am I not." We coded all responses and developed a specific taxonomy. The lion's share of responses (22 %) which included attributes such as friendly, nice or helpful, were classed as "agreeable." These morally good attributes were the most frequently named category in students' spontaneous self-concept. This finding matches the Shell Youth Study which showed that mandatory social and moral rules are important to youths (Albert et al., 2010). The next most frequently mentioned categories were leisure activities and interests (14 %) followed by physical descriptions (11 %; e.g. height, weight, hair/eye colour, etc.). Apart from differences in points of emphasis, that is, stronger language focus at the

European school or more mentions of leisure activities (sports and music) at the German school, there were few significant differences between the two school contexts. Youth-specific topics dominated the responses.

Nationality markers were defined as any mentions of a specific nationality, native country or country of birth. Overall, nationality markers were not mentioned so frequently (0.87 % of the total responses). This result is, however, in line with McGuire et al.'s study. In their sample of N = 560 respondents, only 3 % of the children made any mention of ethnicity. By design, only half (n = 104) of our total sample (N = 221) was nationally mixed and following hypothesis 1, we expected mentions of nationality markers only coming from half or our total sample. Thus, proportionally, the absolute number of mentions is comparable. In the following we will test whether or not the school context influenced the rate of mentions.

Salience of Nationality in the Homogeneous versus Heterogeneous Context

We did indeed find that context matters: There were significantly more mentions of nationality at the European school compared to the German school. The Chi-square test (with Yates Continuity Correction) indicates a highly significant association between school context and the occurrence of nationality markers, $\chi^2(1, 221)$ = 13.35, p = 0.00, phi = 0.26. Thus present data support the hypothesis that a mixed national context increases students' awareness of nationality. Within the European school, 16.3 % of students mentioned nationality within their spontaneous self-concept, compared to 1.7 % at the German school. When analysing the data, we also noticed that 11 students, 10 of which attended the European school, mentioned in the negated self-concept "I am not racist." Even though this statement is not a nationality marker in the above defined sense, this statement suggests an awareness of nationalities. If these mentions are also considered, the percentage of mentions rises to 26 % and 2.6 % respectively. The Chi-square test is also highly significant with stronger effect size, $\chi^2(1, 221)$ = 23.37, p = 0.00, phi = 0.34, medium effect using Cohen's (1988) criteria. In line with McGuire et al.'s

(1978) findings, there was no gender effect within our student sample, $\chi^2(1, 221) = 0.42$, $p = 0.26$, phi $= 0.06$.

Salience of Nationality in the Majority versus Minority Group

Within the German school sample, all students mentioned German as their first nationality and all but one student were born in Germany. As differentiator between minority and majority we chose the "second named nationality" and defined those with more than one nationality as "minority." Overall, there were only two mentions of nationality and indeed one of these mentions was from a minority child in the above defined sense ("I am half German, half Cameroonian") which is commensurate with hypothesis 2. The other mention was by a (majority) German student ("I am not Italian"), but without further context information this statement is difficult to interpret. A within-group comparison between minority and majority is thus not applicable for the German school.

Whilst we did not observe sufficient minority members within the homogeneous school context, we had to determine a meaningful definition of minority versus majority in terms of nationality that reliably covered the huge variability observed within the heterogeneous context. By default, the school is composed of different language sections and we decided to look at each language section separately as a reference group. However, the language sections themselves are composed of different nationalities, such as French and French-speaking Belgians for the French section or the different nations of the UK, Ireland plus Malta in the English section. The language L1 is actually the lowest common denominator between the students and does not show the complex mix of nationalities at the individual student level. This point will be illustrated using the French section as an example. In Table 4.7 nationality attributes are listed in the form of country of birth (CoB) of the student, CoB parents, first nationality and first named mother tongue. Second or third nationality or mother tongues are not included as these do not apply to all students.

Highlighted in bold are the francophone "mononational" students ($n = 6$). Who should be defined as minority within this class? Those

Table 4.7 National background analysis: nationality marker grid French language section

	Nationality markers				
Student	CoB student	CoB mother	CoB father	1st nationality	1st mother tongue
1	DK	DK	PT	LUX	FR
2	FR	FR	FR	FR	FR
3	FR	FR	FR	FR	FR
4	BE	BE	IT	BE	FR
5	LUX	FR	UK	IR	EN
6	IT	IT	IT	IT	IT
7	BE	BE	BE	BE	FR
8	FR	FR	FR	FR	FR
9	LUX	UK	BE	BE	FR
10	LUX	BE	PT	BE	FR
11	FR	FR	GK	FR	FR
12	FR	FR	FR	FR	FR
13	LUX	LUX	LUX	LUX	FR
14	FR	FR	FR	FR	FR

whose first nationality is not French or Belgian? Those whose parents are of mixed nationality or even the highlighted francophone students who are in fact, numerically, in the minority?

To define "majority" within the language sections, we created a "homogeneity" index, which will be illustrated using the French class as an example: A total of 70 attributes defining the composition of the national background are possible (five nationality markers × 14 students = 70). We considered the French-speaking countries (France and Belgium) as default group and for this class a total of 47 FR or BE entries can be counted. We then calculated the proportion of main group entries to the total (47/70 × 100) which shows that 67 % of attributes belong to the two "default" countries (majority). The various language sections differ regarding nationality mix, with the Finnish language section at 90 % being most homogeneous, followed by the Danish section (85 %), French (67 %), English (60 %) and finally the German section at 56 %. Thus, the Scandinavian sections are more homogeneous than the other language sections. Homogeneity is overstated, especially for the English section, as the pool of "default" nationalities is already quite wide. For the Finnish section, "majority" will be easier to define than for the heterogeneous English sections.

Table 4.8 Number of nationality markers mentioned by language section

Language section:	Number of students belonging to:			Nationality marker by student belonging to:		
	Minority	Majority	Total	Minority	Majority	Total
French	8	6	14	3	2	5
German	21	4	25	2	1	3
Finnish	4	6	10	0	2	2
Danish	5	4	9	2	0	2
English	31	14	45	5	0	5
Total	69	34	103	13	4	17

We classified students' responses into "majority" and "minority" according to the nationality marker grids, prepared for each language section separately (see French e.g. Table 4.7) and noted the mentions of nationality markers. The findings are summarized in Table 4.8.

Table 4.8 illustrates two points: The cell size for some entries makes statistical analysis difficult and within the heterogeneous environment, minority children are in fact in the majority. Against this background, qualitative findings regarding mentions of nationality markers will be presented, starting with the now familiar French class:

Out of a class of 14, there were five mentions of nationality markers in total. Two "minority" children referred to their mixed parentage status ("I am Portuguese and Danish," "I am Belgian and English"). Two students addressed their relationship with Luxembourg (their host country), distancing themselves from Luxembourg ("I am not Luxembourgish"), asserting their nationality (one each from the majority/minority). As pointed out above, the mononational students are in the minority within this particular French class and one student actually comments: "Je suis d'une seule nationalité"—I am of one nationality (all nationality attributes were French). Following our definition this student belongs to the "majority"—but his status within this group is actually "minority" so this comment can also be explained using the distinctiveness postulate and is in line with hypothesis 2. Within the English section all five responses came from what we defined as "minority" students: Three times origins were mentioned (two times "I am Lithuanian" and "I am Slovakian") and one student stated mixed parentage "I am half Dutch and half Scottish." A further student commented on the relationship with Luxembourg and asserts his nationality "I am English, I live in Luxembourg, speak Luxembourgish, but I am English."

The German section was the most heterogeneous in this study. One student commented on his mixed nationality (half French, half German) and another student asserted his nationality "I am Luxembourgish." One Austrian girl mentioned in first place within the negated self-concept "Ich bin keine Deutsche. Manche meinen das, da ich so spreche, aber ich hasse das" (I am not German. Some think that I am because I speak German, but I hate that). This student belongs to the pre-defined majority group, but belongs to a minority within the majority. A fifth of the students in this class mentioned anti-racism statements. In the fairly homogeneous Danish section, two children of mixed nationality mentioned this (I am Danish and French). Both mentions of "not being racist" were made by majority Danish children. Finally, the Finnish section: Two (majority) students asserted "being from Finland" in their spontaneous self-concept.

As indicated above, the definition of majority versus minority is quite complex within the European school context. However, a closer look at the responses within the context of each language section shows that if nationality markers are mentioned, they are mentioned by minorities. Yet the definition of minority varies. Minority may constitute having a different nationality from the "language section default" as is the case with the Lithuanians/Slovaks in the English section or the "minority default" as exemplified by Austrians within the German section. Alternatively, minority status may refer to being of mixed nationalities or even being of *one* nationality. Minority status may also be defined in reference to the wider school context. The Finnish section, for example, is quite small compared to other language sections which may explain the number of mentions of the Finnish origins. Some students also raise the issue of living in Luxembourg, their current country of residence and assert their nationality. Concluding, our qualitative data tend support hypothesis 2.

Discussion

Context does matter: Commensurate with the distinctiveness postulate, salience of nationality was significantly higher in the heterogeneous school context than in the homogeneous school context. A qualitative and quantitative analysis of responses also points to the acceptance of hypothesis 2, salience of nationality being higher in minority members. It should however be mentioned that overall, mentions of nationality markers were relatively small. We would like to point out several specific observations.

The European School's credo "Without ceasing to look to their own lands with love and pride, they will become in mind Europeans" was quoted above. The results within our present study suggest that the first part of the school's credo is achieved—the students do not forget about where they are from; awareness of the nationality is in fact enhanced. Yet not a single child mentioned "European" as an attribute. This supra-national category did not feature in students' spontaneous self-concept. This finding may be explained by the fact that different domains are evoked when evaluating group membership regarding nationality and supra-national entities. Social identity theory differentiates three components, namely cognitive, affective and evaluative structures of identification. Within the European school credo, the home country is couched in the terms "love and pride," which evoke affective and evaluative connotations, and emotions are important in inferring postulates. On the other hand, one should become "in mind" European—a cognitive aspect. An attribute mainly anchored in the cognitive sphere may not be triggered in the spontaneous self-concept. The survey of orientations of young men and women to citizenship and European identity of several regions in the EU (Grundy & Jamieson, 2003; Jamieson, 2005) also showed that high exposure to Europe does not ensure high personal identification with Europe.

European school students did not only produce nationality markers, but also the vast majority of "I am not racist statements" in the negated self. This suggests that there is an awareness of other nationalities and *tolerance*. Five of the ten mentions came from students attending the German section. In his recent comparative study of personal and social identity construal across Europe, Schmidt-Denter (2011) found that Europeans on the whole are becoming more homogeneous regarding their description of their personal identity. However, there is diversity in the sphere of social identity as this construal process is more influenced by cultural and socio-historic factors. He found that Germans are, in general, highly self-critical and aware of the aftermaths of World War II.

It comes therefore as no surprise that half of the anti-racism mentions originated in the German section.

Across language sections, the issue of third-country nationality was broached. Usually, the children distanced themselves from their (current) host country, asserting their nationality. Those students usually expressed discomfort with their current situation, which probably explains the salience of this issue.

Another interesting finding in this context is the emphasis on regions, which was particularly showing in the Anglophone sample, but also in the German school sample. In the English section, most students were quite specific regarding their country of origin—England, Scotland, Wales and N.Ireland were mentioned—very few students said "British" and no student mentioned "UK." This matches Condor's (1996, 2000) finding that self-identification "UK" was never used. The particularity of "regionalism" was also found within the German school context, where one student mentioned Bavarian as second nationality and three named their mother tongue to be Bavarian, one even specifying *lower* Bavarian. "Bavarian" was not triggered in the spontaneous self-concept, but in the quantitative part these students volunteered this additional information. We can thus infer that this must have been important to them—that these students possibly wanted to differentiate themselves from the wider national context.

This aspect touches on one of the limitations of the study: We can only analyse *if* nationality was mentioned, but we can only *speculate* on why. Distinctiveness does play a key role; we could show that minority status increases salience. However, not all students of minority status did mention nationality and we don't know what prompted those who did mention nationality markers. Does being of mixed nationality, for example, provide a sense of pride or a unique feature that serves the core motive of self-enhancement (Fiske, 2010)? From the data, we cannot tell which reference group (e.g. class, school, family, country and nation) the students used for social comparison. Furthermore, we cannot tell how nationality is evaluated. These questions will be addressed in a further empirical study to be reported in the next chapter. In this study we specifically looked at how different nationalities are experienced and organized by students.

A further limitation of the study was the relatively small class sizes of some language sections, which did not allow statistical analysis across the language sections. In addition, not all language sections of the European school were represented in the study. Furthermore, the homogeneous sample was provided by a school based in Germany. As alluded to above, the German responses may be influenced by the Holocaust and may have caused less salience of nationality within this sample. It would be interesting to complement data from homogeneous contexts in different countries and different educational settings.

Conclusion

The purpose of this study was to investigate salience of nationality as a function of school context in students' spontaneous self-concept. We used a non-directive, qualitative measure, allowing students to answer spontaneously. Great care was taken not to prime students or to direct them in any way. The answers should thus be authentic, reflecting attributes that are important to the students and characterize them. We could show that a nationally heterogeneous context raises awareness of nationalities, especially for minority students, even though the definition of "minority" is quite complex in itself. The hypotheses were drawn from the distinctiveness postulate and our findings confirm McGuire et al.'s (1978) results.

We would like to point out several specific observations. As context does seem to matter regarding students' self-identification with nationality, it is important for school practice to consider the present results. Just bringing students of different nationalities together does not mean that nationalities are ignored and a supra-national category such as "European" or "international" is adopted. On the contrary, we could show empirically that awareness of nationalities is enhanced in a nationally heterogeneous context. The results from the Anglophone section also suggest that a sense of regional pride is reinforced. However, putting students together under a European "cloak" does not seem to enhance identification with Europe to the extent that "European" becomes salient in students' spontaneous self-concept. We could also show that the definition of majority/minority was quite fluid within the heterogeneous context. This could also be seen as an enhanced opportunity to practise perspective taking—alternating between the majority and minority perspective, depending on context. Increased exposure to different nationalities raises not only awareness of differences but also, as evidenced by the spontaneous mentions of anti-racism statements, awareness of respectful living with each other. At a time when international mobility and trade are becoming the norm (Karim, 2012), it is important to appreciate these complex dynamics when bringing people of different nationalities or backgrounds together. Within the multicultural context of Luxembourg, nationality is likely to be a defining feature, providing orientation for self and others, rather than diminishing in importance.

Concluding Remarks

This chapter started out with a digression into human phylogenies and highlighted that for the longest time in human evolution, human beings have lived in small bands of around 20 to 30 individuals with (personal) familiarity regulating altruistic behaviour. The number of relations to be formed within this setting is also small. Evolution is characterized by few revolutions, but each of these is typified by an increase in population density, a higher degree of specialization, an accumulation of wealth and an escalation of needs. The pace of change has accelerated exponentially, possibly leaving insufficient time for human beings to adjust to each phase.

Within larger groups, familiarity has to be *created*. Measures include, for example, a common language, customs and a unifying moral code. Groups within groups are formed and the number of relationships is potentially infinite within modern urban settings. This semi-familiarity can also be experienced as stressful. Baumeister (1999) noted that the modern Western world is characterized by an instability of social relations. Social and geographical mobility has made social relationships highly unstable and where the relationships are unstable, the self must constantly act to attract new partners. This can be experienced as stressful, as *belonging* is one of the core motives of human development. As was shown, human beings are characterized by a need for strong, stable relationships. The need to belong can also be satisfied by non-interpersonal relationships. Within complex societies the number of potential in-groups increases, which imposes the issue of choice for individuals, another challenge for identity formation, as a hierarchy of criteria have to be applied. As was pointed out by Baumeister (1987), the identity components of the self-definition process have become more complex. Affluence and complexity lead to increasingly individualistic societies, where own interests are placed increasingly above group interest. Affluence allows individuals to be independent of in-groups (Triandis, 1989). As was shown, the cultural context influences the basis for identity definition and its content. The empirical study showed that nationality may actually become a self-defining feature in a multi-cultural environment. Bringing people of different nationalities together might actually heighten rather than lessen awareness of nationalities. This study thus touched on the individual living within a multicultural society and this theme will be developed further in the next two chapters.

References

Albert, M., Hurrelmann, K., & Quenzel, G. (2010). *16. Shell Jugendstudie—Jugend 2010*. Retrieved from Die Shell Jugendstudie 2015 website: http://www.shell.de/home/content/deu/aboutshell/our_commitment/shell_youth_study/downloads/ (accessed 22 April 2013)

Anderson, B. (2006). *Imagined communities: Reflections on the origin and spread of nationalism*. London: Verso Books.

Arts, W., & Halman, L. (2006). National identity in Europe today: What the people feel and think. *International Journal of Sociology, 35*(4), 69–93. doi:10.2753/IJS0020-7659350404.

Barrett, M., Flood, C., & Eade, J. (Eds.) (2011). *Nationalism, ethnicity, citizenship: Multidisciplinary perspectives*. Newcastle: Cambridge Scholars Publishing.

Baumeister, R. F. (1986). *Public self and private self*. New York: Springer.

Baumeister, R. F. (1987). How the self became a problem: A psychological review of historical research. *Journal of Personality and Social Psychology, 52*(1), 163. doi:10.1037/0022-3514.52.1.163.

Baumeister, R. F. (Ed.) (1999). *The self in social psychology*. Philadelphia: Psychology Press.

Baumeister, R. F., & Leary, M. R. (1995). The need to belong: Desire for interpersonal attachments as a fundamental human motivation. *Psychological Bulletin, 117*(3), 497–529. doi:10.1037/0033-2909.117.3.497.

Billiet J. (2002). Questions about national, subnational and ethnic identity. European Social Survey: Core Questionnaire Development. Retrieved from: http://www.europeansocialsurvey.org/index.php?option=com_docman& task=doc_view&gid=129&Itemid=80 (accessed 22 April 2013).

Billig, M. (1995). *Banal nationalism*. Loughborough University: Sage.

Bischof, N. (1975). A systems approach toward the functional connections of attachment and fear. *Child Development, 46*(4), 801–817. doi:10.1111/j.1467-8624.1975.tb04024.x.

Bischof, N. (1980). On the phylogeny of human morality. In G. S. Stent (Ed.), *Morality as a biological phenomenon: The pre-suppositions of sociobiological research* (pp. 48–66). Berkeley: University of California Press.

Bischof-Köhler, D. (1985). Zur Phylogenese menschlicher Motivation. In L.-H. Eckensberger & E.- D. Lantermann (Eds.), *Emotion und Reflexivität* (pp. 3–47). München: Urban & Schwarzenberg.

Bischof-Köhler, D. (1991). Jenseits des Rubikon. Die Entstehung spezifisch menschlicher Erkenntnisformen und ihre Auswirkung auf das Sozialverhalten. *Mannheimer Forum*, 143–193. München: Piper.

Bischof-Köhler, D. (1994). Selbstobjektivierung und fremdbezogene Emotionen. Identifikationen des eigenen Spiegelbildes, Empathie und prosoziales Verhalten im 2. Lebensjahr. *Zeitschrift für Psychologie, 202*, 349–377.

Bischof-Köhler, D. (2007). Zusammenhänge zwischen Bindung, Erkundung und Autonomie. In K. H. Brisch & T. Hellbrügge (Eds.), *Die Anfänge der Eltern-Kind-Bindung* (pp. 325–340). Stuttgart: Klett-Cotta.

Boldt, E. D. (1978). Structural tightness and cross-cultural research. *Journal of Cross-Cultural Psychology, 9*(2), 151–165. doi:10.1177/002202217892003.

Bond, M. H., & Cheung, T. S. (1983). College students' spontaneous self-concept: The effect of culture among respondents in Hong Kong, Japan, and the United States. *Journal of Cross-Cultural Psychology, 14*(2), 153–171. doi:1 0.1177/0022002183014002002.

Brewer, M. B., & Gardner, W. (1996). Who is this "We"? Levels of collective identity and self representations. *Journal of Personality and Social Psychology, 71*(1), 83–93. doi:10.1037/0022-3514.71.1.83.

Broadbent, D. E. (1958). *Perception and communication*. London: Pergamon Press.

Campbell, A. (1981). *The sense of well-being in America: Recent patterns and trends*. *Psychological Medicine, 12*(2), 436–437. doi:10.1017/S003329170004681X.

Chen, S. X. (2013). *Psychological responses to globalization: Bicultural identities and beyond.* Presentation held at Conference "Identity in a globalized world," 31st May – 3rd June 2013, Isle of Vilm, Germany.

Cohen, J. W. (1988). *Statistical power analysis for the behavioral sciences* (2nd ed.). Hillsdale, NJ: Lawrence Erlbaum Associates.

Condor, S. (1996). Unimagined community? Some social psychological issues concerning English National Identity. In G. M. Breakwell & E. L. Speri (Eds.), *Changing European identities: Social psychological analyses of social change.* Oxford: Butterworth Heinemann, pp. 41–64.

Condor, S. (2000). Pride and prejudice: identity management in English people's talk about 'this country'. *Discourse & Society 11* (2): 175–205.

Condor, S. (2011). Towards a social psychology of citizenship? Introduction to the special issue. *Journal of Community & Applied Social Psychology, 21*(3), 193–201. doi:10.1002/casp.1089.

Cousins, S. D. (1989). Culture and self-perception in Japan and the United States. *Journal of Personality and Social Psychology, 56*(1), 124–131. doi:10.1037//0022-3514.56.1.124.

Ehrenberg, A. (1998). La fatigue d'être soi. Dépression et la société. Paris, FR: Odile Jacobs.

Epstein, S. (1973). The self-concept revisited. Or a theory of a theory. *American Psychologist, 5*, 404–416.

Epstein, S. (1979). Entwurf einer Integrativen Persönlichkeitstheorie. In S. H. Filipp (Ed.), *Selbstkonzept-Forschung: Probleme, Befunde, Perspektiven* (pp. 15–45). Stuttgart: Klett-Cotta.

Epstein, S. (1994). Integration of the cognitive and the psychodynamic unconscious. *The American Psychologist, 49*(8), 709–724. doi:10.1037/0003-066X.49.8.709.

Epstein, S. (2003). Cognitive-experiential self-theory of personality. In T. Millon, M. J. Lerner & I. B. Weiner (Eds.), *Handbook of psychology. Personality and social psychology* (Vol. 5, pp. 159–184). New York: Wiley-Blackwell.

Filipp, S.-H., & Mayer, A.-K. (2005).Selbstkonzept-Entwicklung. In J. B. Asendorpf (Ed.), Enzyklopädie der Psycholgie. Band 3. Soziale, emotioinale und Persönlichkeitsentwicklung (pp. 259–334). Göttingen: Hogrefe

Fiske, S. T. (2010). *Social beings: Core motives in social psychology.* Hoboken, NJ: Wiley.

Geertz, C. (1973). *The interpretation of cultures.* New York: Basic.

Greve, W. (Ed.) (2000). *Psychologie des Selbst.* Beltz: Weinheim.

Grundy, S., & Jamieson, L. (2003). *Are we all Europeans now? Local, national and supranational identities of young adults*, British Sociological Association Annual Conference, Belonging & Isolation. York, UK, 11–13 April 2003.

Halkoaho, J. (2012). *Identity-related mediaconsumption a focus on consumers' relationships with their favorite TV programs.* PhD Dissertation, University of Vaasa, Finland.

Helmchen, A. (2005). *Die Entstehung der Nationen im Europa der Frühen Neuzeit: ein integraler Ansatz aus humanistischer Sicht* (Vol. 10). Bern: Peter Lang.

Jamieson, L. (2005). *Orientations of young men and women to citizenship and European identity* (Final Report). (Project no: SERD-2000-00260). Retrieved from: http://www.sociology.ed.ac.uk/youth/final_report.pdf

Karim, S. (2012). The co-existence of globalism and tribalism: A review of the literature. *Journal of Research in International Education, 11*(2), 137–151. doi:10.1177/1475240912452465.

Keupp, H., & Höfer, R. (Eds.). (1997). *Identitätsarbeit heute: klassische und aktuelle Perspektiven der Identitätsforschung* (Vol. 1299). Suhrkamp.

Kuhn, M. H., & McPartland, T. S. (1954). An empirical investigation of self-attitudes. *American Sociological Review, 19*(1), 68–76. doi:10.2307/2088175.

Linville, P. W., & Jones, E. E. (1980). Polarized appraisals of out-group members. *Journal of Personality and Social Psychology, 38*(5), 689–703. doi:10.1037/0022-3514.38.5.689.

Markus, H. (1977). Self-schemata and processing information about the self. *Journal of Personality and Social Psychology, 35*(2), 63–78. doi:10.1037/0022-3514.35.2.63.

Markus, H. R., & Kitayama, S. (1991). Culture and the self: Implications for cognition, emotion, and motivation. *Psychological Review, 98*(2), 224. doi:10.1037//0033-295X.98.2.224.

McGuire, W. J., McGuire, C. V., Child, P., & Fujioka, T. (1978). Salience of ethnicity in the spontaneous self-concept as a function of one's ethnic distinctiveness in the social environment. *Journal of Personality and Social Psychology, 36*(5), 511–520.

Murdock, E., Hirt, F. S., & Ferring, D. (2014). Salience of nationality in students' spontaneous self-concept: A comparative study of a nationally homogeneous and a heterogeneous school context, *Journal of Research in International Education*, 1–16. doi:10.1177/1475240914539797

Niebergall, J. A. (2010). *Promoting positive identity among children in a school curriculum.* Master's Thesis, University of Kansas. Retrieved from: https://kuscholarworks.ku.edu/handle/1808/6789?show=full

Péporté, P. (2011). *Constructing the middle ages: Historiography, collective memory and nation-building in Luxembourg* (Vol. 3). Leiden: Brill.

Pinquart, M., & Silbereisen, R. K. (2000). Das Selbst im Jugendalter. In W. Greve (Ed.), *Psychologie des Selbst* (pp. 75–95). Weinheim: Beltz.

Rumpel, E. (1991). *Kulturelle Identität. Eine Konzeptanalyse im interdisziplinären Raum*. Unpublished master's thesis, University of the Saarland, Germany.

Schmidt-Denter, U. (2011). *Die Deutschen und ihre Migranten: Ergebnisse der europäischen Identitätsstudie*. Beltz Juventa: Weinheim.

Schola Europaea. (n.d.) School homepage. Available at: http://www.eursc.eu/index.php?id=132 (accessed 29 April 2013).

Sedikides, C., & Brewer, M. B. (Eds.) (2001). *Individual self, relational self, collective self*. New York, USA: Psychology Press.

Sedikides, C., Olsen, N., & Reis, H. T. (1993). Relationships as natural categories. *Journal of Personality and Social Psychology, 64*(1), 71.

Sennett, R. (1998). *Der flexible Mensch. Die Kultur des neuen Kapitalismus*. Berlin: Berlin-Verlag.

Sherif, M., Harvey, O. J., White, B.J. Hood, W. R., & Sherif, C. W. (1988). *The Robbers Cave Experiment. Intergroup conflict and cooperation*. Middletown, CT: Wesleyan University Press.

Triandis, H. (1989). The self and social behavior in differing cultural contexts. *Psychological Review, 96*(3), 506–520. Retrieved from http://doi.apa.org/psycinfo/1989-36454-001

Triandis, H. C. (2001). Individualism-collectivism and personality. *Journal of Personality, 69*(6), 907–924. doi:10.1111/1467-6494.696169.

Valsiner, J. (1997). *Constructing identity: A theoretical problem for social sciences*. Presentation at the Workshop Identitätsdiskussionen in der Psychologie, Martin-Luther-Universität, Halle an der Saale, 18 April 1997.

Valsiner, J. (2007). *Locating the self … looking for the impossible? Or may be the impossible is the only possibility*. Presentation at the Conference: Culturalization of the Self, Chemnitz, 1 December 2007.

Von Schlippe, A., & Schweitzer, J. (1996). *Lehrbuch der systemischen Therapie und Beratung*. Göttingen: Vandenhoeck & Ruprecht.

Wallace, P. C., Condor, S., & Boehnke, K. (2005). *Final Report* Contract no : HPSE-CT-2001-00077 Project no : SERD-2000-00260 Title : *Orientations of Young Men and Women to Citizenship and European Identity* (pp. 1–99). Retrieved from: http://www.sociology.ed.ac.uk/youth/final_report.pdf

Weinreich, P. (2003). Identity structure analysis. In P. Weinreich & W. Saunderson (Eds.), *Analysing identity: Cross-cultural, societal and clinical contexts* (pp. 7–76). Hove: Routledge.

Weinreich, P., & Saunderson, W. (Eds.) (2003). *Analysing identity: Cross-cultural, societal and clinical contexts*. Hove: Routledge.

Weinreich, P., Bacova, V., & Rougier, N. (2003). Basic primordialism in ethnic and national identity. In P. Weinreich & W. Saunderson (Eds.), *Analysing identity: Cross-cultural, societal and clinical contexts* (pp. 115–171). Hove: Routledge.

5

On Being Bicultural in a Multicultural Environment

Introduction

In the preceding chapter the influence of the cultural context on identity was shown. The question how two or more cultures are experienced by and organized within the individual will be addressed in this chapter. Within an acculturation framework (Berry, 1990), individuals are described as integrated, if they identify with and participate in both the ethnic and mainstream culture. Integrated individuals have thus also been called *bicultural*. Yet what does biculturalism or being bicultural actually entail? Brannen and Thomas (2010) noted that surface characteristics are not always indicative of biculturalism, and demographic or ethnic labels may only serve as a first clue as to whether a person is bicultural or not. In this chapter, I will first present definitions of biculturalism which have been suggested and explain why biculturalism is different from bilingualism, also drawing on results from an empirical study which explored the relationship between language competence and biculturalism. Going beyond language *competence*, the question whether bilingual persons have two personalities is also investigated. I will review both theoretical and empirical evidence. The second part of this chapter addresses

© The Author(s) 2016   **189**
E. Murdock, *Multiculturalism, Identity and Difference*,
DOI 10.1057/978-1-137-59679-6_5

the question how a second culture is actually acquired and experienced by individuals. Early models of second culture acquisition are presented first, followed by more recent models which focus on the reconciliation of the different cultures at individual level. Combining theory with practice the next empirical study investigates how adolescents growing up in a multicultural environment experience this culture contact situation. I will present the findings from this recent study and discuss the implications in the concluding part to this chapter.

Definition of Biculturalism

Biculturalism has been equated with having two cultures (Nguyen & Benet-Martínez, 2012), but there is more than one way to being bicultural (Phinney & Devich-Navarro, 1997). To date, no commonly agreed psychological definition of biculturalism exists. Nguyen and Benet-Martínez (2007) stated: "Loosely defined, bicultural individuals may be immigrants, refugees, sojourners (international students or expatriates), indigenous people, ethnic minorities, those in interethnic relationships and mixed ethnic individuals" (p. 102). Admittedly, all persons included in this list have experienced second culture exposure, but whether they can actually be described as being bicultural depends on the definition of biculturalism applied. Benet-Martinez, Leu, Lee and Morris (2002) add an important component to the mere second culture exposure: Bicultural individuals are those who have been exposed to and have internalized two cultures that guide their feelings, thoughts and actions (Nguyen & Benet-Martínez, 2007; Ramírez-Esparza et al., 2006). Thus, the condition of *internalization* of two or more cultures is added to second culture exposure. In fact, bicultural individuals are thought to identify with two (or more) cultures because they have internalized more than one set of cultural schemas. Cultural schemas in turn are defined as socially constructed cognitive systems that represent one's knowledge about the values, attitudes, beliefs and behavioural assumptions of a culture as well as relations amongst these attributes (Fiske & Taylor, 1991). A further definition of biculturalism stresses a behavioural component: Biculturalism entails the ability to switch between cultural schemas, norms and behaviours in response to cultural cues (Hong, Morris, Chiu, & Benet-Martínez, 2000). More explicitly, bicultural individuals are those who display multicultural competence as reflected in their language use, choice of friends or media use which are representative of two or more cultures (LaFromboise, Coleman, & Gerton, 1993). It is important to distinguish between cultural identification and cultural knowledge. A person can have knowledge of another culture without identifying with it. The final definition to be introduced here focuses on this identification aspect. According to this definition bicultural individuals are simply defined as those who self-label as bicultural (e.g. "I am bicultural") or group self-categorize (e.g. "I am Chinese-American") in a way that reflects cultural dualism (Benet-Martínez, 2012c; Nguyen & Benet-Martínez, 2007). Language competence is an important aspect of cultural knowledge and Ramírez-Esparza et al. (2006) have stated that "bilinguals tend to be bicultural" (p. 100). Yet is this really the case? Does bilingualism equal biculturalism?

Language and Biculturalism

The difficulty in finding bilingual participants for their studies was also commented on by Ramírez-Esparza et al. (2006). Given the fact that Luxembourg is a trilingual country, Luxembourg is the perfect place to recruit bi- or even trilingual participants. It is not uncommon to find people who are fluent in four or even five languages: Teenagers speaking five or more languages were recruited for an exhibition about Luxembourg's multilingualism in the summer of 2013 (Multilingual teens wanted for an exhibition, Wort.lu 27.05.2013). The high language competence within this country therefore provides an ideal background to explore the relationship between bilingualism and biculturalism. We designed an empirical study to test the alleged relationship between bilingualism and biculturalism. Specifically, we tested the hypotheses that participants who self-identify as bilingual will also self-identify as bicultural (Hypothesis 1). We also explored the relationship between language use and personality which will be explained in the subsequent section.

Empirical Study: Bilingualism = Biculturalism?

Ninety-nine adults participated in this study. Their mean age was 24 years (*SD* = 5.84), and 61 of the participants were female. Fifty-seven participants stated Luxembourg as their first nationality, 23 German and the remaining 19 participants stated a wide range of nationalities. Nine participants also named a second nationality. The only criterion for participation in this study was high competence in at least two of the following four languages: Luxembourgish, French, German or English. The majority of the participants were recruited through flyers at the University of Luxembourg. Participants were presented with a questionnaire which included questions about their language competence and language use. Participants were also asked to give their definitions of a bilingual and a bicultural person. In a second step they were asked to state if they considered themselves to be bilingual and bicultural. If either was negated, participants were asked to explain why not. A further series of questions explored the relationship between language use and personality.

Language Competence

All participants indicated high competence in at least two of the four languages stated above and therefore fulfil the condition for participation in this study. In fact, all but one stated to be competent in three languages with 90 % naming a fourth and 39 % a fifth language. Luxembourgish was most frequently mentioned as first language, German as second, French as third and English as fourth language. Participants were also asked to rate the competence in their languages for the domains of speaking, understanding and writing on a scale from 1 (quite poor) to 5 (mother tongue level). On average, competence in all three areas was rated close to 5 for the first language, with somewhat lower scores for writing. Competence in the second language was rated in all categories above the mid-point 3 (good), but below the mother tongue level. All participants acquired their second and third language skills during their childhood years, but the Luxembourgish participants at a significantly younger age than the other participants. The early language acquisition is a reflection of the Luxembourgish school system, where alphabetization takes place in German, followed by immersion in French in the second half of the primary school years.

The Relationship between Bilingualism and Biculturalism

Of the 99 participants, 22 participants described themselves as *monolingual*. Conversely, 77 % of all participants defined themselves as bi- or trilingual, rising to 91 % for participants of Luxembourg nationality. Less than half of the participants (45 %) agreed with the statement that they feel bicultural, dropping to 40 % within the Luxembourg sample. The association between bilingualism and biculturalism fails to reach statistical significance, $\chi^2(1, 99) = 2.89$, $p = 0.09$. As illustrated in Fig. 5.1, only half (50.6 %) of the bilinguals also feel bicultural. The percentage drops to 44 % within the Luxembourg sub-sample. On the other hand, the majority (72.7 %) of the monolingual participants does not self-identify as bicultural.

Based on these findings, Hypothesis 1, the assertion that bilinguals tend to be bicultural, is refuted. The association between bilingualism and biculturalism is in fact *not* significant.

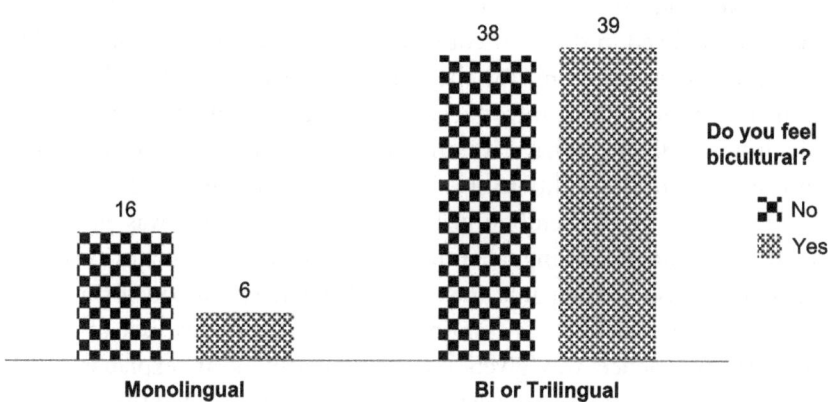

Fig. 5.1 Relationship between bilingualism and biculturalism for total sample (*N* = 99)

The analysis of the qualitative findings illustrates why there is not a stronger association between bilingualism and biculturalism. We had asked participants to provide their definition of a bilingual person. Ninety-eight participants responded and a content analysis of the answers showed that the vast majority of the responses were language-specific. At the most basic level participants described a bilingual person as someone who speaks two languages. Just under half of the participants added that the languages need to be spoken at a high level or fluently, others (n = 11) focused on the length of exposure to a language ("have to be raised with two languages") and 17 mentioned competence in different language areas (speaking, reading, writing). Only eight persons mentioned a relationship to culture in the broadest sense (e.g. "a person who can fit in anywhere") and only one person actually mentioned the term "bicultural."

The picture is very different when looking at the definitions of bicultural persons. Just over a third of the participants (n = 36) mentioned that "one has to have lived in different cultures." Thirty-three participants emphasized that an identification with cultures must have happened, that a person "needs to feel at home" in different cultures. Cognitive factors were also mentioned (n = 13, "need to have knowledge about a culture") as well as affective factors (n = 16, have an "attachment to" different cultures). If language is mentioned, it is mentioned as a necessary, but not sufficient condition: "A person who not only speaks different languages, but has also lived in different countries." These explanations provided by the study participants mirror the definition of biculturalism by Benet-Martínez et al. (2002) introduced above. These authors postulate that bicultural individuals have internalized their cultures. Biculturalism is thus more than the ability to speak languages to a high standard.

Amongst the Luxembourgish participants there was a strong sense of being *multi*-lingual, but *mono*-cultural. The majority of the Luxembourgish participants (68 %) had not lived abroad for a longer period of time (defined as 6 months or more) and this lack of foreign country experience was given most frequently as an explanation for feeling monocultural. Other explanations offered included the comment that the "German and Luxembourgish culture are too close" or "feeling close only to the European culture." A further participant provided a *fusion* explanation (see Chap. 3): "Die Summe der Kulturen, die einen beeinflussen, ergibt eine neue Kultur"[1] and yet another participant is an example for an *individualist marginal*[2]: "Ich akzeptiere die verschiedenen Kulturen, fühle mich ihnen jedoch nicht nahe."[3]

The analysis of the qualitative statements demonstrates that immersion in and identification with another culture has to take place before someone can self-identify as "bicultural." This immersion can be gained in different ways, for example by living in another culture or, as will be shown later, by being exposed to two different cultures from birth. The results illustrate that language is a necessary, but not sufficient condition for biculturalism.

Language and Personality

Several studies have shown that language can serve as a prime for cultural frame switching (i.e. Hong et al., 2000; Ross, Xun, & Wilson, 2002). Trafimow, Silverman, Fan and Fun Law (1997), for example, asked bilingual Hong Kong Chinese students to complete the Twenty Statement Test (TST, Kuhn & McPartland, 1954). If the TST was presented in English, the students produced more trait adjectives associated with independent, "Western" self-construal. In contrast, under the Chinese language prime condition the students described themselves more in terms of their social roles, thus the interdependent self-construal was elicited. Similar results were found by Ross, Xun and Wilson (2002) who suggested that culture-specific knowledge structures are activated by the associated language. In a replication study Kemmelmeier (2004) found support for the notion "that for bicultural individuals, reading a particular language is sufficient to effect temporary shifts in the salience of self-construals" (p. 709). Ramírez-Esparza et al. (2006) investigated whether bilinguals have two personalities. In presenting English and Spanish language versions of the Big Five Personality Inventory (BFI, Benet-Martínez & John, 1998) to

---

[1] The sum of cultures influencing us results in a new culture.

[2] The "individualist marginal" will be explained later in Chap. 5.

[3] I accept the different cultures, but I don't feel close to either of them.

Mexican bilinguals, they found cross-language differences in three of the five personality traits. The results therefore support the hypothesis that language does serve as a prime, triggering a response pattern that is either in line with Mexican or American personality dimensions. As Ramírez-Esparza (2012) explained, people from Mexico put value on *simpatía*—the quality of being likeable, easygoing, polite, affectionate and sharing feelings with others. Modesty is another quality associated with *simpatía*. She found that bilingual Mexicans described themselves lower on *simpatía* when completing a questionnaire in Spanish rather than English. Ramírez-Esparza concluded that these bilinguals do switch personalities "in the sense that their cultural biases are influencing the way they respond to self-reports." Benet-Martínez (2012b) asserted that "Language is one of the main vehicles of culture" and suggests that people can pick up part of another culture by learning another language:

> If you speak perfect Russian, your read Russian novels, you go to Russia sometimes, you watch Russian movies—before you know it, you are internalizing that culture and you are becoming bicultural. It is a matter of degrees. You may not become as Russian as Vladimir Putin, but you will still have a bit of Russian in you.

Empirical Study: Do Bilinguals Have Two Personalities?

Within our empirical study we also wanted to explore the relationship between language and personality. Specifically, we wanted to investigate whether participants would perceive a change in language as influencing their personality. As noted above, bicultural individuals are defined as those who have internalized cultures that guide their feelings, thoughts and actions (Nguyen & Benet-Martínez, 2007; Ramírez-Esparza et al., 2006). We therefore predicted that only those individuals who self-label as bicultural would also experience the change in language as influencing their personality (Hypothesis 2).

We asked participants if they believe that the language they speak influences their personality. Just under half ($n = 47$) of the participants agreed with the statement. The relationship between feeling *bicultural*

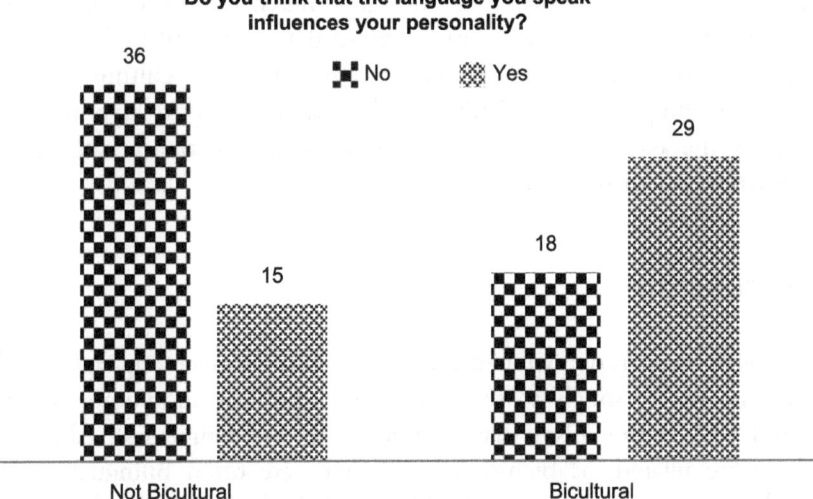

Fig. 5.2 Association between biculturalism and the belief that language influences personality (n = 98)

and the belief that language influences personality is statistically highly significant, $\chi^2(1, 98) = 9.06$ $p < 0.01$, $phi = 0.3$. As Fig. 5.2 illustrates, participants who describe themselves as bicultural also tend to believe that the language they speak influences their personality, whilst monocultural participants don't consider language influencing their personality.

The association between language and personality was explored further. Participants were asked to rate to what extent they agree with the following statements (on a scale ranging from 1 = don't agree at all to 6 = completely agree): (1) I spontaneously adapt my language to the situational context. (2) I am always conscious of which language I am speaking. (3) Switching between languages is effortful for me. (4) When I change language, I am also transferred into a different culture. (5) Bilinguals are automatically bicultural.

Mono- and bicultural participants differed in how they answered these questions. Bicultural individuals agreed more with the statement that they adapt their language to the situational context; they are less conscious of which language they are speaking at a given moment in time and experience the change in language as less effortful. These differences are statistically significant.[4] Even stronger differences exist for the last two statements: Biculturals agree much more than monoculturals with the statement that a change in language means a change in culture and they consider bilinguals to be bicultural. These results support Hypothesis 2, namely the assertion that bicultural individuals experience language as influencing their personality.

Discussion

This empirical study explored the relationship between language, biculturalism and personality. As was noted, biculturalism should not be confused with bilingualism (having fluency in two languages). Although these are related, as bicultural individuals are often bilingual, bilingual persons are not necessarily bicultural. In line with the definitions of biculturalism, the analysis of qualitative statements illustrate that an *internalization* of culture is a necessary condition for biculturalism. Within the Luxembourg sample we did find a high self-identification as bi-or trilingual, coupled with strong monocultural identification ("I am Luxembourgish"). Thus, it is possible to have high language competence in several languages and to feel monocultural. Going beyond language competence, an important finding of this study was also that mono- and biculturals differ regarding their perception whether language influences personality. In fact, the findings suggest that mono- and bicultural individuals differ regarding the extent to which they have *internalized* their languages. Those who identify as bicultural also tend to agree with the statement that language influences their personality. Furthermore, biculturals agreed much more with the statement that a change of language also means a change in culture. Finally, bicultural individuals seem to be less conscious of the language they currently speak; they adapt *automatically* to situational demands and perceive a change of language as a

---

[4]Relationship between language and personality: Item 1 Context: $t(97) = -2.00$, $p < 0.05$, $\eta^2 = 0.04$ $M_{mono} = 5.06$, $M_{bicultural} = 5.49$; Item 2 Conscious: $t(97) = -2.25$, $p < 0.05$, $\eta^2 = 0.05$ $M_{mono} = 4.89$, $M_{bicultural} = 4.30$; Item 3 Effort: $t(96) = 2.1$, $p < 0.05$, $\eta^2 = 0.04$ $M_{mono} = 2.96$, $M_{bicultural} = 2.43$; Item 4 Culture: $t(96) = -3.59$, $p < 0.001$, $\eta^2 = 0.12$, $M_{mono} = 2.52$, $M_{bicultural} = 3.48$; Item 5 Bilingual: $t(97) = -3.58$, $p < 0.001$, $\eta^2 = 0.12$, $M_{mono} = 2.28$, $M_{bicultural} = 3.31$.

change in culture. These findings can be interpreted in accordance with the cultural frame switching research which was briefly outlined above: Bicultural individuals have actually internalized their language and the language serves as prime for cultural frame switching. The process of second culture acquisition will be elaborated in the next section.

Second Culture Acquisition—Theoretical Framework

Bicultural individuals have simultaneous awareness of being a member of two (or more) cultures and they exhibit the behavioural repertoire that stems from having access to two distinct cultural knowledge traditions, sometimes switching between schemas in response to cultural cues. Research on biculturalism focuses on the process of *how* the cultures are integrated, how people experience and reconcile their bicultural identities. In the following, variations in bicultural identification will be explained. I will outline early models first, as they lay the foundations for subsequent research. Building on these frameworks, more recent models will be presented, in particular the *Bicultural Identity Integration* (BII) model and the *Acculturation Complexity Model* (ACM). These models have been applied to a further empirical study and the findings amongst adolescents growing up in a multicultural environment will be presented and discussed.

Early Models of Second Culture Acquisition

As early as 1993, LaFromboise, Coleman and Gerton conducted a literature review on the psychological impact of biculturalism. One of the objectives driving this review was the authors' intention to show alternatives to the assumption of a linear model of culture acquisition. The authors identified five different models of second culture acquisition namely *assimilation, acculturation, alternation, multiculturalism* and *fusion*. At first sight these orientations look very similar to Berry's (1990) model. However the nuances are quite important for the understanding of how the two cultures are organized and I will provide a brief description of each orientation.

The *assimilation* model refers to the ongoing process of absorption into the culture that is perceived as dominant or more desirable. In the process of absorption, the individual loses his or her original cultural identity. This conceptualization corresponds with Berry's (1990) understanding of assimilation. *Acculturation* looks, at first sight, similar to Berry's integration strategy, as the individual seeks to become a competent member of the majority culture whilst continuing to be a member of the minority culture. LaFromboise et al.'s (1993) acculturation model however differs from the integration orientations in an important way: The acculturation process is assumed to be *involuntary*. The underlying relationship between the two cultures is hierarchical and unidirectional. In contrast, the *alternation* model is described as "an additive model of cultural acquisition parallel to the code-switching theories found in the research on bilingualism" (LaFromboise et al., 1993, p. 399). Thus it is possible to know and understand two cultures and have a sense of belonging to two cultures without compromising the sense of cultural identity. The alternation model firstly posits a bidirectional and orthogonal relationship between the culture of origin and second culture. Secondly, the model does not assume a hierarchical relationship between the two cultures. It is therefore possible to maintain a positive relationship with both cultures. The *multicultural* model is referred to more as a hypothetical model as it posits that an individual can maintain a positive identity as a member of his or her culture of origin, whilst simultaneously developing a positive identity engaging in complex institutional sharing with the larger political entity comprised of other cultural groups. The authors question if such a multicultural society can be maintained in reality, as "cultural separation of groups demands the institutional protection and ethnocultural compartmentalization" (Fishman, 1980), quoted in LaFromboise et al., (1993, p. 401). An example for this choice of a culture living within a different culture is the Old Amish in the USA. The *fusion* model epitomizes the assumptions behind the melting-pot ideology. Cultures merge and fuse together until they are indistinguishable and form a new culture. The model assumes no cultural superiority, but in practice it is likely that minority groups become fused into the majority groups. Examples of true fusion, in the sense of a third culture emerging, are rare. This point was already noted when discussing acculturation outcomes.

Table 5.1 Models of second culture acquisition and associated process variables

Model	Contact with:	Loyalty to:	Involvement with the:	Acceptance by members of:	Contact with:	Affiliation with:	Acceptance by members of:
	The culture of origin		*The second culture*				
Assimilation	Low	Low	Low	Low	High	High	High
Acculturation	Low	Low	Low	High	Low	Low	Low
Alternation	**High**	**High**	**High**	**High**	**High**	**High**	**High**
Multicultural	High	High	High	High	Moderate	Low	Low
Fusion	Low	Low	Low	Low	High	High	High

Source: LaFromboise et al. (1993, p. 402)

LaFromboise and colleagues identify these models and analyse them with a view to which models are more conducive for effective functioning of individuals operating in dual cultures. The models and process variables involved in culture acquisition are summarized in Table 5.1.

Bicultural Competence

Following on from these considerations, LaFromboise et al. (1993) developed the construct of *bicultural competence* which grows mainly out of the alternation model. The authors stress that individuals, not groups, become biculturally competent and provide six dimensions an individual may need to develop to become effective in two cultures. These dimensions are:

1. Knowledge of cultural beliefs and values
This dimension refers to the degree to which an individual is knowledgeable (cognitive component), is appreciative (affective component) and internalizes (behavioural aspect) the everyday practices, rituals and values of a given culture. Differences in world view and value conflicts may be the primary sources of stress of bicultural individuals (Trimble, 1981).

2. Positive attitudes to both minority and majority groups
The individual recognizes bicultural competence as a desirable goal in its own right and each of the cultural groups is held in positive, but not necessarily equal regard. The authors note the importance of *contact* in developing positive attitudes towards both groups.

3. Bicultural efficacy
The belief that *one can* develop and maintain effective interpersonal relationships in two cultures is directly related to one's ability to develop bicultural competence. LaFromboise defines bicultural efficacy as "the belief or confidence that one can live effectively and in a satisfying manner within two groups without compromising one's sense of cultural identity" (p. 404).

4. Communication ability
This dimension refers to an individual's effectiveness in communicating ideas and feelings to members of a given culture, both verbally and non-verbally. Language competency may be a major building block in

bicultural competence. "Each of a bilingual's languages is the mediator between differing cultural identities within one and the same person" (Northover, 1988, quoted in LaFromboise et al., 1993, p. 405).

5. Role repertoire

This component concerns the range of culturally or situationally appropriate behaviours or roles an individual has developed. The assumption is that the greater the range of behaviours or roles, the higher the level of competence.

6. Sense of being grounded

"Every culture provides the individual some sense of identity, some regulation or belonging and some sense of personal place in the school of things" (Adler, 1975, p. 20, quoted in LaFromboise et al., 1993, p. 407). The skill of developing stable social networks is conducive to a bicultural existence. As the authors write, one must have the skill to recruit and use external support networks. They have labelled the experience of having a well-developed social support network "a sense of being grounded" (p. 407).

Summing up, the authors conclude that bicultural competence is a difficult set of skills to achieve and maintain, but they are *acquirable* skills. The authors don't claim that this list of skills is exhaustive—other skills may be necessary. They also stress that more research is needed regarding the relationship between these skills. Some dimensions may be more important than others and some may be developed before others. The authors also concede that the model assumes a reciprocal relationship between a person and the environment. As was noted in the discussion of the acculturation taxonomy, context factors such as the nature of the society of origin and the host culture also need to be taken into consideration. Yet the model of bicultural competence is a starting point in identifying skills that may be required by an individual to be effective in two cultures.

Phinney and Devich-Navarro's Model on Being Bicultural

Focusing primarily on identity construal process, Phinney and Devich-Navarro (1997) developed a model for different ways of being bicultural working primarily with ethnic minorities (African-Americans and

Mexican-Americans) living in the mainstream culture of America. These authors explored how adolescents think of themselves in relation to the two cultures to which they are exposed. Specifically, they looked at how ethnic minority groups actually identify with and participate in their ethnic culture and the larger society. Phinney and Devich-Navarro's Model is reproduced in Fig. 5.3 and illustrates how elements of the earlier models have been amalgamated. The circles in the diagram represent ethnic and American cultures respectively, and the "X" represents the individual's position with respect to the two cultures.

The top panel in Fig. 5.3 illustrates *assimilation* and *fusion* patterns. As postulated by the fourfold model, an individual following the assimilation orientation gives up the ethnic culture and becomes part of the mainstream culture which is indicated by the "X" in the American culture circle. The ethnic culture continues to exist, but the person is no longer part of it. As described by the authors, under the fusion model, both cultures are combined and form a new pattern, a new culture. The two original cultures can no longer be distinguished, which is illustrated in the model by the complete overlap of both circles. As previously stated, there are only few examples of fusion. The bottom panel of Fig. 5.3 provides an illustration for separation, the orientation only towards the ethnic culture, illustrated by an "X" in the ethnic circle. Under the marginalization condition the "X" is placed between the circles, demonstrating that the individual feels being neither part of the larger society nor the ethnic culture.

The middle part of the panel represents two different ways of being bicultural: "An individual who occupies primarily the area of overlap can be considered *a blended bicultural* (...) The overlap allows for a new identity as a combination of both cultures. On the other hand, those who move between the two non-overlapping areas can be considered *alternating* biculturals" (Phinney & Devich-Navarro, 1997, p. 7). The authors consider this diagram as a starting point for conceptualizing ways of being bicultural. They stress that the degree of overlap may vary as well as the positions of the individual between the two cultures. Furthermore, the bicultural experience differs widely across groups due to differing historical and societal factors. The authors conclude by stating that "biculturalism is a complex and multidimensional phenomenon; there is not

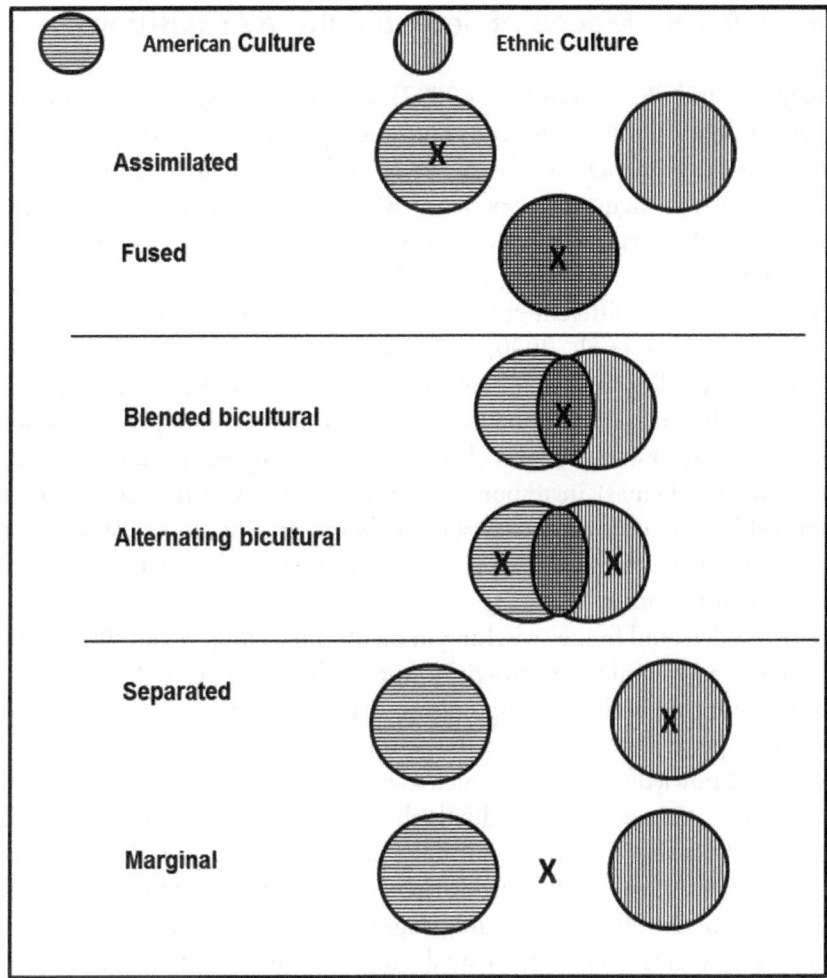

Fig. 5.3 Identification patterns based on individual's perception of American and ethnic cultures (*Source*: Phinney & Devich-Navarro [1997, p. 6])

just one way of being bicultural" (p. 29). They acknowledge that the patterns they describe are oversimplifications but maintain that the patterns provide a useful heuristic for future research. In the following section new research and more recent theories, building on these models, will be presented.

More Recent Models of Second Culture Acquisition

Nguyen and Benet-Martínez (2007) criticized Phinney and Devich-Navarro's (1997) model for the confounding of identity and behavioural markers. Labels such as "fused" or "blended" refer to identity-related aspects of the bicultural experience whereas "alternating" refers to the behavioural domain that is the ability to engage in *cultural frame switching* (CFS). Frame switching is the ability to shift between interpretive frames rooted in different cultures in response to cues in the social environment (Hong et al., 2000; Hong, Benet-Martinez, Chiu, & Morris, 2003). According to this model, biculturals navigate through their cultural worlds by switching between different cultural interpretive frames or meaning systems (e.g. culture-reinforced cognitive, affective and emotional schemas) in response to cultural cues. Cultural cues can be embedded in contextual cues such as home or school environment or symbols such as language which are psychologically associated with one culture or the other.

To understand frame switching in biculturals, Hong et al. (2000) have adopted a dynamic, constructivist approach to understanding culture. Following this understanding culture is not internalized in the form of a highly general structure, but in the form of loose networks of domain-specific knowledge structures, such as categories and/or implicit theories. A second premise is that individuals can acquire more than one such cultural meaning system, even if these meaning systems contain conflicting theories. Contradictory constructs can be simultaneously possessed, but cannot simultaneously guide cognition. According to this assumption at any given time only a small subset of an individual's knowledge comes to the fore and guides the interpretation of stimuli. Pieces of an individual's knowledge structure vary in accessibility. The more accessible a construct, the more likely it is to come to the fore in the individual's mind and to guide interpretation. Accessibility in turn will be influenced by use. The frame switching research uses the concept of accessibility and the technique of priming: Specific icons are chosen as "cultural triggers for knowledge." The assumption is that bicultural individuals who have been socialized into two cultures have access to the cultural meaning systems of these cultures. Priming individuals with icons referring to one culture would activate the networks of cultural constructs of that particular culture. This is exactly what Hong et al. (2000) could show in their series of priming studies with bicultural Hong Kong Chinese students: When primed with Westernized symbols, students displayed attribution styles associated with Western cultures (i.e. predominantly internal attribution) and when primed with Chinese symbols, external attributions dominated, a characteristically Asian behaviour. Exposure to culture-specific cues triggered culture-appropriate behaviour. Exposure to cultural icons activated cultural frame switching. Cultural frame switching is usually automatic, but the authors note that acculturating individuals may engage in active priming: Those wishing to acculturate quickly into the host culture may surround themselves with symbols and situations that prime the meaning of the host culture. Conversely, those who wish to retain accessibility of their home country may wish to surround themselves with symbols (music, food, pictures) of their home country. In the literature this form of cultural self-priming, serving the function of cultural self-affirmation, is referred to as *nostalgia* (Routledge et al., 2011; Sedikides, Wildschut, Routledge, Arndt, & Zhou, 2009). Thus active priming processing may help in the ongoing effort to negotiate cultural identity processes.

From Cultural Frame Switching to the Bicultural Identity Integration (BII)

Hong et al.'s (2000) studies provided the first empirical evidence that biculturals can move between cultural meaning systems. The ensuing question was whether the process of cultural frame switching is uniform across bicultural individuals. Benet-Martinez et al. (2002) suggested that cultural frame switching is moderated by perceived compatibility (vs. opposition) between the two bicultural orientations: Whether a bicultural individual perceives his or her cultural identities as complimentary and compatible or as oppositional and contradictory will moderate the process of frame switching. The authors proposed the construct *Bicultural Identity Integration* (BII) as individual difference variable moderating cultural frame switching. BII is understood as a continuum variable with high BII individuals perceiving their cultural identities as compatible and low BII individuals experiencing their cultural identities as oppositional. High and low BII individuals identify with both mainstream and ethnic culture, but they differ in their ability to create a synergistic, integrated cultural identity.

Further research into the structure and antecedents of BII revealed that BII actually encompasses two separate independent constructs: the perception of *distance* versus overlap and perceptions of *conflict* versus harmony (Benet-Martínez & Haritatos, 2005; Haritatos & Benet-Martínez, 2002). The components of BII are summarized in Fig. 5.4.

Perceptions of cultural *distance* were closely related to traditional acculturation variables such as language proficiency, length of stay in each culture and identification with mainstream culture. In contrast, the experience of cultural *conflict*, the feeling of being caught or trapped between cultural orientations, may be linked to identity confusion (Baumeister, 1986) or role conflict. Thus cultural distance more so than cultural conflict is related to objective, learning and performance-based aspects of acculturation. In other words, cultural distance is linked to performance-related personal and contextual challenges such as cognitive rigidity, low linguistic fluency or the cultural composition of the environment. In contrast, cultural conflict stems from strains that are largely intra- and

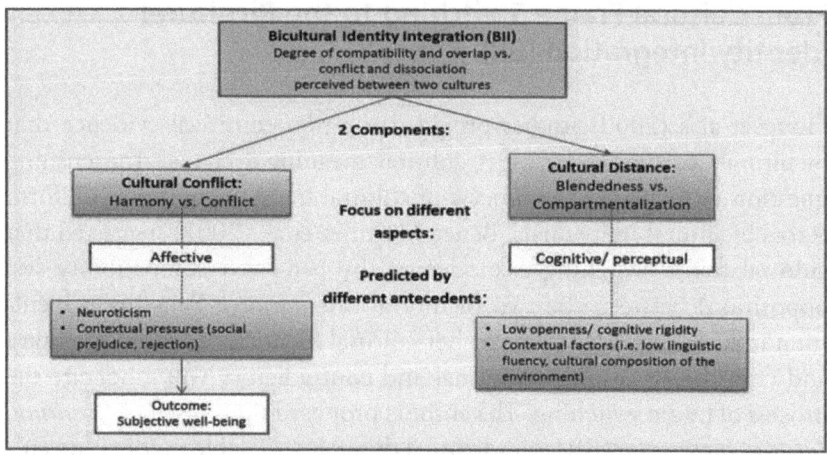

Fig. 5.4 Components of Bicultural Identity Integration (BII) (*Source*: Benet-Martínez [2012a])

interpersonal in nature, for example nervousness or the experience of social prejudice and rejection. The cultural conflict component may capture uniquely affective (vs. perceptual) aspects of the bicultural experience and is predicted by neuroticism and contextual pressures such as linguistic, interpersonal or discrimination stress. These factors may challenge feelings of efficacy in maintaining consistent and harmonious self-image and predict subjective well-being (SWB, Nguyen & Benet-Martínez, 2007). Cultural distance on the other hand may capture uniquely cognitive/perceptual (vs. affective) aspects of the bicultural experience. This component is predicted by low openness and contextual factors such as living in a culturally isolated environment which may lead to the perception that two cultures have rigid boundaries and cannot "come together" (Benet-Martínez, 2012).

The role of affective aspects in the adjustment process for expatriate workers was confirmed by research conducted by van der Zee and van Oudenhoven (2000) and van Oudenhoven, Mol and van der Zee (2003). They developed the multicultural personality questionnaire (MPQ) which includes five traits for multicultural effectiveness, namely cultural empathy, open-mindedness, social initiative, emotional stability and flexibility. In line with the predictions by the BII, the authors found that emotional stability had the strongest relationship with personal adjustment. Low neuroticism was identified as important predictor for psychological well-being in expatriates.

The relationship between biculturalism and adjustment was explored further in a meta-analysis. Nguyen and Benet-Martínez (2012) included 40 studies in their meta-analysis and found that biculturalism had a significant, weak and positive relationship ($r = 0.10$) with psychological and socio-cultural adjustment. However, this relationship was influenced by the way biculturalism was measured: If only unidimensional measures were included in the meta-analysis, the relationship was zero. If studies using bidimensional scales were included, that is studies that measured biculturalism via scores above the median on both cultural orientations, the relationship between biculturalism and adjustment was significant, moderate and positive ($r = 0.23$). Biculturalism is thus related to better adjustment, but only if biculturalism is measured bidimensionally. Nguyen and Benet-Martínez (2007) reasoned that involvement with two cultures may lead to social and cognitive flexibility and wider behavioural repertoires and competencies that buffer the bicultural individual against psychological maladjustment (e.g. anxiety or loneliness) or socio-cultural maladjustment (e.g. interpersonal conflict, intercultural miscommunication). The cognitive benefits of biculturalism will be discussed in more detail, after a brief look at the measurement of biculturalism.

The Measurement of Bicultural Identity Integration (BII)

Benet-Martínez and colleagues proceeded to develop an instrument to measure BII. First, a short vignette referred to as Bicultural Identity Integration Scale-Pilot Version (BIIS-P) was developed to measure the bicultural integration of Chinese-American biculturals (Benet-Martinez et al., 2002). The wording in this instrument reflected these cultural groups. Using a scale ranging from 1 (definitely not true) to 8 (definitely true), participants were asked to rate how well this statement described their experiences as Chinese-American:

> I am a bicultural who keeps American and Chinese cultures separate and feels conflicted about these two cultures. I am simply a Chinese who lives in America (vs. a Chinese-American), and I feel as someone who is caught between two cultures. (Benet-Martinez et al., 2002, p. 498)

The authors conceded that the use of the single-item measure is exploratory in nature and a new multi-item scale measure was developed. As noted above, BII actually encompasses two separate independent constructs: the perception of distance (vs. overlap) and perceptions of conflict (vs. harmony) and the new scale includes items that tap into these constructs. For a detailed overview of the associated scale development I would like to refer to Huynh (2009). The latest version, the Bicultural Identity Integration Scale Version 2 (BIIS-2R, Huynh & Benet-Martínez, 2010) consists of 20 items and has been tested with different ethnic groups (Asian Americans and Latinos in America) and can be adapted to different cultural contexts. The American culture is given and participants are asked to fill in their culture in the blank space provided. Items assessing the Harmony dimension include, for example: *I find it easy to harmonize*

_____ and American cultures; or *I find it easy to balance both* _____ *and American cultures.* Conflict is measured by items such as: *I feel torn between* _____ *and American cultures*; or *Being bicultural means having two cultural forces pulling on me at the same time.* Blendedness is, for example, reflected in the statement *I feel* _____ *and American at the same time,* whereas Separateness is captured by items such as *I keep* _____ *and American cultures separate in my life (that is, I don't mix them).* These items are rated on a scale from 1 (strongly disagree) to 5 (strongly agree).

To date there are very few instruments available that focus specifically on the experience of biculturalism. A search in June 2014 with Google Scholar using the key words "biculturalism + measurement" produced only one other measure, namely the Bicultural Involvement Questionnaire—Short version (BIQ-S, Guo, Suarez-Morales, Schwartz, & Szapocznik, 2009). This measure focuses on Hispanic-American biculturals. Thus, the BIIS-2R is currently one of the few publicly available measures focusing specifically on the question how bicultural individuals experience and organize their different cultures. The authors provide information about scoring instructions and psychometric properties of the scale.

Biculturalism, Cultural Frame Switching and Cognitive Consequences

Research has also shown that individuals high in BII are more effective in appropriately employing their cultural knowledge in specific contexts (Benet-Martínez & Haritatos, 2005; Nguyen & Benet-Martínez, 2007). High BII is also associated with creativity. Cheng, Sanchez-Burks and Lee (2008), for example, could show in a series of experiments that high BII Asian Americans came up with more innovative fusion restaurant dishes than did low BII Asian Americans. Yet benefits are not only associated with high BII. Benet-Martinez, Lee and Leu (2006) demonstrated that low BII individuals may be cognitively more complex. The reasoning behind this finding is that in negotiating their inner cultural conflict, these biculturals are more careful and systematic in processing cues from cultural representations, resulting in cultural representations that are more complex. This finding is mirrored by Tadmor, Tetlock and Peng (2009) and Tadmor and Tetlock (2006) who found that the more severe the cultural conflict is experienced, the greater the need to engage in more effortful and complex sense-making, resulting in higher levels of cognitive complexity. Individuals who had to engage in an effortful process of dealing with their conflicting cultural identities may therefore be better equipped to deal with dynamic, complex cultural situations. This finding may also explain why those expatriates who had the most difficult time in adjusting to their foreign assignment in the first place have been found to be the most effective in the long-term (Thomas, 1998). These individuals had to repeatedly confront and manage their different cultures, which may allow them to develop higher order cognitive skills that are not specific to one culture.

Benet-Martinez et al. (2006) explored what cognitive consequences the repeated experience of CFS may have for biculturals. They wondered if biculturals, by virtue of their frequent engagement in CFS, are cognitively different from individuals for whom CFS is not a common experience. The authors hypothesized that biculturals will think about culture in more complex ways than monoculturals. Cognitive complexity is understood to be an individual difference variable and has been defined as "the capacity to construe people, objects and ideas in a multidimensional way" (Benet-Martinez et al., 2006, p. 388). The authors base their understanding of cultural representation on Hall (1997) thus referring to shared meaning systems of a particular culture that are socially created through language, images and practices. In their empirical studies Benet-Martínez and colleagues found support for their hypotheses and provide the following reasons: Firstly, biculturals have repeated experience in detecting, processing and reacting to cultural cues in the environment and secondly, cultural knowledge is highly self-relevant for biculturals. The authors assert that they do not imply that monoculturals are culturally naïve. However, monoculturals may be less likely to recognize cultural perceptions and beliefs as norms that may differ from other groups. In contrast, "CFS creates a perspective that grasps the relativism and multidimensionality of each cultural system, leading to more complex representations of both cultures" (p. 388).

The authors also draw attention to the finding that biculturals in their study displayed more complex representations of the mainstream culture than did monoculturals. This finding contradicts the common notion that majority members have a deeper understanding of their culture than immigrants would have. Instead, this finding suggests that minorities may have a unique grasp on the complexities and nuances of the main, dominant culture. This is explained by the experience of having to navigate between two cultures and being forced to reason about their differences and similarities, leading to more complex and multidimensional cultural representations. Another implication of this finding is that the ability to think about one's culture(s) in complex ways can be learned and facilitated. Benet-Martinez et al. (2006) propose that biculturals acquire more complex cultural representations largely through the experience of CFS. Therefore, daily immersion into a multicultural environment (e.g. being married to a person with a different cultural background or extensive travelling) may help monocultural individuals develop a more complex understanding of their own culture. The cognitive component plays also a key role in the Acculturation Complexity Model (ACM) which will be explained next.

Acculturation Complexity Model (ACM)

Tadmor and Tetlock (2006) model the impact of second culture exposure on acculturation choice and on individual cognition and coping skills. Similar to Benet-Martinez et al., (2006) the authors emphasize the differential effects second culture exposure can have on cognitive complexity of socio-cognitive functioning. Tadmor and Tetlock (2006) focus on *integrative* complexity, which they define as "the capacity and willingness to acknowledge the legitimacy of competing perspectives on the same issue and to forge conceptual links among these perspectives" (p. 174). Thus they emphasize not only the variety of aspects, but especially the connections that are made amongst differentiated characteristics (Tetlock, 1986). Applied to the cross-cultural context, integrative complexity refers to

the degree to which a person accepts the reasonableness of different cultural perspectives on how to live, both at the micro interpersonal level and at more organizational-societal levels and, consequently, is motivated to develop integrative schemas that specify when to activate different worldviews and/or how to blend them together into a coherent holistic mental representation. (Tadmor & Tetlock, 2006, p. 174)

The authors suggest that the integrative complexity of functioning will depend on the type of acculturation strategy people will choose when experiencing second culture exposure. That choice in turn hinges on the value and role conflicts activated by this exposure. If individuals internalize the values of both groups, that is become bicultural, these individuals will respond in more complex ways, as they need to cope with social and cultural conflict situations, than individuals who adhere to the values of one cultural group, following the separation or assimilation strategy. Up to this point, Tadmor and Tetlock's approach is very similar to the one outlined above. But then Tadmor and Tetlock introduce a new component: The choice of acculturation strategy depends on internal and external *accountability* pressures.

Accountability refers to the need to justify one's thoughts and actions to significant others. Accountability has been shown to motivate more complex, effort-demanding information processing, such as consideration of a variety of options and evidence, tolerance for inconsistency, receptiveness for new evidence (Tetlock, 1983). Cvetkovich (1978) for example, found that accountability leads to "less intuitive" and "more analytic" modes of thought (p. 149). Accountable subjects aim to comprehend and evaluate topic-relevant arguments. Accountability pressure is rooted in people's fundamental need for social approval: "Bad" judgements that could lead to embarrassment and loss of self-esteem should be avoided and "good" judgements, leading to praise and enhanced status are sought. Accountability pressure can come from inside or outside the individual. As Tadmor and Tetlock (2006) explained: "External accountability pressure refers to the matrix of interpersonal accountability relationships in which an individual is engaged with significant others" (p. 178). Within the cultural context, a single audience refers to one composed of perspectives with a unified cultural orientation, whereas a mixed audience refers to one composed of at least two distinct cultural perspectives. The Acculturation Complexity Model (ACM) is summarized in Fig. 5.5 and will be explained in more detail, below.

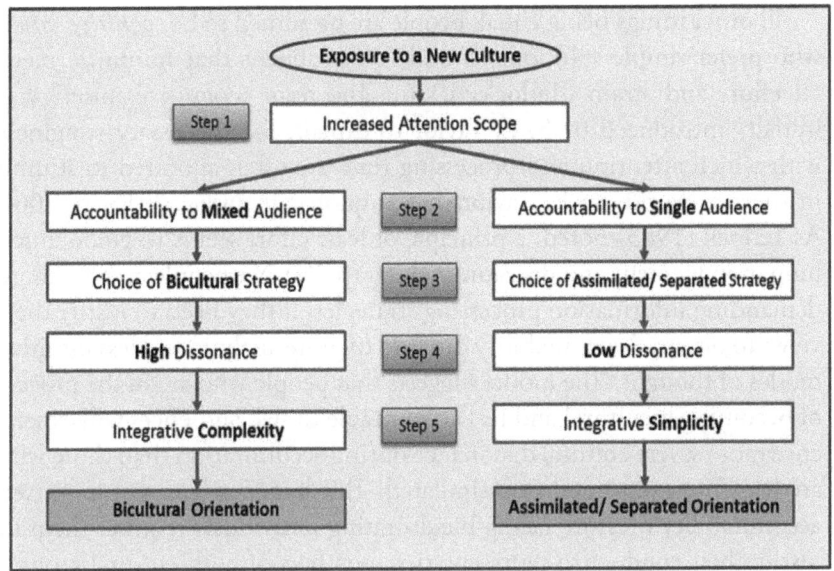

Fig. 5.5 Acculturation Complexity Model (ACM)—Model overview (*Source*: Tadmor & Tetlock [2006, p. 176])

As shown in Fig. 5.5, starting point is the *exposure to a new culture*. When people enter a new cultural setting, the cultural stimulus cues that would normally provide orientation and would automatically activate habits and responses are no longer present. An individual may switch to a more conscious information processing mode and the attention scope will increase as a result. Another consequence of moving to a different cultural context is that specific identity dimensions may become salient. Tadmor and Tetlock (2006) suggested a five-step progression of acculturation strategies. When people initially move to a new culture, they become sensitized to the value conflicts between their old and new cultures (Step 1). The type of accountability pressures encountered shapes their subsequent choice of acculturation strategy (Step 2) and determines the level of conflict experienced during second culture exposure (Step 3) and the cognitive effort required to resolve it (Step 4). Repeated exposure to cultural conflicts leads to the gradual development of automatic coping responses and relatively stable individual differences in integrative complexity (Step 5).

All other things being equal, people are presumed to be *cognitive misers* who prefer simple solutions to trade off problems that minimize mental effort and strain (Tetlock, 1986). The term "cognitive miser" was initially introduced by S. E. Taylor to explain the "necessary stinginess with which attention and processing time are often allocated to stimuli in the real world" (S.E. Taylor, 1981, quoted in Fiske, 2013, p. 206). As Tetlock (1983) noted, a principle of least effort seems to guide much human judgement and decision-making (p. 74). Yet people employ more demanding information processing strategies, if they need to justify their views to others. Accountability can lead to more analytic and less intuitive modes of thought. The model suggests that people who are in the process of becoming bicultural and feel accountable to two audiences will experience more severe cultural dissonance during acculturation than those who are becoming separated or assimilated. This happens because the mixed accountability pressure facing biculturating individuals requires them to justify their conduct to representative members of both cultural groups. By contrast, assimilating and separating individuals are held accountable to a single cultural constituency and experience less conflict.

When dissonance is low, people will prefer information that supports their opinion and will ignore alternative viewpoints. As Tadmor and Tetlock (2006) explain: "When strong dissonance is experienced, the simple solution of bolstering one culture's values and denying the other culture's values will not alleviate the conflict" (p. 182). Drawing on cognitive-consistency theories (e.g. Roccas & Brewer, 2002) the model stipulates that the more severe the cultural conflict, the greater the need to resort to more effortful, integratively complex solutions. Repeated exposure to cultural conflicts will lead to the development of increasingly automatic coping responses, either simple (for assimilating and separating individuals) or complex (for biculturating individuals). Whereas Benet-Martinez et al. (2006) argued that continued cultural frame switching accounts for cognitive complexity, Tadmor, Tetlock and Peng (2009) noted that the acculturative stress that biculturals experience which is not shared by monoculturals may also account for increased cognitive complexity (p. 108). The ACM model works best when the differences between two cultures are large enough to be challenging, but not overwhelming. As Tadmor and Tetlock (2006) noted, there appears to be an inverted U-shaped relationship between the size of the cultural differences experienced and the amount of cognitive change that could be expected. At the extreme difference end, the differences may be too large to be integrated. At the low difference end, even those with high trait complexity may be underwhelmed by the subtle differences.

Extension of Cognitive Complexity

In a next step, Tadmor et al. (2009) explored, whether the greater complexity of biculturals would generalize to other domains. The authors did indeed find that biculturals are more integrative complex *across* domains than assimilated or separated individuals. However, levels of complexity are lower for generalized complexity than for cultural complexity across participants. This finding supports the notion that the further removed the context is from the specific cultural domain, the lower the effects of acculturation on complexity. The authors did address the question of direction of causality, whether greater levels of complexity lead to biculturalism or whether biculturalism leads to greater complexity. Their findings point towards acculturation pressures driving complexity. The authors also noted that not all biculturals are equally complex. Biculturalism and complexity should thus not be viewed as synonymous, but are distinct, continuous variables.

Mere exposure to a second culture is insufficient to bring about the cognitive benefits associated with biculturalism. The key is how individuals internally represent the different cultures. As illustrated in Fig. 5.5, if individuals identify with and value one culture, this path leads to lower dissonance and lower complexity. If both cultures are held in high regard, sharper dissonance may be felt and greater pressure to be integratively complex. This ACM framework could also explain the higher cognitive complexity in low BII individuals found by Benet-Martinez et al. (2006): These individuals may still be in the process of becoming bicultural and have not yet resolved the tension between the two cultures. They could still be in the high dissonance phase (Step 4, Fig. 5.5) and once resolved, they may experience their cultures as more compatible.

Finally, Tadmor et al.'s (2009) research sheds some light on "marginals." As explained within the acculturation framework and illustrated in Fig. 5.3, marginalization is the acculturation orientation where an individual identifies with neither culture. ACM offers an alternative interpretative framework. Marginals' level of identification may be lower than that of biculturals, but the key is that they show an equal preference for both. Bourhis et al. (1997) introduced the distinction between "anomic" and "individualist" marginals. The anomic marginals can be understood in the traditional marginalized sense as being alienated individuals. The "individualists," however, may simply prefer to identify themselves as individuals rather than as members of one culture or another. They may want to be identified in terms of who they *are* rather than by genes or ancestors. As Tadmor et al. (2009) noted, these individuals will want to pick and choose from each culture in accordance with what they deem appropriate rather than allowing society to dictate ascribed expectations. This latter finding underscores once more that there are different ways of being bicultural.

Implications of Biculturalism

Thus both the BII and ACM model emphasize the *cognitive* benefits of biculturalism. As Tadmor et al. (2009) showed, the cognitive benefits extended beyond the cultural domain. Bicultural individuals develop higher order cognitive processes required to manage this complexity. Biculturals can thus possess greater empathy, flexibility and creativity as they integrate ideas in novel or more creative ways (Brannen & Thomas, 2010). In a recent series of studies Tadmor, Galinsky and Maddux (2012) demonstrated that biculturals exhibit more fluency, flexibility and novelty on a creative use task, as well as more innovation at work.

Biculturalism was also shown to have benefits for adjustment. The meta-analysis conducted by Nguyen and Benet-Martínez (2012), mentioned above, indicated that there is a significant, strong and positive association between biculturalism and adjustment. Nguyen and Benet-Martínez (2007) conjecture that the bicultural orientation leads to social and cognitive flexibility and a wider behavioural repertoire and competencies that buffer the bicultural individual against the psychological maladjustment (e.g. anxiety, loneliness) or socio-cultural maladjustment (e.g. interpersonal conflicts, intercultural miscommunication) that often characterize acculturation experience.

Bicultural individuals also have skills (such as language competence, cultural frame switching, intercultural sensitivity) that are crucial for success in our increasingly globalized business world. The role of bicultural individuals as mediators between and within cultures has been recognized for organizational performance. Pekerti and Thomas (2012) asserted that multicultural individuals are an asset for companies, as they are "creative, conscientious, empathetic, *unconstrained* (as they don't fit stereotypes), boundary spanners and synthesizers." The authors argue that multicultural individuals have to deal with competing identity pressures and are therefore also better placed to deal with competing perspectives in business situations. Working in international teams, biculturals may be more effective as they can build on their multicultural knowledge systems and integrate diverse information more effectively. They may work as a bridge in cultural diverse settings and become boundary spanners in that sense. However, biculturals may be perceived as experts in anything relating to either of their cultures. Given their hybrid upbringing this ascription cannot always be fulfilled (Brannen & Thomas, 2010).

Is there a limit to the number of cultures an individual can identify with? Pekerti and Thomas (2012) coined the term "n-cultural" individuals and state that the "n-cultural is capable of creatively synthesizing all facets of their multicultural identities through metacognition." I asked Dr. Pekerti whether he would put a limit on the cultures people can meaningfully integrate. In his reply, Dr. Pekerti conceded that the answer is not yet known but stated that "I am unwilling to put limits on the human brain and its capacity, especially since with some people and cultures it is possible that some of the cultures and associated axioms are complementary (...). If so then the number may get as high at 14 plus 2 etc." (personal communication, 29.07.2012). This answer clearly reflects an emphasis on cognitive abilities, at the expense of the affective components illustrated by the question: "But how many languages can you speak from the heart?" (Question addressed to panel during the symposium "Business in Luxembourg. Multilingualism: driver of competitiveness?" on 27.09.2011). As was noted above, there are indeed practice effects and the assertion that elements of cultural competence can be learnt. Perspective taking, for example, and the switching between cultural reference points are probably techniques that can be transferred to different cultural contexts. However, as noted by Tadmor and Tetlock, achieving bicultural orientation is an effortful process and value differentials between the cultures are an important factor which may impede integration. It is most likely a question of degree and further studies will need to determine the "n" of cultures a person can meaningfully integrate. A much wider range of factors would need to be taken into consideration.

Within the business context, bi- or multicultural individuals are increasingly valued. Biculturalism may also have significant implications for society as a whole. As Nguyen and Benet-Martínez (2007) stated, if biculturalism is found to be associated with better psychological adaptation, greater productivity and achievement and fewer interpersonal conflicts, then a public policy supporting bi-or multiculturalism might lead to greater national success and well-being (p. 109). The authors conclude by saying that an understanding of biculturalism can contribute to the understanding of intercultural relations. The techniques that acculturating individuals employ to negotiate and resolve cultural differences within themselves and with others may be applied to negotiate and resolve cultural differences across individuals and groups of individuals.

Empirical Study: On Being Bicultural

In this study, I wanted to test the theoretical models introduced above, empirically. How are different forms of culture contact experienced and reconciled by individuals? I turned to the European School of Luxembourg (EE) again to recruit participants. With its nationally diverse student body (see Chap. 4) the EE is an ideal place to research the question of what it means to be bicultural in a multicultural society. Students attending the EE experience different forms of second culture exposure—from birth, by having mixed nationality parents, by having moved to a different country and given the multinational composure of Luxembourg in general and the EE in particular, in day-to-day encounters. How do these different forms of culture contact affect the choice of acculturation strategies? As explained above, exposure to a different culture can lead to a bicultural orientation or an assimilated/separated monocultural orientation, depending on feeling accountable to a single or a mixed audience. Therefore, the first question concerns the orientation. The second question is how different forms of culture contact are experienced by the students: as harmonious and compatible or as conflicted and difficult to integrate.

Children growing up with mixed nationality parents are accountable to a mixed audience from birth and I expected that these students are likely to self-identify as bicultural. Many students attending the EE can be described as *Third Culture Kids* (TCKs, Pollock, van Ruth, van Reken, 2009) in the sense that they spend a significant part of their lives outside their parents' passport culture. Their stay in the current host country is often not permanent as it is linked to the parents' work contract. Given this fleetingness, there are lower accountability pressures to the host country. Therefore, for children of mononational[5] parents identification as monocultural is expected, even for children who were born in Luxembourg or have lived in Luxembourg for the most part of their lives. The following hypothesis was thus derived: Students with mixed nationality parents are more likely to self-identify in a bicultural way, whereas students with same nationality parents will self-label as monocultural (Hypothesis 1). An association between the type of culture contact exposure, through parents from birth versus moving to a different country in later life and the experience of culture contact as conflicted or not, is also expected. Following on from this, the second hypothesis was derived: Those who self-identify as bicultural will experience their two nationalities as harmonious and integrated. Monocultural students are more likely to experience the culture contact situation as conflictual (Hypothesis 2).

Method

Two measures were used to assess the students' bicultural orientation. In line with Benet-Martínez' (2012c) definition of biculturalism as "those who self-label as bicultural," a self-definition measure in the form of the

---

[5] The term "mono-national" is used here to emphasize that the parents have the same nationality. Since the term "bicultural" is used for identification with two or more cultures, the term "monocultural" will be used for the identification with one culture.

following question was included: "When people ask you 'What is your nationality?' How do you answer the question?" The second measure was the adapted BIIS-V2 scale[6] measuring bicultural identity integration. I considered the question of belonging an important issue on theoretical grounds (Fiske, 2010; Baumeister & Leary, 1995) and particularly relevant for the sample included in the study. Therefore, two items covering the sphere of belonging were added to the scale. An extensive demographic section covering language competence and use, length of stay in Luxembourg, nationality of students and parents was also included as well as questions relating to behavioural aspects such as spending time with people from different language sections within the school and with people outside school. The relationship between language use and personality, as discussed in the previous study was also assessed. The students also had the opportunity to add comments or observations in an open comments field. The questionnaires were made available in English, German and French and students had the choice between any of the language versions. High language competence in at least one of these languages could be expected amongst the EE students. The surveys were administered in the students' classrooms by a trilingual psychology student who had developed a script in the three languages to ensure

---

[6] An adaption of the Bicultural Integration Scale (BIIS-2R, Huynh & Benet-Martínez, 2010) was necessary for several reasons: Firstly, the BIIS-scale was originally designed for immigration-based acculturation involving two cultures, that is monocultural immigrants moving/being exposed to one other culture. This dual conceptualization does neither reflect the European school context or the wider demographic composition of Luxembourg, nor the composition of some of students' families. Secondly, within such a multinational context, separation or compartmentalization of nationalities is difficult to apply. Thirdly, the sample is composed of nationally heterogeneous students where scale items have to be formulated in a "culturally neutral" way. In the BIIS-2R scale, American cultural orientation is noted in the items as the "given" culture, with the respondents filling in their respective cultural background in spaces provided. Within the present sample, there is no single "given" culture. A final consideration concerns the question of conceptual equivalence in different languages. All material was made available in three languages (English, French and German), as a high level of competence could be expected in at least one of these languages by all European school students. The translations must capture the meaning of concepts in all three languages. We employed the method of translation and back-translation by native speakers and discussed with the respective native speakers whether the meaning of an item can be considered the same in all three languages. As a result of this process the items had to be adapted linguistically. The adapted items were also tested with target students for clarity. The final measure, consisted of 16 items, representing the two dimensions postulated by Huynh and Benet-Martínez (2010) plus two items tapping into the sphere of belonging (*No matter where I am, I am always the foreigner*, and *I never know where I belong*).

consistency in explaining the project in general and the procedure in filling in the questionnaire in particular. She was also able to answer any questions the students may have.

Description of the Student Sample

Two hundred and four students[7] attending the EE II[8] in their fourth and fifth year of their secondary education participated in the study. Just over half (54 %) of the participants were male. The average age was 15.2 years (SD = 0.84). All language sections of EE II (Danish, English, French, German, Greek and Italian) were included in the sample but the children represented a much wider range of nationalities, as well as their parents. Forty-four different countries of birth were given for mothers and 32 for fathers. Just under half of the students (n = 98) had parents of different nationalities. In terms of numbers of nationalities, 51 % of the students listed one, 38 % listed two and the rest three or more nationalities. A wide interpretation of nationality was possible, with students, for example, also naming the different nations of the UK.

Forty-eight percent of the students (n = 98) were born in Luxembourg. Only one student in the sample was born in Luxembourg to parents who were each also born in Luxembourg. Of those students who moved to Luxembourg, 39 % did so during pre-school, 37 % during primary and 25 % when at secondary school. All students indicated competence in a minimum of three languages with a mode of four languages. English is the one language all students mentioned, 90 % indicated competence in French and 65 % in German. The language competence was not formally assessed—the students were only asked to list "their" languages.

The majority of the students (n = 140) belong to a Christian religion; 44 stated that they have no religious affiliation and two students indicated that they belong to a non-Christian community. Parents enjoy a

---

[7] The project outline was presented to the Headmaster of the European School II and permission to conduct the study was granted. As subjects were minors, parent consent forms were distributed well ahead of the study. Only one parent refused participation of their child. The European school management organized and provided a timetable for the administration of the surveys during second language lessons.

[8] This second European School of Luxembourg (EEII) was opened in September 2012.

high educational level with 90 % of the mothers (89 % of the fathers) having completed secondary school or above. Sixty-five percent of the mothers (54 % of the fathers) were reported to hold a university degree, 10 % of the mothers and 18 % of the fathers even a doctoral degree. The majority of the students live with both parents (83 %), 12 % with their mother, 2 % with their father and the rest alternate between both.

Results

First the results of the self-labelling measure will be presented, followed by the relationship between the self-labelled groups and the bicultural integration scale measures. The relationship between other factors and the bicultural measures will then be explored, followed by an examination of the relationship between self-labelled groups and other measures. Finally, the results from the qualitative analysis will be presented.

Self-Labelling

All students answered the self-definition question and I categorized the answers in the following way: When students listed only one nationality (I am Greek; I am Czech) they were classified as "monocultural" ($n = 105$). The remaining answers ($n = 99$) were grouped into different subcategories. The largest category is made up of what I called "Blended" students ($n = 70$). Within this category some students ($n = 30$) *added* nationalities (English *and* Danish; Greek *and* a little bit Australian), a further group ($n = 25$) gave detailed percentages (2/4 Luxembourger, 1/4 German, 1/4 Italian or Française 50 %, Italienne 50 %) and 15 students provided "*hyphenated* identities" (Portuguese-Korean; Franconéerlandaise). Students within the "Blended" group describe themselves as a mixture of two or more nationalities, but they find different ways of expressing this. A second group ($n = 19$) stated their nationality and made reference to living in Luxembourg in the form of a "but" statement (from Malta, *but* I live in Luxembourg; Danish, *but* I live in Luxembourg). I labelled this group "Nationality but Luxembourg" students or "Nat but Lux" for short. A further group ($n = 8$) made reference to their origin in

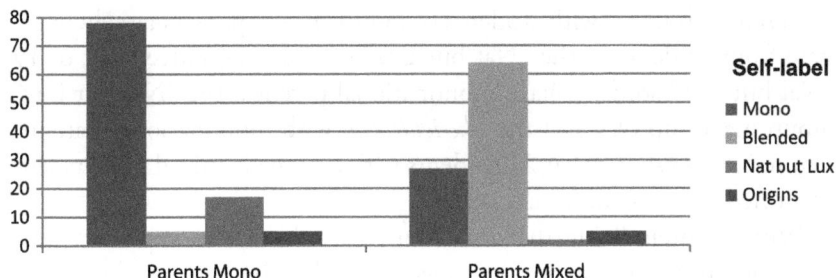

Fig. 5.6 Relationship between parents (mono vs. mixed) and self-labelling of students as mono- or pluricultural

addition to their nationality such as "Welsh, descendant from Scotland." Two students made references to supra-national groups (one European, and one global reference "An Afro-European who feels American"). The latter two groups were combined to form the "Origins" group (n = 10). The self-definition measure thus resulted in four broad categories: Mono (51 %), Blended (34 %), Nationality plus Lux (9 %) and Origins (5 %). Together, the three *non*-monocultural groups will be referred to as *pluricultural* (n = 99). The students born in Luxembourg are almost equally distributed between the two groups (n = 46 in the mono—and n = 52 in the pluricultural group).

There is a strong, statistically significant[9] association between having parents of mixed nationality and the students' self-definition as pluricultural. The χ^2 test exploring the relationship between the parents (mono vs. mixed) and the more differentiated breakdown of the self-label groups is also highly significant.[10] These findings strongly support Hypothesis 1, which postulated a strong association between the parental composition and self-labelling.

Even though there is a strong relationship between parents (mono vs. mixed national) and the self-labelling as mono- versus pluricultural there is not a one-to-one relationship. As Fig. 5.6 above illustrates, the pluricul-

---

[9] The χ^2 test (with Yates Continuity Correction) examining this relationship is highly significant χ^2 (1, 203) = 40.71, p < 0.001 *phi* = 0.46. The effect size is just short of a large effect using Cohen's (1988) criteria.
Cohen's (1988) effect size criteria for phi coefficient: 0.10 small effect, 0.30 medium effect and 0.50 large effect.
[10] χ^2 (3, 203) = 86.93, p < 0.001 and *phi* = 0.65 (large effect).

tural self-definitions with students of monocultural parents largely originate from students in the "Nat but Lux" category. Seventeen out of 19 "Nat but Lux" students have mononational parents. The "Nat but Lux" group makes up 69 % of the *pluriculturals* with mononational parents. Figure 5.6 also shows that 27 students with nationally mixed parents self-identified as monocultural.

Without prejudicing the discussion, I would like to explain at this stage briefly the rationale for categorizing the "Nationality, but I live in Luxembourg" students as "pluricultural." It could be argued that the "Nat but Lux" students actually self-define as monocultural. In contrast to the "Blended" group who use the conjunction "and" to describe themselves by placing both nationalities on an equal footing, the use of the conjunction "but" suggests the linkage of contrastive clauses. The students indicate that they *are* from one country, but they *live* in another. Because of this differentiation between being and living, it could be argued that the "Nat but Lux" students actually self-define as monocultural. However, as the students explicitly *acknowledge* the culture contact situation by stating that they live in Luxembourg, in contrast to the monocultural students, I decided to include the "Nat but Lux" students in the pluricultural group.

Being born in Luxembourg does not affect the self-labelling as mono- or pluricultural, but the time of moving to Luxembourg does. Students moving during pre-school are more likely to self-label as pluricultural than those moving to Luxembourg at a later stage.

Bicultural Identity Integration Scale (BIIS) Measures

As explained above, the bicultural identity measure assesses whether the nationalities are experienced as conflictual or harmonious and whether they are integrated or kept separate in daily life. In a first step I compared only two groups, the mono- and pluricultural students. I found no statistically significant differences for the Conflict, Separateness and Belongingness scales. On average, both student groups did not experience growing up with different nationalities as a source of conflict. Yet pluricultural students expressed higher levels of harmony and experience their nationalities as

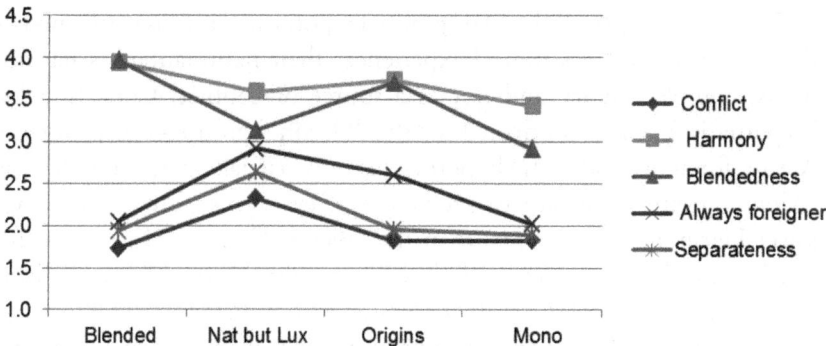

Fig. 5.7 Self-labelled groups and scores on biculturalism scales (scale range 1–5)

more blended than the monocultural students.[11] This latter finding is not surprising, as lower levels of Harmony/Blendedness can be expected for students who self-identify as monocultural.

In a second step the four groups formed following the self-labelling question were compared concerning the five biculturalism scale measures. One-way between group analyses of variance were conducted to explore the relationship between self-labelled group membership and the five biculturalism scale measures. Statistically significant differences were found for all five scales[12]: These results are visually represented in Fig. 5.7. The "Blended" students experience their nationalities as harmonious, blended and low in conflict. The "Origins" students are very similar to the "Blended" group except for higher mean scores on the Always foreigner scale. The "Mono" students expressed low conflict, but lower levels of Blendedness and Harmony. The "Nat but Lux" group had higher Conflict scores than the other three groups, coupled with lower scores in Harmony and Blendedness.

---

[11] Harmony scale $t(194)$ = -3.64, p < 0.001, η2 = 0.06, M_{Mono} = 3.43 (0.89), M_{Pluri} = 3.84 (0.68); Blendedness scale t(192) = -6.42, p < 0.001, η2= 0.18, M_{Mono}= 2.90 (1.03), M_{Pluri} = 3.78 (0.86). The mean difference of -0.87 for the "Blendedness" scale is substantial as indicated by the large effect size.

[12] Conflict scale $F(3, 186)$ = 3.2, p < 0.05 with an effect size calculated using $η^2$ = 0.05; Harmony F (3, 192) = 5.79, p < 0.01, $η^2$ = 0.08; Blendedness, $F(3, 190)$ = 18.14, p < 0.001, $η^2$ = 0.22; Foreigner $F(3, 195)$ = 4,56, p < 0.01, $η^2$ = 0.07 and Separateness $F(3,194)$ = 4.43, p < 0.01, $η^2$ = 0.06.

With regards to the "Blended" group, Hypothesis 2 is thus confirmed—this group of students indeed experiences their nationalities as harmonious, complementary and not as a source of conflict. Conditionally, Hypothesis 2 is also confirmed for the "Origins" group—except for the Always foreigner scale. The hypothesis is only partially confirmed for the "Mono" group. Contrary to prediction, they express low conflict, but lower Harmony/Blendedness than the "Blended" group. The "Nat plus Lux" group displays an entirely different pattern. These findings will be examined in more detail in the discussion section below, also taking into consideration findings regarding other factors influencing the bicultural integration measures.

The Influence of Other Factors on the Bicultural Measures

Gender, personality factors, as measured by the *Short Version of the Big Five Inventory* (Rammstedt & John, 2007) and length of stay in Luxembourg revealed no significant differences regarding the biculturalism scales. Yet differences were found for other measures:

Pride. There is a highly significant difference between the four self-labelled groups regarding the pride expressed in having more than one nationality. Students belonging to the "Blended" and "Origins" group expressed significantly higher pride in having more than one nationality than the other two groups.[13] The students were also asked if they consider it an advantage to have more than one nationality. The average mean for this item is $M = 4.13$, $SD = 0.90$ (Scale maximum = 5) indicating high overall agreement with this statement. The "Blended" group has a Mean score of $M = 4.35$ ($SD = 0.84$), which is significantly higher than that the "Mono" group $M = 3.95$ ($SD = 0.94$). The students were also asked if they consider it a disadvantage to have more than one nationality. The difference on this item (reverse scored) does not reach statistical significance, but as shown in Fig. 5.8 the "Nat but Lux" group disagreed less with this statement (without reaching statistical significance) than the other two

---

[13] $F(3,184)=18.33$, $p < 0.001$, $\eta^2 = 0.23$; post hoc Tukey HSD showed the mean for the "Blended" group $M = 4.46$ (0.83) and the "Origins" group $M = 4.50$ (0.71) are significantly higher than those for the other two groups.

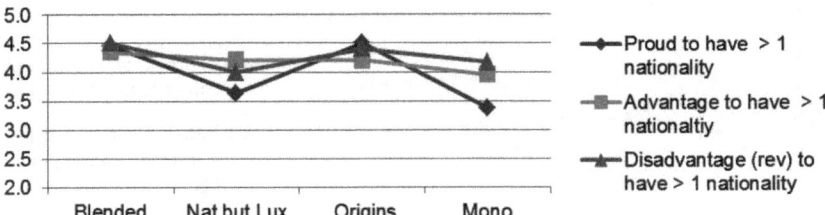

Fig. 5.8 Mean scores of mono- and pluricultural groups on Items regarding pride and advantages of having more than one nationality

pluricultural groups. The relationship between group membership and scores on the pride and advantages measures is illustrated in Fig. 5.8.

Contact Behaviour. Between group differences were found, when examining time spent with people from *other* language sections.[14] The "Nat but Lux" group showed significantly lower mean scores than the other three groups for all three measures as represented in Fig. 5.9.

Difficulty in stating nationality. Ninety-eight percent of the monocultural students found it easy or very easy to answer the question regarding their nationality. This figure drops to 80 % for the pluricultural students. The χ^2 test (with Yates continuity correction) examining the association between self-labelling and ease of description of nationality is highly significant, $\chi^2(1,203) = 12.64$, $p < 0.001$ *phi* = 0.27. The analysis of the pluricultural students shows that (only) 12 % of "blended" students indicated difficulty in stating their nationality, with proportionally more "Nat but Lux" students (37 %) and 40 % of the "Origin" students being amongst those who found it difficult to state their nationalities.

Language use. As in the previous study, students were asked to rate the statement "The language I am currently speaking influences the way I think and feel" (Item 1) and "If I change the language I speak, I also switch to a different culture" (Item 2). Item 1 reaches significance $F(3,200) = 3.84$, $p < 0.05$, $\eta^2 = 0.05$. and post hoc analysis shows that the

---

[14] The between group analysis reached statistical significance for "the amount of time spent with people from other language sections at break time " $F(3, 200) = 4.95$, $p < 0.01$, $\eta^2 = .07$; for "the amount of time spent with people for other language sections after school" $F(3, 200) = 2.89$, $p < 0.05$, $\eta^2 = 0.04$ and "the amount of time spent with Luxembourg nationals" $F(3, 200) = 4.92$, $p < 0.01$, $\eta^2 = 0.07$. Post hoc analyses using Tukey HSD showed that the "Nat but Lux" group showed significantly lower mean scores than the other three groups for all three measures.

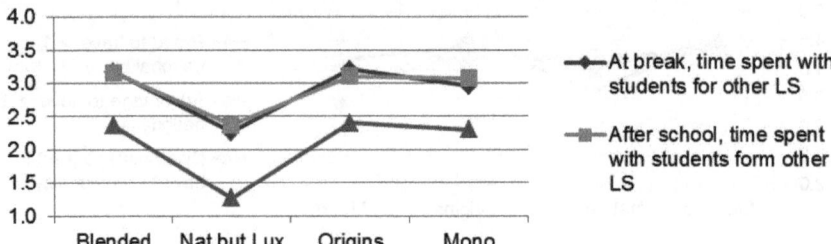

Fig. 5.9 Mean scores of mono- and pluricultural groups on Items regarding contact behaviour

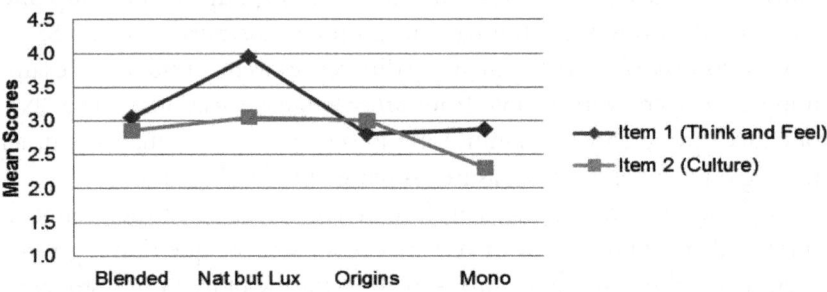

Fig. 5.10 Mean scores of mono- and pluricultural groups on Items related to language use

"Nat but Lux" group has significantly higher mean scores than the other two groups. Item 2 also reaches significance $F(3,200) = 6.46$, $p < 0.01$ $\eta^2 = 0.06$ and post hoc analysis shows that the monocultural group has significantly lower mean scores than the other three groups. These findings are represented in Fig. 5.10.

Multiculturalism. The relationship between self-labelling and the attitude towards the plurally composed society was assessed using the Multicultural Ideology Scale which will be explained in Chap. 6. The overall mean score for the scale was $M = 5.09$ $(SD = 0.81)$, indicating endorsement of multiculturalism. No group differences were found comparing the four self-labelled groups. As previous research on multiculturalism has indicated that immigrants tend to show higher endorsement of multiculturalism, I assessed the influence of country of birth (born in Lux vs. not born in Lux). A significant difference was

Table 5.2 Qualitative findings. Frequency of categories

Categories:	Merged categories	Monocultural	Pluri-cultural	Total	Merged cat. in %
LUX—acknowledgement/positive	Luxembourg	5	3	8	23
LUX—dissociation/negative		6	2	8	
Belonging—country of origin	Belonging	1	0	1	23
Belonging—relative relationship between two nationalities		2	6	8	
Belonging—always the foreigner		2	4	6	
Belonging—at home in 2 countries		1	0	1	
Difficulty in completing BII measure	Biculturalism measure	14	1	15	22
Regret at being monocultural	Advantages of being multicultural	2	0	2	19
Advantages of being multicultural		4	7	11	
Context determines nationality	Context	1	2	3	7
Cultural distance negative experience		0	2	2	
Pride	Pride	2	2	4	6
Other comment	other	1	0	1	
Total		41	29	70	100

found between students born in Luxembourg versus not in Luxembourg $t(186) = -2.67$, $p < 0.01$, $\eta^2 = 0.04$, with students born in Luxembourg showing lower mean scores: Lux born $M = 4.93$ ($SD = 0.82$), not Lux born $M = 5.24$ ($SD = 0.78$). However, the effect size is quite small.

Analysis of the Qualitative Comments

A total of 70 open comments or observations were made. Both, mono- and pluricultural students commented, with the "Nat but Lux" students being strongly represented with almost half of them providing comments. A content analysis of all 70 comments was conducted, which resulted in 13 categories. These were then combined into six merged categories. The categories alongside their frequency of mentions, given separately for mono- and pluricultural students are listed in Table 5.2.

The relationship with Luxembourg, as well as issues relating to belonging were the most frequently mentioned topics, each making up 23 % of the total. Monoculturals also commented on the difficulty in filling in the biculturalism scale measure (22 %). The next major category consists of comments in relation to advantages of having more than one nationality. It should also be noted that the relationship with Luxembourg was covered from different angles, with half of the comments being positive and the other half reflecting a distancing from the host country. The subject matter of "Belonging" is also broached in different ways with some students focusing on the problem of "always being the foreigner," "not to belong" whilst others describe their relationship with their different nationalities.

Discussion

The results of the study confirm a strong association between growing up with mixed nationality parents and self-identification in a bicultural way. Hypothesis 1 could thus be confirmed. Being born in Luxembourg does not affect the self-classification as pluri- or monocultural. However, if students have moved to Luxembourg after birth, the likelihood of self-classification as monocultural increases with the age of the student at the time of arrival in Luxembourg. Hypothesis 2 postulated that those who self-identify as bicultural will experience their two nationalities as harmonious and integrated, whereas monocultural students are more likely to experience the culture contact situation as conflictual. The self-labelling measure highlighted that there are different ways of being bicultural and in the following each group will be discussed separately.

The "Blended" group of students, who expressed their bicultural orientation by using the conjunction "and," by providing percentages or hyphenated identities, experienced their nationalities as predicted by Hypothesis 2. Having two (or more) nationalities is experienced as harmonious, complementary and not as a source of conflict. These students expressed pride in having more than one nationality and consider this an advantage. Judging by the number of languages students mentioned and the number of nationalities students listed, it can be inferred that within the context these students are growing up, language capability and having more than one nationality is a source of pride and distinction. The students experience the multinational status as a source of self-enhancement and uniqueness (Fiske, 2010). This feeling of pride is also reflected in the qualitative comments, for example: "Being multinational can get you raised eyebrows, for sure! But the ease in which blending with other people is so much of an advantage." The majority of the observations, pointing out advantages of having more than one nationality, originated from pluricultural students. For the majority of the "blended" students (88 %), stating their nationalities is not difficult. The question of "belonging" is solved by belonging to *two* cultures. On average, the "blended" students had low scores on the "Always foreigner" scale. The students have experience of and knowledge in their two cultures. The level of reflection and perspective taking was high as is exemplified by the self-definition of a 14 year old student "I am half German, half Italian—sometimes the other way round, depending on the situation, the place or the person I am talking to." To summarize, there is evidence that these students display the dimensions LaFromboise, Coleman and Gerton (1993) have identified as supporting the development of a bicultural identity: At the cognitive level, the students have knowledge of their cultures. At the affective level they show a positive attitude towards both nationalities—they consider both to be part of who they are. They have the language capability and can communicate in both cultures effectively. Furthermore, they can depend on support networks in both cultures (groundedness). Those students of blended national identity may find it easier to navigate through a multicultural environment as they are sensitive to cultural primes and navigate *automatically*, without conscious effort, between cultural frames. As exemplified by the quote above, perspective taking and switching is ingrained and applied automatically to the situation and context.

The "Origins" group is similar to the "Blended" group, but the relationship between the nationalities is expressed differently. Whereas the "Blended" group expresses a belonging in the here and now (I *am* Belgian and Italian), the "Origins" group derives their self-definition from historic roots (i.e. Francaise, mais d'origine belge et italienne[15]; Welsh, descending from Scotland; Italian, but my grandmother is English). This group has higher scores on the "Always foreigner" scale than the "Blended" group, but the difference in mean scores does not reach statistical significance. Within this relatively small group (*n* = 10), four students indicated that they find it difficult to state their nationality, but apart from these differences, the "Origins" group is very similar to the "Blended" group in terms of how the nationalities are experienced.

The "Nat but Lux" group, however, displays a different pattern. As noted above, this group was classified as pluricultural, because this group of students stated their (single) nationality, but acknowledges the culture contact situation of living in a different country. As illustrated in Fig. 5.7, these students display higher Conflict scores as well as lower Blendedness scores than the other pluricultural groups. Even though this group considers it an advantage to have more than one nationality, less pride is experienced than by the other two pluricultural groups (Fig. 5.8). Interestingly, this group also spends significantly less time with *other*-nationals than the other three groups (see Fig. 5.9) Yet this group agreed significantly more than the other three groups that the language they speak influences the way they think and feel (see Fig. 5.10). These findings can be explained within the Acculturation Complexity (ACM) framework (Tadmor & Tetlock, 2006). According to ACM accountability to two cultures fosters the development of a bicultural orientation. Most of the blended and origin students will have experienced exposure to different cultures from birth through their mixed

---

[15] French of Belgian and Italian origin.

nationality or origins of the parents. As it can be assumed that they feel accountable to both parents, it can be inferred that they also feel account-able to two cultures. The high Harmony and Blendedness scores as well as the self-definitions these students provided indicate that the "Blended/ Origins" students have internalized two cultures; having two nationalities is part of who they are. In contrast, the majority of the "Nat but Lux" students has mononational parents and has experienced the culture contact situation later in life. This culture contact situation has provoked reflection and the students experience dissonance—the culture contact situation is experienced as a source of conflict. This phase of dissonance is described by Tadmor and Tetlock (2006) as succeeding the culture contact experience. The "Nat but Lux" students don't experience the benefits of biculturalisms (i.e. source of pride, self-enhancement) and don't have the sense of belong-ing that the monocultural students express. They are caught between both worlds—their current state could be described as *moratorium* (Marcia, 1993). The culture contact situation provoked reflection (exploration), but commitment is vague at this stage and their orientation could go either way—as mono- or bicultural. The students also show what Benet-Martínez and colleagues (2002) have described as *reactance* or the reverse priming effect in biculturals as they spend *less* time with people from other nation-alities than any of the other groups. On the other hand they agree *more* than the other three groups that the language they speak influences the way they think and feel. Within this group, the level of reflection appears high—another indicator for the phase of *dissonance* as described by Tadmor and Tetlock (2006). These students could be on their way to a bicultural orientation as expressed by one "Nat but student": "Although I live in a foreign country, I still feel connected to my country of origin, but I con-sider Luxembourg as a big part of who I am and have become" or possibly more of a monocultural orientation: "It is an advantage to be born/live in Luxembourg and experience many different cultures and be able to speak different languages, but I think of myself as Irish."

This latter quote illustrates the difference between the "Nat but Lux" group and the self-labelled monocultural students. The student quoted above acknowledges the culture contact situation—which the monocultural students do not, at least as examined by the self-label measure. When designing the questionnaire we realized that the biculturalism measure may be more difficult to complete for children of mononational parents. On the other hand, there was only one student who was "fully" Luxembourgish, if defined in terms of country of birth of student and parents. All other students will have at least experienced second culture exposure by living in Luxembourg. The majority of the monocultural students also answered the biculturalism measure with this in mind. However, 13 % of the monocultural students commented on the difficulty in completing the biculturalism scale measure (see qualitative analysis).

In the preceding study, language capability was identified as a necessary, but not sufficient condition for being bicultural. The analysis of the qualitative comments in this pilot study had shown that the condition of "having lived in two cultures" was frequently cited as a necessary condition for being considered bicultural. As was already outlined above, students of mixed national parents are more likely to self-identify in a bicultural manner. The opposite is also true—students of mononational parents are less likely to self-identify in a bicultural manner, even if they have lived in a different country for most of their lives. Judging by the analysis of the open comments, when students point out (and underline) the fact that they are only of <u>one</u> nationality, the implied assumption in the minds of these students is that having parents of mixed nationality is the necessary condition to qualify as a "bicultural" student. Living in a different country is not a sufficient condition for self-labelling as pluricultural. Within this context, growing up in a mixed national family is the necessary condition to be considered bicultural. This may be a reflection of the TCK phenomenon. For those children, Luxembourg is a transient place and accountability pressures to their current country of residence may be low. This is also reflected in some of the open comments regarding Luxembourg—it is a country where they happen to live, but not a country these TCKs identify with. Only three of the 105 monocultural students indicated that they find it difficult to state their nationality. Thus the ease of self-labelling is associated with being mononational. The conflict scores, as measured by the biculturalism scale measures, did not differ from the "Blended/Origins" group. Based on these scores, Hypothesis 2 cannot be confirmed for this group. However, there are also different ways of being monocultural. As evidenced by some of the open comments, some of the monocultural students seem to be less aware of culture contact situation and live as monoculturals in a third country. Others are very conscious of living in a different country and for those "always being the foreigner" is experienced as stressful. As anticipated, the question of belonging was broached by students—23 % of the open comments refer to the topic of "belonging."

In terms of attitude towards living in plural society—no significant difference between the mono- and pluricultural students was found. With an average score of M = 5.09, SD = 0.81 the students *endorse* living in a plurally composed society. This average score is higher than those found in empirical studies in the Netherlands, where respondents showed neutral scores towards multiculturalism as measured by the MIS scale (Arends-Tóth & van de Vijver, 2003; Breugelmans et al., 2009; Schalk-Soekar et al., 2009). The country of birth (Luxembourg vs. not Luxembourg) did not influence any of the biculturalism measures. However, interestingly, the "immigration" effect was shown for the multiculturalism scale, with those students having moved to Luxembourg having significantly higher scores than those who were born in Luxembourg. Monocultural students also consider it an advantage to have more than one nationality, but they have significantly lower scores on this item than the "Blended" group, although the effect size is small. In terms of time spent with people with other language sections/nationalities, the monoculturals don't differ from the "Blended/Origin" group. However, the monoculturals agree significantly less than the pluriculturals with the statement that the language implies a cultural switch. Thus the monocultural students experience language less as a prime for cultural frame switching than the pluricultural students.

Gender does not influence self-labelling as mono- or pluricultural and only had a minor influence on the biculturalism scales. Personality traits, as measured by the short personality inventory scale, did not have any influence on the biculturalism measures. The European School language sections did not differ regarding the biculturalism measures with one small exception: the participants from the Danish section recorded a significantly higher mean score on the "Always foreigner scale" than those from the French language section. With France and Belgium being geographically so close to Luxembourg and French being one of the official languages of Luxembourg, the question of "belonging" may be less of an issue for these francophone students than for the Danish students as is exemplified by a quote from a Danish language section student: "I feel Danish when I'm in Lux, because I can't speak the language, but I feel more Luxembourgish when I'm in Denmark".

The student sample is quite homogeneous—except for the range of nationalities. The educational level of the parents is very high and only two students indicated a non-Christian background. Even though the range of nationalities is wide, most children have a European background. Thus the cultural distance as expressed in the cultural distance map by Inglehart and Welzel (2010), introduced in Chap. 2, is in fact quite close. Therefore, the value structures of the nationalities are quite close and thus the level of dissonance in negotiating these will be more manageable. This could also explain why the conflict scores were low for all groups, except for the "Nat but Lux" students. This relative homogeneity of the sample may be considered an advantage as other confounding factors are eliminated. It would be interesting to replicate this study with a more diverse student body in terms of socio-economic background and wider cultural distance between countries involved.

Conclusion

One student commented: "I found that this survey was a bit pointless for someone who only has one nationality and the questions concerning culture were a bit strange, because I've never really thought that much about it and am still unsure that it really is and also found it puzzling about how personality would be affecting or affected by culture." Another student commented: "Ich habe keinen 'richtigen' Bezug zu einem Land, sondern wohl eher zu einer Sprache oder Menschen, die ich dort kenne. Ich empfinde den Kontakt zu verschiedenen Kulturen als eine Bereicherung, die Einfluss auf meine Persönlichkeit hat. Ich bin stolz darauf, auf eine europäische Schule zu gehen, weil es einem 'viel' mitgibt und durch die Vielfältigkeit an Sprachen immer Neues zu entdecken gibt. Man muss auch mehr nachdenken und sich anpassen können an verschiedene Gruppen, um sich verständigen zu können."[16]

These two students attend the same school and are of roughly the same age, but culture contact is experienced completely differently. The first quote originates from a student of mononational parents. For this student, the culture contact situation is seemingly not a salient issue. For other students with mononational parents, in particular the "Nat but Lux" group, the culture contact experience triggered reflection. Within the present research project it can only be observed that children of mononational parents may react very differently to the culture contact situation. Further research is required to investigate which individual difference factors or context variables trigger reflection—leading some students to embrace the culture contact experience, whilst others remain mononational within the multicultural environment.

The study also confirmed the ACM model, which postulates that being accountable to a mixed audience furthers a bicultural orientation. The study demonstrated that students of mixed national parents are very likely to self-identify as pluricultural. Being of more than one nationality is experienced as enrichment, a source of pride. Mentions of supra-national categories were scarce. Only one student (out of 204) mentioned "European" as a self-label and one other student described herself as "multi-cultural, an afro-European who feels American." This finding mirrors that of the empirical Study presented in Chap. 4 where none of the European School children mentioned "European" in their spontaneous self-concept. Thus becoming "in mind European," as hoped for by the founding fathers of the European Union, does not find its expression in terms of self-identification with the supra-national category. This could also be explained by differential information processing. The supra-national category is rational, cognitively construed, whereas belonging to a "homeland" has emotional connotations (Epstein, 1979, 1994). This may also explain why the students don't lose the connection

---

[16] I don't have a "real" relationship with a country, but rather with a language or with people whom I know there. I experience the contact to different cultures as an enrichment, which influences my personality. I am proud to go to a "European school" because you can learn a lot and the multitude of languages always offer the opportunity to discover something new. One has to reflect more and to be able to adapt to different groups to get along.

with their homeland. A large number of students also go beyond a self-identification in terms of a single national category. These students lead the way in terms of going beyond expressions of mononationalism and provide reflected bicultural self-definitions as a matter of course. As mentioned above, students, on average, expressed a positive attitude towards living in a plurally composed society and the pluricultural students show that it is *possible* to identify with more than one nationality. Some of these students resent being forced into one category and demonstrate that "old" models of nationality don't suffice in today's globalized world. The students incorporate different nationalities and experiences in their sense of self. They integrate complexity—it is for the others to adjust, as exemplified by another quote by a 14-year-old student: "My mother is German, my father is Irish, I was born in England and I grew up in Luxembourg. You decide! PS. If all these don't work for you, then Luxembourgish."

Summary and Conclusions

Biculturalism is closely intertwined with acculturation and specifically associated with the integration acculturation orientation—the extent to which an individual is motivated or allowed to retain identification and involvement with the culture of origin and the mainstream culture. Domain-specificity also applies to biculturalism. As Nguyen and Benet-Martínez (2007) emphasized, bicultural individuals do not internalize their two cultures globally and uniformly. Experimental studies have shown that individuals can hold two or more cultural orientations simultaneously and that bicultural individuals can move between their orientations by engaging in cultural frame switching (CFS, Hong et al., 2000). CFS in turn impacts on cognitive complexity.

Benet-Martinez and her collaborators introduced the construct of bicultural identity integration (BII), referring to the degree of compatibility perceived between two cultures. BII is composed of two independent components—cultural distance and cultural conflict. BII has been shown to moderate CFS. Both high and low BII individuals have access to multiple cultural knowledge systems which they have learned as a result of exposure to more than one culture. This research on BII has extended the understanding of bicultural individuals to show how the degree of integration of bicultural identities relates to behavioural, cognitive and other psychological variables. Benet-Martinez et al. (2006) showed, for example, that cultural information is self-relevant, highly accessible in memory and more richly elaborated. Contextual cultural clues are interpreted as primes for CFS. CFS in turn may help biculturals to develop more integrated cultural schemas.

One aspect related to biculturalism not yet mentioned is what Benet-Martínez and Haritatos (2005) have referred to as the "dichotomy and paradox" experience (p. 1019). Biculturals may feel special and confused at the same time, being both cultures at the same time and neither. Thus, biculturalism can be a source of self-enhancement and pride and at the same time challenge the feeling of belonging and become a source of identity confusion and value clashes. This source of dissonance is a central theme of the ACM. Tadmor and Tetlock emphasize the importance of accountability pressures in determining which acculturation route an individual may follow. Individuals who feel accountable to two cultures are likely to feel more dissonance, but once this has been resolved it will lead to integrative complexity. The authors acknowledge that the process of negotiating and balancing two cultural value systems may be stressful. Once resolved, the greater integrative complexity achieved in the cultural domain may extend to other areas and has also been shown to boost creativity. The mere exposure to another culture does not produce a multicultural individual. An individual has to feel attachment with and loyalties to both cultures.

The deliberations above have shown that there is clearly more than one way of being bicultural. One of the reasons why research on biculturalism was discussed in detail is that "an understanding of biculturalism can contribute to the understanding of intercultural relations" (Nguyen & Benet-Martínez, 2007, p. 110). As these authors explained the techniques that acculturating individuals employ to negotiate and resolve cultural differences within themselves and with others may be applied to negotiate and resolve cultural differences across individuals and groups of individuals. The empirical study therefore explored how adolescents growing up in a multinational context experience and organize their nationalities. Bicultural identity integration was measured using an adapted version of

BIIS-V2 and a self-definition measure. The results are interpreted in the ACM framework. In this chapter the focus was on cultural plurality at the individual level. In the next chapter, cultural plurality is extended to the collective or society level.

References

Adler, P. S. (1975). The transitional experience: An alternative view of culture shock. *Journal of Humanistic Psychology*, *15*, 13–23. Retrieved from http://psycnet.apa.org/psycinfo/1976-27992-001

Arends-Tóth, J., & van de Vijver, F. J. R. (2003). Multiculturalism and acculturation: Views of Dutch and Turkish-Dutch. *European Journal of Social Psychology*, *33*(2), 249–266. doi:10.1002/ejsp.143.

Baumeister, R. F. (1986). *Public self and private self.* New York: Springer.

Baumeister, R. F., & Leary, M. R. (1995). The need to belong: Desire for interpersonal attachments as a fundamental human motivation. *Psychological Bulletin*, *117*(3), 497–529. doi:10.1037/0033-2909.117.3.497.

Benet-Martínez, V. (2012a). *Bicultural identify integration: Components, dynamics, correlates.* 21st International Congress for Cross-Cultural Psychology, 17–21 July 2012. Stellenbosch, South Africa.

Benet-Martínez, V. (2012b). Speaking your mind. In: http://www.psychologicalscience.org/index.php/publications/observer/2012/may-june-12/speaking-your-mind.html

Benet-Martínez, V. (2012c). Multiculturalism: Cultural, social, and personality processes. In K. Deaux & M. Snyder (Eds.), *Handbook of personality and social psychology* (pp. 623–648). Oxford, UK: Oxford University Press.

Benet-Martínez, V., & Haritatos, J. (2005). Bicultural identity integration (BII): Components and psychosocial antecedents. *Journal of Personality*, *73*(4), 1015–1049. doi:10.1111/j.1467-6494.2005.00337.x.

Benet-Martínez, V., & John, O. P. (1998). Los Cinco Grandes across cultures and ethnic groups: Multitrait multimethod analyses of the Big Five in Spanish and English. *Journal of Personality and Social Psychology*, *75*(3), 729–750. doi:10.1037//0022-3514.75.3.729.

Benet-Martinez, V., Lee, F., & Leu, J. (2006). Biculturalism and cognitive complexity: Expertise in cultural representations. *Journal of Cross-Cultural Psychology*, *37*(4), 386–407. doi:10.1177/0022022106288476.

Benet-Martinez, V., Leu, J., Lee, F., & Morris, M. W. (2002a). Negotiating biculturalism: Cultural frame swsitching in biculturals with oppositional versus compatible cultural identities. *Journal of Cross-Cultural Psychology, 33*(5), 492–516. doi:10.1177/0022022102033005005.

Berry, J. W. (1990). Psychology of acculturation. In J. Berman (Ed.), *Cross-cultural perspectives. Nebraska symposium on motivation* (Vol. 37, pp. 201–234). Lincoln: University of Nebraska Press.

Bourhis, R., Moise, L., Perreault, S., & Senécal, S. (1997). Towards an interactive acculturation model: A social psychological approach. *International Journal of Psychology, 32*(6), 369–386. doi:10.1080/002075997400629.

Brannen, M. Y., & Thomas, D. C. (2010). Bicultural individuals in organizations: Implications and opportunity. *International Journal of Cross Cultural Management, 10*(1), 5–16. doi:10.1177/1470595809359580.

Breugelmans, S. M., van de Vijver, F. J. R., & Schalk-Soekar, S. G. S. (2009). Stability of majority attitudes toward multiculturalism in the Netherlands between 1999 and 2007. *Applied Psychology, 58*(4), 653–671. doi:10.1111/j.1464-0597.2008.00368.x.

Cheng, C.-Y., Sanchez-Burks, J., & Lee, F. (2008). Connecting the dots within: Creative performance and identity integration. *Psychological Science, 19*(11), 1178–1184. doi:10.1111/j.1467-9280.2008.02220.x.

Cohen, J. W. (1988). *Statistical power analysis for the behavioral sciences* (2nd ed.). Hillsdale, NJ: Lawrence Erlbaum Associates.

Cvetkovich, G. (1978). Cognitive accommodation, language, and social responsibility. *Social Psychology, 41*(2), 149–155. doi:10.2307/3033574.

Epstein, S. (1979). Entwurf einer Integrativen Persönlichkeitstheorie. In S. H. Filipp (Ed.), *Selbstkonzept-Forschung: Probleme, Befunde, Perspektiven* (pp. 15–45). Stuttgart: Klett-Cotta.

Epstein, S. (1994). Integration of the cognitive and the psychodynamic unconscious. *The American Psychologist, 49*(8), 709–724. doi:10.1037/0003-066X.49.8.709.

Fishman, J. (1980). Bilingualism and biculturism as individual and as societal phenomena. *Journal of Multilingual & Multicultural Development, 1*(1), 3–5.

Fiske, S. T. (2010). *Social beings: Core motives in social psychology.* Hoboken, NJ: Wiley.

Fiske, S. T. (2013). *Social cognition: From brains to culture.* London: Sage.

Fiske, S. T., & Taylor, S. E. (1991). *Social cognition.* New York: Mcgraw-Hill.

Guo, X., Suarez-Morales, L., Schwartz, S. J., & Szapocznik, J. (2009). Some evidence for multidimensional biculturalism: Confirmatory factor analysis and measurement invariance analysis on the Bicultural Involvement Questionnaire–Short Version. *Psychological Assessment, 21*(1), 22.

Hall, S. (1997). *Representation: Cultural representations and signifying practices.* Bristol, PA: The Open University.

Haritatos, J., & Benet-Martinez, V. (2002). Bicultural identities: The interface of cultural, personality, and socio-cognitive processes. *Journal of Research in Personality, 36*(6), 598–606. doi:10.1016/S0092-6566(02)00510-X.

Hong, Y., Morris, M. W., Chiu, C., & Benet-Martínez, V. (2000). Multicultural minds: A dynamic constructivist approach to culture and cognition. *American Psychologist, 55*(7), 709–720. doi:10.1037//0003-066X.55.7.709.

Hong, Y.-Y., Benet-Martinez, V., Chiu, C.-Y., & Morris, M. W. (2003). Boundaries of cultural influence: Construct activation as a mechanism for cultural differences in social perception. *Journal of Cross-Cultural Psychology, 34*(4), 453–464. doi:10.1177/0022022103034004005.

Huynh, Q.- L. (2009). Variations in biculturalism: Measurement, validity, mental and physical health correlates, and group differences (Doctoral dissertation, University of California, Riverside).

Huynh, Q.- L., & Benet-Martínez, V. (2010). Bicultural identity integration scale—version 2: Development and validation. Manuscript in preparation.

Inglehart, R., & Welzel, C. (2010). Changing mass priorities: The link between modernization and democracy. *Perspectives on Politics, 8*(2), 551–567. doi:10.1017/S1537592710001258.

Kemmelmeier, M. (2004). Language and self-construal priming: A replication and extension in a Hong Kong sample. *Journal of Cross-Cultural Psychology, 35*(6), 705–712. doi:10.1177/0022022104270112.

Kuhn, M. H., & McPartland, T. S. (1954). An empirical investigation of self-attitudes. *American Sociological Review, 19*(1), 68–76. doi:10.2307/2088175.

LaFromboise, T., Coleman, H. L. K., & Gerton, J. (1993). Psychological impact of biculturalism: Evidence and theory. *Psychological Bulletin, 114*(3), 395–412. doi:10.1037/0033-2909.114.3.395.

Marcia, J. E. (1993). The ego identity status approach to ego identity. In J. E. Marcia, A. S. Waterman, D. R. Matteson, S. L. Archer, & J. L. Orlofsky (Eds.), *Ego identity* (pp. 3–21). New York: Springer.

Nguyen, A.-M. D., & Benet-Martinez, V. (2012). Biculturalism and adjustment: A meta-analysis. *Journal of Cross-Cultural Psychology, 44*(1), 122–159. doi:10.1177/0022022111435097.

Nguyen, A.-M. D., & Benet-Martínez, V. (2007). Biculturalism unpacked: Components, measurement, individual differences, and outcomes. *Social and Personality Psychology Compass, 1*(1), 101–114. doi:10.1111/j.1751-9004.2007.00029.x.

Northover, M. (1988). Bilingual or "dual linguistic identities"? In J. W. Berry & R. Annis (Eds.), *Ethnic psychology: Research and practice with immigrants, refugees, Native peoples, ethnic groups and sojourners* (pp. 207–216). Berwyn, PA: Swets North America.

Pekerti, A. A., & Thomas, D. C. (2012). *n -Culturals : Modeling the multicultural experience.* 21st International Congress for Cross-Cultural Psychology, 17–21 July 2012, Stellenbosch, South Africa.

Phinney, J. S., & Devich-Navarro, M. (1997). Variations in bicultural identification among African American and Mexican American adolescents. *Journal of Research on Adolescence, 7*(1), 3–32. doi:10.1207/s15327795jra0701_2.

Pollock, D. C., Van Ruth, E. R., & Van Reken, R. E. (2009). *Third culture kids: Growing up among worlds.* Boston/London: Nicholas Brealey Publishing.

Ramírez-Exparza, N. (2012). Speaking your mind. Retrieved from: http://www. psychologicalscience.org/index.php/publications/observer/2012/may-june-12/speaking-your-mind.html

Ramírez-Esparza, N., Gosling, S. D., Benet-Martínez, V., Potter, J. P., & Pennebaker, J. W. (2006). Do bilinguals have two personalities? A special case of cultural frame switching. *Journal of Research in Personality, 40*(2), 99–120. doi:10.1016/j.jrp.2004.09.001.

Rammstedt, B., & John, O. P. (2007). Measuring personality in one minute or less: A 10-item short version of the Big Five Inventory in English and German. *Journal of Research in Personality, 41*(1), 203–212. doi:10.1016/j. jrp.2006.02.001.

Roccas, S., & Brewer, M. B. (2002). Social Identity complexity. *Personality and Social Psychology Review, 6*(2), 88–106. doi:10.1207/S15327957 PSPR0602_01.

Ross, M., Xun, W. Q. E., & Wilson, A. E. (2002). Language and the bicultural self. *Personality and Social Psychology Bulletin, 28*(8), 1040–1050. doi:10.1177/01461672022811003.

Routledge, C., Arndt, J., Wildschut, T., Sedikides, C., Hart, C. M., Juhl, J., et al. (2011). The past makes the present meaningful: Nostalgia as an existential resource. *Journal of Personality and Social Psychology, 101*(3), 638–652. doi:10.1037/a0024292.

Schalk-Soekar, S. R. G., Breugelmans, S. M., & van de Vijver, F. J. R. (2009). Support for multiculturalism in The Netherlands. UNESCO. Retrieved from http://onlinelibrary.wiley.com/doi/10.1111/j.1468-2451.2009.00698.x/full

Sedikides, C., Wildschut, T., Routledge, C., Arndt, J., & Zhou, X. (2009). Buffering acculturative stress and facilitating cultural adaptation: Nostalgia as a psychological resource. Retrieved form: http://psycnet.apa.org/psycinfo/2008-17689-021

Tadmor, C. T., Galinsky, A. D., & Maddux, W. W. (2012). Getting the most out of living abroad: Biculturalism and integrative complexity as key drivers of creative and professional success. *Journal of Personality and Social Psychology, 103*(3), 520–542. doi:10.1037/a0029360.

Tadmor, C. T., Tetlock, P. E., & Peng, K. (2009). Acculturation strategies and integrative complexity: The cognitive implications of biculturalism. *Journal of Cross-Cultural Psychology, 40*(1), 105–139. doi:10.1177/0022022108326279.

Tadmor, C. T., & Tetlock, P. E. (2006). Biculturalism: A model of the effects of second-culture exposure on acculturation and integrative complexity. *Journal of Cross-Cultural Psychology, 37*(2), 173–190. doi:10.1177/0022022105284495.

Tetlock, P. E. (1983). Accountability and complexity of thought. *Journal of Personality and Social Psychology, 45*(1), 74–83. doi:10.1037//0022-3514.45.1.74.

Tetlock, P. E. (1986). A value pluralism model of ideological reasoning. *Journal of Personality and Social Psychology, 50*(4), 819–827. doi:10.1037//0022-3514.50.4.819.

Thomas, D. C. (1998). The expatriate experience: A critical review and synthesis. *Advances in international comparative management, 12,* 237–273.

Trafimow, D., Silverman, E. S., Fan, R. M.-T., & Fun Law, J. S. (1997). The effects of language and priming on the relative accessibility of the private self and the collective self. *Journal of Cross-Cultural Psychology, 28*(1), 107–123. doi:10.1177/0022022197281007.

Trimble, J. E. (1981). Value differentials and their importance in counselling American Indians. In P. B. Pedersen, W. J. Lonner, J. G. Dragnus, & J. E. Trimble (Eds.), *Counselling across cultures* (pp. 203–226). Honolulu: Sage.

Van Der Zee, K. I., & Van Oudenhoven, J. P. (2000). The multicultural personality questionnaire: A multidimensional instrument of multicultural effectiveness. *European Journal of Personality, 14*(4), 291–309. doi:10.1002/1099-0984(200007/08).

Van Oudenhoven, J. P., Mol, S., & Van der Zee, K. I. (2003). Study of the adjustment of Western expatriates in Taiwan ROC with the multicultural personality questionnaire. *Asian Journal of Social Psychology, 6*(2), 159–170. doi:10.1111/1467-839X.t01-1-00018.

6

On Living in a Multicultural Environment

Introduction

In Chap. 3 the origins of multiculturalism were explained. As was noted, multiculturalism can have different meanings—referring to the demographic composition of society, a policy promoting diversity and equality and finally an *attitude* towards a culturally plural society. Whereas acculturation refers to the psychological consequences of prolonged exposure to another culture, multiculturalism at the individual level refers to the acceptance of and support for the culturally plural composition of societies at large (Celenk & van de Vijver, 2014). The focus of this chapter is the individual living in a multicultural environment and the factors influencing an individual's attitude towards a plurally composed society. First, multiculturalism as a psychological concept will be explained, before two empirical studies will be presented. These studies investigate the attitude to multiculturalism, and in particular specific factors thought to influence this attitude. Previous studies have shown that even though

© The Author(s) 2016
E. Murdock, *Multiculturalism, Identity and Difference,*
DOI 10.1057/978-1-137-59679-6_6

multiculturalism is a broad, multifaceted concept, the attitude towards multiculturalism is actually a unidimensional construct, even though the support for multiculturalism across domains varies.

Multiculturalism as an Ideology

Multiculturalism as a psychological concept denotes "an *attitude* related to the political ideology, which refers to the acceptance of and support for, the culturally heterogeneous society" (italics in the original, van de Vijver et al., 2008, p. 93). Before discussing multiculturalism as an attitude, a brief detour will be made to explain multiculturalism as an ideology since the ideology may influence the attitude towards multiculturalism. Multiculturalism as an ideology entails that cultural differences *should* be accepted and valued by all groups of society. Ideologies are *normative* in nature and ideologies will determine acculturation options for minorities. In Chap. 3 the Interactive Acculturation Model (IAM, Bourhis et al., 1997) was mentioned as an example for an acculturation model which takes context considerations explicitly into consideration. The model holds that there is a relationship between immigration and government policies on integration and acculturation orientations of both the majority and immigrant communities. The model distinguishes four ideologies, which differ in their approaches of how to accommodate immigrants. The ideologies and associated principles are summarized in Table 6.1. The ideologies are arranged hierarchically going left to right,

Table 6.1 Multiculturalism ideologies as identified by the IAM

Principle:	Pluralism ideology	Civic ideology	Assimilation ideology	Ethnist ideology
Adoption of public values and laws of the host country by immigrants	✓	✓	✓	☐
Respect of private values of the immigrants	✓	✓	x	x
Public funds spent on private activities of immigrants	✓	x	x	x

with increasing pressure put on immigrants by the nation state to adopt values of the main society and leaving less room for cultural expression (van de Vijver et al., 2006).

Canadian multiculturalism policies are derived from the pluralism ideology. Immigrants are expected to participate in Canadian civic life, but the heritage culture is explicitly respected and public funds are made available both for language classes and sustaining heritage-related activities. The extreme contrast is provided by the ethnist ideology, which is based on *ius sanguinis*. Only blood members can gain full recognition and become rightful members of the host society. According to this *exclusive* ideology, immigrants cannot become equal members of the society. This is indicated by the "blank" square in Table 6.1.

Majority and minority members will hold implicit assumptions towards acculturation processes in culturally diverse societies. The ideologies about multiculturalism will act as guiding principles of how to treat immigrants and what in turn is expected of them. Conversely, the ideology will influence the range of acculturation choices available to immigrants, but will also impact on the majority attitude regarding the acculturation behaviour expected by immigrants. The perception of immigrants by the larger society will thus also influence the acculturation strategies open to minority groups. Under both the pluralism and civic ideology, immigrants are expected to abide by civic rules governing society in public, but cultural maintenance in the private sphere is respected. Under the pluralism ideology cultural maintenance is supported by public funding. Within the assimilationist framework, adaptation to the host society is also expected in the private domain. Under the ethnist ideology complete assimilation is expected, even though immigrants can never become rightful members of the host society.

As discussed in Chap. 3, Berry's fourfold model provides a useful systematization of acculturation orientation options. The ideologies differentiated by the Interactive Acculturation Model (IAM) highlight the normative ideas behind the concept of multiculturalism. The multifaceted nature of multiculturalism was also noted: Multiculturalism ideologies include ideas about minority acculturation as well as mainstream support; they cover life in the public domain as well as the private sphere, and they are about policies and individual rights (van de Vijver et al., 2008).

The preferred ideology will guide majority expectations in relation to minority acculturation. As Bourhis et al. (1997) have posited congruence between majority and minority acculturation expectations and state policies facilitate harmonious relations. The recognition of the importance of the majority attitude has sparked a growing body of research into attitudes towards multiculturalism. Whereas concepts such as acculturation orientation or prejudice focus on attitudes of a single group or on intergroup aspects, multiculturalism focuses on society as a whole. The extent to which mainstream and immigrant citizens accept and support the plural composition of their society is an important factor in determining the dynamics of this society. As repeatedly noted, societies are becoming increasingly diverse around the world; migration flows are on the increase both globally and within Europe. In front of this background, research into attitudes towards the plurally composed society has grown in importance.

Measuring Attitudes to Multiculturalism

Multicultural Ideology Scale (MIS)

The first survey of multicultural and ethnic attitudes was carried out as early as 1991 in Canada (Berry & Kalin, 1995). Recognizing the multifaceted nature of the concept of multiculturalism, these authors developed scales to assess attitudes towards multiculturalism ideology, the perceived consequences of multiculturalism and specific policy programmes. The initial survey also assessed attitudes towards specific ethnic immigrants as well as tolerance and *Canadianism*. The Multicultural Ideology Scale (MIS) was developed for this survey (Berry & Kalin, 1995) and covers three domains: diversity, the question whether diversity is good for society, acculturation strategies by minorities (assimilation or cultural maintenance by immigrants) and finally acculturation strategies by the majority, for example whether the majority should be more proactive in getting to know the minorities. This scale has also been adapted and used in the Netherlands, and van de Vijver et al. (2008) summarized: "The Multiculturalism Ideology Scale provides a short, reliable measure of majority attitudes toward multiculturalism" (p. 96). This scale includes ten items, measured on a Likert scale from 1 to 7. The scale is balanced (five items are reversed scored). Example items for the general attitude towards diversity include: "Dutch should recognize that the Dutch society consists of groups with different cultural backgrounds." The attitude towards acculturation strategies by immigrants is covered by items such as "People who come to the Netherlands should change their behaviour to be more like the Dutch" (reverse scored). Acculturation behaviour by the majority population is covered by items such as "Dutch natives should do more to learn about the customs and heritage of different cultural groups in this country."

Multicultural Attitude Scale (MAS)

The MIS scale has been amended and extended which resulted in the 28-item Multicultural Attitude Scale (MAS, Breugelmans & van de Vijver, 2004; Schalk-Soekar, van de Vijver, & Hoogsteder, 2004). This extended scale includes the basic domains covered by the MIS scale, that is (dis-) approval of diversity, minority and majority acculturation strategies in more depth. An additional domain was added namely equal societal participation and interaction between ethnic majority and minority groups. As the name suggests, this subscale covers specific measures of societal participation as well as the equal treatment of immigrants. This fourth subscale focuses on specific aspects of living together. Example items include "I think that non-natives and mainstreamers should have equal rights" or "I think that Dutch children should have both non-native and Dutch teachers." This societal Participation Subscale (soPat) has eight items and is also measured on a Likert Scale from 1 to 7.

Ethnic Prejudice Scale

For completeness it should also be noted that Maykel Verkuyten (2005) used a different measure composed of five items to assess the endorsement of multiculturalism. These items were taken from prior Dutch research (Verkuyten & Masson, 1995) and were originally developed to assess ethnic prejudice in the Netherlands. The items are "You can learn a lot from other cultural groups"; "It is better that every ethnic group stays in its own country" (reverse coded); "It is never easy to understand people from another culture" (reverse coded); "The more cultural groups there are, the better it is for a society"; and "Ethnic groups should mix as much as possible." Items were measured on scales ranging from 1 (disagree strongly) to 5 (agree strongly). Verkuyten (2005) reported that the five-item scale was internally consistent with Cronbach's α = 0.82, with a higher score indicating a stronger endorsement of multiculturalism. This instrument was developed for use with adolescents and does not tap into the areas of cultural maintenance by immigrants nor acculturation by majority members.

Psychometric Properties

Arends-Tóth and van de Vijver (2003) administered an adapted version of the ten-item MIS scale to a sample of N = 1565 Dutch majority group members and found that the attitude towards multiculturalism was a unidimensional construct with high degree of internal consistency. Even though the multiculturalism scales cover several dimensions, multiculturalism has a *unifactorial* structure. Support across domains varies, however (Breugelmans & van de Vijver, 2004). The distribution of scores showed a bell-shaped distribution, not lending support to the assumption that there is polarization (Kremer, 2013). "Multiculturalism for majority members is a unidimensional construct, that can be measured with high reliability, and the level of support for multiculturalism depends on the specific domain that is addressed" (van de Vijver et al., 2008, p. 97). The question of construct validity was addressed by Schalk-Soekar (2007). She compared quantitative and qualitative answers of Dutch majority members (N = 1285). She found significant correlations across measurement modes also lending support to the construct validity of the measures of multiculturalism.

The attitude to multiculturalism has also been shown to be a stable construct. The Dutch case study in terms of trajectory of multiculturalism policies was presented in Chap. 3. The Netherlands have not only experienced changes in policy and the associated discourse, but also politically motivated murders—the politician P. Fortuyn in 2002 and the film director T. van Gogh in 2007. Two studies investigated whether the shift in public discourse in relation to multiculturalism is also reflected in changes in the attitude towards multiculturalism. One study employed a cross-sectional design, comparing data from 1999 through to 2007 (Breugelmans, van de Vijver, & Schalk-Soekar, 2009) and the other study employed a longitudinal design (Schalk-Soekar, van de Vijver, & Croon, 2008). Contrary to popular belief, the support for multiculturalism has remained remarkably stable across this time period in the Netherlands: "Strong shifts in discussions about multicultural society in political debate and in the media are probably not adequate reflections of the attitudes towards multiculturalism held by the Dutch population" (Schalk-Soekar, Breugelmans, & van de Vijver, 2009, p. 279). The authors suggest that the attitude towards multiculturalism is a *strong* attitude which is not easily refuted by external events. As ethnic attitudes, strong attitudes are deeply rooted through socialization and resistant to change. It is possible that the attitude towards multiculturalism represents a higher order postulate (Epstein, 1979, 1994), as was discussed in Chap. 4. The stability of the attitude towards multiculturalism in the Netherlands at a time of change in government policies also suggests that the attitude to multiculturalism and government immigrant policy are not related.

Level of Endorsement of Multiculturalism

There have been few studies empirically testing the attitude of majority members towards multiculturalism specifically. A detailed review of studies covering related subject matters such as attitudes towards acculturation and prejudice (e.g. Zick, Wagner, van Dick, & Petzel, 2001) goes beyond the remit of this book, which is focused on multiculturalism. Berry and Kalin (1995) found endorsement for multiculturalism in Canada. Attitudes towards multiculturalism were moderately positive, and tolerance was moderately high. There was also a relatively high sense of attachment with and commitment to Canada. In fact, attachment to Canada is considered as a bracket, holding the diverse society together. Both the multiculturalism and *Canadianism* scales received moderate support, with no apparent contradiction between feeling attachment to

Canada and the endorsement of multiculturalism. This is supported by a positive correlation ($r = 0.25$) between the two scales.

Studies in the Netherlands found mainly neutral attitudes to multiculturalism—majority members do not oppose multiculturalism, but they do not actively support cultural diversity in their own country. Comparative studies also including the minorities (e.g. Turkish in the Netherlands) consistently find higher endorsement of multiculturalism by minority members (Arends-Tóth & van de Vijver, 2003; Breugelmans & van de Vijver, 2004; Schalk-Soekar et al., 2009; Schalk-Soekar & van de Vijver, 2008; Verkuyten & Martinovic, 2006; Verkuyten, 2005). The higher level of endorsement by minority members is explained by the fact that these groups have more to gain from multiculturalism—they can engage with the host society whilst staying attached also to their country of origin. As mentioned above, although multiculturalism is a one-dimensional construct, support across domains varies. In the Netherlands, overall support for multiculturalism was found to be neutral. This neutral score is the result of endorsement and rejection of domains cancelling each other out. Majority respondents in the Netherlands tend to be neutral about diversity, negative about acculturation of ethnic groups (they prefer assimilation over cultural maintenance by the immigrant groups in all domains), neutral about acculturation by the majority group (the extent to which Dutch majority have to adjust) and positive about societal participation. One consistent finding across the studies is that immigrant groups make a distinction between private and public domains in their acculturation strategies, with most preferring cultural maintenance in their private lives but integration in the public domains. Majority members prefer integration in both private and public domain. Within the majority the view predominates that it is not possible to show adequate attachment to two countries. Dutch majority members believe that it is impossible for immigrants to combine cultural maintenance and adjustment to Dutch society. However, as van Oudenhoven et al. (1998) found, for Moroccan and Turkish immigrants, integration (both the original culture and contact with the majority culture are considered important) was the preferred acculturation strategy. Dutch majority members in this study preferred assimilation or integration by immigrants and they assumed that separation would be the preferred attitude by immigrants—even though the study clearly showed that this was the least preferred strategy by immigrants themselves.

When comparing studies across countries, the measures used to assess the attitude towards multiculturalism have to be taken into consideration. As van de Vijver et al. (2006) pointed out, if surveys focus on cultural maintenance by immigrants, support tends to be lower. This was the case, for example, with studies carried out in Spain (Medrano, 2005) and the UK (Heath & Tilley, 2005) where a slightly negative attitude towards multiculturalism was reported. Citrin and Sears (2001) investigated multiculturalism in the American public opinion. Within the American context it is important to note that the core idea of multiculturalism, the enduring significance of ethnicity is fundamentally opposed to the melting-pot idea. Furthermore, the idea of granting special status to minority groups is opposed to individual liberalism. It therefore comes as no surprise that the "hard" form of multiculturalism, affirming group differences, is rejected by all ethnic groups. The authors observed an opposition to a tendency that articulates ethnic identities in a form that *competes* with rather than *complements* the older liberal ideal of a common civic identity. This is also reflected in a pervasive tendency to identify oneself as "just an American" rather than as a member of a particular racial or ethnic group. "The elevation of *pluribus* over the *unum*" (p. 266) is rejected. Ethnic cleavages are more pronounced when it comes to specific policies rather than general principles and then the nature of the differences depends on the issues raised. A liberal political self-identification boosted the general support for multiculturalism. For another "classical" immigration country, Australia, Moran (2011) argued that multiculturalism is used as nation-building tool, building an inclusive national identity whilst embracing diversity. However, he also remarked that like other immigrant societies, Australia is marked by national "status anxieties" related to its "newness." Yet this "uncertainty, newness, and future orientation has allowed Australia and Canada to embrace multiculturalism as a project of national identity renewal" (p. 2156). Moran (2011) argued further that these nations have had a chance to practice perpetual reinvention and the promotion of inclusive national identities, less organized by dominant ethnicity and have therefore had an advantage over other countries which have only recently experienced heterogeneous immigration. However, a survey by Ho (1990) found only neutral support for multiculturalism amongst the native Australian-born population.

Several studies in the Netherlands have found a strong positive effect of educational background on multiculturalism (Arends-Tóth & van de Vijver, 2003; Breugelmans & van de Vijver, 2004; van de Vijver et al., 2008). The latter two studies also found a small effect of gender, with women having a more positive attitude. The 2008 study also found a small effect of age, with younger members having a more positive attitude than older participants. Thus the findings for age and gender are inconclusive. As mentioned above, in comparative studies with immigrant groups, immigrants have consistently shown higher levels of endorsement than majority members. Strong ethnic identification was related to higher endorsement by minorities, but lower level of endorsement by majority members (Verkuyten & Martinovic, 2006). These authors also found that out-group friendships had a positive effect on multiculturalism for majority members.

Interim Summary

Breugelmans and van de Vijver (2004) concluded that "majority support for multiculturalism is a simple construct with a complex manifestation" (p. 418). Several studies have shown that the attitude towards multiculturalism is a unidimensional construct, but the support across domains varies. Cultural maintenance by immigrants is the aspect of multiculturalism that is often least supported by majority members. Majority members in the Netherlands have been shown to be neutral towards multiculturalism, strongly supporting equal rights and opportunities for all, but reluctant to actively support multiculturalism. Majority members also think that immigrants are insufficiently adapted to Dutch society. Whereas immigrants tend to favour cultural maintenance in the private domain and adaptation (notably integration) in the public domain, majority members favour assimilation in both domains. In reference to the IAM (Bourhis et al., 1997) this may lead to problematic or even conflictual relationships over the private domain, but consensual relations in the public sphere.

Introduction to Empirical Studies

Building on these findings, I set out to investigate the attitude towards multiculturalism in a country where the majority population finds itself increasingly in the minority. As was shown in Chap. 2, Luxembourg and especially the capital, Ville de Luxembourg (VdL), can be described as multicultural, certainly in terms of demographics. Within the capital, 68 % of the residents are not of Luxembourg nationality, representing 160 different nationalities (Etat de la population, Statistiques sur la Ville de Luxembourg, 2014). Studies on multiculturalism in the Netherlands have investigated the Dutch *majority* attitudes towards multiculturalism (Breugelmans et al., 2009; Breugelmans & van de Vijver, 2004). The Luxembourg context provides a unique opportunity to examine the attitude of the Luxembourg native-born population towards multiculturalism from a "majority in the minority" perspective. Within the Dutch context several factors have been identified which influence the attitude towards multiculturalism. These factors include demographic variables (such as age, gender and education), intergroup relation variables (e.g. direct contact scales, ethnic distance scales) and individual person characteristics (e.g. life satisfaction, personality traits). Leong and Ward (2006) have also suggested a relationship between the human values (Schwartz, 1992, 1994) and multiculturalism. However this study used archival data and aggregated data at country-level focusing on Schwartz's seven cultural value dimensions. I wanted to investigate the role of human values at the individual level and multiculturalism. The theory of human basic values will be presented next.

Theory of Human Basic Values

Schwartz (1992) proposed the theory of basic values, which has since been refined and amended (e.g. see Schwartz et al., 2012 or Cieciuch, Schwartz, & Vecchione, 2013). Schwartz and Bilsky (1987) theorized that values form a circular motivational structure. Schwartz (1992) organized the value domains into ten motivationally distinct, basic human values, forming a circular motivational continuum. This continuum is reproduced in Fig. 6.1 below. The ten value types can then be combined into four value dimensions of two conflicting pairs: Openness to change versus Conservation and Self-Enhancement versus Self-Transcendence.

Values nearby in the circle are expected to relate similarly and variables at the opposite side of the circle are expected to exhibit opposite associations. Adjacent values express compatible motivations and opposing values express conflicting motivations. Values on the left side of the circle (subsumed under Self-Transcendence and Conservation) regulate more how individuals relate socially to others, whilst the values on the right side regulate how individuals express personal interest and characteristics. Values on the bottom of the circle are grounded in anxiety and express

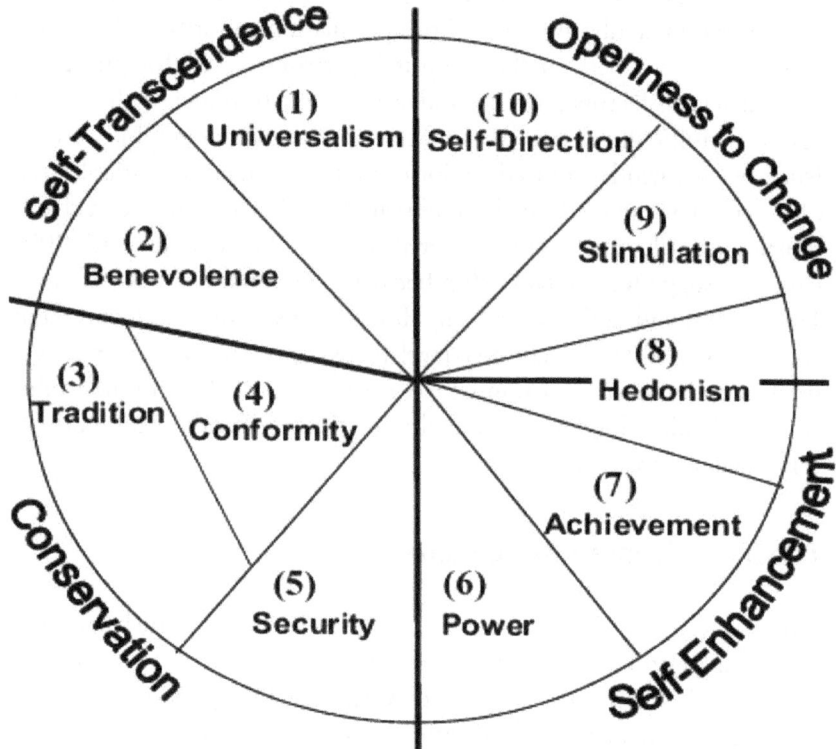

Fig. 6.1 Circular motivational continuum of ten values (*Source*: Cieciuch et al. [2013, p. 1219])

self-protective motivations, whereas values at the top of the circle are relatively free from anxiety and express growth motivations (Cieciuch et al., 2013). Several studies have shown the Schwartz values to be culturally universal, but the importance and weight accorded to each value type may vary across cultures (Schwartz & Sagiv, 1995). For the purposes of the present study, I considered the inclusion of human values important as values provide guidance to individuals *across* situations. Motives are often unconscious, but values are cognitively accessible. People can and will think about their values and can communicate their values to others. Values are also used to justify behaviours (e.g. "I help, because I think that it is important to help others"). Traits, motives or needs can be positive or negative, but values are inherently desirable. Values are ranked according to subjective importance and form a personal value hierarchy (Roccas & Sagiv, 2010). Given this centrality to human behaviour, I considered it important to investigate the relationship between the Schwartz values and the attitude towards multiculturalism, testing the hypothesis that values regulating interpersonal relations would be conducive to endorsement of multiculturalism, whereas those values pertaining to anxiety and self-protective motives should have the opposite effect.

Empirical Study: Human Values and Multiculturalism

Based on findings in Canada and the Netherlands, I derived several hypotheses which I wanted to test within the Luxembourg context: (1) The attitude towards multiculturalism is expected to be neutral to positive. (2) No gender differences are predicted. (3) Younger participants are expected to have higher multiculturalism scores. (4) Immigrants have a more positive attitude towards multiculturalism than the native-born participants. (5) Culture contact impacts positively on the attitude towards multiculturalism. The primary objective for this study was to test the proposed relationship between the Schwartz values and multiculturalism: (6) The Schwartz Value dimensions Openness and Self-Transcendence correlate positively with endorsement of multiculturalism. A further aim of this study was the testing of the multiculturalism scales developed in the Canada and the Netherlands within the Luxembourg context and to test the online methodology.

Method

The dependent measure, the acceptance of and support for the culturally heterogeneous composition of society, was measured using the following instruments: The MIS, as explained above, and the soPat of the MAS. Two further items asking whether multiculturalism is considered to have more advantages (item 1) or disadvantages (item 2) were also included. Together, these two items formed the Multiculturalism Advantages subscale (MCadv). These three measures (MIS, soPat and MCadv) were also combined and formed the Total Multiculturalism Scale (TMC). The original scales were only available in English and written for the Dutch context. Therefore, the items had to be adapted to the Luxembourg context and translated into German. As was noted already in previous chapters, translations must capture conceptual equivalence. We used a method of translation and back translation into English, enlisting the help of a professional translator.

The independent variables included 21 Schwartz value items, as used in the European Social Survey (EES, Schwartz, S.H. (n.d.) Chapter 7), which were combined to form the ten Schwartz value types (Schwartz (n.d.) Computing scores scores for the 10 human values), which in turn, when combined, form the four value dimensions: Openness for Change versus Conservation and Self-Enhancement versus Self-Transcendence (Schwartz, 1992, 1994). An extensive demographic section, covering also nationalities, language competence as well as a question concerning the composition of the circle of friends completed the measure.

Procedure

The questionnaire was designed as an online survey using software which allowed the use of different language versions. The survey was made available in German and English. The link to the "Multikulti-survey" was distributed via Facebook, flyers and the uni.lu intranet. Participation was voluntary and anonymous. A reward of 8 × Euro 25 Amazon vouchers was offered to participants who agreed participate in the lottery of vouchers. The contact data of the participants taking part in this lottery were kept separate from the actual survey data.

Sample

A total of N = 640 persons participated in the survey of which 66 % were female. The mean age was M = 24.6 (SD = 9.0) with a range = 54. Thirty-nine percent of the participants were students at the uni.lu, 8 % staff of the uni.lu and 53 % had no association with the uni.lu. Over two-thirds (69 %) of the participants stated to be Luxembourg nationals, 12 % German, a "francophone" group (8 %) was composed of French, Portuguese, Belgian and Italian nationals and the remaining participants represented a wide range of nationalities (mixed group—11 %). The majority of the participants (83 %) opted for the German version of the questionnaire.

Results

In the following, the results will be presented in relation to the hypotheses formulated.

Hypothesis 1:
The attitude towards multiculturalism is expected to be neutral to positive. The psychometric properties for all four multiculturalism measures are provided in Table 6.2. The means for all four scales are above the neutral scale mid-point of four. Therefore, the attitude is slightly positive for all four measures, with the soPat subscale reaching the highest mean scores. Hypothesis 1 was thus confirmed.

Hypothesis 2:
No gender differences are predicted. Independent samples t-tests conducted for all four multiculturalism were not significant. Male and female participants did not differ regarding the multiculturalism measures. Hypothesis 2 could thus be confirmed.

Table 6.2 Psychometric properties of the multiculturalism measures

Scale	n	M	SD	Sk	Ku	No of items	α	r_{tt}
MIS	612	4.42	0.91	−0.35	0.38	10	0.75	
soPat	623	5.40	1.03	−0.79	1.26	7	0.74	
MC adv	626	4.99	1.51	−0.49	−0.24	2		$r_{tt} = 0.68**$
TMC	592	4.83	0.88	−0.59	0.78	19	0.86	

Note: Sig (2-tailed) **$p < 0.01$; [a] For "MC adv" the Pearson-correlation is computed as an estimate of r_{tt}

Hypothesis 3:
Younger participants are expected to have higher multiculturalism scores. The age structure of the sample reflected recruitment within a student setting with a majority of participants being in their early twenties. As indicated by the age range, older participants did participate, but they were proportionally fewer. I grouped the participants into five age bands with approximately similar sample sizes.[1] The one-way ANOVA comparing the between group differences of these five groups regarding the TMC measure is highly significant: $F(4,587) = 11.23$ $p < 0.001$, $\eta^2 = 0.07$. As Fig. 6.2 below illustrates, the four younger age groups hardly differ and post hoc analysis using Tukey HSD confirmed that the "28+" group had a significantly higher mean score ($M = 5.30$, $SD = 0.82$) than the four other groups. Within this sample, older participants had significantly higher mean scores than the younger participants and Hypothesis 3 is therefore refuted.

Figure 6.2 shows results for the combined scale (TMC), as well as for each subscale separately and illustrates that the mean scores for all scales are above the neutral position of the scale mid-point 4, as was pointed out in relation to Hypothesis 1.

Hypothesis 4:
Immigrants have a more positive attitude towards multiculturalism than the native-born participants. Participants were grouped into two groups—those born in Luxembourg ($n = 427$) and those not born in Luxembourg

---

[1] <20 years, $n = 131$; 20–21 years, $n = 164$; 22–23 years, $n = 103$; 24–27 years, $n = 84$; 28+ years, $n = 110$

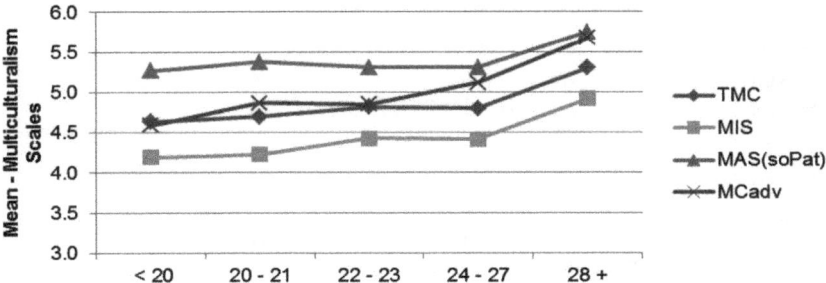

Fig. 6.2 Relationship between age bands and mean scores on multicultural-ism scales

(n = 213) and independent sample t-tests were carried out comparing these two group on the four multiculturalism measures. The results show that participants not born in Luxembourg had significantly higher mean scores than the Luxembourg-born participants on all multiculturalism measures, confirming Hypothesis 4.[2]

Hypothesis 5:
Culture contact impacts positively on the attitude towards multiculturalism.
The participants were asked how many of their friends have a different country of birth to themselves. They could indicate this on a five- point scale ranging from 1 = none, 2 = a few, 3 = about half, 4 = more than half and 5 = all. The responses were combined into three groups result-ing in Group 1 (none/few) n = 175, Group 2 (about half) n = 197 and Group 3 (more than half/all) n = 263. The one-way ANOVA comparing these three groups and the multiculturalism measures showed a statisti-cally highly significant relationship for all measures.[3] For the combined TMC measure, the result is $F(2, 586) = 30.67, p < 0.001, \eta^2 = 0.09$. The more mixed the circle of friends, the higher the multiculturalism scores. Hypothesis 5 could thus be confirmed.

---

[2] MIS $t(610) = -5.86, p < 0.001, \eta^2 = 0.05; M_{LuxBorn} = 4.27 (0.89), M_{notLuxborn} = 4.72 (0.85)$; MAS $t(621) = -7.33, p < 0.001, \eta^2 = 0.08, M_{LuxBorn} = 5.20 (1.05), M_{notLuxborn} = 5.81 (0.86)$; Advantages $t(624) = -5.90, p < 0.001, \eta^2 = 0.05, M_{LuxBorn} = 4.75 (1.50), M_{notLuxborn} = 5.49 (1.41)$ and TMC $t(590) = -7.41, p < 0.001, \eta^2 = 0.09, M_{LuxBorn} = 4.65 (0.89), M_{notLuxborn} = 5.20 (0.74)$.

[3] For the combined TMC measure, the result is $F(2, 586) = 30.67, p < 0.001, \eta^2 = 0.09$.

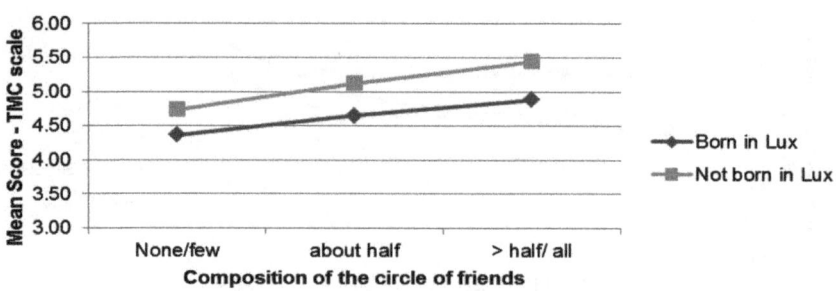

Fig. 6.3 Relationship between country of birth, composition of circle of friends and the TMC scale

The effect of country of birth (Lux vs. not born in Lux) and the composition of the circle of friends on the combined multiculturalism score (TMC) was examined using a two way between group analysis of variance. There was no interaction effect between composition of circle of friends and country of birth. The main effect for both independent factors was significant: Country of birth $F(1,583)$ = 38.52, $p < 0.001$, partial η^2 = 0.08, with higher mean scores for those not born in Luxembourg (see Hypothesis 4). Composition of circle of friends $F(2, 583)$ = 24.24, $p < 0.001$, partial η^2 = 0.06. This relationship is presented in Fig. 6.3: Persons not born in Luxembourg express higher openness to multiculturalism than those born in Luxembourg and for both groups endorsement rises in line with an increasingly mixed circle of friends.

Hypothesis 6:
The Schwartz Value dimensions Openness and Self-Transcendence correlate positively with a positive attitude towards multiculturalism. The correlations between the value dimensions and the TMC scale are presented in Table 6.3.

As highlighted in Table 6.3, there is indeed a highly significant positive relationship between the value dimension *Self-Transcendence* and the multiculturalism scale ($r = 0.42^{**}$), confirming part 1 of Hypothesis 6. However, there is only a slightly positive, but not statistically significant relationship between *Openness* and TMC ($r = 0.06$). Therefore the second part of Hypothesis 6 could not be confirmed. Even though the correlation between *Openness* and TMC did not reach significance, the corresponding dimension *Conservation* did: There is a strong negative, highly significant relationship between *Conservation* and TMC (r = –0.72**).

Discussion

The results mirror those found in the Netherlands in terms of the mean scores in the different domains as covered by the multiculturalism measures (Schalk-Soekar et al., 2009). As in the Netherlands, the support for societal participation (soPat) was higher than the support for the multiculturalism ideology measure (MIS). However, within this study sample, the attitude across the scales is more positive than the results reported for the Netherlands which centred more on the mid-point of the scale. As in previous research, no gender differences were found, but in contrast to previous findings, the "older" participants had a more positive attitude towards the plurally composed society than the younger participants. A possible explanation for this may be a sampling effect. The link to the "Multikulti" survey was passed on from students, to parents to friends creating a "snow ball effect." Participation was voluntary and only a small reward was offered with the chance of winning one of the eight vouchers being small. Therefore it can be inferred that participants were intrinsically motivated. They may have either been interested in the topic or may have wanted to help a friend/acquaintance by completing the questionnaire. The relationship between age groups and *Self-Transcendence* was examined by means of a one-way ANOVA and a statistically significant difference between the age groups was found, $F(4, 635)$ = 9.56, $p < 0.001$, η^2 = 0.06. A post hoc test using Tukey HSD shows that the (28+) group had significantly higher *Self-Transcendence* scores than all four younger age groups. *Self-Transcendence*

Table 6.3 Correlations between TMC scale and the value dimensions

	1	2	3	4	5
TMC	1	–.13**	.42**	0.06	–.30**
Conservation		1	–.30**	–.72**	–.13**
Self-Transcendence			1	0.034	–.59**
Openness				1	–.25**
Self-Enhancement					1

Note: *$p < 0.05$, **$p < 0.01$

taps into the social dimension. Care and concern for others are emphasized rather than the personal focus which is captured by the dimension *Self-Enhancement*. It is likely that there is a link between this social concern and the motivation for participation in this survey for the "older" participants. The "older" participants in this sample had a significantly higher mean score on the *Self-Transcendence* dimensions than the younger participants and the strong correlation between TMC and *Self-Transcendence* was discussed. If participants have higher *Self-Transcendence* scores, they are also more likely to express a more positive attitude towards multiculturalism.

As predicted, the participants not born in Luxembourg expressed a more positive attitude towards multiculturalism than the native-born participants. This is in line with previous findings. As Verkuyten (2005) explained "multiculturalism is typically seen as identity threatening for the majority group and identity supporting for minority groups" (p. 122). One simple explanation, already mentioned above, is that minority members benefit more from multiculturalism, as they can stay connected to their home country *and* gain the benefits of living in a new host country. An alternative explanation may be that immigrants have *chosen* to live in another country, in this case Luxembourg. Of course there are "push-and-pull factors" influencing a migration decision as was outlined in Chap. 3, but nevertheless there is at least an element of control exercised over the move, and control is one of the core motives of human development (Fiske, 2010) as explained in Chap. 4. People born in Luxembourg do not have control, at individual level, over the composition of "their" society. The voluntary decision by persons moving to Luxembourg will, at first instance, lead to "involuntary" culture contact for the resident population. This experience of *lack of control* may also be an explanation for the weaker endorsement of multiculturalism by the resident population. This feeling of lack of control may be exacerbated by a feeling of weakened predictability of daily life, as foreigners may bring with them unknown customs or unfamiliar ways of doing things. Therefore, another core motive namely that of understanding may be infringed. Of course, in a second step, a native-born person may *voluntarily* seek second culture exposure by choosing friends or a partner from a different background. As was shown above, a more diverse circle of friends is also associated with a more positive attitude towards multiculturalism.

Finally, the association between the value dimension *Self-Transcendence* and multiculturalism could be confirmed. This dimension is composed of value types with a social dimension, focusing on the well-being of others. Persons scoring high on this dimension share a strong concern for the equal treatment and well-being of all human beings. On the other hand, persons with high scores on *Self-Enhancement* focus stronger on the personal well-being and personal achievement. The student participants within this sample are in a phase of life where they need to "find their place in the world," to establish themselves. This may explain why the values related to *Self-Enhancement* were more dominant for this group than for the "older" participants and then in turn why multiculturalism was less strongly endorsed by the younger than the older participants. The low association between the value dimension *Openness* and TMC was not expected. However, as was noted above, there is a strong negative correlation between *Conservation* and multiculturalism. Therefore, it may not be *Openness to change* that is decisive for the relationship with multiculturalism, but rather the absence of *Conservation*, values related to security, tradition and conformity.

Conclusion

As noted above, one objective associated with this study was to test the multiculturalism scales within the Luxembourg context. The findings regarding the endorsement of multiculturalism in Luxembourg are in line with empirical findings in the Netherlands. The reliability of the scales, as indicated by Cronbach's alpha from ranging $0.74 < \alpha < 0.86$, was satisfactory.[4] However, feedback from participants also indicated that the wording of some items could or should be simplified.

Another key objective was to examine whether the proposed relationship between the Schwartz value dimensions and multiculturalism could be shown. As was discussed, there is indeed a strong relationship between the dimension *Self-Transcendence* and multiculturalism. The data also suggest an association between the absence of a need for *Conservation*

---

[4] A more detailed analysis of the psychometric structure of the scales will be provided as part of the second empirical study.

and multiculturalism, rather than with *Openness to change*. For the purposes of this study the human value items as used in the European Social Survey were employed. The European Social Survey is administered in an interview format, but we administered an online questionnaire. Feedback from several users indicated a need to simplify the wording for an online survey. However, overall the online methodology worked well. In conclusion, the results from this online study were encouraging and allowed the fine-tuning of the test battery for the second study.

Empirical Study: Multiculturalism—Majority in the Minority Perspective

Introduction

Luxembourg's capital, Ville de Luxembourg (VdL), uses the slogan "multiplicity" in its external branding. As explained on VdL's website (www. vdl.lu), the slogan expresses the diverse and polyglot nature of the city: "Multinational: a city welcomes the world. The city has a long history of welcoming foreigners. Indeed it is the blend of traditional Luxembourgish culture and the influence of many nationalities of our residence that have given the city its unique cosmopolitan diversity" (p. 2, *multiplicity of Luxembourg*, 2011). To the outside world, the city presents diversity as an asset. Yet how is this diversity perceived by the native-born Luxembourg population? What is the attitude of those working in the capital towards the plurally composed society? Is this external positioning matched by the internal position of native-born Luxembourgers working in the capital? I managed to obtain approval to conduct a study examining the attitude towards multiculturalism amongst the workforce of a large employer (workforce of approx. 3700 in 2013). Crucially, this company offers a wide range of services and employs a cross section of the population, but mainly Luxembourg nationals. This is in turn important, as I wanted to investigate the "majority in the minority" perspective and a key objective was to identify *within* group differences regarding the attitude towards multiculturalism amongst Luxembourg nationals who find themselves increasingly in the minority within their capital. Apart from human values, I wanted to include a wider range measures which I expected to have a bearing on the level of endorsement of multiculturalism.

After the permission to conduct research was granted by the company's management, a meeting was set up with the Heads of Human Resources, Communications and IT to present the proposed study in detail and to discuss the feasibility of implementation. During this initial meeting it was decided that the questionnaire would need to be made available in German and French and that no material incentives should be offered. Following this meeting, I developed the full sets of questionnaires in French and German and submitted the first draft for approval. Approval was granted, but with a request to shorten the questionnaire. The variables included in the final questionnaire and specific hypotheses derived will be outlined next.

Measures

Assessment of Multiculturalism

Several measures of multiculturalism were used and each will be presented in turn. The MIS was already introduced above. The scale showed good reliability with representative sample of Canadian citizens (α = 0.80, Berry & Kalin, 1995). The version adapted for use in the Netherlands (Arends-Tóth & van de Vijver, 2003) yielded a single factor solution and good reliability (α = 0.82). Verkuyten (2005), in his use of the scale, achieved an even higher reliability coefficient of α = 0.90. The items were translated into German and adapted to the Luxembourg context for the previous study. Based on the feedback obtained, these translations were revised and a French translation added. One item of the original scale, "A society that has a variety of cultural groups has more problems with national unity than societies with one or two basic cultural groups" was judged too complex for the online survey and was omitted. The items, translated into English, are presented in Appendix 1. The nine-items scale yielded a high reliability coefficient α = 0.87 and the factor analysis a single factor solution. The Scree plot is shown in Appendix 2 and factor loadings for each item are listed in Appendix 3. Only the first factor had an Eigenvalue > 1 (4.50) and explained 50 % of the total variance.

Societal participation was assessed using the subscale of the MAS as explained above. The items and psychometric properties for the MAS societal participation (soPat) subscale are included in Appendix 4. This subscale also yielded good reliability (α = 0.83). Factor Analysis showed that the soPat is also unidimensional. The Scree plot is included in Appendix 5. Two factors had Eigenvalues greater than 1 (3.86 and 1.11 respectively). Together, both factors explain 60 % of the variance, whilst factor 1 explains 46 % of the variance. Factor loadings for each item are provided in Appendix 6. Schalk-Soekar (2007) in her research also adapted and extended the MAS scale. She added two subscales, one focusing on the advantages of multiculturalism and another one on the disadvantages of multiculturalism. Based on this extension, one further item was added as a "closing" question in the questionnaire "Alles in allem haben multikulturelle Gesellschaften mehr Vorteile als Nachteile."[5] After this question participants had the opportunity to insert open comments or observations. The MIS and soPat scale as well as the advantages (adv) item were combined to form a combined multiculturalism scale (TMK). The combined scale thus consisted of 18 items and had high internal consistency (α = 0.92). Factor analysis for the combined scale showed that three factors had Eigenvalues greater 1: Factor 1 (7.75), factor 2 (1.33) and factor 3 (1.17). Together, these three factors explain 56.9 % of the variance, factor 1 alone explaining 40.05 % of the variance. The Scree plot for the combined scale (TMK) is shown in Appendix 7. The combined scale also shows a unifactorial structure, suggesting that issues of cultural diversity are perceived on a single dimension. If people are positive in one domain, they tend to be positive in other domains. This is supported by the high positive correlation between the MIS scale and the soPat scale r = 0.75, p < 0.01 (Correlation between MIS and adv item r = 0.74, p < 0.01, soPat and adv item r = 0.63 p < 0.01). However, the level of support varies across these domains. Based on research findings in the Netherlands (Schalk-Soekar et al., 2009) and the results of the previous study we expected neutral to slightly positive support for the idea of multiculturalism (MIS) (Hypothesis 1) and slightly more positive support for the social participation measure (soPat) (Hypothesis 2).

---

[5] On balance, multicultural societies have more advantages than disadvantages.

Relations of Multiculturalism with Other Variables

Demographic Variables

Three demographic variables have been found to influence the attitude to multiculturalism, namely gender, age and level of education. The latter has been found to have the strongest impact, with higher educational levels being positively related to support for multiculturalism. The results regarding gender and age as predictors have been less clear cut. Some studies have shown that females have slightly higher scores than males and younger participants also show higher scores than older participants; however, effect sizes have been small (van de Vijver et al., 2008). In the previous study no gender effect, but an age effect was found with older participants showing stronger endorsement of multiculturalism, but this was explained as a likely sampling effect. In line with these previous findings we expected for the present study that support for multiculturalism will rise in line with the level of education, as well as a slight effect for gender and age (Hypothesis 3).

Intergroup Relations

Culture contact can be experienced in different ways. Persons can grow up with parents of different nationalities; they can have a partner with a different country of birth, a circle of friends with different nationalities or have lived in another country. All forms of culture contact are normally conducive to a more open attitude towards multiculturalism. Predictors for higher levels of endorsement of multiculturalism include (1) having a mixed circle of friends (half or above), (2) having lived abroad for at least 6 months, (3) a partner with a different country of birth to oneself, (4) having moved to Luxembourg and (5) growing up with parents of mixed nationalities. The first four forms of culture contact listed are characterized by their voluntariness. This voluntary nature is one explanation why persons born in Luxembourg are predicted to show lower endorsement of multiculturalism than persons who have moved there (predictor 4). As explained in the context of the previous study, voluntariness, the experience of control are decisive as well as the fact that immigrants are thought to benefit more from openness to multiculturalism (Verkuyten, 2005). Growing up with mixed national parents (predictor 5) is an involuntary culture contact experience, but as shown in Study *on being bicultural* in Chap. 5, the students perceived the experience as beneficial and the vast majority of students defined themselves in a bicultural way. We therefore expected that this bicultural orientation would extend to openness to multiculturalism. All forms of culture contact are thus expected to contribute to openness towards multiculturalism (Hypothesis 4); however it is not clear which form of culture contributes the most in relation to openness towards multiculturalism.

Perception of cultural distance has also been shown to influence intergroup relations and the attitude towards multiculturalism (Schalk-Soekar, 2007; Schalk-Soekar et al., 2004). Therefore, the cultural distance between the main resident migrant groups (see Figs. 2.6 and 2.7, Chap. 2) was also assessed. Participants were asked to rank the groups as shown in Fig. 6.4 regarding their perceived closeness to Luxembourg nationals.

In the online questionnaires, participants were asked to drag the respective groups into their perceived position. On the paper questionnaire, participants were asked to draw a line between the group and the perceived position in terms of closeness to Luxembourg nationals.

Language. Participants were also asked about their language competence and language use. A high level of language competence was expected. In Study *Bilingualism = Biculturalism* (Chap. 5) within group differences regarding the perception of language as a prime for a switch in culture were identified. The expectation for the present study was that those participants who perceive a change in language as a change in culture will also show higher endorsement of multiculturalism (Hypothesis 5).

Interindividual Difference Variables

Personality traits. Differences can be observed regarding the distribution of personality traits within cultural groups. Sociability or openness to new experiences could, for example, influence to what degree a person is seeking contact with persons of different backgrounds. On the other hand persons who get stressed easily may be less prone to seek culture

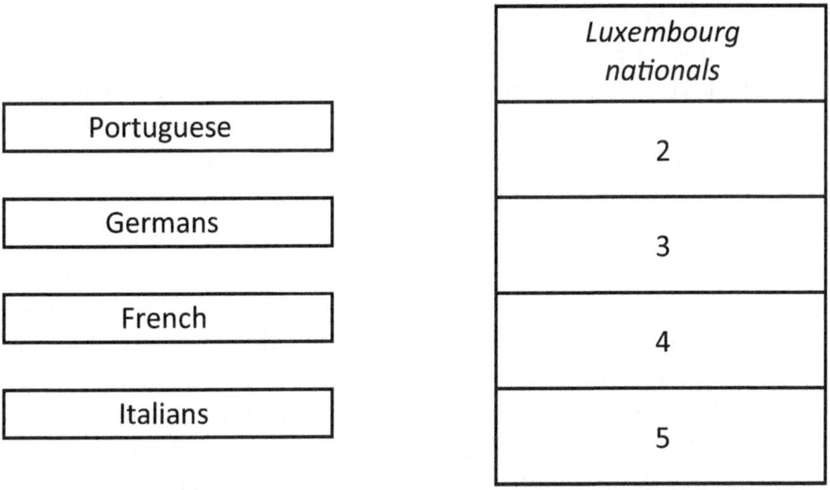

	Luxembourg nationals
Portuguese	2
Germans	3
French	4
Italians	5

Fig. 6.4 Perceived distance of main resident groups to Luxembourg nationals

contact experiences. The *Big Five Inventory* (BFI, John & Srivastava, 1999) measures the five big personality traits, *extraversion, agreeableness, conscientiousness, neuroticism* and *openness*. Agreeableness refers to altruistic, sensitive dealings with others. Openness denotes interest in new experiences. The trait extraversion includes sociability, warmth and proactiveness. Neuroticism refers to differences regarding emotional stability. Conscientiousness signifies discipline, ambition and the willingness to do a task well and thoroughly (Maehler & Schmidt-Denter, 2013). In the present study the "Big 5" traits are measured using as short scale, developed by Rammstedt and John (2007) for use in Germany. In relation to multiculturalism, a positive association is expected between high scores in agreeableness, openness and extraversion and multiculturalism and negative association with neuroticism. Conscientiousness is not expected to have an impact on multiculturalism. Personality-trait-related predictions are summarized as Hypothesis 6.

Subjective well-being. Does a relationship between subjective well-being and multiculturalism exist? This question is examined in an exploratory manner. Subjective well-being is measured using the German version of the *Satisfaction with Life Scale* (*SWLS*, Glaesmer, Grande, Braehler, & Roth, 2011).

Value structure. As explained above, values provide guidance for decisions and orientation *across* situations. Values are inherently desirable and are ranked according to subjective importance and form a personal value hierarchy (Roccas & Sagiv, 2010). As noted above, the human values are assessed as part of the European Social Survey (ESS) and in the previous study the exact wording of the German version was used. However, some of these items actually included more than one concept. Furthermore, feedback obtained was that some items were too long and complicated for an online questionnaire. Therefore, the items were adapted seeking guidance from Boll (1999). This revision resulted in 23 items which are presented in Appendix 8. Appendix 8 also shows how these items were combined to form the value types which were then in turn combined to form the value dimensions. Psychometric properties are also indicated.

Leong and Ward (2006) examined country-level relations between multiculturalism, socio-economic indicators and Schwartz's and Hofstede's cultural value orientations. Their studies showed that the Schwartz values benevolence and universalism (forming the value dimension Self-Transcendence) had a positive relation with multiculturalism. Conservation on the other hand was negatively related. The preceding study also confirmed the positive correlation between the value dimension Self-Transcendence as well as the negative association with Conservation. The following hypotheses were thus deduced for the present study: Participants, for whom Conservation values are important, will endorse multiculturalism less than participants who express strong Openness for change (Hypothesis 7). Participants who express strong interest in universalism and benevolence (Self-Transcendence) will have a more positive attitude to multiculturalism than those who are more self-focused (achievement and power, forming Self-Enhancement, Hypothesis 8).

Understanding of Nationality

As was shown in Chap. 4, two conceptualizations of nationality can be distinguished; the primordial or essentialist and the socially constructed understanding (see also Péporté (2011). According to the primordial understanding, nationality is passed on through lineage and nationality is therefore acquired through birth. According to this understanding, one can therefore only belong to one nationality, nationality being an *exclusive* category. Under the alternative view, nations themselves are perceived as socially constructed and it is acknowledged that nations can change and are the result of political decisions. Consequently, it is also possible to acquire a nationality after birth and it is also possible to belong to more than one nationality. The socially constructed understanding allows for a more *inclusive* perception of nationality.

Even though history tells us that borders can change, and Luxembourg is a case in point, many people adhere to the primordial understanding of nationhood (Weinreich & Saunderson, 2003). These authors also explain that the primordial—socially constructed understanding of nationality is thought to form a continuum. This is why the questions concerning the understanding of nationality have been operationalized in the form of a series of bipolar statements. The expectation is that those participants who perceive nationality as passed on through lineage (primordial end of the spectrum) will endorse multiculturalism less than those who gravitate towards the socially constructed end of the spectrum (Hypothesis 9).

Sample

Sampling

Participation in the survey was open to all employees and all members of staff were informed through a note in their pay slips about the survey, ensuring that everybody was informed about the survey at the same time and in the same way. Team leaders of those employees who do not have access to computers were contacted ahead of the study to enquire about the number of paper questionnaires required. The distribution of the questionnaires was organized through the Communication Department. The link to the online questionnaire was published on the company's intranet and was open for access from 13 May until 5 July 2013. Questionnaires were made available in French and German. Participation was voluntary and participants could log out at any time. The voluntary aspect was underlined by the fact that questions could also be skipped (such as age).

In the online questionnaire, filters were used directing participants only to relevant parts of the questionnaire. Only these filter questions were programmed as mandatory.

A total of 521 employees opened the online questionnaire. Of these, 100 only opened the link or filled in the questionnaire too incomplete to allow an analysis. This left a total of 421 valid online questionnaires. Eighty-six paper questionnaires were returned which resulted in a total of N = 507 participants. For both methods, German was the preferred language (77 % online, 89.5 % paper).

Description of the Sample

A total of 67.2 % of the participants are male, which closely matches the male percentage of 69.2 % (as of 01.06.2013) of the total workforce. The mean age is 42 years (SD = 10 years) and the age distribution of the participant sample closely matches that of the total sample.

The career paths fall into three broad categories (Lower, middle and upper career path) and participants from all three career structures participated: 35 % from the lower band, 47 % middle band and 18 % upper band. On average, participants have been working 15 years (SD = 11 years) for the company. Just under a quarter of the participants (n = 120) have been working there for five years or less. Only a minority (n = 17) have no or low (only primary school) level of education. The majority of the participants (91.5 %) were born in Luxembourg. A large percentage of participants' parents were also born in Luxembourg (77.9 % of the mothers, 80.4 % of the fathers). For 72.3 % of the participants, Luxembourg was place of birth as well as for both parents. 85 % of the participants indicated to have a partner. For 78.1 %, participant and partner had the same country of birth. Ninety-seven percent of the participants are Luxembourg citizens, the majority (82.3 %) since birth and 13.8 % have acquired Luxembourg citizenship. Forty-one percent of the participants live in the Canton[6] of Luxembourg and 28.3 % in the capital. The catchment area for

---

[6] Luxembourg is subdivided into 3 Districts and 12 Cantons.

the employees is wide, but the majority of the employees live in the Cantons geographically closest to the capital. A detailed breakdown of countries of origins, nationalities, geographic spread, and so on can be found in Murdock and Ferring (2013, 2014).

Selectivity Analysis

The 507 participants mirror a rate of return of 14 %. In the following section I will examine whether this sample can be considered representative of the workforce. As noted above, all employees were informed about the study in the same way and at the same time. All employees had the same chance for participation. It was emphasized that participation was voluntary and anonymous. For the sake of anonymity, no material incentives were offered for participation to avoid any suspicion of identification, even though any data relevant for identification would, of course, be held separately from those in the questionnaire. In all communications the academic nature of the survey was stressed.

The respondents represent a self-selective sample. The results do not represent a random selection and cannot be interpreted in a strict mathematical–statistical sense as being representative of the total sample. However, central measures reflect some key characteristics of the total sample. As was noted above, the percentage of male participants (67.2 %) closely matches the percentage of males working for the company (69.2 %). The average age of the sample ($M = 42$ years) closely matches that of the total workforce ($M = 41$ years). Because of this convergence of central characteristic and convergence with results of the previously reported study with $N = 640$ participants, there is no reason to assume that the results constitute a biased or imprecise representation of the attitudes of the employees regarding the plurally composed society.

Results

In the following, the results will be presented again in relation to the hypotheses formulated.

Attitude towards Multiculturalism

On average, the participants have a slightly positive attitude towards the idea of multiculturalism, as measured by the MIS scale. The mean score $M = 4.25$ ($SD = 1.08$) is statistically significantly higher than the scale mid-point of 4: $t(487) = 5.28$, $p < 0.001$. The mean for the soPat scale, $M = 3.84$ ($SD = 1.32$), is statistically significantly lower than the scale mid-point $t(491) = -2.55$, $p < 0.05$. Based on the scores on the respective scales, participants were divided into five groups: negative (Scores 1–2.5), slightly negative (2.51–3.5), neutral (3.51–4.5), slightly positive (4.51–5.5) and positive (5.51–7) (see also Schalk-Soekar et al., 2009). The percentage of participants falling into each of these five categories for the MIS and soPat scale is shown in Fig. 6.5.

The level of endorsement of the idea of multiculturalism is stronger than that for specific measures of participation. Diversity ("It is good that many different groups with different cultural backgrounds live in Luxembourg") and ethnic maintenance ("Ethnic minorities should preserve their ethnic heritage in Luxembourg") are affirmed but a majority also expects assimilation by immigrants ("Immigrants to Luxembourg should change their behaviour to be more like the Luxembourgish people," reversed item). The general endorsement of multiculturalism is also reflected in the high agreement with the summary statement "Overall, multicultural societies have more advantages than disadvantages" $M = 4.74$ ($SD = 1.82$), mode = 6. Based on these findings, Hypothesis 1, predicting neutral to slightly positive support for the idea of multiculturalism, can be confirmed.

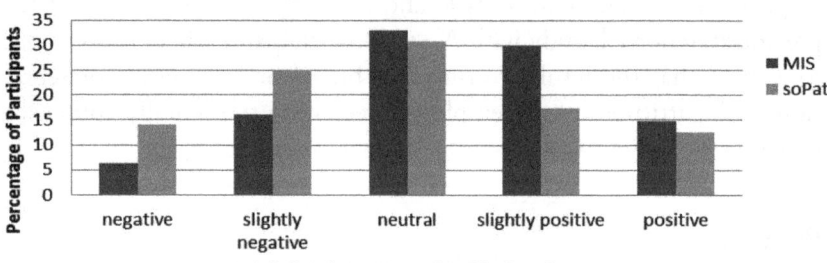

Fig. 6.5 Endorsement of multiculturalism measured by MIS and soPat: participants in percent

The societal participation scale covers very specific forms of living together. The charged debate concerning the use of the Luxembourg language (see Chap. 2) is reflected in very high agreement with the statement "It is annoying not to be served in Luxembourgish in shops." $M = 5.38$ ($SD = 1.97$), mode = 7. Forty-six percent of the participants totally agreed with this statement (which is reverse scored). As can be seen in Fig. 6.6, very strong disagreement was also found regarding the recruitment of more non-Luxembourgers into the police force, more non-Luxembourgish teachers and granting voting rights to foreigners after five years. The mode for all three items is one. Descriptive statistics for all items can be found in Appendix 4.

Hypothesis 2 had predicted higher endorsement for societal participation measures than for the idea of multiculturalism. This hypothesis could not be confirmed. Specific societal participation measures are less endorsed, with 43 % of the participants expressing a negative attitude towards societal participation measures.

The Influence of Other Variables on Multiculturalism

As shown above, the idea of multiculturalism, as measured by the MIS scale, was endorsed more strongly than specific measures regarding societal participation. The highly significant positive correlation between both

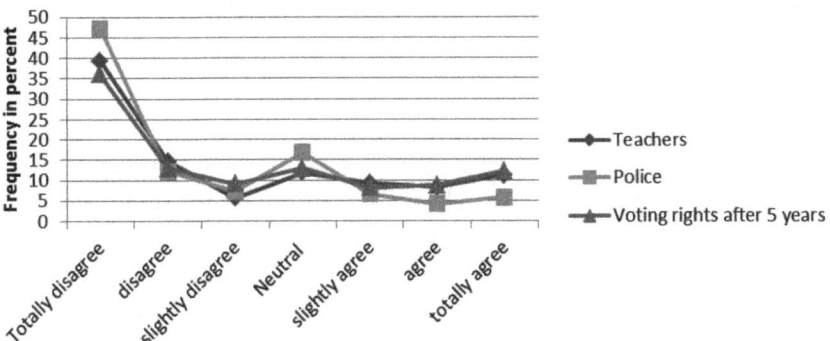

Fig. 6.6 SoPat scale: distribution of answers for three items relating to specific forms of societal participation

scales was pointed out ($r = 0.75$) and the *unifactorial* structure of the combined scale (TMK) was noted, suggesting that issues of cultural diversity are perceived on a single dimension. Therefore, when discussing influence of other variables, results will be reported for the combined scale.

Demographic Variables

Conform to Hypothesis 3, female participants expressed a more positive attitude towards multiculturalism. There is a statistically highly significant difference between the mean scores of male and female participants, but the effect sizes are small; $t(455) = 4.14$, $p < 0.001$; women $M = 4.34$ ($SD = 1.15$), men $M = 3.84$ ($SD = 1.22$), $\eta^2 = 0.04$. The relationship between the age of the participants and multiculturalism was not statistically significant.

As expected, higher levels of education were found to be strongly related to support for multiculturalism. The ANOVA comparing groups with different levels of educational achievement reaches statistical significance; $F(6, 436) = 12.14$, $p < 0.001$, $\eta^2 = 0.14$. Post hoc analysis using Tukey HSD show that those participants who have completed secondary school with an academic degree (bac) or above have significantly higher scores than those who have achieved a lower level school leaving qualification. The effect size is much stronger ($\eta^2 = 0.14$ medium effect) than for gender. Hypothesis 3 predicting that the support for multiculturalism will rise in line with the level of education can be confirmed.

Intergroup Relations

Nearly all participants ($n = 502$, 99 %) answered the question concerning the composition of their circle of friends. The results show that 6 % of the participants have "no" friends with a different country of birth to themselves, 52.8 % stated "few," 23.5 % "about half" and 17.7 % "many" which includes the one person who had indicated "all." The ANOVA examining whether these four groups differ regarding their attitude towards multiculturalism, as measured by the TMK scale, reaches statistical significance $F(3, 454) = 13.21$, $p < 0.001$, $\eta^2 = 0.08$. Post hoc tests using Tukey HSD show that the groups with "about half" and "many" friends with a different country of birth have significantly higher scores than the other two groups.[7]

The majority of the participants (70.5 %) indicated that they have not lived abroad for an extended period of time (> 6 months). A comparison of participants with and without foreign country experience shows that those who have lived abroad show higher levels of endorsement than those participants without this experience, but the effect size is small.[8]

Within this sample, the country of birth of parents (same vs. different) had no impact on the multiculturalism scores. However, a statistically significant difference was found for participants who have a partner with the same versus different country of birth. Those participants who have a partner with a different country of birth to themselves expressed a more positive attitude to multiculturalism than those with a same country of birth partner.[9]

As predicted, those participants who were not born in Luxembourg endorsed multiculturalism more strongly than participants born in Luxembourg.[10]

The results show that all *voluntary* forms of culture contact are conducive to endorsement of multiculturalism, confirming Hypothesis 4. To ascertain which form of culture contact has the strongest impact on the attitude towards multiculturalism, a linear hierarchical regression analysis was conducted. The results of this analysis are presented in Table 6.4. In a first step, the influence of gender and education was statistically controlled for. As shown above, the country of birth showed the strongest effect size ($\eta^2 = 0.08$) amongst culture contact variables. Therefore, this

---

[7] "none" $M = 3.20$ ($SD = 1.20$), "few" $M = 3.79$ ($SD = 1.22$), "about half" $M = 4.27$ ($SD = 1.05$) and "many" $M = 4.49$ ($SD = 1.18$).

[8] A comparison of the two groups (with and without foreign country experience) using a *t*- test for independent samples showed that both groups significantly differed regarding their attitude towards multiculturalism, $t(456) = -4.43$, $p < 0.001$, $\eta^2 = 0.04$, but the effect size is small. Participants with foreign country experience had a mean score of $M = 4.38$ ($SD = 1.19$) than participants without foreign country experience $M = 3.84$ ($SD = 1.20$).

[9] $t(350) = -3.51$, $p < 0.001$, $\eta^2 = 0.04$, partner's country of birth different $M = 4.34$ ($SD = 1.29$), partner's country of birth same $M = 3.76$ ($SD = 1.17$).

[10] $t(453) = -5.97$, $p < 0.001$, $\eta^2 = 0.8$; participants not born in Luxembourg $M = 5.12$ ($SD = 0.99$), participants born in Luxembourg $M = 3.90$ ($SD = 1.19$).

Table 6.4 Hierarchical regression. Intergroup relation variables as predictors for multiculturalism (TMK scale)

Variable	Demographic variables Block 1 β	Country of birth participant Block 2 β	Other forms of culture contact Block 3 β
Gender	−0.13*	−0.12*	−0.13**
Highest level of education	0.29***	0.27***	0.24***
Country of birth participant		0.24***	0.18***
Country of birth partner			0.06
Circle of friends			0.19***
Foreign country experience			0.02
R^2	0.12	0.17	0.22
Adjusted R^2	0.11	0.17	0.21
Δ R^2	0.12	0.06	0.05
Fchange	25.21***	25.97***	7.37***
Δ df	2/379	1/378	3/375

Note: * $p < 0.05$, ** $p < 0.01$, *** $p < 0.001$, highest β values are marked bold

variable was entered next. In a final step, all forms of voluntary contact (country of birth partner, circle of friends and foreign country experience) were entered. This final model explains 21 % of the differences in TMK scores, with level of education having the strongest effect explaining 11 % of the variance in TMK scores. Culture contact variables together explain an additional 10 %. In the final model, the composition of the circle of friends is the strongest predictor followed by country of birth of the participant, each explaining about 5 % of the variance in TMK scores.

The ranking exercise showed that the participants view the German national group to be closest to Luxembourg nationals, followed by French, Italians and Portuguese. However, the results for the positions 3 to 5 are not as clear as those for the nominations of "Germans" as having the least perceived distance to Luxembourg nationals.

The majority of the participants described themselves as multilingual (86 %), followed by bilingual (8.4 %) and only 5 % as monolingual. Participants were asked to indicate the languages they speak with friends (multiple options possible) and Luxembourgish was most frequently mentioned (98 %), followed by French (67 %), German (61 %) and English

(40 %). In a single choice question, participants were asked in which language they "consume" news. Luxembourgish was mentioned most frequently (43 %), followed by German (34 %) and French (16 %). There is statistically significant relationship between the preferred language use for news consumption and the endorsement of multiculturalism, as indicated by the ANOVA comparing the three groups regarding their TMK scores $F(2, 428) = 38.92, p < 0.001, \eta^2 = 0.15$. A planned comparison of those with a preference for the Luxembourgish with those with a French or German preference is statistically significant. $t(437) = 4.74, p < 0.001, \eta^2 = 0.05$; $M_{Lux} = 3.61$ ($SD = 1.17$), $M_{FR} = 4.95$ ($SD = 1.00$), $M_{DE} = 4.03$, ($SD = 1.12$).

The study reported in Chap. 5, *Bilingualism = Biculturalism?* had shown that the majority of the Luxembourg participants considered themselves to be multilingual but monocultural. Within the present study just over half of the participants (51.6 %) agreed with the statement, that language influences the way they think and feel, but for only a quarter (25.5 %) of the participants, a change in language is also considered a change in culture. Conversely, 59 % disagreed with the statement that a change in language is experienced as a change in culture (15.5 % were neutral).

The relationship between the question of "The language I speak influences the way I think and feel" and multiculturalism was statistically not significant ($p > 0.05$). The relationship between multiculturalism and the experience of a change in language as a change in culture is however statistically significant: Those participants who do not consider the change in language as a change in culture have significantly lower mean scores on the TMK scale $M = 3.77$ ($SD = 1.20$), than the other two groups, "neutral" group $M = 4.30$ ($SD = 1.15$) and the "agree" group $M = 4.38$ ($SD = 1.20$); $F(2, 438) = 12.48, p < 0.001, \eta^2 = 0.05$. The effect size is small, but for those participants neutral or in agreement with language serving as a prime for cultural frame switching, there is a positive relationship regarding openness towards multiculturalism. Hypothesis 5 could thus be confirmed.

Interindividual Difference Variables

Personality traits. Relatively weak correlations were found between the "Big 5" and the TMK scale, the correlation coefficients ranging from $r = 0.06$ (Extraversion), $r = 0.08$ (Conscientiousness), $r = -.09, p < 0.05$

(Neuroticism) to $r = 0.24$, $p < 0.01$ for Agreeableness and Openness. ANOVAs comparing the five groups (negative to positive attitude to multiculturalism) in relation to the "Big 5" scores showed no statistically significant relationship regarding Neuroticism ($p > 0.05$), but statistically significant relationships with Agreeableness and Openness: Agreeableness $F(4, 421) = 6.79$, $p < 0.001$, $\eta^2 = 0.06$, Openness $F(4, 422) = 5.96$, $p < 0.001$, $\eta^2 = 0.05$. For Agreeableness, the highest mean difference was between Group 1 (negative) and 5 (positive) $M_{dif} = -.63$, $p < 0.001$ as indicated by Tukey HSD. For Openness also only the mean difference between the Group 1 (negative) and 5 (positive) is significant $M_{dif} = -.62$, $p < 0.001$. To summarize, only the personality traits Agreeableness and Openness showed a statistically significant relationship with the TMK measure. No relationship was found with either Conscientiousness or Extraversion. The former was predicted, but the latter was not. The only weak negative correlation with Neuroticism was also not predicted. Hypothesis 6 could therefore only partially be confirmed.

For *subjective well-being* (*SWLS*), a statistically significant relationship with multiculturalism was found, but the effect size was small: The five TMK groups were compared regarding their relationship with SWLS and the ANOVA is statistically significant, $F(4, 422) = 3.63$, $p < 0.01$, $\eta^2 = 0.03$. The Dunnet C post hoc test showed that Group 5 (positive) has a significantly higher mean score ($M = 29.13$, $SD = 4.58$), than Group 2 (slightly negative) ($M = 25.63$, $SD = 5.84$) and Group 1 (negative) ($M = 26.76$, $SD = 5.14$) both ($p < 0.05$). In conclusion, there is a weak, positive association between subjective well-being and openness towards multiculturalism.

Human values. The results confirm that there is a relationship between the human values and TMK. The Pearson correlations between the ten value types and the two sets of value dimensions are presented in Table 6.5.

This analysis shows that all value types except for tradition have a statistically significant correlation with TMK, but the correlations vary in strength. The value types related to the social dimension, universalism and benevolence, show a strong relationship (all $p < 0.01$). Consequently, the value dimension Self-Transcendence also shows a highly significant and strong correlation with the TMK scale ($p < 0.01$). This finding is confirming Hypothesis 8. The value types related to Openness to change show statistically significant, but weak correlations. The correlations for

Table 6.5 Pearson correlations between value types, value dimensions and TMK scale

Value dimension	Value type (centered)	Pearson correlation	TMK
Openness to Change	Stimulation		0.15**
	Self-Determination	−0.04	−0.12**
	Hedonism		0.10*
Conservation	Security		**−0.34****
	Conformity	−0.25**	−0.26**
	Tradition		0.09
Self-Transcendence	Universalism	**0.51****	**0.43****
	Benevolence		**0.36****
Self-Enhancement	Achievement	−0.29**	−0.27**
	Power		−0.20**

Note: *< 0.05, **< 0.01, r > 0.30 values are marked in bold

the opposing dimension are much stronger: As predicted, the value types security and conformity, which combine to form the value dimension Conservation, show a strong negative relationship with TMK ($p < 0.01$). These findings conform with Hypothesis 7.

To examine the relationship between the value dimensions and openness towards multiculturalism, participants were first divided into five groups of approximately equal sizes depending on their scores on each on the Self-Enhancement and Self-Transcendence scales. Then the relationship between "very low," "low," "neutral," "high" and " very high" scores on the value dimensions and the TMK scale was examined. The ANOVA for the TMK scale shows a highly significant statistical relationship between the high in Self-Transcendence group and openness towards multiculturalism.[11] The effect size is large for all three scales. The opposite effect can be shown for the corresponding value dimension Self-Enhancement. Participants who expressed a strong preference for Self-Enhancement-related values showed lower endorsement of multiculturalism and the related ANOVAs are all statistically highly significant.[12]

---

[11] TMK scale, $F(4, 453) = 38.21$, $p < 0.001$, $\eta^2 = 0.25$; MIS scale $F(4,475) = 35.97$, $p < 0.001$, $\eta^2 = 0.23$ and soPat $F(4,478) = 29,97$, $p < 0.001$, $\eta^2 = 0.20$.

[12] The related ANOVAs are all statistically highly significant, but the effect sizes are smaller: TMK $F(4,446) = 11.11$, $p < 0.001$, $\eta^2 = 0.09$, MIS, $F(4,464) = 10.76$, $p < 0.001$, $\eta^2 = 0.08$ and soPat $F(4, 467) = 10.44$, $p < 0.001$, $\eta^2 = 0.08$.

A linear hierarchical regression analysis was carried out to examine the predictive qualities of the individual difference variables, which were identified as having a relationship with multiculturalism as measured by TMK. In step 1, demographic variables were statistically controlled for. In step 2, the personality traits Agreeableness and Openness were entered. In a final step the value dimensions Self-Transcendence and Conservation were entered. The results, as presented in Table 6.6 below, show that the value dimension Self-Transcendence makes the largest contribution in explaining the differences in TMK scores.

As before, gender and education (this time operationalized as career level) explain 11 % of the variance in TMK scores. The personality traits Agreeableness and Openness explain a further 9 % of the differences. Value dimensions have the strongest impact explaining a further 18 % of the differences. Together, these six variables explain 37 % of the variance in the TMK scores, with the value dimension Self-Transcendence making a major contribution as indicated by the high β value. The analysis of the part correlation shows that this variable alone explains 14.56 % of the variance of the TMK scores.

Table 6.6 Hierarchical regression: individual difference variables as predictors for multiculturalism (TMK scale)

Variable	Demographic variables Block 1 β	Personality traits Block 2 β	Value dimensions Block 3 β
Gender	−0.16***	−0.13**	−0.10**
Career path	**0.28***	**0.25***	0.20***
Agreeableness		0.22***	0.12***
Openness		0.20***	0.13***
Self-Transcendence			**0.41***
Conservation			−0.14***
R^2	0.12	0.2	0.38
Adjusted R^2	0.11	0.19	0.37
ΔR^2	0.12	0.09	0.18
Fchange	27.42***	22.51***	60.25***
Δ df	2/418	2/416	2/414

Note: *p < 0.05, **p < 0.01, ***p < 0.001. Highest β values are marked in bold

Understanding of Nationality

Participants differ regarding their understanding of nationality as socially constructed or primordial. The frequency distribution of answers along the primordial (P)—socially constructed (S) spectrum is presented in Fig. 6.7.

The spread of answers shows that participants differ concerning their understanding of nationality. For statement 1 (Nationality), 40 % of the participants gravitate towards the primordial end of the spectrum, believing that it is only possible to have one nationality, 9 % are undecided and just over half of the participants consider it possible to have more than one nationality. Regarding item 2 (Birth), 27 % of the participants agree more with the statement that nationality is determined at birth, again 9 % are undecided and 64 % gravitate towards the constructivist pole, believing that it is possible to acquire nationalities after birth. The Pearson correlation between both statements is $r = 0.55$, $p < 0.01$. For each bipolar statement I divided participants into three groups (primordial, neutral and constructivist),[13] depending on their position on the primordial-constructivist spectrum. In a second step I assessed the association between the understanding of nationality and the level of endorsement of multiculturalism. For the first statement (Nationality) the association is highly significant: Those participants who believe that it is only possible to have one nationality have significantly lower multiculturalism scores than those who are of the

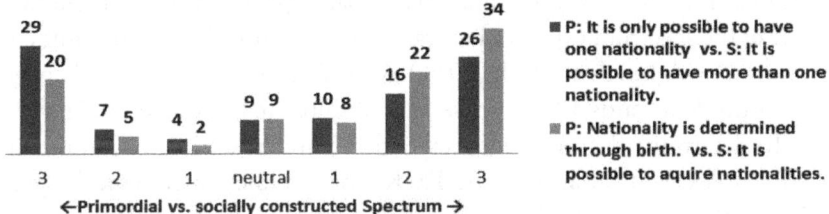

Fig. 6.7 Bipolar statements regarding understanding of nationality—answers in percent

[13] Group sizes, statement 1: primordial $n = 196$, neutral $n = 44$ and constructivist $n = 253$, statement 2: primordial $n = 132$, neutral $n = 46$ and constructivist $n = 313$.

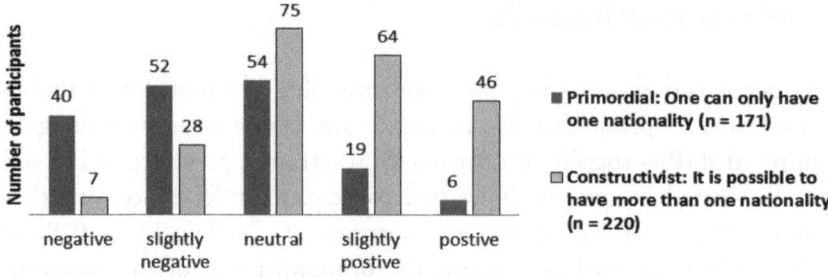

Fig. 6.8 Understanding of nationality (one versus several nationalities) and multiculturalism

opinion that it is possible to have more than one nationality. The relationship is visually represented in Fig. 6.8. As can be seen, participants on the constructivist end of the spectrum, indicated by the light grey bars, have a more positive attitude toward multiculturalism. The χ^2 test is highly significant $\chi^2(8, 429) = 92.07, p < 0.001$, Cramer's V = 0.33.

Findings are even stronger for bipolar statement 2 (Birth). The χ^2 test for statement 2 is also highly significant $\chi^2(8, 429) = 90.35, p < 0.001$, Cramer's V = 0.36. Overall, fewer participants gravitated towards the primordial end of the spectrum for this item. The majority of those who believe that nationality is determined at birth show a negative to slightly negative attitude towards multiculturalism. Of this group only 8 % endorse multiculturalism. Conversely, the majority of participants on the constructivist pole of the spectrum express a neutral or positive attitude towards multiculturalism, with less than a fifth (19 %) expressing a negative or slightly negative attitude towards TMK. These relationships are illustrated in Fig. 6.9.

To determine if and to what extend the understanding of nationality is able to explain variance in the TMK scores, a linear hierarchical regression analysis was carried out. In a first step, the effects of demographic variables were statistically controlled for. In a second step the nationality variables were entered. The results are presented in Table 6.7.

This analysis shows that the understanding of nationality does explain part of the variance in TMK scores. After controlling for the effects of gender and education, the understanding of nationality explains 25 % of the differences in the TMK scores, with the item 1 (nationality) making the larger contribution ($\beta = 0.35$).

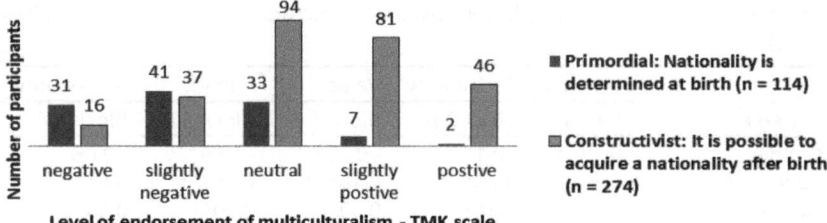

Fig. 6.9 Understanding of nationality (nationality is determined at birth) and multiculturalism

Table 6.7 Hierarchical regression: understanding of nationality as predictor for differences in TMK scores

Variable	Demographic VA Block 1 β	Nationality Block 2 β
Gender	−0.13**	−0.06
Level of education	0.29***	0.17***
Item1, Nationality		**0.35*****
Item2, Birth		0.25***
R^2	0.12	0.37
Adjusted R^2	0.11	0.36
ΔR^2	0.12	0.25
Fchange	29.27***	86.24***
Δ df	2/440	2/438

Note: * $p < 0.05$, ** $p < 0.01$, *** $p < 0.001$. Highest β values are marked in bold

Interim Summary—Variables Influencing Multiculturalism

In a final step all variables which were shown to have a statistical significant relationship were compared regarding their impact on the explanation of variance in TMK scores. Which variable would be the best predictor? A hierarchical regression analysis was carried out. First, the impact of demographic variables was statistically controlled for, followed by a stepwise inclusion of the other variables. For the human values, the value types which were shown to have the largest impact were entered. The results of this analysis are presented in Table 6.8.

As this analysis shows, this model explains 50 % of the variance in TMK scores. This analysis also demonstrates the importance of the

Table 6.8 Hierarchical multiple regression—predictors of multiculturalism (TMK scale)

Variable	Dem. VA Block 1 β	Personality Block 2 β	Value Block 3 β	Friends Block 4 β	Nationality Block 5 β
Gender	−0.13**	−0.11*	−0.09*	−0.09*	−0.06
Education	0.29***	0.26***	0.16***	0.15***	0.01**
Agreeableness		0.21***	0.10**	0.10**	0.06
Openness		0.20***	0.13**	0.11**	0.09*
Security(z)			−0.23***	−0.23***	−0.18***
Universalism (z)			0.29***	0.28***	0.20***
Benevolence(z)			0.23***	0.22***	0.18***
Circle of friends				0.16***	0.11**
Item1— Nationality					0.21***
Item2—Birth					0.17***
R^2	0.12	0.20	0.40	0.43	0.51
Adjusted R^2	0.11	0.20	0.39	0.42	0.50
ΔR^2	0.12	0.09	**0.20**	0.02	**0.09**
Fchange	29.27***	23.22***	49.03***	17.50***	37.38***
Δ df	2/440	2/438	3/435	1/434	2/432

Note: * $p < 0.05$, ** $p < 0.01$, *** $p < 0.001$

human values—the three value types explain 20 % of the variance in TMK scores. The composition of the circle of friends makes a smaller contribution, but the understanding of nationality explains a further 9 % of the variance in TMK scores.

Analysis of the Qualitative Findings

Just under a third of the participants (n = 158) used the option to comment. The question was: "From your point of view, what are the advantages of a multicultural society? If you like, please write down your comments." The comments were analysed according to three different criteria (1) Level of complexity, (2) positive or negative comment and (3) themes mentioned.

A scientific collaborator and I separately coded the comments according to these three criteria. The instances when coding differed were discussed and the coding criteria were refined. In terms of classifying the answers into positive or negative comments, agreement was nearly perfect. Regarding complexity, the criteria for the 2nd and 3rd category had to be tightened. The agreement for the categorization into topics was high. For those cases where there were disagreements, the criteria were clarified and after this clarification phase complete consensus regarding the themes could be achieved.

Level of Complexity

The answers were coded into the following four categories, depending on their level of complexity: (1) *one* word or concept (n = 35), (2) List of up to four words or concepts (n= 77), (3) one or two sentences with logical conjunction (n = 34) and (4) a complex paragraph (n = 10). Two answers could not be interpreted.

Positive and Negative Comments

The question was phrased focusing on advantages and therefore it is not surprising that the majority of comments mention advantages of multiculturalism (n = 139). Thirteen participants made critical statements and four participants mention both advantages and disadvantages. Participants taking advantage of the open comments field were compared with those who did not comment regarding their attitude to multiculturalism. The independent samples t-test showed that the group who commented had significantly higher mean scores than those participants who did not comment.[14]

Content Analysis of Open Comments

The topical categories were created in a "bottom-up" process, that is, the categories were created based on the themes and concepts mentioned. The goal was to be as parsimonious and comprehensive as possible. A total of

---

[14] MIS $t(487)$ = 4.63, p < 0.001, η^2 = 0.04, $M_{comment}$ = 4.58 (SD = 1.06), $M_{no\ comment}$ = 4.10 (SD = 1.06). The difference is even stronger for the soPat scale $t(491)$ = 5.33, p < 0.01, η^2 = 0.05, $M_{comment}$ = 4.31 (SD = 1.25), $M_{no\ comment}$ = 3.26 (SD = 1.25).

388 contributions were counted which were divided into 24 categories. A separate analysis was carried out for the positive and critical comments. The themes and their frequencies are listed in Appendix 9 (negative) and Appendix 10 (positive).

Critical comments. Several participants used the invitation to state advantages of multiculturalism to point out that in fact, multiculturalism, in their view, does not have any advantages:

> *Die in Luxemburg propagierte multikulturelle Gesellschaft sind in Wirklichkeit Parallelgesellschaften und der Luxemburger ist der Jenige (sic) der sich im eigenen Land den einzelnen ausländischen Gruppen anpassen muss.* Study participant.[15]

The most frequently mentioned theme was the need for adaptation by the immigrant groups ($n = 9$) and the fear of being overwhelmed by foreign influences (Überfremdung) ($n = 6$).

Positive comments. Whereas the critical comments focus on specific forms of living together, the positive comments centre on more idealistic topics. The most frequently mentioned theme was broadening of the horizon ("über den eigenen Tellerand blicken"), getting to know different perspectives and ideas ($n = 70$). Diversity, experienced as enrichment, was mentioned 59 times. In third place, with 50 mentions was the cognitive component of getting to know different customs and traditions. A participant's comment touching on tolerance and the economic benefits is provided next:

> *D'une part la société multiculturelle permet à chaque citoyen de développer quotidiennement sa notion de tolérance. Cette réflexion personnelle se fait alors de manière tacite, non forcée, progressive, chaque groupe culturel apprenant peu à peu toujours plus sur la manière de vivre du voisin. D'autre part, dans une réalité économique définitivement tournée vers la mondialisation, la société multiculturelle participe clairement à la performance économique du pays qui l'accueille, car ses habitants intègrent la mondialisation comme une réalité*

---

[15] The much propagated multicultural society in Luxembourg is in reality a parallel society and the Luxembourg people are those who have to adapt to the various foreign groups in their own country.

quotidienne, et non comme une pression venue de l'étranger. Study participant.[16]

Conclusion

Attitude towards Multiculturalism

This study with 507 participants working within Luxembourg's capital showed that the idea of multiculturalism, as measured by the MIS scale, is more strongly endorsed than specific measures of societal participation. Only about a quarter of the participants expressed a negative attitude towards the idea of multiculturalism, but 43 % of the participants were critical towards societal participation, as measured by the soPat subscale. The analysis at item level showed that specific measures such as employing more non-Luxembourgers within the police force or as teachers were rejected by the majority of participants. A possible explanation for this finding could be the "principle–implementation gap." Yogeeswaran and Dasgupta (2014) investigated the effect of multiculturalism construals on attitudes towards ethnic minorities. When taking an abstract "bird's eye" view of the multiculturalism construal, participants showed higher endorsement of the concept than when "zooming-in" to focus on specific details on how this goal can be achieved.

As mentioned before, few empirical studies have been carried out so far investigating specifically the majority attitudes towards multiculturalism. Canada is one of the few countries where a positive level of support, as measured by the MIS scale, has actually been found. The mean reported by Berry and Kalin (1995) $M = 4.59$ $(SD = 1.20)$ is significantly higher than that for the present study $M = 4.25$ $(SD = 1.08)$ as the one sample t-test shows, $t(487) = -6.81$, $p < 0.001$. However, the mean obtained

---

[16] On the one hand the multicultural society allows every citizen to develop a notion of tolerance on a daily basis. This personal reflection happens tacitly, unforced and progressively with each cultural group gradually learning more and more about each other. On the other hand, at a time when globalization is an economic reality, a multicultural society is also better positioned to take on this challenge, as the inhabitants have already integrated the force of globalization into their daily lives and do not perceive it as an external pressure.

for the Luxembourg sample is significantly higher than that reported for Dutch majority members M = 4.10 (SD = 1.02) (Arends-Tóth & van de Vijver, 2003, p. 259) $t(487)$ = 3.23, p < 0.001. Whilst Dutch majority participants have shown a *neutral* attitude towards multiculturalism ideology, the Luxembourg participants have shown slight endorsement. The Luxembourg mean score is statistically significantly higher than the scale mid-point. In contrast, the societal Participation domain was the most strongly endorsed in Dutch studies (Schalk-Soekar et al., 2009). For the Luxembourg sample, the finding is clearly reversed and may be the effect of the "majority" in the "minority" position. As noted in Chap. 2, Luxembourg is characterized by looking outward economically, but looking inward in relation to national identity. Protectionism may become stronger in an environment where outsiders in fact outnumber the resident population. At 4 %, the percentage of foreign citizens in the Netherlands is much lower than the 43.1 % in Luxembourg (Eurostat, 2011). The analysis at item level of the societal Participation subscale also shows that those items which "zoom-in" on specific forms of participation are the most strongly opposed. "Softer" forms of participation, such as mutual co-operation or children playing with non-Luxembourg children are actually endorsed.

The analysis of the open comments also pointed at a difference in emphasis between the positive and negative comments. Whereas the positive comments focused on "soft," ideational aspects such as "Esprit," broadening of the horizon and so on, the critical comments addressed specific aspects of living together. Again, the abstract *idea* or the principle of diversity is embraced, but the *reality* in terms of practical implementation and consequences less so. Schalk-Soekar (2007) had asked participants to state what they thought multiculturalism meant. She obtained seven main categories. The most frequently mentioned category (1) at 62 % was a demographic meaning (a state/society in which many different cultures are living), but the subsequent subject areas mentioned closely match the answers provided in the open section (see Appendix 10). In second place Schalk-Soekar's respondents mentioned (2) doing things/ being together (59 %); (3) acceptance of plurality (59 %) (e.g. being tolerant, open); (4) Learning from each other, mixing cultures (27 %); (5) Insistence that the Netherlands is the main culture (27 %); (6) Equality

(12 %) and finally negative aspects of multiculturalism (9 %) (e.g. NL will lose values, social security spongers, criminality, differences too large). The positive associations were very similar across the two studies. Furthermore, in both studies the positive associations by far outnumber the negative comments.

The unidimensionality and high reliability of the multiculturalism scales were confirmed also for this study. The distribution of the scores follows a normal curve, which is an indication that there is no polarization into proponents and opponents of multiculturalism. A comparison with Dutch data shows that the variance is higher in the Luxembourg sample. As with the present studies, the Dutch participants were divided into five groups depending on their level of endorsement of multiculturalism (Schalk-Soekar & van de Vijver, 2008). However, the full MAS scale as developed by Breugelmans and van de Vijver (2004) was administered, so the data are not directly comparable. As was explained above, the MAS scale covers the same domains as MIS plus societal Participation. Therefore, the MAS scale and the combined TMK scale constructed for this study measure the same domains and therefore, in terms of content measured, there is a high degree of overlap. For the Dutch study the mean score on the MAS scale was $M = -.06$ (Scale mid-point = 0; 7 point Likert scale, SD not provided for the MAS total scale). A comparison of the frequency of answers for the two samples is given in Fig. 6.10.

Figure 6.10 illustrates several points: The distribution for the Dutch sample is peaked—with nearly half of the participants taking a neutral

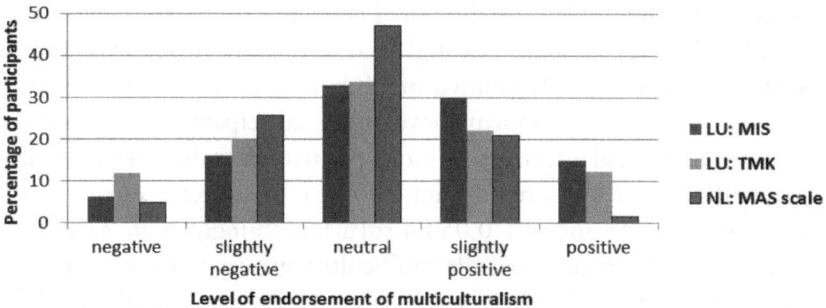

Fig. 6.10 Endorsement of multiculturalism: comparison of Dutch and Luxembourg participants

stance and very few showing endorsement or outright rejection. Within the Luxembourg sample only a third of the participants take a neutral position—with 45 % endorsing the idea of multiculturalism (MIS) and somewhat lower endorsement of the combined scale, which includes the societal participation measures. Schalk-Soekar et al. (2009) explained the "neutral" position by the fact that the overarching concept of multiculturalism contains both positive and negative aspects which cancel each other out. The varying support across domains has already been mentioned. Although not polarized, the findings suggest that stronger positions regarding multiculturalism are held within the Luxembourg sample.

In this context, I would also like to address the question of the representativeness of the sample in the present study again. As noted above the sample can be considered representative in terms of key characteristics, but in light of the analysis of the qualitative findings, it is possible to assume that self-selection may have taken place. Just under a third of all participants provided an open comment. The question was phrased asking for *advantages* of multiculturalism. Therefore, it was expected that the majority of comments would refer to benefits associated with multiculturalism. I assumed that those who are of the opinion that multiculturalism does not bear advantages would also take the opportunity to express their views. Ten percent of the participants used the open comment field in this way. These comments, which defy an instruction, should possibly be given stronger weight than would be given to a question asking explicitly for disadvantages. Ninety percent answered the question conforming to the instruction and 10 % did not. Taking this proportion of 9:1 into consideration, the conclusion could be drawn that persons with a more positive attitude towards multiculturalism were more inclined to complete the survey. As was shown above, those participants who completed the comments field expressed a more positive attitude towards multiculturalism than those who did not, although the effect sizes were small ($\eta^2 = 0.04$ for MIS and $\eta^2 = 0.05$ for soPat). Seemingly, more employees with a positive attitude towards multiculturalism may have completed the survey. It is possible that a positive bias influences the reliability of the data and the results should possibly be corrected downward.

The Influence of Other Variables on Multiculturalism

In the following paragraphs, the variables explaining the differences in the attitude towards multiculturalism will be discussed in turn.

As in previous studies on multiculturalism a relationship between the level of education and multiculturalism was found. Endorsement of multiculturalism rises in line with the highest level of education achieved. This finding could be explained by the fact that a higher level of education generally increases options in the private and professional sphere. As Brandstädter (2007) noted, higher self-complexity increases the scope for compensation. In case of a threat to the self-concept in one area, this threat can then be compensated with success in another area. Transferred to the multicultural society this may mean that persons with a higher level of education feel less threatened in their existence. On the contrary, foreign influences may be perceived as stimulating, as enrichment rather than as a threat.

All forms of *voluntary* culture contact experience had a positive influence on multiculturalism. By design, the majority of participants were Luxembourg-born. As in previous studies, immigrants to Luxembourg endorsed multiculturalism more strongly than native-born participants. Even within the Study *On being bicultural* as reported in Chap. 5, the students who were *born* in Luxembourg showed lower level of endorsement of multiculturalism than those who have moved to Luxembourg. A mixed circle of friends, a partner with a different country of birth and having lived in a foreign country are all associated with a higher level of endorsement of multiculturalism. This finding suggests that there is a virtuous cycle between culture contact and endorsement of multiculturalism, but the challenge is the first step. If my partner comes from a different country, the likelihood increases that the circle for friends becomes more mixed. Living abroad increases the chances of finding a partner with a different country of birth and then again finding friends who have a different country of birth. Amongst various forms of culture contact, the composition of the circle of friends was identified as strongest predictor for differences in the TMK scores, with a positive attitude towards multiculturalism rising in line with an increasingly heterogeneous circle of friends.

Usually, language is a key barrier for entering into culture contact, but in Luxembourg, trilingualism is the norm. As expected, the vast majority of participants described themselves as bi- or even multilingual, speaking at least three languages. Being able to speak three different languages does not mean that there is an equal preference for the languages. Luxembourgish was the most frequently mentioned language for communication with friends, followed by French, German and English (multiple choice). Luxembourgish was also the preferred language for news, followed by German and French in third place (forced choice question). As in other countries, languages are taught at school (Study 1 in Chap. 5) and it is not necessary to move to another country to learn a language. In fact, 70 % of the participants have not lived abroad. For language learning this means that languages are actually *learnt* for the most part as foreign languages, albeit at an early age. This may also explain why for the majority of participants the change of language is not experienced as a change in culture. About half of the participants acknowledge that language influences the way they think and feel, but only a quarter consider languages to be a cultural prime. These findings are in line with Study 1 in Chap. 5 which identified monoculturalism combined with multilingualism as a characteristic for the Luxembourg participants. A link between the language perception as cultural prime and a more positive attitude to multiculturalism could be identified.

As noted above, the majority of the participants have not lived in another country. For 72 % of the participants, Luxembourg is country of birth for participant as well as both parents. The majority of participants (78 %) have also a partner with the same country of birth—which is Luxembourg for the vast majority (95 %). In terms of daily contact, Luxembourg nationals were also mentioned most frequently for the work domain as well as in the private sphere. Naturally, the centre of life for individuals born and raised in Luxembourg will be Luxembourg, which finds its expression in the language preference and contact behaviour. These findings also show that it is possible to lead a monoculturally centred life within a demographically heterogeneous context. This is also supported by the indication concerning the composition of the circle of friends. Whilst only 6 % of the participants stated that they have no friends with a different country of birth, over half (53 %) stated that they have "few" friends with a different country of birth.

Van de Vijver et al. (2006) argued that the distinction between ethnic and civic citizenship does not play a role in the understanding of individual differences in attitudes towards multiculturalism. In the present study, a strong relationship between the understanding of the concept of nationality as socially constructed as opposed to primordial could be shown. After controlling for gender and education, understanding of nationality explained 25 % of the variance in TMK scores. In the final model (see Table 6.8), nationality explained 9 % of the variance in multiculturalism scores. Participants on the primordial end of the spectrum endorse multiculturalism significantly less than those who have constructivist understanding. It is also important to note that within the present sample, 29 % strongly agreed with the statement that is possible to have only one nationality and 20 % strongly agreed with the statement that nationality is determined at birth. Persons are not necessarily aware of their understanding of nationality. For people who assume that nationality is acquired through birth, the concept of *multi*-culturalism is inherently contradictory, as they assume that it is only possible to have *one* nationality. For these individuals nationality is determined through lineage. By definition, such an ethnic interpretation of nationality is *exclusive* as it is then only possible to belong to one nationality. The new Luxembourg Law on Nationality allows for dual citizenship—explicitly stating that it is possible to have attachment to two nationalities. This point of view will be difficult to share by a sizeable minority within the present sample. The challenge is then to build a more *inclusive* understanding of nationality. This finding has policy implications, as celebrating differences may not be a path which will convince persons who hold an exclusive understanding that it is possible to be both committed to Luxembourg and at the same time to a different country of origin.

Overall, personality traits were shown to have only a weak relationship with multiculturalism. Only Openness and Agreeableness had a statistically significant relationship, but effect sizes were weak. This may be due to the use of the short measure assessing the "Big 5." For pragmatic reasons the short version was used and a personality test with a larger range of items may have yielded stronger relationships. The data suggest that human values are the more important predictor for the attitude towards multiculturalism. Values are usually reflected, as they provide the justification for daily actions; they provide guidance and orientation in how we lead our daily lives. As explained above, two basic conflicts need to be negotiated—orientation towards others (Self-Transcendence) versus orientation towards self (Self-Enhancement) and preference of stability (Conservation) versus Open-mindedness to change. People differ regarding the emphasis they place on either pole.

The value types universalism and benevolence, which together form the value dimension Self-Transcendence, were shown to be strong predictors for the endorsement of multiculturalism. These value types tap into the social dimension and in particular the concern for the well-being and equal treatment of all human beings. It is therefore no surprise that persons who express a strong interest in these value types will also endorse multiculturalism as the equal treatment of all is also a core dimension of multiculturalism. As noted above, Openness to change only showed a low, statistically not significant correlation with multiculturalism. On the other hand the value types security and to a lesser degree conformity showed a statistically significant, negative correlation with multiculturalism. Persons with a strong need for security therefore also expressed a more negative attitude towards multiculturalism. Since values guide behaviour these findings are noteworthy and have implications for policies.

Policy Implications

These findings amongst Luxembourg natives, who find themselves increasingly in the minority, point to an endorsement of the *principle* of multiculturalism. Thus, the idea of a plurally composed society is widely endorsed. However, specific measures of integration are largely opposed. The analysis of the open comments shows that those who perceive multiculturalism as an advantage stress the "soft" factors such as broadening of horizon, learning from different cultures, tolerance and enrichment. Those who are critical focus on specific aspects of living together. The data suggest that there is an appreciation of differences, that differences are perceived as enrichment and different customs and traditions are perceived as a welcome way of broadening the horizon. Tolerance and respect for different cultures exist, at the same time as reluctance towards acceptance of concrete forms of societal participation. Aspects that were described under the "misleading" model of multiculturalism in Chap. 3 are endorsed, and the data suggest that those aspects mentioned under the shared citizenship approach also described in Chap. 3 need to be addressed by policy-makers. The critical voices, for example, raised the question of limits. Within the concept of shared citizenship this falls under the heading of stressing human rights and individual freedom over respect for cultural traditions. Secondly, persons with strong self-enhancement values and those with a primordial (exclusive) understanding of nationality were shown to be more reluctant towards endorsing multiculturalism. The challenge is to build and foster a more inclusive understanding of nationality. This may be achieved by stressing commonalities, rather than celebrating differences. Celebrating differences might actually exacerbate the divide, rather than accepting immigrants as fellow citizens. This point of building inclusive identities over the recognition of ancestral cultural identities was also raised under the shared citizenship model as well as cultural change and cultural mixing over the reification of static cultural differences. This latter point is also borne out by the data as all forms of voluntary culture contact were shown to have a beneficial effect on the attitude to multiculturalism. As was noted in Chap. 4, "in-group" members tend to be classified on a trait-base, whereas "out-group" members are classified category-based. Personal contact may lead to a more trait-based classification process, but the challenge is to introduce a virtuous cycle. More than half of the participants indicated that they have no or few friends with a different country of birth to their own. Therefore, there is scope for more inter-mixing. On the other hand, there is also the issue of reciprocity—the incoming population must also be willing to engage. Within Luxembourg, the yardstick for this engagement is often language competence, and more specifically Luxembourgish language competence (see Chap. 2). The final point emphasized by the model of shared citizenship is political participation and economic opportunities over the symbolic politics of cultural recognition. The door towards political participation has been opened through the New Law on Luxembourg Nationality, although the debate is on-going whether the hurdles in terms of residence clause and language level are too high. However, in principle, foreign residents have the opportunity to apply for (dual) citizenship if they wish and if their home country allows this to happen. The concession that foreigners can apply for Luxembourg citizenship without having to give up their other nationality can be considered a milestone. It is acknowledged that nationality can be adopted by choice/volition rather than lineage. The political elite consider citizenship as a means to facilitate integration (mid-point) whereas the public debate often focuses on the "symptoms" of integration. Immigrants have to prove integration first and may be rewarded by citizenship (end-point). The "symptom" of integration is mainly reduced to the question of (Luxembourgish) languages competence in the public debate. Apart from this debate, the core question is whether economic participation should depend on citizenship. The findings suggest that within majority population there is reluctance to accept this aspect of societal participation of multiculturalism.

Appendix 1: Multiculturalism Ideology Scale (MIS)—psychometric characteristics

Item/Scale	N	M	SD	Sk	Ku	r_{it}	p	α
1 It is good that many different groups with different cultural backgrounds live in Luxembourg.	503	4.83	1.86	−0.53	−0.73	0.76	0.69	
2 Ethnic minorities should preserve their ethnic heritage in Luxembourg.	499	4.28	1.78	−0.17	−0.80	0.71	0.61	
3 It would be best if all people forgot their background as soon as possible.(R)	503	5.34	1.76	−0.87	−0.17	0.56	0.76	
4 A society that has a variety of cultural groups is more able to tackle new problems as they occur.	502	4.02	1.82	−0.11	−0.91	0.63	0.57	

	N	M	SD	Sk	Ku	r_{it}	p	α
5 The unity of the country is weakened by non-Luxembourgers. (R)	503	4.00	2.11	−0.01	−1.32	0.61	0.57	
6 If immigrants want to keep their own cultures they should keep to themselves. (R)	504	3.95	2.11	−0.05	−1.32	0.62	0.56	
7 Native Luxembourgers should do more to learn about the customs and traditions of the other cultural groups.	503	3.78	1.84	0.03	−1.02	0.56	0.54	
8 Immigrant parents must encourage their children to retain the culture and traditions of their homeland.	503	3.58	1.73	0.13	−0.81	0.55	0.51	
9 Immigrants to Luxembourg should change their behavior to be more like the Luxembourgish people.(R)	504	2.33	1.47	1.16	0.80	0.47	0.33	
Total MIS Scale	489	4.25	1.08	−0.23	−0.51			0.87

Note: Items Likert scale 1–7; (R) reversed item; M = mean; SD = standard deviation; Sk = skewdness; Ku = Kurtosis, r_{it} = corrected Item—total correlation, p = item difficulty; α = Cronbach's alpha

Appendix 2: Screeplot MIS scale

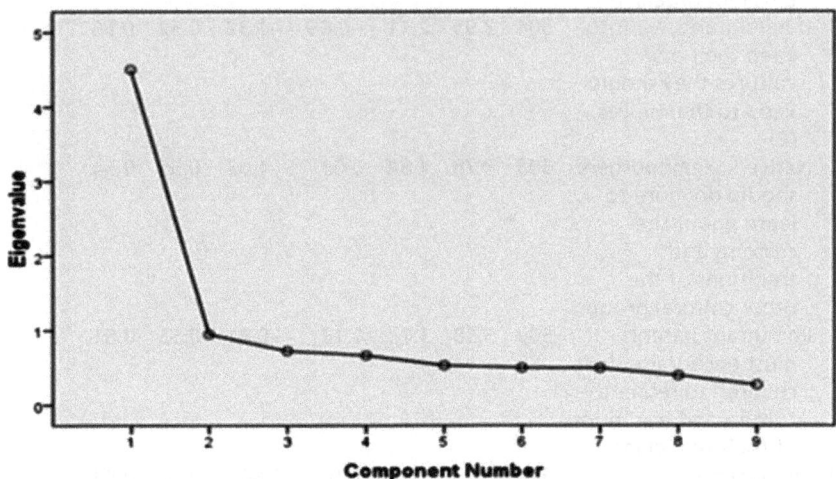

Scree Plot

Appendix 3: Factor loadings MIS scale

Item	Loading
1 It is good that many different groups with different cultural backgrounds live in Luxembourg.	0.838
2 Ethnic minorities should preserve their ethnic heritage in Luxembourg.	0.794
3 A society that has a variety of cultural groups is more able to tackle new problems as they occur.	0.728
4 If immigrants want to keep their own cultures they should keep to themselves. (R)	0.713
5 The unity of the country is weakened by non-Luxembourgers. (R)	0.709
6 Native Luxembourgers should do more to learn about the customs and traditions of the other cultural groups.	0.670
7 Immigrant parents must encourage their children to retain the culture and traditions of their homeland.	0.656
8 It would be best if all people forgot their background as soon as possible. (R)	0.653
9 Immigrants to Luxembourg should change their behavior to be more like the Luxembourgish people. (R)	0.570

Appendix 4: Multiculturalism Attitude Scale (MAS) social Participation Subscale (soPat)— psychometric characteristics

Item/Skala	N	M	SD	Sk	Ku	r_{it}	p	α
1 Luxembourgers and non-Luxembourgers should cooperate more to solve problems in Luxembourg.	502	4.80	1.76	−0.54	−0.50	0.58	0.69	
2 When shopping, I get annoyed if I get not served in Luxembourgish. (R)	504	2.62	1.97	0.98	−0.32	0.45	0.37	
3 I think that Luxembourgers and non-Luxembourgers should seek more contact with one another.	503	4.82	1.65	−0.52	−0.25	0.56	0.69	
4 Children should be taught by Luxembourgish and non-Luxembourgish teachers.	500	3.06	2.18	0.59	−1.14	0.55	0.44	
5 I think that more non-Luxembourgish persons should work for the Luxembourg police.	501	2.59	1.89	0.90	−0.38	0.61	0.37	

Item/Skala	N	M	SD	Sk	Ku	r_{it}	p	α
6 I think that Luxembourgish children should play more with non-native children.	504	4.81	1.69	−0.46	−0.41	0.60	0.69	
7 I would not like to have a non-native boss at work. (R)	503	4.82	2.24	−0.57	−1.17	0.48	0.69	
8 I think that after a period of 5 years Luxembourgers and immigrants should have the same voting rights.	503	3.19	2.17	0.51	−1.18	0.61	0.46	
Total MAS	493	3.84	1.32	0.16	−0.45			0.83

Note: Items Likert scale 1–7; (R) reversed item; *M* = mean; *SD* = standard deviation; *Sk* = skewdness; *Ku* = Kurtosis, r_{it} = corrected Item—total correlation, p = item difficulty; α = Cronbach's alpha

Appendix 5: Screeplot MAS social Participation (soPat) subscale

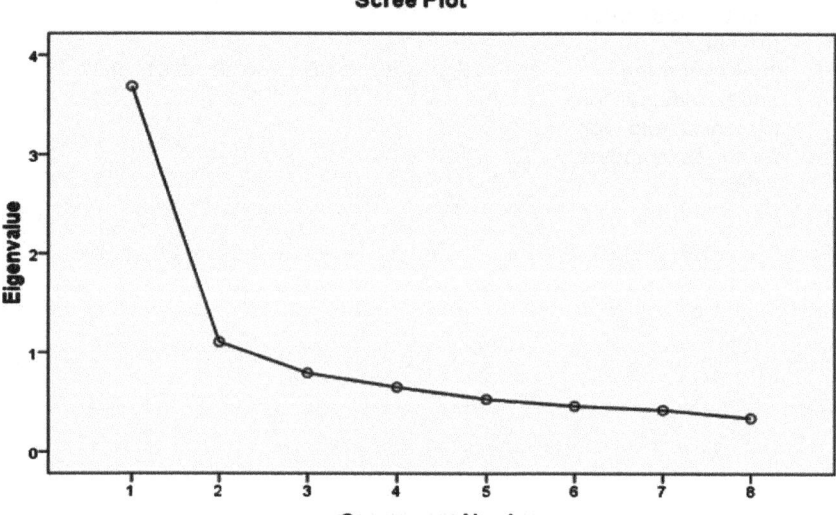

Appendix 6: Factor loadings MAS social Participation (soPat) subscale

Item/Skala	Loading
1 I think that Luxembourgers and non-Luxembourgers should seek more contact with one another.	0.764
2 Luxembourgers and non-Luxembourgers should cooperate more to solve problems in Luxembourg.	0.713
3 I think that Luxembourgish children should play more with non-native children.	0.695
4 I think that after a period of 5 years Luxembourgers and immigrants should have the same voting rights.	0.587
5 I think that more non-Luxembourgish persons should work for the Luxembourg police.	0.583
6 Children should be taught by Luxembourgish and non-Luxembourgish teachers.	0.567
7 When shopping, I get annoyed if I get not served in Luxembourgish. (R)	0.540
8 I would not like to have a non-native boss at work. (R)	0.342

Appendix 7: Screeplot combined multiculturalism scale (TMK)

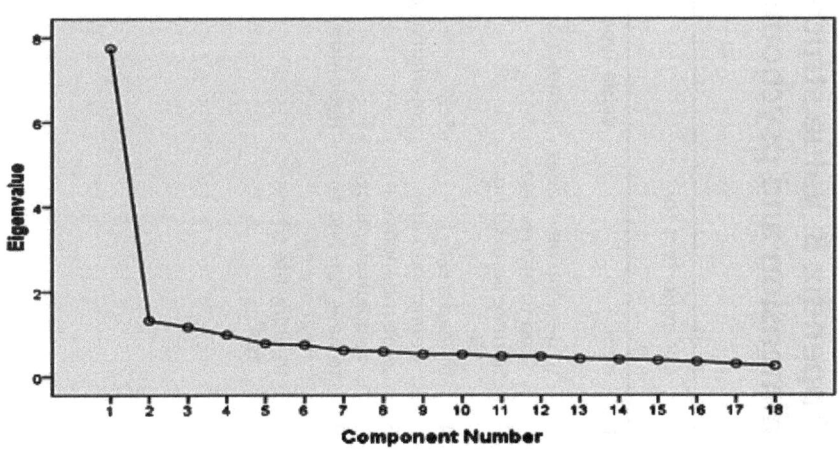

Scree Plot

Appendix 8: Value structure: individual items, value type, value dimension and psychometric properties

It is important for me, …			Item properties (raw scores)			Value Type		Value Dimension
No	Item	Value Type	Value Dimension	N	M	SD	r_{12}	r_{13} r_{23}	r_{it}
1	to develop new ideas and to be creative.	Stimulation	Openness for Change	493	5.24	1.41	0.400**		0.343
7	to have an exciting life.			493	5.65	1.25			0.523
4	to lead a self-determined life.	Self-determination		492	5.82	1.05	0.490**		0.497
5	to be independent and autonomous.			493	5.91	1.17			0.686
9	to have fun and to treat myself.	Hedonism		493	5.92	1.13	0.734**		0.642
11	to enjoy life to the full.			493	5.66	1.36			0.570
									$\alpha = 0.79$

#	Item	Subcategory	Group	N	Mean	SD			Loading
6	to advocate law and order.	Security	Conservation	494	5.54	1.28	0.369**		0.485
14	to live for the well-being and security of the family.			487	6.36	0.94			0.530
12	to show good manners.	Conformity		494	5.98	1.08	0.448**		0.400
21	to always comply with law and order.			483	5.48	1.33			0.213
17	to be modest and restrained.	Tradition		485	4.79	1.47	0.174**		0.414
19	to show respect for customs and traditions.			483	4.72	1.53			0.564
									$\alpha = 0.71$
2	to preserve nature.	Universalism	Self-Transcendence	492	5.67	1.31	0.376**	0.377**	0.390
8	to support human rights for all.			491	5.68	1.36		0.534**	0.612
16	to show understanding for others.			486	5.74	1.11			0.431
10	to take on responsibility for others.	Benevolence		490	5.10	1.53	0.278**	0.379**	0.675
20	to be there for friends and family.			485	6.26	0.97		0.235**	0.332
23	to support the socially disadvantaged.			486	4.80	1.57			0.642
									$\alpha = 0.77$

It is important for me, …		Item properties (raw scores)			Value Type		Value Dimension
	Self-Enhancement				0.174^{**}	0.219^{**}	*0.344*
3	Achievement	to be zealous and work hard.	488	5.17	1.20		
13		to achieve a high standard of living and wealth.	485	5.10	1.28	0.346^{**}	0.451
18		to achieve social recognition and status.	484	4.51	1.50		0.535
15	Power	to be successful.	486	5.81	1.06	0.282^{**} .	0.508
22		to exercise power.	484	4.04	1.54		0.489
							$\alpha = \mathbf{0.71}$

Appendix 9: Open comments—analysis of critical themes

Themes	Number	Percent
Adaptation by foreigners incl. ability to speak Luxembourgish, need to follow rules	9	20.5
Fear of being overwhelmed by foreigners (Überfremdung)/ fear of having more foreigners than native people in their own country, who have to adapt in their own country	6	13.6
Principle of mutuality/Basic values	6	13.6
No advantages	5	11.4
Religion as "poison"	5	11.4
Formation of parallel societies/lack of feeling of cohesion/ lack of integration	4	9.1
Criminality/violence	3	6.8
Foreigners only have rights, but no duties	2	4.5
Costs/Imbalance Lux—Nicht-LUX (cost to society « auf der Tasche liegen »)	2	4.5
If critical, risk of being called a racist	1	2.3
It is not possible speak own language in own country.	1	2.3
Total	44	

Appendix 10: Open comments—analysis of positive themes—advantages of multiculturalism

Themes	Number	Percent
Broadening of horizon/different perspectives/exchange of ideas (mutuality)	70	20.35
Diversity/enrichment/more interesting society	59	17.15
Getting to know other traditions/customs/cultures (cognitive focus, acquisition of knowledge)	50	14.53
Tolerance	31	9.01
Openness/"esprit"	31	9.01
Langue/multilingualism/variety of languages	27	7.85
Peace/Living together in peace and harmony/reduce hostility—general focus on living together peacefully	24	6.98

Themes	Number	Percent
Food	19	5.52
Reduce fear of the unknown/less racism/reduction of prejudice/discrimination	11	3.20
Respect	8	2.33
Mutual empathy, interest in each other, understanding, (focus on emotional aspects)	6	1.74
Solutions to problems in society, progress	6	1.74
More beautiful people (Schönere Menschen)	2	0.58
Total	344	100.00

References

Arends-Tóth, J., & van de Vijver, F. J. R. (2003). Multiculturalism and acculturation: Views of Dutch and Turkish-Dutch. *European Journal of Social Psychology, 33*(2), 249–266. doi:10.1002/ejsp.143.

Berry, J., & Kalin, R. (1995). Multicultural and ethnic attitudes in Canada: An overview of the 1991 National Survey. *Canadian Journal of Behavioural Science, 27*(3), 301–320. doi:10.1037/0008-400X.27.3.301.

Boll, T. (1999). *Verfahrensbeschreibung zur "Werte-Liste": Problemhintergrund, Konstruktionsprinzip, Dimensions-und Skalenanalysen.* Universität Trier, FB Psychologie. Internal Report.

Bourhis, R., Moise, L., Perreault, S., & Senécal, S. (1997). Towards an interactive acculturation model: A social psychological approach. *International Journal of Psychology, 32*(6), 369–386. doi:10.1080/002075997400629.

Brandtstädter, J. (2007). Das flexible Selbst. Selbstentwicklung zwischen Zielbindung und Ablösung. Heidelberg: Elsevier/SpektrumAkademischerVerlag.

Breugelmans, S. M., & van de Vijver, F. J. R. (2004). Antecedents and components of majority attitudes toward multiculturalism in the Netherlands. *Applied Psychology, 53*(3), 400–422. doi:10.1111/j.1464-0597.2004.00177.x.

Breugelmans, S. M., van de Vijver, F. J. R., & Schalk-Soekar, S. G. S. (2009). Stability of majority attitudes toward multiculturalism in the Netherlands between 1999 and 2007. *Applied Psychology, 58*(4), 653–671. doi:10.1111/j.1464-0597.2008.00368.x.

Celenk, Ö., & van de Vijver, F. J. R. (2014). Assessment of psychological acculturation and multiculturalism: An overview of measures in the public domain. In V. Benet-Martínez & Y.-Y. Hong (Eds.), *Oxford handbook of mul-*

ticultural identity: Basic and applied psychological perspectives. Oxford, UK: Oxford University Press.

Cieciuch, J., Schwartz, S. H., & Vecchione, M. (2013). Applying the refined values theory to past data: What can researchers gain? *Journal of Cross-Cultural Psychology, 44*(8), 1215–1234. doi:10.1177/0022022113487076.

Citrin, J., & Sears, D. (2001). Multiculturalism in American public opinion. *British Journal of Political Science, 31*(2), 247–275. doi:10.1017/S0007123401000102.

Epstein, S. (1979). Entwurf einer Integrativen Persönlichkeitstheorie. In S. H. Filipp (Ed.), *Selbstkonzept-Forschung: Probleme, Befunde, Perspektiven* (pp. 15–45). Stuttgart: Klett-Cotta.

Epstein, S. (1994). Integration of the cognitive and the psychodynamic unconscious. *The American Psychologist, 49*(8), 709–724. doi:10.1037/0003-066X.49.8.709.

Eurostat (2011). *Migrants in Europe. A statistical portrait of the first and second generation. Eurostat statistical books* (2011 ed.). Luxembourg: Publications Office of the European Union. doi:10.2785/5318.

Etat de la Population. (2014). Ville de Luxembourg. Sstatistique sur la Ville de Luxembourg.

Fiske, S. T. (2010). *Social beings: Core motives in social psychology*. Hoboken, NJ: Wiley.

Glaesmer, H., Grande, G., Braehler, E., & Roth, M. (2011). The German version of the satisfaction with life scale (SWLS). European Journal of Psychological Assessment.

Heath, A., & Tilley, J. (2005). British national identity and attitudes towards immigration. *International Journal on Multicultural Societies, 7*(2), 119–132.

Ho, R. (1990). Multiculturalism in Australia: A survey of attitudes. *Human Relations, 43*(3), 259–272.

John, O. P., & Srivastava, S. (1999). The Big Five trait taxonomy: History, measurement, and theoretical perspectives. *Handbook of personality: Theory and research, 2*(1999), 102–138.

Kremer, M. (2013). *The Netherlands: From national identity to plural identifications*. Transatlantic Council on Migration, Washington, DC: Migration Policy Institute.

Leong, C.-H., & Ward, C. (2006). Cultural values and attitudes toward immigrants and multiculturalism: The case of the Eurobarometer survey on racism and xenophobia. *International Journal of Intercultural Relations, 30*(6), 799–810. doi:10.1016/j.ijintrel.2006.07.001.

Maehler, D., & Schmidt-Denter, U. (2013). *Migrationsforschung in Deutschland: Leitfaden und Messinstrumente zur Erfassung psychologischer Konstrukte*. Springer-Verlag.

Medrano, J. (2005). Nation, citizenship and immigration in contemporary Spain. *International Journal on Multicultural Societies, 7*(2), 133–156.

Moran, A. (2011). Multiculturalism as nation-building in Australia: Inclusive national identity and the embrace of diversity. *Ethnic and Racial Studies, 34*(12), 2153–2172. doi:10.1080/01419870.2011.573081.

Murdock, E., & Ferring, D. (2013). Multikulturalismus—Multiplicity. Eine Meinungsumfrage zur Frage des Zusammenlebens in einer multikulturellen Gesellschaft. University of Luxembourg, INSIDE, Internal Report.

Murdock, E., & Ferring, D. (2014) On being bicultural in a multicultural society. European Association for Research on Adolescences (EARA) Newsletter, May 2014, 9–12.

Péporté, P. (2011). *Constructing the middle ages: Historiography, collective memory and nation-building in Luxembourg* (Vol. 3). Leiden: Brill.

Rammstedt, B., & John, O. P. (2007). Measuring personality in one minute or less: A 10-item short version of the Big Five Inventory in English and German. *Journal of Research in Personality, 41*(1), 203–212. doi:10.1016/j.jrp.2006.02.001.

Roccas, S., & Sagiv, L. (2010). Personal values and behavior: Taking the cultural context into account. *Social and Personality Psychology Compass, 4*(1), 30–41. doi:10.1111/j.1751-9004.2009.00234.x.

Schalk-Soekar, S. (2007). Multiculturalism. A stable concept with many ideological and political aspects. (Doctoral Dissertation, University of Tilburg, The Netherlands).

Schalk-Soekar, S. R. G., Breugelmans, S. M., & van de Vijver, F. J. R. (2009). Support for multiculturalism in The Netherlands. UNESCO. Retrieved from http://onlinelibrary.wiley.com/doi/10.1111/j.1468-2451.2009.00698.x/full

Schalk-Soekar, S. R. G., & van de Vijver, F. J. R. (2008). The concept of multiculturalism: A study among Dutch majority members. *Journal of Applied Social Psychology, 38*(8), 2152–2178. doi:10.1111/j.1559-1816.2008.00385.x.

Schalk-Soekar, S. R. G., van de Vijver, F. J. R., & Hoogsteder, M. (2004). Attitudes toward multiculturalism of immigrants and majority members in the Netherlands. *International Journal of Intercultural Relations, 28*(6), 533–550. doi:10.1016/j.ijintrel.2005.01.009.

Schalk-Soekar, S. R. G., Van de Vijver, F. J. R., & Croon, M. A. (2008). Strength of multicultural attitudes: A longitudinal study among Dutch mainstreamers. Submitted for publication. Quoted in Van de Vijver, F. J., Breugelmans,

S. M., & Schalk-Soekar, S. R. (2008). Multiculturalism: Construct validity and stability. *International Journal of Intercultural Relations*, 32(2), 93–104.

Schwartz, S. H. (1992). Universals in the content and structure of values: Theoretical advances and empirical tests in 20 countries. *Advances in Experimental Social Psychology*, 25(1), 1–65.

Schwartz, S. H. (1994). Are there universal aspects in the structure and contents of human values? *Journal of Social Issues*, 50(4), 19–45. doi:10.1111/j.1540-4560.1994.tb01196.

Schwartz, S. H. (n.d.). Chapter 7: A proposal for measuring value orientations across nations. 259–319. Retrieved from: http://www.europeansocialsurvey. org/docs/methodology/core_ess_questionnaire/ESS_core_questionnaire_ human_values.pdf

Schwartz, S. H. (n.d.) Computing scores for the 10 human values. Retrieved from: http://www.europeansocialsurvey.org/docs/methodology/ESS1_ human_values_scale

Schwartz, S. H., & Bilsky, W. (1987). Toward a universal psychological structure of human values. *Journal of Personality and Social Psychology*, 53(3), 550–562. doi:10.1037//0022-3514.53.3.550.

Schwartz, S. H., Cieciuch, J., Vecchione, M., Davidov, E., Fischer, R., Beierlein, C., et al. (2012). Refining the theory of basic individual values. *Journal of Personality and Social Psychology*, 103(4), 663–688. doi:10.1037/a0029393.

Schwartz, S. H., & Sagiv, L. (1995). Identifying culture-specifics in the content and structure of values. *Journal of Cross-Cultural Psychology*, 26(1), 92–116. doi:10.1177/0022022195261007.

Van de Vijver, F. J. R., Breugelmans, S. M., & Schalk-Soekar, S. R. G. (2008). Multiculturalism: Construct validity and stability. *International Journal of Intercultural Relations*, 32(2), 93–104. doi:10.1016/j.ijintrel.2007.11.001.

Van de Vijver, F. J. R., Schalk-Soekar, S. R. G., Arends-Tóth, J., & Breugelmans, S. M. (2006). Cracks in the wall of multiculturalism? A review of attitudinal studies in the Netherlands. *International Journal on Multicultural Societies*, 8(1), 104–120.

Van Oudenhoven, J. P., Prins, K. S., & Buunk, B. P. (1998). Attitudes of minority and majority members towards adaptation of immigrants. *European Journal of Social Psychology*, 28(6), 995–1013. doi:10.1002/ (SICI)1099-0992(1998110)28.

Verkuyten, M. (2005). Ethnic group identification and group evaluation among minority and majority groups: Testing the multiculturalism hypothesis. *Journal of Personality and Social Psychology*, 88(1), 121–138. doi:10.1037/0022-3514.88.1.121.

Verkuyten, M., & Martinovic, B. (2006). Understanding multicultural attitudes: The role of group status, identification, friendships, and justifying ideologies. *International Journal of Intercultural Relations, 30*(1), 1–18. doi:10.1016/j.ijintrel.2005.05.015.

Verkuyten, M., & Masson, K. (1995). 'New racism', self-esteem, and ethnic relations among minority and majority youth in the Netherlands. *Social Behavior and Personality: An International Journal, 23*(2), 137–154. doi:10.2224/sbp.1995.23.2.137.

Weinreich, P., & Saunderson, W. (Eds.) (2003). *Analysing identity: Cross-cultural, societal and clinical contexts.* Hove: Routledge.

Yogeeswaran, K., & Dasgupta, N. (2014). The devil is in the details: Abstract versus concrete construals of multiculturalism differentially impact intergroup relations. *Journal of Personality and Social Psychology, 106*(5), 772–789. doi:10.1037/a0035830.

Zick, A., Wagner, U., van Dick, R., & Petzel, T. (2001). Acculturation and prejudice in Germany: Majority and minority perspectives. *Journal of Social Issues, 57*(3), 541–557. doi:10.1111/0022-4537.00228.

7

Final Conclusions

Introduction

Increasingly complex societies pose a challenge to human identity development, and culture contact adds an additional dimension. The reach of globalization was noted in Chap. 3: People experience an increase in the frequency and intensity of intercultural exposure even without necessarily physically relocating. Culture contact presents additional challenges to core human motives (Chap. 4): At the cognitive level, the culture contact experience may represent a challenge to understanding and the experience of control. As was noted, belongingness is a core motive, and within multicultural societies, the boundaries between in- and out-groups become increasingly blurred and categorization processes become more and more difficult. As was also noted, belongingness shapes cognition and people classify in terms of social relationships. Information about in- and out-group members is cognitively processed differently, with information about in-group members being processed in more complex ways (attribute-based) and out-group information more simplistically (category-based). As Baumeister and Leary (1995) observed, prejudice can be employed towards out-groups to which individuals have no

© The Author(s) 2016   **317**
E. Murdock, *Multiculturalism, Identity and Difference,*
DOI 10.1057/978-1-137-59679-6_7

opportunity to belong (e.g. ethnicity or gender). The in-group is then bolstered at the expense of the out-group—serving the need to enhance self-worth—self-enhancement being another core motive. In the context of proliferation of groups within complex societies, it was also remarked that if complexity reaches a certain degree, a move towards simplification as a counter-reaction emerges. As noted in Chap. 3, Alibhai-Brown (2001) observed that the reaction to this bewildering opening up of our lives has been a greater (and more idealized) identification with old histories and smaller, neater identities. Thus at a time of proliferation of choice of in-groups, a counter-reaction may be observed in the form of (over-) simplification or nostalgia.

Culture contact presents a challenge to the *need for stability*, but offers opportunity of stimulation (*need for arousal*). People differ regarding the amount of stimulation they can tolerate as well as tolerance for ambiguity. Those individuals with high need of stability and low levels of tolerance for ambiguity will find the navigation of a world where people of different, often competing worldviews live side by side quite challenging. Others experience diversity as enriching. Within multicultural settings the basis of *familiarity*, as source for developing trust, also has to be negotiated. A plurally composed society offers a wider choice regarding potential in-groups. The basis of comparison (at personal and group level) is even more complex. Furthermore, culture contact may also pose a challenge to existing meaning systems, values and ways of doing things. Growing diversity has a profound effect on people's identities, and the comparison of identity processes in individualistic and collectivistic societies in Chap. 4 highlighted the fundamental differences in qualities that are important in forming identity. In the culture contact situation, these differences become apparent and can be reflected upon. The cultural experience is an issue of continual development and reformulation of identity in the contexts of alternative cultural norms.

This book started out with a review of Luxembourg's nation-building process with particular emphasis on the evolution of the demographic profile. I wanted to anchor the processes outlined above in a real-life case study and Luxembourg provides an ideal "natural laboratory" to illustrate various processes pertinent to a multicultural context. As noted in Chap. 2, Luxembourg has just celebrated 175 years of independence and the

search for and research into the Luxembourg national identity continues. There are many reasons for Luxembourg's current demographic
composition and linguistic landscape, which can best be understood in
retrospect. As stipulated by the Bioecological Model (Bronfenbrenner,
1986), an archival study into the external context was carried out first,
charting the transformation from a poor, agrarian country of emigration
to a highly developed, target country for immigration. As was shown in
Chap. 2 the process of nation-building (looking inward) has, from the
beginning, been accompanied by looking outward economically. Today's
demographic composition is the product of several different immigration
waves. Key themes emerging from this archival case study of Luxembourg
and the analysis of discourse on national identity were "size" of the country in all its facets and language. The debate concerning language includes
both multilingualism and Lëtzebuergisch. The discourse concerning the
latter is often at the heart of the national identity debate. These themes
were then explored further in several empirical studies, each addressing a different aspect of living within a multilingual and multicultural
environment. However, at the heart of all studies lies the culture contact
situation. All studies explore how culture contact is experienced from
different angles within the natural laboratory the multilingual, multinational Luxembourg context provides.

In Chap. 4 the study *on salience of national identity as a function of context* ("Study 1") was introduced. This study can be considered a "baseline"
study demonstrating that salience of nationality increases as a function of
context—especially for minorities, even though the delineation between
majority and minority is increasingly fluid. As was concluded, within
the multicultural context of Luxembourg, nationality is likely to be a
defining feature, providing orientation for self and others, rather than
diminishing in importance. In line with the hypothesis derived from the
distinctiveness paradigm the study also found that salience of nationality increases especially for minority members. Based on this finding, a
higher salience of nationality within the Luxembourg population can be
expected, as the Luxembourg native population finds itself increasingly
in the minority.

The difference between *bilingualism and biculturalism* ("Study 2")
was addressed in Chap. 5 as well as the question how the integration of

different cultures is actually achieved at individual level. As was shown in Chap. 5 there are different ways of being bicultural. The path towards achieving biculturalism may be experienced as stressful, as the culture contact situation implies that existing values and ways of doing things may be questioned. If integration is achieved following this period of dissonance, integrative complexity may be extended to other areas. The empirical study *on being bicultural* ("Study 3") addresses the question how adolescents growing up in a nationally heterogeneous context organize and experience their nationalities. As was shown, growing up with mixed nationality parents facilitates a bicultural orientation which then, in turn, is experienced as a source of pride and enrichment. Finally, in Chap. 6 the question of attitudes towards a multicultural society was explored. First, the role of human values and endorsement of multiculturalism ("Study 4") could be confirmed before a wider range of factors influencing the attitudes towards multiculturalism was explored in empirical "Study 5." In the following sections, findings *across* the empirical studies will be discussed. The first theme concerns the question of language and identity. Secondly, the implications of culture contact will be discussed and finally, the multiculturalism will be linked to human motivation.

Language and Identity

The empirical studies offer new insights concerning language and identity. The starting point for Study (2) was Ramírez-Esparza et al.'s (2006) statement that "bilinguals tend to be bicultural." However, the results within the Luxembourg context show that it is possible to self-identify as *multi*-lingual, but *mono*-cultural. Language competence was clearly identified as a necessary, but not sufficient condition for biculturalism. The majority of the Luxembourgish participants had not lived abroad and the sequence of languages acquisition was Luxembourgish, German, French and English—following the Luxembourg school curriculum. Similar findings were obtained for Study (5), where the majority of the participants (87 %) described themselves as multilingual (8 % bilingual), but the majority (70 %) has never lived abroad. In both studies, the degree of internalization of language was examined. In Study (2), a significant difference between those participants who described themselves as bicultural versus monocultural could be identified. The self-identified bicultural Luxembourg participants described the switch in language as effortless and *automatic*. They also agreed significantly more than the monocultural participants with the statement that a change in language means a change in culture. In Study (5), just over half of the participants agreed with the statement that the language they speak influences the way they think and feel, but only 25 % consider a change in language as a change in culture.

These findings suggest that for the majority of the Luxembourgish participants, the change in language involves a conscious effort. Languages have been learnt as a second (foreign) language, but the language has not been internalized as part of a second culture. The languages can be practiced on a daily basis, but learning the languages has not required a physical relocation, a total immersion in another culture. Immersion was mentioned by Study (2) participants as condition for becoming bicultural. For some participants an immersion has taken place, but for the majority of the Luxembourg participants, the language does not function as a cultural prime. As was noted, those who perceive language as a cultural prime also have a more positive attitude towards multiculturalism. One explanation for this finding may be that this cultural frame switching just happens automatically for this group of persons—there is no effort involved. Even though there is such a high degree of language competence within Luxembourg, which can partly be explained by the early onset of language learning, the change in language involves a conscious effort for the majority of Luxembourgers. The usefulness of multilingualism, the added value of being able to speak multiple languages, is widely recognized. Multilingualism is a source of pride—a unique feature of Luxembourg. Nevertheless, the need to switch between languages can also be a burden—requiring cognitive effort. This extra effort may also be one simple explanation why participants in Study (5) agreed so strongly with the statement that it is annoying not to be able to speak Luxembourgish in shops. However, as explained in Chap. 2, competence in the Luxembourgish language is *the* contentious issue in the debate on Luxembourg nationality, which is the more likely explanation for the strength of response to this item. Language lies at the core of the national identity debate.

To summarize, the empirical studies show that language competence is a necessary, but not sufficient condition for biculturalism. Even though language competence is very high within Luxembourg, only around a quarter of the study participants have internalized the languages to an extent that language actually serves as a cultural prime. Therefore shifting between cultural frames is automatic only for a minority. For the majority of participants shifting between languages is associated with conscious effort. As indicated by the Study (2), there is a strong sense of being multilingual, but monocultural. This is an important finding for a society that is multilingual and increasingly multicultural.

Culture Contact as First Step

The natural laboratory of Luxembourg offers opportunity for second-culture experience from very different angles. Within a multicultural society, the opportunity of culture contact is only the first step: The crucial question is what happens next.

Forms of Culture Contact

Different forms and types of culture contact can be distinguished. At a first level there is the distinction between globalization- and immigration-based culture contact. The former refers to the ubiquitous nature of globalization as described in Chap. 3. Through advances in technology people all over the world come indirectly in contact with different forms and expression of culture—through media exposure (music, films, social media, news, etc.) and manufactured goods including food products. Immigrant-based culture contact involves mobility of people and leads to direct culture contact. Immigration-based culture contact can be voluntary, from the perspective of the initiator of the move or involuntary, from the perspective of residents within the receiving society. Within the acculturation research, the majority of the studies concern the adjustment of the (minority) immigrant to the (majority) host society. As also discussed in Chap. 3, in terms of acculturation orientation, the key question is if and to what extent immigrants retain identification with the country of origin and to what extent they wish to integrate with the host society. As was explained further, the acculturation question is actually more complex, as the characteristics of the home and host society play a role, as well as the domain concerned and the characteristics of the immigrants themselves. Within domains, the main distinction is between the public and the private sphere. Visible or objective criteria for integration in the public domain include competence in the host country language, employment/schooling, respecting local law and order and voting. Criteria for the more private domain include number of host country friends or engagement in local activities/clubs.

As was shown in Chap. 2, immigrants to Luxembourg are in fact a heterogeneous group or super-diverse as defined by Vertovec (2007). Whereas some immigrants only spend a working day in Luxembourg, others will stay on a limited contract with an intention to return to their country of origin whilst others move to Luxembourg with an intention to stay. There is a constant flux of "new" foreigners next to some established foreign populations who have stayed in Luxembourg for one or more generations. These different frames of reference will also influence the depth or level of engagement with the host country. Foreigners make up 68 % of the resident population in the capital, spread over 170 nationalities. This also means that incoming persons don't need to adjust simply to one host society and one language, or three languages as is the case in Luxembourg; they also need to find their position within the diverse foreign population.

In acculturation research, the focus has been predominately on minorities moving to a new host society and the "mainstream" perspective has only recently been taken into consideration (Breugelmans et al., 2009). The host country perspective is usually researched in the form of the study of attitudes towards multiculturalism. As was shown in Chap. 6, the multiculturalism *ideology* will influence the acculturation options an immigrant may have. Within Luxembourg, the vast majority of immigrants are voluntary migrants—the migrants chose to come to Luxembourg. Even though local businesses may actively seek and attract migrants, for the majority of the resident population, the incoming population represents *involuntary* culture contact in the first instance. In addition, the incoming population is diverse. As noted in Chap. 4, familiar in-group members tend to be classified trait-based ("who they are") and for non-familiar out-group members category-based classification is applied. This is an economical information processing strategy, but in an increasingly multicultural world, the initial classification into "in-" and "out-group" is more and more fluid. Country of birth and nationality may not correspond; there are persons of dual nationality or as noted in Chap. 3, there are persons who in terms of visual appearance don't correspond to the group prototype. The classification processes are becoming ever more complex. The plurally composed society that is Luxembourg illustrates the complexities of culture contact in an increasingly multicultural society and shows that the fourfold acculturation model needs to be extended to include a broader spectrum of context and outcome variables, as for example suggested by Arends-Tóth and van de Vijver (2006) in their taxonomy of acculturation variables.

The Experience of Culture Contact

In the preceding section, different forms or classifications of the culture contact situation were provided and this section will focus on the actual culture contact experience. The first part "culture" stands for a unifying principle and stability. Members of a culture share a common language and meaning systems which are understood and passed on from one generation to the next. These meaning systems provide orientation, members act accordingly and behaviours are thus predictable. A culture can be described as "cycling with the wind"—the force carries its members along and the force itself does not need to be questioned. In Chap. 4, Harry Triandis (1989) was quoted who also commented on this economical aspect of culture as custom can be used as a substitute for thought and thus time can be saved. Even though cultures change, this change is usually gradual and difficult to notice by the members. However, this changes in the actual culture *contact* situation.

As Tadmor and Tetlock (2006) explained in the Acculturation Complexity Model (ACM, Chap. 5), exposure to a new culture leads to an increased attention scope in the first instance. The cultural meaning systems that have been taken for granted may be reflected upon and actually questioned. This period of reflection, when long-held beliefs, values or ways of doing things are challenged can be experienced as stressful. The amount of stress experienced will also depend on the value differences between the cultures in question. Tadmor and Tetlock introduced the concept of *accountability* to a mixed or single audience as a key factor determining a bi- or monocultural orientation in working through this period of dissonance. Study (3) suggests that growing up with mixed nationality parents is conducive to developing accountability towards a mixed audience and consequently a bicultural orientation. The vast majority of students who had grown up with two nationalities from birth self-identified in a bicultural way. For these children, perspective taking, switching between cultural frames is engrained since birth and has become an automatism. As was also shown in Study (3), mere exposure to culture contact does not lead to a bicultural orientation. The majority of students of monocultural parents self-identified in a monocultural way, even if they were born in a different country or have lived in another country to their country of birth for an extended period of time. Yet some students of monocultural parents showed a reaction to the culture contact situation. The students who self-identified as "I am from …, but I live in Luxembourg" showed an increased attention scope, and crucially, experienced dissonance. Getting to know a different culture, questioning and reflecting upon one's own value systems and ways of doing things, addressing the question of "belonging" can be experienced as stressful, which was reflected in these students' higher conflict scores. As noted by Tadmor and Tetlock, the path to achieving a bicultural orientation may be quite demanding, but once achieved, integrative complexity may be extended to other areas beyond nationality. The benefits of biculturalism are discussed by Brannen and Thomas (2010). The crucial point however is that these students experienced dissonance and that they were willing to engage in the process of questioning. Other students were not expressing an awareness of living in a different culture. This may be because they feel accountable only to a single audience and don't feel the need. Others may just choose the "path of least resistance." The concept of "cognitive miser" was introduced as an explanatory framework to show why people may opt to surround themselves with like-minded individuals who do not challenge assumptions.

Several key aspects can be learnt from this study: As postulated by Tadmor and Tetlock, the culture contact situation can lead to an increased attention scope and dissonance. Secondly, not everybody will take on this challenge (cognitive miser) and thirdly there is a strong association between being raised by mixed national parents and biculturalism, confirming the condition of mixed audience and fourth—bicultural students expressed their dual nationality as a matter of fact, demonstrating clearly that it *is* possible to have more than one nationality. Having two nationalities was perceived as a doubling of resources and a source of self-enhancement and pride. The high degree of internalization also means that the switching between cultural frames of reference is "automated," requiring less conscious effort.

Schmidt-Denter (2011) observed that at least within the European context, individuals are becoming increasingly similar in terms of self-descriptions. Therefore, in terms of personal identities, people are becoming more homogeneous and national identification offers an opportunity for differentiation to satisfy the need for uniqueness. The phenomenon of "stroke-identities" has been critically commented on by Bissoondath (Chap. 3). He noted that the "exoticism" and unique identity these stroke-identities provide are also double edged, as the cost of uniqueness may be a lack of sense of belonging, belonging being a central motive of human development. This cost of uniqueness was indeed mentioned by the European school students in Study (3) as a concern.

The stroke-identities symbolize another change. As alluded to above, the categorization of people has become more complex. The simple question—"Where are you from?" may produce a series of answers, as evidenced by the student quoted in Study (3) ("My mother is German, my father is Irish, I was born in England and I grew up in Luxembourg—You decide!"). For some, this intermixing and blurring of categories may be experienced as liberating, as going beyond the confines of a single culture. For others this blurring may be experienced as a challenge and a threat.

As Alibhai-Brown (2001) noted, the reaction to this bewildering opening up of our lives has been a greater (and more idealized) identification with old histories and smaller, neater identities. Alternatively, people may seek refuge in religion, as religions are stable and independent of place (Hirschman, 2003).

In this context it is interesting to note that in diverse cultures across the world, globalization tends to be associated with an increase in competence, but a loss in warmth. There is an appreciation of technological advances as well as fears for the closeness of community. Movement of people, which is one aspect of globalization, is perceived as an advantage by those who move, but not necessarily by recipient countries. Kremer (2013) explained the link between cultural insecurity and politics within the Dutch context. She observed that the "ethnic competition theory" whereby people fear that jobs will be taken away from the local population does not hold true for the Netherlands. Anti-immigrant attitudes do not fluctuate predictably with economic cycles. Furthermore, voters for the right-wing parties tend to live in areas where there is little competition for work and housing, though it is possible that some *perceive* this to be the case. The analysis of voters in the Swiss referendum on immigration showed that those living in cantons with the lowest numbers of foreign residents were most in favour of a restriction of immigration. Rather than being based on personal experience, there is more a diffuse feeling of cultural insecurity. Kremer (2013) wrote: "This cultural insecurity—when people fear their norms and values are being taken over, and their national identity is at stake—leads people to turn to authoritarianism, rigid social order, and intolerance towards others" (p. 6). This argument is mirrored in a recent commentary by Germany's former Foreign Secretary Joschka Fischer (2016). He argues that the threat or perception of loss of white, western supremacy is met by fear, actually a lot of fear. Quite often less educated people have less cultural capital and Kremer concluded that therefore "intolerance seems to be primarily rooted in the *cultural* background of the less educated rather than as a result of competition over resources, and as such, people who are ethnically and/or culturally different are considered a cultural rather than an economic threat" (italicized in the original document, p. 6). This may explain the link between education levels and the attitude towards multiculturalism, which was also confirmed in Study (5). Kremer (2013) explained "While more educated people feel better able to deal with globalization and are more able to cope with uncertainties, less-educated people become more insecure and try to keep what they have" (p. 7). Populist parties tap into this cultural insecurity. To quote Kremer again: "Parties or the populist right do not stand out for their economic profile yet. It is on the cultural issues where they support a demarcation strategy much more strongly than the mainstream parties (…) globalization has opened up a new demarcation line between those who feel they are not in control and do not have a 'grip' over their lives, and those who are able to cope with diversity" (p. 8).

The high parental level of education of the European school students was mentioned in Chap. 5. This, what some might consider privileged upbringing, might produce a climate where the majority of students consider it an advantage to have more than one nationality, regardless whether they grow up in a mono- or mixed national home. Studies (1) and (3) have also highlighted the low salience of a supra-national identity. Despite schooling at a *European* school "European" was neither mentioned in the spontaneous self-concept in Study (1) nor a as part of the self-identification in Study (3). A likely explanation is that the supra-national category is a cognitive category, which does not satisfy the emotional aspect of sense of belonging and feeling connected. The founding fathers of Europe actually postulated that the students should become "in mind" Europeans—making a specific cognitive reference. The connection with the homeland is couched in affective terms "Without ceasing to look to their own lands with love and pride." Empirical evidence supports the salutogenic effects of national identity (Schmidt-Denter, 2011).

Finally, it should also be noted that the empirical evidence points to a virtuous culture contact cycle. For both studies in Chap. 6 it could be shown that the more mixed the cycle of friends, the higher the endorsement of multiculturalism. Any form of *voluntary* culture contact contributed to openness towards multiculturalism—thus the challenge is the first step.

Multiculturalism—A Strong Attitude

For acculturation orientation preferences, Arends-Tóth and van de Vijver (2006) suggested that acculturation can be seen as a hierarchical concept with unidimensionality at the top. At the apex, there is thus a general global preference for either adaptation or cultural maintenance. The second level is constituted of the public versus private domain. In style of Epstein's (1973, 1979) self-concept theory (see Chap. 4), it could be argued that this global preference represents a higher order postulate, giving orientation for and guiding behaviour in the lower domains. These findings relate to the acculturation orientation by the immigrant. The attitude towards multiculturalism can also be assessed from the host country perspective.

The unidimensional nature of the multiculturalism construct was confirmed for the present study. Breugelmans et al. (2009) have shown the stability of attitudes towards multiculturalism over time. Schalk-Soekar et al. (2009) argued that the attitude towards multiculturalism is a *strong* attitude. These findings, together with the strong association identified in Studies (4 and 5) between the value orientation and multiculturalism suggest that the attitude towards multiculturalism may also be a higher order postulate. The strong association with value orientations indicates that this construct gives guidance across situations. As was explained in Chap. 4, the schemas at the centre are usually stable and not easily invalidated. This could explain why the external events in the Netherlands had little impact on the attitude of multiculturalism. On the other hand, educational programmes aimed at changing the attitudes towards multiculturalism will also have limited impact if they only affect the periphery and fail to reach the centre. Furthermore, information obtained through educational programmes will be mostly processed through the rational information processing system, whereas the pre-conscious experiential system will have largely contributed to the development of the implicit theory of multiculturalism in the first place. As schemas function as selective filters for information processing, those who are open towards multiculturalism will seek and process information that will confirm their attitude, whereas those with a negative attitude are less likely to seek cultural encounters, which may then in turn change the basic attitude. Thus the challenge for any educational programme is to remove the blinkers and to reach the centre.

Outlook

People differ—also with regard to acculturation strategies and their ways of dealing with the culture contact situation. Some people wish to assimilate, as was the case with Americans of Asian descent discussed in relation to identity denial; others want to express their dual nationalities in the form of stroke-identities. A further group remains rooted in their pride for their country of origin. A sense of belonging to a collective identity such as a nation state has salutogenic benefits. Evolutionarily we are primed to live in groups. Humans are social and survival depends on groups. Within affluent, individualistic societies the choice of groups one can potentially belong to has widened. And as Schmidt-Denter (2011) has pointed out, as personal identities are becoming more similar, self-enhancement or uniqueness is expressed through collective categories. As he further noted, patriotism, the expression of an emotional attachment to a country has a stabilizing effect for an individual. Not acceptable is nationalism which implies the devaluation of others.

Some people thrive in a multicultural environment—they are happy to go beyond the confines of a nation state. Those who have internalized more than one culture will also switch effortlessly from one cultural frame to the next. For those with multicultural competencies, the navigation within a multicultural context is easier. Van der Zee, van Oudenhoven, Ponterotto and Fietzer (2013) developed the Multicultural Personality Questionnaire. The fact that such a questionnaire was developed in the first instance highlights the fact that certain dispositions are conducive for living in a multicultural environment. The subscales of the scale, namely *Cultural Empathy, Flexibility, Social initiative, Open-mindedness* and *Emotional stability* show a strong overlap with the cultural competencies highlighted by LaFromboise et al. (1993) outlined in Chap. 5. Conversely, individuals with a strong need for stability, low ambiguity tolerance and low self-efficacy may feel less comfortable in a multicultural environment. It is a truism that people differ. Within Studies (4) and (5) for example, participants displayed different emphasis in terms of values. Some participants are more self-focused, emphasizing personal achievement, whereas other participants placed a stronger emphasis on needs of others. These value preferences in turn had an impact of the attitude towards multiculturalism. Study (5) has also shown that some people seemingly prefer to lead a monocultural life within the plurally composed society that is Luxembourg.

Banting (2010) asked the question about the "glue" that holds everything together within a multicultural society. Luxembourg has been mentioned several times as a "natural laboratory," as well as its remarkable transition from being a poor country of emigration to a wealthy target country for immigration. Initially, hesitance at embracing the sovereign state could be observed, but today, as confirmed also by the empirical studies, there is strong identification with the country. For a country of its size, it is remarkably diverse. The northern part is largely rural and green, the southern part is dominated by its industrial past and the multicultural side is concentrated in the centre. The foreign population is also very diverse as explained in Chap. 2. The analysis of the demographic section of participants in Study (5) suggests that some Luxembourg nationals prefer to live a monocultural life, whereas others engage with the international community. If human rights and civic values as are taken as the basic guiding framework, the next unifying principle or "glue" could be what the Dalai Lama described as "the Indian example of many religions living together in harmony" (Appendix 1, personal communication). A plurally composed society offers a much wider range of opportunities for self-expression, for different types of *Lebensentwürfe* (ways of living). This does not mean "anything goes." As Appiah (2006) noted, we need to develop habits of coexistence. Human rights and civic values provide the basic operating framework. As noted in the report on competences for democratic culture (Council of Europe, 2016) we need to nurture a set of common values around which to organize. Young minds have to be taught to understand diversity, rather than to fear it. The aim is to teach students not what to think, but *how* to think "in order to navigate a world where not everyone holds their views, but we each have a duty to uphold the democratic principles which allow all cultures to co-exist" (p. 7). Thus the next transformation could be the commitment to pluralism, offering a wider range of ways of living together in harmony. Living with difference is a reality of today. Emphasizing difference may exacerbate the divide, remembering that we all belong to one human family may bridge the divide. Living together in harmony is the theme of the main oeuvre of a famous Luxembourg-native US citizen.

The Family of Man—A Personal Epilogue

The world famous photographer Edouard Jean Steichen was born on 27 March 1879 in Bivange, Luxembourg. His family emigrated to Chicago, USA, in 1881 and he became a naturalized US citizen in 1900, signing his papers as Edward J. Steichen. From 1947 to 1962 Steichen was Director of Photography at the New York Museum of Modern Art (MoMA). In this function he was curator of the Family of Man exhibition. Following the experience of World War II and the Cold War period that followed, the collection was aimed to convey a message of peace. Over 500 photos depicted life, love and death in 68 countries. In the period of 1955–1962 the travelling exhibition was seen by 10 million people throughout the world and on completion of the tour, the US Government donated the last complete version of the exhibition to Luxembourg. Edward Steichen visited his native country and expressed his wish for The Family of Man to be exhibited permanently at Clervaux Castle. The exhibition is now installed at Clervaux and in 2003, the inscription on the UNESCO Memory of the World register followed. This exhibition, curated by Steichen, is a perfect example of showing what we, as human beings, have in common. An example image, representing happiness, is given below (Fig. 7.1).

This theme of focusing on what we as human beings have in common is also the core message in a recent communication by the Dalai Lama (see Appendix 1) to a small, Luxembourg-based group called InterFaith (http://www.interfaith.lu), who aim to bring people of different faiths groups together in running for peace. This group explicitly seeks the dialogue between people of different faiths. In the introduction to this book, the twenty-first century was introduced as the "age of migration."

Fig. 7.1   The Family of Man exhibition (*Source*: http://www.loc.gov/pictures/
item/fsa2000023030/PP/)

The Dalai Lama postulates that the twenty-first century should be the
"age of dialogue" (p. 13, Der Appell des Dalai Lama an die Welt, 2016).
We can't change the past, but we can learn and create a better future.
In his words of welcome to InterFaith the Dalai Lama provides guidance on how to achieve this: "In our world these days we are ever more
interdependent and yet we spend too much time dividing people into
'us' and 'them', thinking that overcoming 'them' will be a victory for 'us.'
As human beings we are all the same. We all want a happy life and have
a right to lead it, which is why it is important to remember that we all
belong to one human family."

Appendix 1: Message to InterFaith by His Holiness the Dalai Lama

THE DALAI LAMA

MESSAGE

Warm greetings to everyone participating in the *"Interfaith Run for a United World"* as part of the ING Night Marathon, Luxembourg, on 31st May this year. I am very moved to hear that so many people are planning to take part in this run. I am always impressed when, in addition to words of support, people actually undergo some physical effort and hardship to express their support for some cause. It takes courage. I am reminded of the way down the centuries in Tibet, people would set out on pilgrimage, or embark on a journey to join a monastery to further their education. Either way, like those who are running on this occasion, they would dedicate their efforts to the welfare of others.

In our world these days we are ever more interdependent and yet we spend too much time dividing people into 'us' and 'them', thinking that overcoming 'them' will be a victory for 'us'. As human beings we are all the same. We all want a happy life and have a right to lead it, which is why it is important to remember that we all belong to one human family.

Similarly, since religious faith is one of the factors that help us temper our negative emotions, it is particularly sad when religion becomes a source of conflict. I think this occurs when there is not enough contact and understanding between us. We need to make greater efforts to emulate the Indian example of many religions living together in harmony. Religious harmony is not just a matter of making diplomatic gestures but of demonstrating our respect and mutual admiration in action. Your coming from different faiths and running together sets a strong example to millions of religious followers all over the world. It expresses our need to reach out to each other and work together for the common human goal of peace and happiness.

The key to genuine world peace is inner peace and the foundation of that is a sense of understanding and respect for each other as human beings, based on compassion and love. As you take part in the Luxembourg Night Marathon and gather at the end, let us pray that these qualities grow within us all, contributing to a happier, more peaceful world for all sentient beings now and in the future.

May 22, 2014

References

Alibhai-Brown, Y. (2001). After multiculturalism. *The Political Quarterly Publishing Co., 72*(1), 47–56. doi:10.1111/1467-923X.72.s1.7.

Appiah, K. A. (2006). *Cosmopolitanism. Ethics in a world of strangers.* New York: W. W. Norton & Company.

Arends-Toth, J., & van de Vijver, F. J. R. (2006). Conceptual and measurement issues in family acculturation research. In M. H. Bornstein & L. R. Cote (Eds.), *Acculturation and parent-child relationships: Measurement and development* (pp. 33–62). Mahwah, NJ: Lawrence Erlbaum.

Banting, K. G. (2010). Is there a progressive's dilemma in Canada? Immigration, multiculturalism and the welfare state. *Canadian Journal of Political Science, 43*(04), 797–820. doi:10.1017/S0008423910000983.

Baumeister, R. F., & Leary, M. R. (1995). The need to belong: Desire for interpersonal attachments as a fundamental human motivation. *Psychological Bulletin, 117*(3), 497–529. doi:10.1037/0033-2909.117.3.497.

Brannen, M. Y., & Thomas, D. C. (2010). Bicultural individuals in organizations: Implications and opportunity. *International Journal of Cross Cultural Management, 10*(1), 5–16. doi:10.1177/1470595809359580.

Breugelmans, S. M., van de Vijver, F. J. R., & Schalk-Soekar, S. G. S. (2009). Stability of majority attitudes toward multiculturalism in the Netherlands between 1999 and 2007. *Applied Psychology, 58*(4), 653–671. doi:10.1111/j.1464-0597.2008.00368.x.

Bronfenbrenner, U. (1986). Ecology of the family as a context for human development: Research perspectives. *Developmental Psychology, 22*(6), 723–742. doi:10.1037/0012-1649.22.6.723.

Council of Europe (2016). *Competences for democratic culture. Living together as equals in culturally diverse democratic societies.* Strasbourg, France: Council of Europe Publishing.

Dalai Lama, A. F. (2016). *Der Appell des Dalai Lama and die Welt. Ethik ist wichtiger als Religion.* Wals bei Salzburg: Benevento Publishing.

Epstein, S. (1973). The self-concept revisited. Or a theory of a theory. *American Psychologist, 5,* 404–416.

Epstein, S. (1979). Entwurf einer Integrativen Persönlichkeitstheorie. In S. H. Filipp (Ed.), *Selbstkonzept-Forschung: Probleme, Befunde, Perspektiven* (pp. 15–45). Stuttgart: Klett-Cotta.

Fischer, J. (2016, January 2/3). Die Alterskrankheiten des Westens. Project Syndicate/Institute für die Wissenschaften vom Menschen, 2015.

www.project-sncicate.org. Quoted in: Luxemburger Wort, Analyse & Meinung, p. 15.

Hirschman, C. (2003). *The role of religion in the origins and adaptation of immigrant groups in the United States.* Paper presented ate the conference on "Conceptual and Methodological Developments in the Study of International Migration" at Princeton University, 23–25 May 2003.

Kremer, M. (2013). *The Netherlands: From national identity to plural identifications.* Transatlantic Council on Migration, Washington, DC: Migration Policy Institute.

LaFromboise, T., Coleman, H. L. K., & Gerton, J. (1993). Psychological impact of biculturalism: Evidence and theory. *Psychological Bulletin, 114*(3), 395–412. doi:10.1037/0033-2909.114.3.395.

Ramírez-Esparza, N., Gosling, S. D., Benet-Martínez, V., Potter, J. P., & Pennebaker, J. W. (2006). Do bilinguals have two personalities? A special case of cultural frame switching. *Journal of Research in Personality, 40*(2), 99–120. doi:10.1016/j.jrp.2004.09.001.

Schalk-Soekar, S. R. G., Breugelmans, S. M., & van de Vijver, F. J. R. (2009). Support for multiculturalism in The Netherlands. UNESCO. Retrieved from http://onlinelibrary.wiley.com/doi/10.1111/j.1468-2451.2009.00698.x/full

Schmidt-Denter, U. (2011). *Die Deutschen und ihre Migranten: Ergebnisse der europäischen Identitätsstudie.* Beltz Juventa: Weinheim.

Tadmor, C. T., & Tetlock, P. E. (2006). Biculturalism: A model of the effects of second-culture exposure on acculturation and integrative complexity. *Journal of Cross-Cultural Psychology, 37*(2), 173–190. doi:10.1177/0022022 105284495.

Triandis, H. (1989). The self and social behavior in differing cultural contexts. *Psychological Review, 96*(3), 506–520. Retrieved from http://doi.apa.org/psycinfo/1989-36454-001

Van der Zee, K., van Oudenhoven, J. P., Ponterotto, J. G., & Fietzer, A. W. (2013). Multicultural personality questionnaire: Development of a short form. *Journal of Personality Assessment, 95*(1), 118–124. doi:10.1080/00223 891.2012.718302.

Vertovec, S. (2007). Super-diversity and its implications. *Ethnic and Racial Studies, 30*(6), 1024–1054. doi:10/1080/01419870701599465.

Index

© The Author(s) 2016
E. Murdock, *Multiculturalism, Identity and Difference*,
DOI 10.1057/978-1-137-59679-6

CPI Antony Rowe
Chippenham, UK
2017-02-15 10:11